NISA

NISA

The Life and Words of a !Kung Woman

by Marjorie Shostak

This edition published in 1990 by Earthscan
Reprinted 1993, 1996, 2000, 2006

First published in the United States by Harvard University Press 1981
First published in Great Britain by Allen Lane 1982

A catalogue record for this book is available from the British Library

ISBN-10: 1-85383-060-7
ISBN-13: 978-1-85383-060-0

Printed and bound in the UK by Biddles Ltd

For a full list of publications please contact:

Earthscan
8–12 Camden High Street
London NW1 0JH, UK
Tel: +44 (0)20 7387 8558
Fax: +44 (0)20 7387 8998
Email: earthinfo@earthscan.co.uk
Web: www.earthscan.co.uk

Earthscan is an imprint of James & James (Science Publishers) Ltd and publishes in
association with the International Institute for Environment and Development

To Nisa and her people in the hope that their struggle to survive
will be as successful in the future as it has been in the past

Contents

I'll break open the story and
tell you what is there. Then, like
the others that have fallen out onto
the sand, I will finish with it,
and the wind will take it away.

Nisa

Introduction

I LAY THERE and felt the pains as they came, over and over again. Then I felt something wet, the beginning of the childbirth. I thought, "Eh hey, maybe it is the child." I got up, took a blanket and covered Tashay with it; he was still sleeping. Then I took another blanket and my smaller duiker skin covering and I left. Was I not the only one? The only other woman was Tashay's grandmother, and she was asleep in her hut. So, just as I was, I left.

I walked a short distance from the village and sat down beside a tree. I sat there and waited; she wasn't ready to be born. I lay down, but she still didn't come out. I sat up again. I leaned against the tree and began to feel the labor. The pains came over and over, again and again. It felt as though the baby was trying to jump right out! Then the pains stopped. I said, "Why doesn't it hurry up and come out? Why doesn't it come out so I can rest? What does it want inside me that it just stays in there? Won't God help me to have it come out quickly?"

As I said that, the baby started to be born. I thought, "I won't cry out. I'll just sit here. Look, it's already being born and I'll be fine." But it really hurt! I cried out, but only to myself. I thought, "Oh, I almost cried out in my in-laws' village." Then I thought, "Has my child already been born?" Because I wasn't really sure; I thought I might only have been

1

sick. That's why I hadn't told anyone when I left the village. After she was born, I sat there; I didn't know what to do. I had no sense. She lay there, moving her arms about, trying to suck on her fingers. She started to cry. I just sat there, looking at her. I thought, "Is this my child? Who gave birth to this child?" Then I thought, "A big thing like that? How could it possibly have come out from my genitals?" I sat there and looked at her, looked and looked and looked.

The cold started to grab me. I covered her with my duiker skin that had been covering my stomach and pulled the larger kaross over myself. Soon, the afterbirth came down and I buried it. I started to shiver. I just sat there, trembling with the cold. I still hadn't tied the umbilical cord. I looked at her and thought, "She's no longer crying. I'll leave her here and go to the village to bring back some coals for a fire."

I left her, covered with leather skins. (What did I know about how to do things?) I took a small skin covering, tied it around my stomach, and went back to the village. While I was on the way, she started to cry, then she stopped. I was rushing and was out of breath. Wasn't my genital area hurting? I told myself to run, but my judgment was gone; my senses had left me.

My heart was pounding and throbbing when I arrived. I sat down by the fire outside my hut to rest and to warm myself. Tashay woke up. He saw me with my little stomach, and he saw the blood on my legs. He asked how I was. I told him everything was all right. He asked, "Where is that which I thought I heard crying?" I told him the baby was lying covered where I had given birth. He asked if it was a boy. I said she was a girl. He said, "Oh! Does a little girl like you give birth to a baby all alone? There wasn't even another woman to help!"

He called to his grandmother, still asleep, and yelled, "What happened to you that you, a woman, stayed here while a little girl went out by herself to give birth? What if the childbirth had killed her? Would you have just left her there for her mother to help, her mother who isn't even here? You don't know that the pain of childbirth is fire and that a child's birth is like an anger so great that it sometimes kills? Yet, you didn't help! She's just a little girl. She could have been so afraid that the childbirth might have killed her or the child. You, an adult, what were you asking of her?"

Just then, the baby started to cry. I was afraid that maybe a jackal had come and hurt her. I grabbed some burning wood and ran back to her. I made a fire and sat. Tashay continued to yell, "Find her. Go over there and cut the baby's umbilical cord. What happened to you that you let my wife give birth by herself?"

His grandmother got up and followed Tashay to where I was sitting with the baby. She arrived and called out softly to me, "My daughter-in-law . . . my daughter-in-law . . ." She talked to the infant and greeted her with lovely names. She cut her umbilical cord, picked her up, and carried her as we all walked back to the village. Then they laid me down inside the hut.

The next day, my husband went gathering and came back with sha roots and mongongo nuts, which he cracked for me to eat. But my insides were still sore and I was in pain. He went out again and killed a springhare. When he came back, he cooked it and I drank the gravy. That was supposed to help the milk come into my breasts, but my milk didn't come down.

We lived in the bush and there was no one else to help feed her. She just lay there and didn't eat for three nights. Then milk started to fill one breast, and the same night the other one filled. I spilled out the colostrum, the bad thing, and when my chest filled with good milk, she nursed and nursed and nursed. When she was full, she went to sleep.

THIS STORY WAS TOLD to me in the !Kung language by Nisa, an African woman of about fifty years of age, living in a remote corner of Botswana, on the northern fringe of the Kalahari desert. It was March 1971, the last month of my twenty-month field stay among the !Kung San, a people who had recently started to leave their traditional means of subsistence—gathering and hunting.

But Nisa, her family, and the people she knew had spent most of their lives as their ancestors had before them—gathering wild plant foods and hunting wild animals in their semi-arid savannah environment.[1]

Gathering and hunting as a way of life has now almost disappeared, but it was the way people lived for nearly 90 percent of the estimated one hundred thousand years of human existence. Adding to this the evolutionary history of our prehuman ancestors would give a period of nearly three million years and a figure closer to 99 percent. Thus this form of human society has been a much more universal human experience than agriculture, which has been practiced for only about ten thousand years, or industrial manufacture, which has existed for only about two hundred years. The uniqueness of the human species was patterned—and the human personality was formed—in a gathering and hunting setting.

This should in no way suggest that the !Kung San or other contemporary gatherer-hunters are less modern as human beings than anyone else. People everywhere are, in a biological sense, fundamentally similar, and have been so for tens of thousands of years. Gatherer-hunters today exhibit the same range of emotional and intellectual potential as can be found in other human societies. What they represent is a way of life that succeeded; in terms of duration, at least, it is the most successful adaptation people have yet made to their environment.

Nisa is a member of one of the last remaining traditional gatherer-hunter societies, a group calling themselves the *Zhun/twasi*, "the real people," who currently live in isolated areas of Botswana, Angola, and Namibia. Referred to in the past as the Sonquas and in Botswana as the Basarwa, they are also known as the !Kung Bushmen, the !Kung San, or simply the !Kung. They are short—averaging about five feet in height—lean, muscular, and, for Africa, light-skinned. They have high cheekbones and rather Oriental-looking eyes. Along with their pastoral neighbors, the Khoi-Khoi, they are distinguished in these and other physical details from the Black African peoples immediately surrounding them, and are considered by population biologists to be part of a separate racial group called Khoisan. (It is

4

from this term that the words currently used to refer to them are derived: "Khoi" for Hottentots; "San" for Bushmen. The terms "Hottentot" and "Bushmen," used for more than three hundred years, although more familiar, are also more derogatory.)

In 1963, Irven DeVore and Richard Lee, anthropologists from Harvard University, first made contact with Nisa's people, a traditional group of !Kung San in the Dobe area of northwestern Botswana.[2] They had in mind a long-term research expedition in which scientists representing a wide range of disciplines would carry out specialized studies of !Kung life. A composite picture would result, including information on health and nutrition, demography, archaeology, infant growth and development, child-rearing practices, population genetics, the ritual healing ceremonies, folklore, and women's life cycles. In 1969, six years after the project began and very close to its end, my husband and I joined it and went to live and work with the !Kung.

Some of the findings from this expedition were available to me before I left for Africa. I welcomed the perspective they gave me on the !Kung and their way of life. But when I asked questions about what they were like as people and how they felt about their lives, I received answers so varied that they seemed to reflect as much the personalities of the individual anthropologists as anything they had learned about the !Kung. No matter whom I talked to or what I read, I did not come away with a sense that I knew the !Kung: How did they feel about themselves, their childhoods, their parents? Did spouses love one another; did they feel jealousy; did love survive marriage? What were their dreams like and what did they make of them? Were they afraid of growing old? Of death? Most of all, I was interested in !Kung women's lives. What was it like being a woman in a culture so outwardly different from my own? What were the universals, if any, and how much would I be able to identify with?

My initial field trip took place at a time when traditional values concerning marriage and sexuality were being questioned in my own culture. The Women's Movement had just begun to gain momentum, urging re-examination of the roles Western women had traditionally assumed. I hoped the field trip might help me to clarify some of the issues the Movement had raised.

5

!Kung women might be able to offer some answers; after all, they provided most of their families' food, yet cared for their children and were lifelong wives as well. Furthermore, their culture, unlike ours, was not being continuously disrupted by social and political factions telling them first that women were one way, then another. Although the !Kung were experiencing cultural change, it was still quite recent and subtle and had thus far left their traditional value system mostly intact. A study revealing what !Kung women's lives were like today might reflect what their lives had been like for generations, possibly even for thousands of years.

Upon arriving in the field, I did everything I could to understand !Kung life: I learned the language, went on gathering expeditions, followed along on hunts, ate bush foods exclusively for days at a time, lived in grass huts in !Kung villages, and sat around their fires listening to discussions, arguments, and stories. I gained an invaluable perspective, participating and watching. I was struck by their broad, subtle knowledge of their environment, by their skill in deciphering animal and human tracks in the sand and in detecting, among mats of dry, tangled vines, the ones that signaled water-storing roots below the ground. I observed their sharing of vegetable foods, meat, and material goods so that no one had substantially more than anyone else. I saw how disputes were defused by discussions that went on for hours, long into the night, in which all points of view were expressed until a consensus was reached. I listened to hunters recount the events of successful hunts, to musicians sing and play their own and other people's compositions, and to storytellers cause body-shaking laughter in their hearers. I noticed in each presentation a modesty akin almost to bashfulness, and I learned that it was considered bad manners to brag or to act in an arrogant way. I sat at their medicine ceremonies and saw the community bound together in a powerful, moving ritual.

I was thrilled to have seen this much in only a few months in the field. Still, I did not feel I knew, except in the most general terms, what these events really meant to the !Kung. I could see, for example, how much they relied on one another and how closely they usually sat together, but I did not understand how they felt about their relationships and their lives. I needed information that could not be observed; I needed the !Kung to start speaking for themselves.

Talking to people and asking questions that encouraged them to talk openly to me became the focus of my fieldwork. Because my own inclination was toward learning about women's lives and because I generally found it easier to talk with them than with men, my work centered almost exclusively on women. I presented myself to them pretty much as I saw myself at the time: a girl-woman, recently married, struggling with the issues of love, marriage, sexuality, work, and identity—basically, with what womanhood meant to me. I asked the !Kung women what being a woman meant to them and what events had been important in their lives.

One woman—Nisa—impressed me more than the others with her ability to describe her experiences. I was struck by her gifts as a storyteller; she chose her words carefully, infused her stories with drama, and covered a wide range of experience. My hundreds of interviews with the !Kung had shown me that much of human emotional life was universal. Nisa's narrative, despite its foreignness, brought that knowledge deeper.

Walking into a traditional !Kung village, a visitor would be struck by how fragile it seemed beneath the expanse of sky and how unobtrusively it stood amid the tall grass and sparse tree growth of the surrounding bush. Glancing at the six or seven small grass huts, the visitor might notice how low they were, how closely one was set beside another, and the more or less circular space they described. The center, where children often play, would be clear of grass and shrubs, making it easier to notice snakes or snake tracks.

A visitor who arrived in the middle of the cold season—June and July—and just at sunrise would see mounds of blankets and animal skins in front of the huts, covering people still asleep beside their fires. Those who had already awakened would be stoking the coals, rebuilding the fire, and warming themselves in the chilly morning air. The morning would start slowly for most of them, a luxury made possible by the cool of the winter season. A visitor on another morning, in the hot, dry months of October and November, would find people moving about, even at dawn, up early to do a few hours of gathering or hunting before the midday heat would force them to rest in the thickest shade.

The Dobe area, on the edge of the Kalahari desert, falls into an ecosystem classified as semi-arid. The land, covered with grass, thorn and scrub brush, and spindly trees, has a flat appearance that disguises a variety of low hills, dunes, flats, and river beds. The rivers are active only about twice a decade. The mean elevation is about 3,300 feet above sea level, and temperatures vary from below freezing in winter to above 100°F in summer. The wet season lasts four to six months; annual rainfall varies from five to forty inches. Then comes a brief autumn (April and May), followed by a three-to-four-month winter with about six weeks of freezing and near-freezing night-time temperatures. Spring begins late in August and turns quickly into a hot dry summer in which temperatures hovering above 110°F are not uncommon.

The area was long sheltered from more than intermittent settlement by outsiders, Europeans and Bantu-speakers alike, by its lack of dependable sources of water, by a vast waterless zone between it and the nearest large population center, and by the general harshness of its environment. This environment must have supported gathering and hunting, however; archaeological excavations demonstrate the continuous occupation of the Dobe area by gathering and hunting people for more than eleven thousand years.

The !Kung are masters of survival in this environment, capable of responding to its ever-changing and often extreme demands. Adaptability is the key to their success. People live in semi-permanent villages, or camps, numbering from about ten to thirty individuals. Personal property must be minimal (the total weight of an average person's belongings is less than twenty-five pounds), because everything has to be carried when the band moves. The technology involved in the manufacture of tools and implements is relatively simple, and each household provides them for itself.

Whatever possessions do exist are owned exclusively by individuals, who are free to dispose of them as they wish. Most items are eventually given away and become part of a network of goods that are frequently exchanged. All !Kung participate in this reciprocal giving of gifts, but each person gives to and receives from only a few partners. Gift-giving is a fairly formal affair, and people remember clearly who gave what to whom and when. These exchange relationships, which may last a lifetime and may even be passed on to one's children, help to even out wealth differentials. An approximation of equality is thus achieved, aided by the daily sharing of food and meat. Generosity also ensures the reciprocal help of others in times of sickness or need.

Both family and village life take place out of doors. Huts are too small to contain much more human activity than sleeping They are set only a few feet apart. A fire burns outside each doorway, in front of the hut, and the area around it is the effective living space for the hut's occupants—the nuclear family—and their visitors. All doors face inward toward a large communal space. The intensity of social life that this fosters seems deliberate, as space is abundant and privacy could easily be arranged. Except for an occasional tryst in the bush, however, privacy is not something most !Kung deem very important. Companionship is cherished and sought at most times.

Residence in a camp is fluid and subject to frequent change, from day to day and from month to month. At its center, however, each camp has a stable core of closely related older people who have proved successful in living and working together. This core may spend years, perhaps the majority of their adult lives, with one another. They share food and material goods, and they travel together while foraging over an area they have access to by tradition. Spacious, yet essentially circumscribed, this region of approximately 250 square miles is generally acknowledged as being "owned" by some male or female descendant of the people who have lived longest in an area, although this association rarely goes back much further than a few generations. Access to land is collective and nonexclusive and, like so much else in !Kung life, flexible: most people live as visitors or residents in a number of different areas during their lives, and establishing

9

short-term residence at one water hole does not jeopardize one's claim to residence at another. Visitors—perhaps from an area with a temporary food shortage—are expected to ask permission of the "owners" before making use of an area's water, game, and vegetable foods. Accepting this favor, however, brings with it an obligation to reciprocate if the occasion arises.

Little in the way of special privilege is gained by ownership, because virtually all members in a band are directly or indirectly related to a core member and thus have free access to the area's resources. A senior descendant coming from a long line of owners may assume a position of dominance, but only if he or she also shows personal leadership qualities. In general the !Kung do not have status hierarchies or legitimized authorities, such as chiefs or headmen. Group decisions are reached through consensus. Although a small number of men and women do function as leaders, their influence is derived primarily from having earned the respect of others, and is essentially informal.

Traditional !Kung groups are economically self-sufficient (except for iron, which is acquired by trade). Children, adolescents under fifteen, and adults over sixty contribute little to the quest for food, and others gather or hunt only about two or three days a week. Additional time is spent in housework, cooking and serving food, child care, and the making and repairing of tools, clothing, and huts. But this still leaves substantial time for leisure activities, including singing and composing songs, playing musical instruments, sewing intricate bead designs, telling stories, playing games, visiting, or just lying around and resting.

The central ritual event in traditional !Kung life is the medicinal trance dance, in which all members of a band participate. Healers enter trance and ritually draw illness out of a sick person's body. Other group members support their efforts with singing, clapping, and dancing. The dance takes place anywhere from a few times a month to several times a week and is grounded in a very old tradition—so old that its origins are beyond speculation, even among the oldest living !Kung. Its long history is confirmed by scenes depicted in rock paintings, by dance circles etched in rock, by archaeological findings, and by the occurrence of dances similar in form, content, and musical style in San groups that speak languages other than !Kung and live several hundred miles away.

Travel—whether in search of food or to visit relatives in distant villages—is usually concentrated during or just after the rainy season, when water is widely available throughout the savannah and food resources are varied and abundant. Travel ceases by nightfall, when living areas are hastily cleared of shrubs and grass, minimal shelters are erected, and huge fires are stoked to establish dominion over the bush and the night. If the group plans to stay, the grass shelters may be made more substantial, especially if the downpours and lightning storms of the rainy season are expected. After a few weeks in one place, however, the group will have depleted the major food resources in the area and will move on. Only if a large animal has been shot will they stay longer, and even then they will move to the site of the kill.

As temporary pools and semipermanent springs dry up, people start moving back toward permanent water, to build new camps for their winter residence. For a while, water trapped in the recesses of large trees may make bush travel possible, but as the temperature and the humidity fall—a signal that winter has arrived and the rains are long over—the only available water may be that squeezed from heavy water roots dug from deep within the sand, or from melons distributed throughout the area. When the nights become bitterly cold and the days cloudless and windy, most bands will settle in for a three-to-five-month stay around one of the permanent springs. The large aggregations of people that result—sometimes more than two hundred—intensify the ritual life of the community as well as the social life of individuals. Trance dances occur more frequently (up to two or three times a week), initiation ceremonies requiring a large number of boys of similar age are performed, gifts are given and reciprocated, and marriages are arranged.

With so many people depending on one set of concentrated resources, tension is inevitable, especially as the distances required to find food increase and the approaching hot, dry season makes travel difficult and unpleasant. Add to this the conflicts that always increase when large numbers of people gather in a small area, and the result is that a greater number of fights occur in these camps. Passionate and explosive, most are resolved quickly and without serious incident. (Before 1948, however, when a Bantu headman was officially appointed to administer Tswana customary law in the Dobe area, significant numbers of fights led to death from poisoned arrows.) By the time the rains finally come, scattering the dry landscape with temporary oases again, the composition of the small groups that leave to forage on their own may have changed, as some members may have left and others joined.

The day-to-day organization of subsistence is as complex as the seasonal round. !Kung women contribute the majority (from 60 to 80 percent by weight) of the total food consumed. Averaging little more than two days a week in the quest for food, they gather from among 105 species of wild plant foods, including nuts, beans, bulbs and roots, leafy greens, tree resin, berries, and an assortment of other vegetables and fruits. They also collect honey from beehives, and occasionally small mammals, tortoises, snakes, caterpillars, insects, and birds' eggs. Intact ostrich eggs are sought both for their nutritional value—equivalent to about two dozen hens' eggs—and for their shells. After the egg is extracted through a hole bored in one end, the shell makes an excellent container for carrying or storing water. Broken eggshells found at old nesting sites are fashioned into beads, to be strung or sewn into necklaces, headbands, and aprons.

The staple of !Kung nutrition is the abundant mongongo (or mangetti) nut, which constitutes more than half of the vegetable diet. It is prized both for its inner kernel and for its sweet outer fruit. Other important plant foods are baobab fruits, marula nuts, sour plums, tsama melons, tsin beans, water roots, and a variety of berries. Most women share what they bring home, but there are no formal rules for distribution of gathered foods and those with large families may have little left over to give others.

Although food resources are located at variable distances from the villages, they are fairly reliable. Groups of about three to five women leave, usually early in the morning, and head for an agreed-upon area. They proceed at a leisurely pace, filling their karosses with a variety of foods as they travel, and return to camp by mid-to-late afternoon. After a brief rest, they sort their piles of food, setting some aside to be given as gifts. Most of the food is distributed and consumed within forty-eight hours.

!Kung women also care for children and perform a variety of daily domestic chores. They average close to four hours a day in maintaining their subsistence tools and in housework: fetching water, collecting firewood, maintaining fires, making huts (frame and thatching), arranging bedding, and preparing and serving food (including cracking nuts for themselves and their young children). Men average three hours a day in making and repairing tools and in domestic work: they chop trees for fires and for building huts, help collect firewood, and butcher, prepare, and serve meat. Devoted and loving fathers, they also participate in child care, though their contribution, in terms of time spent, is minor.

Women's status in the community is high and their influence considerable. They are often prominent in major family and band decisions, such as where and when to move and whom their children will marry. Many also share core leadership in a band and ownership of water holes and foraging areas. Just how influential they really are and how their status compares with that of men is a complicated question: women may, in fact, be nearly equal to men, but the culture seems to *define* them as less powerful. In other words, their influence may be greater than the !Kung—of either sex—like to admit.

Men's principal food contribution is hunted meat, which is very highly valued—perhaps because it is so unpredictable—and which, when brought into the village, is often the cause of great excitement, even dancing. Men average slightly less than three days a week in hunting. They, too, leave early in the morning, alone or in pairs, and usually return by sunset, although overnight stays are possible. Although accomplished hunters, they only succeed about one day in every four that they hunt. Game is sparsely distributed in the northern Kalahari—a marked contrast to the herds of thousands of animals in the Central Kalahari Game Reserve farther south—and has become scarcer over the last fifty years.

Bows, arrows, and spears of minimal size and weight make

up the basic hunting kit, along with a variety of bags and implements. But the hunters depend most on a lethal poison extracted from beetle larvae. It is so potent that an antelope, or even a giraffe, is likely to die within a day of being struck with a well-placed arrow. Harmless to people ingesting the meat, the poison works on the animal's central nervous system; it becomes harmful only when it enters an animal's—or a person's—bloodstream. In the village, poisoned arrows are stored in closed quivers hung out of the way of adults and the reach of children. For additional safety, poison is applied only to the shaft, not to the sharp arrow point, to avoid poisoning from accidental cuts. The arrows are periodically checked and fresh poison applied.

Unlike women, who maintain a fairly constant gathering routine, men rarely adhere to strict hunting schedules. They often hunt intensively for a few weeks, then follow with a period of inactivity. Because success in the hunt is so variable, meat accounts for only 20 to 40 percent of the !Kung diet, depending on the time of year and the number of hunters residing in a camp.

Men are as knowledgeable as women in plant lore, but they collect plants only infrequently and account for about 20 percent of all food gathered. Their primary contribution to subsistence is in the animals they hunt. Most prominent are the large game animals (kudu, wildebeest, gemsbok, eland, roan antelope, hartebeest, and giraffe) and the smaller ones (warthog, steenbok, duiker, and hares). Men also collect reptiles (snakes and tortoises), amphibians, and insects, trap hole-dwelling animals (porcupine, antbear, springhare, and anteater), and snare birds (guinea fowl, francolin, kori and korhaan bustards, sand-grouse, and doves). Honey, a great favorite, is extracted from beehives, often with the help of women. Distribution of all but the smallest game is tied to more formal rules than is the case for gathered foods, but the result is similar.

Perhaps because of the limitations of their hunting methods, the !Kung kill only what they need and use every part of the animal. Bones and hooves are cracked for marrow; skins are either eaten or tanned for blankets; sinew is made into thread or strung on a hunting bow. Even the tails of some animals are used: the hair may become the strings of a musical instrument or be braided into a bracelet, or the entire tail may be carried as a spiritual object in a medicinal trance dance.

Food is rarely stored for any length of time. The environment can be depended on to act as a kind of natural storehouse, with food being gathered only when needed. There are occasional scarcities in some of the important wild vegetable foods, but rarely has there been a shortage in the mongongo nut, which is so well adapted to the Dobe area that even in most years of drought hundreds of thousands of nuts are left on the ground to rot.

Dietary quality is excellent. Richard Lee studied the !Kung diet in 1968 and found their average intake of calories and protein to exceed the United Nations recommendations for people of their size and stature. Their diet is extremely low in salt, saturated fats, and carbohydrates, particularly sugar, and high in polyunsaturated oils, roughage, and vitamins and minerals. In fact, it conforms to most contemporary ideas of good nutrition. The dry season of 1968 was one of the most severe droughts in southern Africa in recent history; thus it is likely that the !Kung diet is even better in normal years. (More recent studies have indicated that during the dry season many !Kung lose weight, suggesting an insufficient calorie intake. They usually regain the weight, however, when the dry season is over. Whatever the actual deficit during this period, the diet remains wide-ranging and high in nutrients.)

Their diet, along with their relaxed pace of life, seems to have protected the !Kung from some of the diseases common in our society: they do not suffer from high blood pressure, hypertensive heart disease or atherosclerosis, hearing loss or senility, varicose veins, or stress-related diseases such as ulcers or colitis.

This does not mean that !Kung health is, in general, good. It is not: nearly 50 percent of children die before the age of fifteen; 20 percent die in their first year, mostly from gastrointestinal infections. Life expectancy at birth is only thirty years, while the average life expectancy at age fifteen is fifty-five. One reason that the illnesses we associate with aging seem to have little impact on them is that only 10 percent of the population is over sixty years old—the age at which they would begin to be more vulnerable to such illnesses. Respiratory infections and malaria are major killers of adults. !Kung health nevertheless compares favorably with that of many nonindustrial societies, and of our own society before the advent of modern public health and medicines.

Given the circumstances the !Kung face, they have been remarkably successful. They survive—even thrive—in an environment that is hospitable only to those who know it intimately. Their traditions, distilled from thousands of years of experience, have been passed on through hundreds of generations. There is neither memory nor legend regarding a time when, for example, the poison they use on their arrows, or their trance ritual, did not exist. They know nearly five hundred species of plants and animals: which are edible, and which have medicinal, toxic, cosmetic, or various other uses. Their skill in exploiting their environment allows them free time in which to concentrate on family ties, social life, and spiritual development. Their life is rich in human warmth and aesthetic experience and offers an enviable balance of work and love, ritual and play.

The !Kung are not exceptional among gathering and hunting peoples. According to scientists who have compared the social and economic organization in different groups of contemporary gatherer-hunters, these societies have more in common with each other than with their agricultural, pastoral, and industrial neighbors. Wherever it is practiced, whatever the climate, whatever the terrain, there is an undeniable "master plan" in contemporary gatherer-hunter life. The best explanation for the similarities among these groups is that within the gathering and hunting mode, there is a limited set of alternatives to choose from. Any group of people who had to live off the land would face similar ecological problems and would probably invent a roughly similar system. It seems reasonable to suggest, then, that this pattern—or more properly, this range of patterns—prevailed in most human societies before the agricultural revolution and during much of the course of human evolution.

But what relevance does all this have for us? What do we gain from knowing about our gathering and hunting past? Most important, perhaps, is the knowledge that the gatherer-hunter legacy is a rich one. Life for our prehistoric ancestors was not characterized by constant deprivation, but rather by usually adequate food and nutrition, modest work effort, fair amounts of leisure, and sharing of resources, with both women and men contributing substantially to the family, the economy, and the social world. Today, gatherers and hunters, the !Kung included, live in the most marginal areas, whereas prehistoric gatherers and hunters occupied areas abundant with water, plant food, and game. If there is any bias in the data from modern-day gatherer-hunters, therefore, it probably leads to an underestimate of the quality of life of their—and our—predecessors.

My first months in the field were spent adjusting to Kalahari life, trying to fit in with three other anthropologists living there, and studying the !Kung language. Books of !Kung grammar and vocabulary did not exist, nor did the people themselves read or write. At the outset, I received help from the anthropologists, who described the basics of the language. There were four different click sounds and two throat sounds, all fairly easy to master with practice. But many words that sounded the same to our Western ears were actually distinguished by the use of four or more different tones—a dimension of speech that was difficult to hear, let alone to master. I learned two important phrases: "What is the name for that?" and "When I do this, what is it called?" Using these two questions, combined with some obvious gestures, I was able to elicit a large vocabulary in a few weeks. But the other anthropologists were scheduled to leave shortly and were busily completing their research. They generously answered my questions, but I was uncomfortable taking up their time and tried, as much as I could, to proceed on my own.

Within the first month I hired two !Kung men to sit with me while I pointed, pantomimed, and repeatedly asked my two questions: "What is the name for that?" and "When I do this, what is it called?" I struggled to write down the answers, which bore no relation to any sounds I had ever heard before. I adopted the standard orthography for writing the clicks: / = dental (the sound that is written in English as "tsk, tsk"); ≠ = alveolar (the clicking sound we sometimes make while tasting something); ! = alveolar-palatal (a pop of the tip of the tongue off the roof of the mouth); and // = lateral (like the click made after saying "giddyap" to a horse). The rest of the vowels and consonants I approximated using the English alphabet.

By the time three months had passed, the !Kung sounds had become a little less strange, the clicks, glottal stops, and fricatives a little more manageable, and I could finally hear the tones (although it took close to twenty months before I started using them correctly). Polite formalities could now be exchanged: "How are you this morning, my niece?" "Why I'm fine, my uncle."

But more was required than finding the !Kung equivalents for English words; it was, of course, necessary to say them correctly, at the appropriate times, and in the culturally accepted manner. My first attempts were awkward and embarrassing. By the time I had lived there six months, however, I was more at ease with the language and occasionally succeeded in asking questions that elicited personal responses. At that point, I started to "interview" anyone who was friendly and willing, trying various ways to ask them about the things they perceived as important in their lives. I questioned them about marriage in general and their marriages in particular. I talked with pregnant women about their pregnancies and their thoughts about having children. I asked women in polygamous marriages how it felt to share a husband with another woman. These talks pointed me in the right direction, but they did not prove as successful as I had hoped. I still needed too many repetitions, and my vocabulary was still too limited to circumvent impersonal, generalized answers. My project demanded a richer and more subtle mastery of the language.

I kept talking, and my language ability steadily improved. During my tenth month there, I had a breakthrough: after weeks of friendly, informal talks with a woman named Bau, she started to confide in me. She told me about things other people had only hinted at, and she told me about her own life. Sexual play was common, she said, even among young children. She told me which children in the village were "coupled" and the kind of sex play they probably engaged in. She said that many people had extramarital affairs, and she told me which men and women in her village were involved with each other. She said that in the past a woman with an unwanted pregnancy would drink herbal medicines that made her menstrual flow return, that "ruined her insides," producing an abortion without affecting her ability to conceive again. She also said that women of her grandmother's generation had occasionally practiced infanticide, but that it was no longer done: the Tswana government prohibited it and there would be severe punishment if it were discovered.

Miraculously, it seemed, Bau talked freely about things I had wanted to hear, but hadn't, until then. We talked seven times over a period of two weeks; I took notes on all that I understood. She explained how children eventually became aware of their parents' sexual intercourse—conducted discreetly at night in the same one-room hut. That was how children got their ideas for sexual play. At first they played that way with friends and sometimes even with their brothers or sisters. As they grew older, they stopped playing with their siblings and played only with children of the opposite sex. She herself had played "house" when she was a child, and she remembered a time when two playmates had been discovered having "sex" under the blankets.

Becoming even more personal, she told about a recent dream in which she and another woman yelled insults at each other. They started to fight and bit and scratched each other's faces. Other women pulled them apart. The woman in the dream reminded Bau of someone her husband had once had an affair with. He had told Bau about it—a grave insult: "Men don't tell their wives about affairs, they just have them." Later she had had a romance of her own. Once she spent a few nights in the mongongo nut groves with her lover while her husband was away. Someone saw them leave and told her husband, who later beat her until "I was almost dead." She stopped seeing her lover after that, and since then had been afraid to have affairs.

Winning Bau's trust had been the first step; trying to understand what her confidences meant came next. I knew enough not to assume that what she told me was necessarily true. Informants often told anthropologists what they thought they wanted to hear. Some even told outright lies—for concealment, from indifference, or just for amusement. It was also possible that the way Bau talked was governed by cultural forms that I didn't know, but which she assumed I understood. Perhaps in interpreting it all literally I was missing the real meaning of her words.

Not knowing the answers, I only hoped that Bau hadn't been lying. I tried to assess how likely that was, considering all I knew about her. She was quiet and reserved and did not constantly seek me out. Only after weeks of talking together had she started to confide in me. She was fair to the people she talked about. She didn't gossip unnecessarily. When she said "Some women have lovers," she mentioned the names of hers and the complications that followed. All in all, I felt quite certain that she had told me what she believed to be true. If so, then, whatever her personal biases, I now had a base from which to explore further. Naturally, I would ask other people similar questions in order to determine the overall validity of Bau's confidences, but she had given me something to go on.

From then until I left the field ten months later, I proceeded in just that way: interviewing people and asking them about their lives. After some trial and error, I settled on a standard approach that was an outgrowth of my talks with Bau. The main difference was that I was now more certain of what I was after and more confident that it would be possible to get.

My technique was straightforward: I would ask someone to "enter work" with me (a !Kung expression), and over the course of about two weeks we would sit together and talk for an hour or more a day. The conversations were taped; recordings could capture the kinds of subtle details invariably missed by note-taking, and would reveal how stories were developed and expressed.

I did not select my subjects completely objectively—that is, by random or strictly representative selection. After interviewing two men, I saw that I could not achieve nearly the same degree of intimacy with them as I could with women. The women I chose were those with whom I felt I could establish good rapport, and who represented a wide range in !Kung conditions of life. I interviewed eight women in addition to Nisa, ranging in age from fourteen to seventy. The fourteen-year-old was unmarried, premenstrual, and living with her parents. The seventy-year-old was the mother of a large extended family and an "owner" of a resource area; she lived with her husband and her sister who, when widowed a few years earlier, had been taken on as a co-wife. The others were a dynamic twenty-two-year-old mother of a little girl, who had married for love; a gifted, barren woman in her early thirties who was married to a Tswana man and having serious marital difficulties; a recent widow in her late thirties, a trance healer, who lived alone with her five-year-old son and near her married daughter; two other women in their thirties—in some sense the ideal !Kung women—who were in stable marriages with several children each; and a reserved, barren woman in her forties, married to a respected healer. These women were fairly representative of the range of life circumstances of !Kung women in the Dobe area in the 1960s and 1970s.

All the women I approached were eager to participate, partly for the payment I offered and partly, it seemed, for the opportunity to talk about themselves. At the outset, I told each woman that I wanted to spend a number of days talking with her about her life. I explained that I wanted to learn what it meant to be a woman in their culture so I could better understand what it meant in my own. With older women, I went further, presenting myself as a child in need of help in preparing for what life might yet have to offer. In all cases, the women were talking specifically to me, as a person and as a woman.

I also mentioned some of the topics I hoped to cover: memories of childhood; feelings about parents, siblings, relatives, and friends; adolescence and experiences with other children; dreams; marriage; the birth of children; childhood sex and adult sex; relationships with husbands and lovers; feelings about death; thoughts about the future; and anything else they felt was important in their lives. I made it clear that everything would be confidential as long as I was there and if and when I returned to the region. I told them I would, however, share the material with people in my own country, so that they could learn about !Kung women's lives.

I encouraged the women to initiate conversations, since the way one memory led to another seemed to be of potential importance. I interrupted as little as possible, primarily to ask for clarifications. I also asked for expansion of topics that seemed to have been covered too briefly. If a woman found it difficult to sustain a topic or to start a new one, I suggested alternatives. With some women I had to direct each interview, while others, once they understood the process, needed little assistance.

The women often expressed their pleasure in working with me. They were proud that they had been chosen to teach me about things that were obvious to them yet were so fascinating to me. These things, they said, would never have been discussed with a man, because "men have their talk and women theirs." They became silent whenever a man walked near the hut we were working in. It would be in a low and excited voice that a woman first mentioned a lover's name, or discussed an early sexual experience, or talked of the time she went from the village, alone, to give birth to her child.

Talking about experiences and telling stories is a main source of aesthetic pleasure for the !Kung. With no written expression, people sit together and talk, often for hours. While hunts or gathering expeditions are being recounted, speakers may gesture broadly, suddenly raise or lower their voices, or imitate the sounds or physical movements of animals, birds, or insects. Elements of the best stories are repeated again and again, with frequent exaggeration and hyperbole. The drama and excitement accompanying the telling of stories elicit almost continual comments from the audience as everyone is drawn into the experience. As with any skill, some people are more proficient at such narration than others. Among the women I interviewed, Nisa stood out. She had an exceptional ability to tell a story in a way that was generous, vibrant, and moving. Her sensitivity and skill made her stories larger and more important than the details they comprised. Sometimes they captured the most subtle and profound experiences in human life; sometimes they revealed a confused human entanglement that was all too recognizable. This was the value that her narrative had for me, and the reason it became so compelling.

I don't remember the first time I met Nisa. Perhaps she had stopped at our camp to ask for tobacco—just one of many who came, each with a special request. But the first time she made an impression on me was two weeks after my talks with Bau ended, the halfway mark in my twenty-month field stay. My husband and I had set up camp for a week near Gausha, an area where a number of !Kung and other villages were situated, and where Nisa lived.

By the time we arrived at Gausha, from Goshi, where we had our main camp, it had long since been dark. We drove the Land Rover past one !Kung village and stopped at a deserted village site farther down the road. The full moon, high in the sky, appeared small and gave off a cold light. Shadows extended from the shrubs and dried thorn bushes momentarily caught in the truck's beams; then the lights of the Land Rover were turned off.

Kxoma and Tuma, two !Kung men traveling with us, suggested we make our camp at this site where Richard Lee and Nancy Howell, other anthropologists, had set their camp four years earlier. Living where someone had lived before was right, they said; it connected you to the past. The slender stick shell of Richard and Nancy's hut was still there. It stood out in the moonlight, a bizarre skeleton set apart from the surrounding bush. Long branches, taken from nearby trees, described a six-foot circle at the base; at the top they were bent toward the middle and tied with strips from the leaf of a fibrous plant: a traditional !Kung frame. The grass had long since been taken and used in Nisa's village. As it stood, the hut offered no protection from the weather, nor any privacy.

Tuma started a fire with dead wood he found nearby. From one of the five-gallon gerry cans we always carried in the Land Rover, he poured water into a kettle and put it on the fire. We didn't expect anyone from the villages. The people must have heard the truck as we passed by and the sudden quiet when the engine sounds stopped. But it was too late for visiting. They knew us by then: we would still be there in the morning. Then they would find out what we planned to do and how long we would stay. The !Kung would ask for medicine and tobacco, and their cattle-herding neighbors, the Herero, would be by with their requests.

The four of us worked slowly taking the blankets and tents

from the truck. Kxoma and Tuma set up their tent beneath a small shade tree; my husband hung our own tent over the frame of Richard and Nancy's hut. I untied the bedding, and shook the sand from the blankets before laying them down. I thought of the time Nancy had found a puff adder in her sleeping bag. I lay down on the newly made bed, slid my hands over the blankets to feel for thorn branches and dried cow dung under the canvas, and then removed them. We had been determined to travel light this time, like the !Kung, and were without our mattresses and pillows.

I joined the men by the fire and drank the freshly brewed, chicory-flavored coffee. I was always amazed how quickly a new place felt less strange: a fire, blankets, and coffee seemed enough. Tired, I sat enjoying the moments of quiet, unpressured time, which had become surprisingly rare. People's voices rose from the nearby villages, laughing or shouting; it was comforting to know they were there. I felt pleasantly drowsy and lay down on my jacket, lulled by the voices and by the fire.

Moving was always exhausting. There were so many things to organize before we even began to pack the truck: gasoline, water and food, notebooks, observation sheets, cameras, tape recorders, lanterns, tents, blankets, clothing, and more. Tension built up and everyone felt it—the people working for us, my husband, myself, and the people whose village we had left that day. It invariably was like that—the longer we stayed in one place, the more people began to depend on us: for tobacco, for medicine, for trade, or just for the interest we created wherever we went—and the more we became a reason for people to stay around, sometimes longer than they would otherwise have done. When we did leave, it was disrupting to their lives, especially at Goshi where we spent much of our time. That day it was very late when we finally left.

Our coffee almost finished, we talked about going to bed. Then we heard people coming. They were only two: Nisa and her husband, Bo. Nisa wore an old blanket loosely draped over the remnants of a faded, flower-print dress, sizes too big; Bo was wearing a pair of shorts, even the patches of which were worn through in places. They greeted us and sat down by the fire, where I could see them better. Both were close to fifty years old. Bo moved slowly, spoke softly and deliberately, with energy and intelligence emanating from his eyes. Nisa was all activity: constantly in motion, her face expressive, she spoke fast and was at once strong and surprisingly coquettish.

No sooner had they settled than Bo, using my husband's !Kung name, said, "Hey, Tashay, give me some tobacco. Tobacco hunger has killed me! Don't you see I'm already dead because of it?" I thought he was about to answer, "Wait until morning. This is our time now. Asking-for-things has killed *us* today." But he didn't. It was too late to argue, and there were only the two of them. Sometimes we found it easier to give whatever was asked for, until the constant demands became too much. Then we fought back and argued, knowing it might be easier if we didn't. It was fine if we argued in the same spirit they did—half-seriously, half just as a way of making contact. But sometimes we couldn't, and the insults thrown at us hurt, "You're rich but stingy," and, "You could help, but you refuse."

My husband got up, opened the rear door of the Land Rover, and came back with some crushed-leaf tobacco. He gave it to Bo and Nisa, saying he would give them more in the morning. That was when we would give it to the rest of the !Kung with whom we planned to work. My husband was studying mother-infant relationships and infant mental and physical growth, and I was hoping to find women who would talk to me about the properties of medicinal roots. Bau had discussed several that supposedly affected fertility, abortion, and miscarriage.

Bo filled an old wooden pipe, one he must have received in trade, with only the bowl section intact. (The mouthpiece is rarely used, even on new pipes.) He opened a small, worn, cloth pouch where he had put the tobacco and filled the bowl. He lit the pipe and inhaled deeply four or five times, trying to hold as much smoke as he could, puffing his cheeks and holding his breath with each inhalation. With the exhalation, he turned, spat in the sand, and handed the pipe to Nisa. She smoked the same way and gave it to Kxoma and Tuma, who each did the same. Kxoma passed what was left of his sweet coffee to Nisa and Bo and together they finished it.

The four of them were talking, exchanging news of their villages. Our presence seemed to have become a matter of indifference to them, and I stopped straining to understand their words. I felt sleepy; the sound of their voices gradually became a meaningless but pleasant hum. Then I became aware that Nisa was calling my !Kung name, talking to me: "Hwantla . . . Hwantla . . . what news is there of my wonderful friends Richard and Nancy? I really liked them! They liked us, too—they gave us beautiful presents and took us everywhere with them. Bo and I worked hard for them, because we are not afraid of work. That's how it was with the four of us. Yes, Nancy and Richard . . . Oh! How I wish they were here!"

She continued to talk about events of four years before, when Richard and Nancy had periodically lived at Gausha. As Nisa spoke I thought, as I did quite often, about some of the difficulties we had had adjusting over the last ten months. We had come near the end of a long line of anthropologists working in these remote villages. Richard had been followed by six others, each of whom had lived there for about two years.

Coming at the end gave us certain advantages. We were taken to Goshi by a colleague we had previously met, and the !Kung were prepared for our arrival. Information collected by our predecessors was available to us, including identifications of the people, their family histories, and records of births, deaths, and marriages spanning the time the others had been there. With so much known before we arrived, we were able to direct our energies to the aspects of !Kung life that most interested us.

But as time passed we became aware that we had also inherited serious problems. The !Kung had been observing anthropologists for almost six years and had learned quite a bit about them. Precedents had been set that the !Kung expected us to follow. That was difficult, because we were critical of much that we saw: a separate elaborate anthropologists' camp, tobacco handouts, payment for labor and crafts in money, and occasional excursions by truck to the nut groves. Determined to do things our own way, we packed away our inherited tent and moved into a !Kung-style grass hut in a !Kung village.

Once we were on our own, our romanticism was attacked

by the !Kung themselves. They wanted us to give them jobs as the others had; they wanted money; they wanted to stop relying on their traditional way of life, which was becoming impossible to sustain.

With money, they said, they could buy goats, clothing, and blankets. They wanted seed to plant crops, to have fields just as the Herero and Tswana had. And they wanted tobacco: "Without tobacco, you wake up and walk around all day with only half your heart and don't know when the sun rises or sets." They didn't care, or even believe us, when we said that tobacco was bad for their health. They argued that without our help they would have to beg it from their Herero neighbors and would feel demeaned. They argued further that we should give them something that made life more enjoyable. After all, they cooperated with us, letting us intrude into their lives; we, in turn, should give them something that we could easily get and they badly wanted.[3]

We weren't convinced, at least not yet. We did not feel justified in yielding to the pressure to give out tobacco or in paying cash or having people work for us. There were too many unanswered questions. Money had no place in their traditional economy and had only come to the area recently; what would be the long-range effects of giving it to some individuals but not to all? If we hired men and women to work for us, how would this affect the amount of hunting and gathering they did, or the attitudes of their sons and daughters toward the skills of the bush? If we encouraged the planting of crops, what would happen when limited rainfall resulted in no harvest?

Perhaps the most important consideration was that after our work was completed we would leave, like the other anthropologists before us. Then what? Would the people be willing to accept the low-paid work offered by the cattle-herders? If not, would they return to full-time hunting and gathering? If they did, could they still make it work? The influx of the Bantu-speakers, bringing both herds of animals and awareness of the outside world, made change inevitable. But how could we as anthropologists justify a short-term input of goods and money? If we yielded to the pressure wouldn't we be behaving irresponsibly?

A confrontation seemed inevitable, and when it came it focused on tobacco. We had begun refusing it to anyone living outside the villages in which we lived or worked at any given time. We hoped eventually to stop supplying it altogether. One morning when my husband drove the truck, loaded with empty water drums, five miles to the permanent well where we drew water, he found a mound of thorn branches barring his passage. The people from a nearby village soon appeared: "Do you expect to draw water where you refuse people tobacco?" They eventually let him through (it was illegal to stop someone from using a well for drinking water), but we realized that we could not ignore such strong protests. The !Kung demanded a relationship on their terms, not ours. Eventually we accepted those terms, as our colleagues had urged us to do months before. Our tobacco handouts became more generous, and we no longer refused tobacco to visitors in the village where we were working.

Later we also acknowledged the responsibility we would continue to have after we left, a responsibility to work with the San in their struggle to determine their future. But as we sat around the fire with Nisa and Bo we had no sense of how we would carry out our obligation. At that time we were still grappling with the question of whether we should practice strict noninterference in the !Kung way of life.

Nisa's praise of Richard and Nancy reminded me of these painful adjustments. Had they really managed better? Had their relationship with Bo and Nisa been as easy as Nisa described it? Nisa's talk whetted my curiosity. Fully awake now, I asked her to tell me more.

"Nancy and Richard? They were the best! Nancy, I greet you! Nancy, hello! Why, she and Richard gave us whatever we wanted: clothes, food and money, all sorts of things. They never refused us anything! Nancy, how I loved her! She was the best white person here. Write and tell her I said so. Ask her for some cloth and money, too. Everyone was stingy compared to her. She was different. She wasn't a European, she was a !Kung! Oh, I would like her to be here right now. She really looked after me."

I felt a familiar despair. What had I expected her to tell me? About the conflicts? About the numerous requests Richard and

Nancy had refused? About the times Nancy had told Nisa to
come back later? No, I knew what it had been like; I didn't have
to ask. The !Kung had treated Nancy and Richard the same way
they treated us.

As Nisa continued to talk, her voice began to strike me as
unpleasant. I hoped that if I didn't say anything more she would
stop, and soon she did. She turned to Kxoma, Tuma, and her
husband and rejoined their conversation. It was very late by
now. Nisa and Bo had smoked, had drunk the sugar-saturated
coffee, and had exchanged news. It was time for them to go. As
they walked away, I felt relieved.

We stayed at Gausha a week that time. Every day Nisa visited our camp, and every day she reminded me how much
Nancy and Richard had done for her. She arrived in the morning,
sat around, watched the confusion our presence always generated, and talked to the people who waited for medicine or tobacco. Her three-year-old niece was always with her, and they
would play and laugh together. After the first day, I started to
dread these times. Her voice was loud, sharp, somewhat frantic,
and constantly seeking attention, and it seemed never to stop.
Whenever she had my attention (and often even when she
didn't), she talked about Nancy and Richard. My dread soon
turned to dislike, first mild, then stronger. I tried to escape to my
tent and close the flaps, but summer was approaching and the
days were already warm; I couldn't stay there long. I spent time
in the !Kung villages, interviewing women, but Nisa was often
there when I came back. Her voice persisted. I couldn't ignore it,
with its barrage of thinly veiled criticisms. I felt I needed a place
to go where I could close my ears and eyes, where I could stop
hearing and stop responding. I had to do something.

Finally I decided that since I had to listen to her anyway, I
might as well get her to talk about something I wanted to hear. I
had asked other women at Gausha about the drug properties of
various roots and plants, but these interviews had not been very
satisfying. The women seemed evasive, or perhaps they did not
know enough about what I was asking. None of them spoke
clearly on which specific roots had which specific effects. They
said I should ask an older woman, perhaps someone who ac-

tually helped others when they had problems. They didn't give me any names. How could I have known one would be Nisa?

At last I approached her: "I have some questions I want to ask you. Would you like to work with me?" She broke from her conversation and smiled broadly. Catching my eye, she said "Aiye!" which means, literally, "Mother!"—but this time it also meant "Of course I will, I'd love to."

It now seems a strange way to have begun a relationship that was to become so important to me, but it was only after I had approached her in this way that her attitude toward me changed. She had been trying to talk to me all along, but it was only on the subject of Nancy and Richard that she felt we had common ground. Now I had asked her to start something new. It was as though she had been waiting for me to see that she had something to offer.

Our first talk lasted an hour. She concentrated on my questions and answered them thoughtfully. She named four medicinal plants and described each one clearly—one, she said, prevented miscarriage, one brought on the menstrual flow, and two produced sterility. She told me about her sister-in-law whose "heart had been ruined by children"; she had given birth to ten, but only four were still alive. After the youngest died, she drank the medicine that makes a woman sterile; their deaths had caused her too much pain and she didn't want to have to go through it again. Throughout our talk, Nisa was considerate and helpful. She repeated things in different ways so as to be sure I understood. Most surprising, perhaps, was that she seemed to be enjoying herself. By the end of the hour, I had to admit that the interview had gone exceptionally well.

In our second talk, I asked her about children—what they did and how they played. She confirmed much of what Bau had told me about children's sexual play. She even described an incident she had seen a few days earlier: a boy, about six, and his sister were standing against the wall of their hut, the boy behind his sister, rubbing their bottoms together. And that wasn't the first time; she had seen them under a blanket once before. Both times she scolded them, telling the little girl that her vagina would become irritated and smell bad if she kept playing like that. But their parents didn't see them, and Nisa didn't tell. Children that age have no sense, she said; and anyway, their mother would have hit them. Nisa, somewhat amused, added that if a girl grows up without learning to enjoy sex, her mind doesn't develop normally and she goes around eating grass, like a crazy Herero woman who lived in the area. Grown women, too, need sex. If a woman doesn't have sex, Nisa claimed, her thoughts get ruined and she is always angry.

Nisa and I talked again the next day, the next, and the next. She began telling me about her own childhood: her homosexual loves, her initial refusal of sex with boys, the boyfriend she loved who taught her to play "house," and her eventual enjoyment of sex. I was entranced by then—the interviews were beautiful. But during our last meeting she told me something I found so puzzling that I began to doubt not only it but much of what she had told me before.

I had asked about her earliest childhood memories. She explained that a child, when very young, isn't aware of anything except nursing and sleeping. Once she walks and later talks, she starts to remember things. Nisa's earliest memories were of nursing, which she had loved. But when her mother became pregnant with her younger brother, Kumsa, Nisa was weaned. This caused her tremendous unhappiness. It happened when she was too young, she said. That was why she was so much smaller than her two brothers. When she wanted her mother's breasts, she found them covered with a bitter paste. She cried and screamed until it was washed off. But her mother said the milk in her breasts belonged to the baby growing inside her. If Nisa continued to nurse, she would get sick and might even die. Her father yelled at her, too. Nisa threw tantrums and was punished for her constant attempts to nurse; she was very unhappy.

So far this made sense. Other women had recounted similar experiences, and my husband had observed young children in the village undergoing intense emotional upsets during weaning.

But there was more. Nisa described a day when she went with her mother to gather food. Not far from the village, her mother sat down in the shade of a tree and gave birth to her brother Kumsa. When the baby was born, her mother told Nisa

31

to get the digging stick so she could bury him. Her mother was worried that Nisa had been weaned too early. If there weren't another baby, Nisa could nurse again. But Nisa cried and told her mother she didn't want to nurse any more; she wanted her baby brother to live. They argued and her mother finally agreed; they would keep the baby and he would nurse, not Nisa. Nisa believed that it was only through her own efforts that her younger brother had lived.

Could I have misunderstood? Infanticide is said to have existed at the time she spoke of, but a little girl would surely not have been involved, especially just after witnessing the birth. "Tell me again," I said, "more slowly this time, what happened when your brother was born." The retelling was essentially the same. Did she remember seeing all she had described, or was it what others had told her? She said, "I remember seeing it with my own eyes."

I didn't know what to make of it. It seemed too strange to be a lie. Perhaps it had to be interpreted another way? As one of her earliest "memories," maybe it was a fantasy she had created when her brother was born, to help her deal with the anger and jealousy she felt toward him. Or perhaps Nisa's mother, never seriously entertaining the idea, actually suggested killing the baby, knowing that Nisa would say no. She might have hoped to make Nisa feel protective toward her brother. Or, more likely, the threat might have been a guilt-inducing weapon to make Nisa stop complaining about weaning. Other explanations also came to mind. What was clear, however, was that Nisa believed the story as she told it.

Still, I began to doubt her again. We were planning to leave Gausha the next day. We could have stayed on, but with my renewed ambivalence about Nisa I felt relieved to be going. Days later I found myself dismissing her and denying the uniqueness of our contact. But I did acknowledge that talking with her had been good for me. Building on my talks with Bau, my discussions with Nisa gave me increased confidence. I was now determined to question other women, in ever-greater depth and intimacy, about their lives.

I interviewed seven women during the next ten months, and for the most part, the interviews were very successful. What Bau and Nisa had told me, the others confirmed and expanded on. By the end I had a reasonable understanding of the subtleties of !Kung women's inner feelings, and of their attitudes toward their lives. That was what I had hoped for initially, and I was pleased to have accomplished it. On another level, however, I was dissatisfied. I had wanted the women to give more than they had. I had hoped that at least a few of the women would become deeply involved in describing their experiences. I had also hoped that close friendships might develop during the course of our work.

In retrospect I could think of many possible reasons why none of this had happened. The interview situation was based, after all, on a business exchange: I paid for each set of interviews with money or gifts. Or perhaps my wealth, status, and foreignness kept the women from trusting me. Or it might have been more subtle, perhaps involving the type of woman I chose—one who had, after all, made sure that I would notice her. Whatever the underlying causes, it took me a long time to realize that neither close friendship nor a really spontaneous, open approach to the interviews would be forthcoming.

The signs had been there from the beginning. Long before I had spoken to Bau or had started the formal interviews, I had developed what seemed to be the beginnings of a pleasant friendship with a woman at Goshi. When I left Goshi, she would tell me how much she was going to miss me, and when I returned, she would be sure to greet me. I occasionally gave her small presents (such as bottles, oil, and beads) she had asked for—things of little monetary value, but highly coveted by the !Kung. I saw these gifts as expressions of my appreciation for her friendship. Over the course of several weeks, however, I noticed that she never gave me anything. Of course, being wealthier, I expected very little in return, but gifts, even those of minimal material value, are one way the !Kung show friendship. (Months later, modest presents from other !Kung confirmed that my expectations of her had been reasonable.) Following the !Kung custom, I approached her directly and said it was time I received a present:

roots, berries, nuts, or any small thing would do. She protested my accusation of stinginess (again, according to custom), but ultimately agreed that she should be more generous. I waited, not giving anything more for a while, but she never came. The next time I left Goshi she failed to tell me how much she would miss me; later still, we spoke only in greeting.

My early encounter with Hwantla was another instance. Beautiful, creative, and charismatic, Hwantla enchanted me perhaps more than any other !Kung woman. On our first day at Goshi, a dispute arose over what my !Kung name was going to be, with Hwantla and an older woman each urging me to accept her name. By taking a !Kung woman's name I would become identified as my namesake's genealogical twin and be incorporated into her social networks, based on kinship and name-sharing. (The !Kung have fewer than thirty-five names for each gender. People with the same name are linked in a special relationship—the name relationship—which can substitute for close kinship ties and which connects them to each other's lives in a way that would be impossible if social relations were based solely on biological kinship.)

I favored Hwantla from the outset, but I didn't want to alienate anyone during my first few days. Still, when she handed me a present, it was easy to accept—and I did, immediately. That day I wrote in my journal:

Hwantla stormed into my tent today after participating in a long, noisy discussion with the people who have been sitting around our camp since we arrived. She not only asked me, again, to take her name, but she came forth with a present—a beaded leather apron. The other women who approached me only talked about how much they expected me—their "little-name"—to give them once I accepted. But Hwantla actually gave *me* something. She didn't even say I'd have to reciprocate, although we both know that I will.

As soon as I understood what was happening—which took quite some time—I told her, with whatever sign language I could invent, that I was happy to accept her offer. I've been practicing calling myself Hwantla all afternoon, and I like the sound of it.

I had hoped our common name would favor a connection between Hwantla and me, perhaps even a meaningful friendship. I was completely taken with her and thrilled to have a pretext for staying near her. She sang, danced, and played her own musical compositions with talent and energy; she also seemed extremely intelligent and witty. I didn't expect much in the beginning, given the language barrier and my frequent trips elsewhere, and for the entire first year, nothing much developed between us.

After the initial interviews with Bau and Nisa were behind me and I had a greater command of the language and customs of !Kung women, I made my first serious effort to establish a closer relationship with Hwantla: I suggested that we work together. She was enthusiastic about the interviews and was responsive throughout, but the connection I had hoped for never materialized. It wasn't that she didn't trust me—once she even precipitated an argument with her husband in front of me. Yet most of the time she seemed reluctant to invest much of herself in our work, even less in her relationship with me. She was preoccupied with her own problems: she was barren, and her Tswana husband was spending more and more time with his mistress, with whom he had recently had a child. After the paid interviews were over, we rarely talked personally and she usually came to my camp only to ask for tobacco.

I wasn't as deeply involved with the next two women I interviewed. Nai, a fourteen-year-old girl on the verge of womanhood, and Nukha, twenty years old and already a mother, were both helpful informants, but neither had the spark, charm, or intelligence of Hwantla, or the clear-headed maturity of Bau. I had hoped to learn how Nai felt about growing up and her hopes and fears for the future. But she was in almost as much conflict about me as she was about her changing self, and she tried to avoid talking about most of the issues raised. With Nukha, it was quite possible to talk about her struggles with her husband and her occasional intimacies with other men, but she did not seem able or willing to articulate her deeper feelings.

The next two women, Naukha and Kxaru, were more problematic. Naukha, about thirty-five years old, a mother of three children, and (by her own account) happily married, told me essentially the same story over and over again. It took me days to

realize it, because the names and places always differed. I sometimes wondered if she was simply (and deliberately) juggling the
names of all the people, places, and foods she knew, fitting them
into a standard pattern, and creating new "memories." It was
her mother, father, sister, brother, aunt, or uncle who, to the
north, south, east, or west, once refused to give her a certain
root, berry, nut, or kind of meat. The next day, week, or month
when she had some root, berry, and so on of her own, and her
father, mother, and so on asked for it, it was her chance to refuse,
and she did! With this formula she could apparently have gone
on indefinitely, and that seemed to me to be her intention. I did
not see much humor in this, and at the time I could not easily
respect her right to be so evasive. I had not pressured her into
working with me, nor was I insisting that she continue. I finally
confronted her, saying that she had talked enough about stinginess and now we had to start talking about other things. But the
interviews never did go anywhere.

There was a different problem with Kxaru. Kxaru, about the
same age as Naukha, was kind, good-natured, and gentle, and
she loved working with me. But she had grown up much farther
south and had enough unfamiliar words in her vocabulary that
following her required tremendous effort and concentration.
Too often, the continuous effort of piecing together her words
became so tedious that I stopped reviewing as we went along.
Later I would realize that I had not understood much of what she
had said.

By the time I worked with Naukha and Kxaru, I had lived in
the field for more than nineteen months, and frustration, rather
than reasoned patience, characterized a good proportion of my
reactions. The strain of having been away from home so long, the
continual pressure of adapting to other people's ways, the hard
work of collecting reliable information about their lives, and the
demands of the physical environment had exhausted me. I
wanted to be finished. Had I had more energy, perhaps I would
have found a way to reassure Naukha, to encourage her to talk
more freely. Had I allowed the interviews with Kxaru to take
three times as long as the other women's did, while things were
clarified, she would have been willing. But I was not; worn down
and impatient, I was no longer as sensitive an interviewer as I

might otherwise have been. I wanted immediate rapport, immediate understanding, immediate confidences. I was lonely and no longer felt capable of exerting the necessary effort to gain acceptance. I was ready to be where living was physically easier, where people really cared about me, and where I could be alone when I wanted to, for hours at a time, undisturbed by requests from anyone.

Everything indicated that it was time to leave. My husband's work was near completion; I would soon be finished working with Naukha and then with Kxaru. We set three weeks as a realistic departure date. That still left enough time to interview Bey, who at seventy-five was the oldest woman at Goshi. She was an able storyteller and had been assuring me for months that I was wasting my time talking to young women. She "really knew" about things. Why hadn't I asked her? Despite my exhaustion, I was intrigued. Perhaps the perspective of age would make a difference. I decided to try.

"Bey, we've already talked about how people still remember some of their childhood experiences, no matter how old they are. You agreed and said that was true for yourself. Won't you tell me about things you still remember?"

"Yes, I certainly remember things from my childhood. I am old and have experienced much. You ask me about something and I'll tell you about it."

"Why don't you tell me about anything that comes into your mind about your childhood, something that has stayed with you over the years."

"Are you saying that people don't remember their childhoods? They do. Ask me and I'll tell you."

"Tell me about the things your mother and father did."

"Fine. They brought me up, gave me food, and I grew and grew and then I was an adult. That's what they did."

"Do you remember any specific time, maybe when they did something wonderful or perhaps, something you didn't like?"

"You are asking me well. Parents sometimes help children and sometimes scold them."

"Did your parents ever scold you?"

"Are you saying that a parent doesn't scold a child? Children do senseless things and their parents scold them."

"What did you do that was senseless?"

"I ruined things, just like my granddaughter. Why this very morning she ruined some things in the hut and my daughter-in-law hit her. Do you think a parent doesn't scold a child? No, a parent scolds a child, then the child learns sense."

"Bey, we are talking very well together; I know you are old and have experienced many things . . ."

"Many things, ehey, mother . . ."

". . . but I want to talk only about you, not about anyone else. I want to know about things you experienced, things your mother did when you were small, and what you did as you grew up, married, and had children. So far we have been talking about things in a general way, in a way that everyone would agree with. That's good. But now, let's talk more specifically about things that happened to you, about any time in your life."

"Yes, we are talking very well. You keep asking me and I'll keep telling you. I am old and know many things."

"I am asking you. But I cannot tell you what memories to speak about. Only you know what you've experienced. Try to tell me about something your parents or your siblings did; or what happened when you menstruated, when you married or had children; or, about your family, your co-wife, your husband . . . anything you'd like. Only it has to be about you."

"Yes . . . we have already talked about my mother and my father and how I ruined things. Now ask me about other things and I will tell you. I am old and *know*. Those other women are children and still haven't taught themselves. I have seen a lot. I really know. You ask me and I'll tell you . . ."

After a few days of just this sort of conversation, we stopped working together. Perhaps the details of her early experiences were no longer easily accessible to her, or the format of the interviews was difficult for her to adapt to. Or perhaps I was just too impatient to frame questions specific enough to draw her out. Just as likely, however, was that she thought she *was* offering what I wanted. She had lived for more than a quarter of a century before the first settlers came to the area; thus she was a bearer of the traditions, customs, and beliefs held by the !Kung as a people and over time. The weight of her opinions was what others most valued and most often asked her for. Wasn't that what anthropologists were supposed to want, anyway?

After these interviews, I had only to finish working with Kxaru and to organize and pack in preparation for leaving. But no sooner did the end seem near than old doubts started to surface again. Was the dissatisfaction I felt with the interviews really a consequence of the limits of the format? Or might I still find someone—someone not as unmalleable as Bey, yet with equally varied experience, who could talk about them from a mature, perhaps even philosophical, perspective? It was clear that most of the nine women had made reasonable attempts to be honest and open about their lives; and yet none of the interviews were especially inspiring.

At last, I thought about Nisa again. I still wasn't sure I could trust her, but something about her held my interest. I thought about how patient she had been with me and how important it had been to her that I understand. She had also been open and warm, even entertaining; and she did say that there was much more to tell. Of course, I had no way of knowing in advance that she would take on the job of teaching me about her life with a seriousness and clarity I had not met in anyone else. I just knew I could not leave without giving the interviews one last chance. The next day I sent a message asking if she would come, live in my camp, and work with me. She could bring her husband and her niece; I would feed the family and would pay her for our work. A few days later her message arrived: she was ready whenever I was.

In Nisa, I finally found what I had been looking for. After she understood the requirements of the interviews, she summarized her life in a loosely chronological order; then, following my lead, she discussed each major phase in depth. In the first interview she repeated the story of her younger brother's birth. Although this version contained more details than the first, the story itself had not changed. This time, however, I was not so badly thrown by it; I accepted it as something I might not understand for awhile. The final interpretation of this story and of some of the others will probably always remain subject to speculation. I came to see that as one of the rules of the game.

Nisa and I "worked very well together." We often joked about how I (her "niece") was a child and she (my "aunt")[4] was

39

a woman of vast experience whose task it was to teach me about life. We were pleasant and friendly and our rapport was easy. She had a determination to make each interview work and seemed to derive considerable pleasure from the entire process. Although she occasionally asked for direction, she led the way most of the time. At the start of an interview, she often asked to review the end of the previous session's tape, to see where we had left off and what still needed to be discussed. She would say things like, "Let's continue our talk about long ago. Let's also talk about the stories that the old people know. I will teach you so that you will learn." Once, in the middle of telling a story, her thoughts crowded with others. Delighted, she exclaimed, "What am I trying to do? Here I am, sitting, talking about one story, and another runs right into my head and into my thoughts!" Restraining them as she might a small child, she added, "I'll speak about those thoughts after I finish, after the ones I'm now talking about are gone."

When she would come to the end of a story, she would let me know by saying, "That is finished, is it not? Let's talk about another now." If I had no question, she would move on. She had another expression, one of my favorites: "the wind has taken that away." Once she elaborated: "I'll tell you another now. I'll break open the story and tell you what is there. Then, like the others that have fallen out onto the sand, I will finish with it, and the wind will take it away."

Most of her stories were described in rich detail and told with a beginning, a middle, and an end. If I questioned her before she had finished, she often said, "Wait. I'm getting to that. Now, listen." Once, however, she was describing the dissolution of one of her marriages—obviously a trying time for her. She ended her story in a fairly usual way, saying, "That's all, and life went on." An unusually long silence followed. Then she added, thoughtfully and slowly, "No. There's still something in my heart about this that isn't finished. My heart is still shaking. The story hasn't come completely out. I'm going to talk more about it until it does. Then, I'll go on to another. Then, my heart will be fine."

During our last interview, we discussed my imminent departure and her plans for the future. She said, "After you leave,

I'll stay around here for a few more days, then go to the bush, to live and to eat. There's still plenty of water, nuts, bulbs, and roots, so even winter will find me there. I won't live with the black people or where the cows stay.

"Because we are people who live in the bush, and who belong in the bush. We are not village people. I have no goats. I have no cattle. I am a person who owns nothing. That's what people say I am: a poor person. Yes, grandmother, a poor person without a goat or a teeny-weeny little cow. Not even a small baby goat that cries out 'Behhh . . . behhh . . .' No donkey, either. I still carry things myself, in my kaross when I travel, and that's why I live in the bush."

She felt that her plans were somewhat jeopardized by a dream—an almost prophetic glimpse of the future—that she had had the previous night. "I dreamed that I was hired to cut grass for a hut being built by the Tswana headman. He praised me, 'You're doing a fine job. After you finish fastening the grass, you'll have some corn meal to eat.' I said, 'I'm not selling my labor for corn meal. I'd rather have money.' The headman agreed, but when I woke up, I thought, 'Why did God[5] tell me I was doing something I didn't want to do?' A long time ago the headman did ask me to do that kind of work and I refused. I told him I wouldn't do it because I wasn't getting paid. Now God is telling me I'll be doing it again." She paused, then added, "But, I don't want to do that kind of work anymore."

Turning to my departure again, she said, "After you leave, I will continue to live. I will see things around me and think about them, as you've asked me to do. When I see something interesting, I'll say, 'Eh, this is something Marjorie and I have talked about. Its very heart is here. Now, there is more about this to tell her.' I will remember it and carry it around with me. When I see something else, I'll carry that, too. I'll carry all the things I have yet to see, and when you come back, I'll give them to you."

Then she said, "Perhaps, some day another white person will come here, perhaps Richard. After he stays for a while, I'll ask him to bring a present to you, Marjorie, from me. I'll find something beautiful—some ostrich eggshell beads or, if I have the leather, I'll sew a pouch with beads so that it will be truly beautiful. I'll say, 'Richard, when you return home, give this to Marjorie for me, only to Marjorie.' I'll also beg him to write the things I want to say to you. I'll say, 'Write down on paper that I am giving this pouch to Marjorie. Take it, along with the pouch, and bring it to her. I like her so much that when she left, my heart almost died.'

"But today, I have no pouch or even kaross, to fill up with bulbs. I don't know where I will get them. So, I still haven't given you a present." She fingered a bracelet on her arm, then pulled it off: smooth copper beads fastened to a band of dark leather. She handed it to me. "I've been looking for something to give you and found this bracelet. It won't go on your hand because it is too small. Here, put it away. Another day, give it to a child." I protested, "How will you do without it?" She said, "I'm giving it to you and want you to have it. Now, don't ever give it to someone else. Hold onto it. When you have your own child, you will name her Nisa and will put it on her leg. You'll tell her that it is her namesake who gave it to her. Then, when you bring her here, I'll carry her around and give her many other presents."

These were very moving moments for both of us—an extension, so it seemed, of the intensity of our conversations. Nevertheless, I did not become Nisa's "best friend," nor did she become mine. She rarely asked much about me, nor did she seem particularly interested in my life, and there was no doubt that the financial arrangements were important to her. Strangely enough, once the interviews gained momentum and I saw what she *was* giving, the rest no longer mattered. Her commitment to the interviews and her willingness to talk openly about all aspects of her life was, in a sense, the most valuable gift of friendship. To her, I wasn't just the "white woman" or the "rich one"; I was a Zhun/twa, a "real person," like herself. For that reason, I was worthy of her best efforts.

Her best efforts were what I got. The fifteen interviews completed during those two weeks and another six completed four years later during a second field trip provided me with the deepest insights I was able to gain into !Kung life. These interviews (constituting about 8 percent of all the interviews I conducted with !Kung women) produced close to thirty hours of tape in the

!Kung language and hundreds of pages of typewritten, literal transcriptions. These were written mostly in English, with many !Kung expressions retained so that the final translation could reflect nuances unique to !Kung. The chronological sequence in which the narrative is presented does not necessarily reflect the order in which the stories appear in the interviews. In a number of places, a memory presented as continuous is taken from more than one account of the same incident. Other changes come from the deletion of clarifying remarks and the modification or elimination of word and phrase repetitions—a dramatic device for emphasis in !Kung but distracting in English, which accomplishes the same purpose with adjectives. Apart from these changes, the narrative is faithful to the interviews. Wherever possible, I have incorporated literal translations of !Kung idioms to reflect some of the beauty and subtlety of the language. This may occasionally invest the narrative with a somewhat more poetic quality than Nisa intended.

Nisa's narrative is just one view of !Kung life. Her history does not represent the whole range of experience available to women in her culture; the life stories of other women are often quite different. Also, it is not possible to take everything Nisa says literally, particularly her descriptions of her earlier years. She enjoyed the interview situation with the "machine that grabs your voice." To make her story lively and dramatic, she often assumed the high, somewhat insistent voice of a young child, as though trying to describe the events of her childhood through the eyes of Nisa, the little girl. It is probable that these early accounts are somewhat exaggerated—a combination of actual memory, information about her childhood related to her when she was older, generalized experiences common to the culture, and fantasy. As the narrative progresses, her voice becomes more mature and independent and her stories are likely to be more reliable. I was able to corroborate much of what she said about her later life from independent sources. Thus her description of her adult life may be considered to be as accurate as it is vivid.

Chapter 1

Earliest Memories

!KUNG CHILDREN spend their first few years in almost constant close contact with their mothers. The !Kung infant has continual access to the mother's breast, day and night, usually for at least three years, and nurses on demand several times an hour. The child sleeps beside the mother at night, and during the day is carried in a sling, skin-to-skin on the mother's hip, wherever the mother goes, at work or at play. (This position is an ideal height for older children, who love to entertain babies.) When the child is not in the sling, the mother may be amusing her—bouncing, singing, or talking. If they are physically separated, it is usually for short periods when the father, siblings, cousins, grandparents, aunts, uncles, or friends of the family are playing with the baby while the mother sits close by. Separation from the mother becomes more frequent after the middle of the second year, but even then it is initiated almost exclusively by the child, who is steadily drawn into the groups of children playing around the village. Still, the mother is usually available whenever needed.

!Kung fathers—indulgent, affectionate, and devoted—also form very intense mutual attachments with their children. Nevertheless, men spend only a small fraction of the time that women do in the company of children, especially infants, and avoid many of the less pleasant tasks of child care, such as toileting, cleaning and bathing, and nose wiping. They are also inclined to hand crying or fretful babies back to the mothers for consolation. Fathers, like mothers, are not viewed as figures of awesome authority, and their relationships with their children are intimate, nurturant, and physically close. Sharing the same living and sleeping space, children have easy access to both parents when they are around. As children—especially boys—get older, fathers spend even more time with them.

Assuming no serious illness, the first real break from the infant's idyll of comfort and security comes with weaning, which typically begins when the child is around three years of age and the mother is pregnant again. Most !Kung believe that it is dangerous for a child to continue to nurse once the mother is pregnant with her next child. They say the milk in the woman's breasts belongs to the fetus; harm could befall either the unborn child or its sibling if the latter were to continue to nurse. It is considered essential to wean quickly, but weaning meets the child's strong resistance and may in fact take a number of months to accomplish. The usual procedure is to apply a paste made from a bitter root (or, more recently, tobacco resin) to the nipple, in the hope that the unpleasant taste will deter the child from sucking. Psychological pressure is also employed, as was clear from one woman's memories of being weaned: "People told me that if I nursed, my younger sibling would bite me and hit me after she was born. They said that, of course, just to get me to stop nursing."

If a child has recently been weaned and the mother miscarries, or if the new infant is stillborn or dies soon after birth, the older child may be allowed to nurse again. But this situation is considered far from ideal. One woman whose baby died and whose young son then resumed nursing was worried because her son had become ill. Other people in the village interpreted his illness as being caused by his mother's milk, which had been meant for his dead sibling. In this time of stress the boy clung to his mother and to the security of her breasts with an intensity that was difficult for her to rebuff. Although she believed she should refuse him the breast, she too was suffering and could not bring herself to do it. A few weeks later she did find the strength, and soon after that her son got better.

Because of the physical and emotional comfort nursing affords, most children do not give it up easily. Also, with no domesticated animals to provide substitute sources of milk, the only alternative to nursing is to eat increased amounts of bush foods, but these do not compare to the appeal of mother's milk. Children, therefore, are likely to be miserable during this period and often express their displeasure quite dramatically. Tantrums are typical, and general psychological distress is usually obvious. One man remembered, "I wanted to nurse after my younger brother was born, but my mother refused. I cried and my grandmother took me to another village so I would forget about nursing. But I thought about it anyway, and asked why she wouldn't take me back to my mother so I could nurse. I was in great pain."

The last-born child of a mother in her late thirties or early forties is spared the pain of abrupt weaning. If the mother does not get pregnant again, a child may nurse until the age of five or older, stopping only when social pressure such as mild ridicule from other children makes it difficult to continue.

When the new baby is born the older child also has to give up the coveted sleeping place immediately beside the mother. Although she may sleep between her parents for a while, an older child is eventually expected to sleep on the far side of her younger sibling. No surprise, then, that resentments and anger are frequently expressed toward the parents and sometimes even toward the new infant. This was clearly the case of a four-year-old who kept asking to hold her newborn brother. The mother finally took the baby from her sling and placed him gently in his sister's arms. The girl sat and rocked the baby, singing to him and praising him, while her mother stood nearby. The next moment, however, hearing the shouts of other children playing, the girl suddenly stood up and dropped her tiny brother in the sand. Without a glance, she ran off, followed by her brother's cries and her mother's admonishments.

Within a year of being weaned from the breast the child is "weaned" from the sling as well. !Kung children love to be carried. They love the contact with their mothers, and they love not having to walk under the pressure of keeping up. As their mothers begin to suggest and then to insist that they walk along beside them, temper tantrums once again erupt: children refuse to walk, demand to be carried, and will not agree to be left behind in the village while their mothers gather for the day. Other people often make this adjustment easier by offering to carry the child, and on long walks a father will usually carry the child on his shoulder. By the age of six or seven, however, a child is expected to walk on her own and is no longer carried, even for short distances.

!Kung parents are concerned that these events not hit their children too hard, but coming as they do one after the other, these times are difficult at best. The father may try to spend more time with the child, or the child may stay with a devoted grandparent or aunt (who will be sure to spoil her) in a nearby village for a while. But parents are aware that the tremendous outpouring of love given each child in the first few years of life produces children who are typically secure and capable of handling this period of emotional stress. The extremely close relationship with their mothers seems to give children strength: the child has the mother's almost exclusive attention for an average of forty-four months, thirty-six of these with unlimited access to the food and comfort afforded by nursing. Also, the child of three or four is no longer as needy of the mother's attention as she had been. The boisterous play of other children ultimately becomes more appealing than continuing the conflict with the mother. Within a few months after the birth of their siblings, many children can be seen playing exuberantly most of the day and only occasionally behaving angrily with their families. Before long even these difficulties are largely overcome as the child starts enjoying the role of older sibling. Because children are between three and five years old when these events occur, many adults remember, if not the actual details, at least the feelings that accompanied weaning, both from the breast and from the sling. Some adults, looking back, see these events as having had a formative influence on their lives.

The !Kung economy is based on sharing, and children are encouraged to share things from their infancy. Among the first words a child learns are na ("give it to me") and ihn ("take this"). But sharing is hard for children to learn, especially when they are expected to share with someone they resent or dislike.

And giving or withholding food or possessions may be a powerful way to express anger, jealousy, and resentment, as well as love.

It is also hard to learn not simply to take what you want, when you want it. !Kung children rarely go hungry; even in the occasional times when food is scarce, they get preferential treatment. Food is sometimes withheld as a form of punishment for wasting or destroying it, but such punishment is always short-lived. Nevertheless, many adults recall "stealing" food as children. These episodes reflect the general !Kung anxiety about their food supply, as well as the pleasure they take in food—both emotions already present in childhood.

!Kung parents are tolerant toward children's angry outbursts. Most youthful transgressions are explained by remarks like "Children have no sense" or "Their intelligence hasn't come to them yet." Behavior is judged, commented on, and occasionally criticized, and scoldings are not uncommon, but parents basically believe children to be utterly irresponsible. There is no doubt in the parents' minds that as children grow up they will learn to act with sense, with or without deliberate training, simply as a result of maturation, social pressure and the desire to conform to group values. Since most !Kung adults are cooperative, generous, and hardworking and seem to be no more self-centered than any other people, this theory is evidently right, at least for them.

Although the !Kung say that children need to be disciplined, their efforts to do so are minimal. Adult attitudes toward discipline are not always clearly understood by a child, however—especially an older child, who may feel stronger pressure to conform. One young girl was convinced that a woman's lack of response to the verbal assault of her young son was just as "senseless" as the boy's behavior: "His mother didn't do anything to him. She didn't even yell at him. That's how adults are—without sense. When a child insults them, they just sit there and laugh."

Still, these early years are often remembered as times of intense conflict between parents and children. Beating and threats of beating are almost universal in the childhood memories of

!Kung adults; yet observational research has shown that !Kung parents are highly indulgent with children of all ages, and physical punishment is almost never witnessed. It is probable that rare instances of physical punishment become exaggerated and vivid in the child's memory. So, too, the much more common *threats* of beatings may be translated, in retrospect, into actual incidents. Whatever the reality, such memories dramatize the very real tensions that exist in !Kung families as in any others.

Grandparents (and often other relatives) are remembered much more favorably. Alternate generations are recognized as having a special relationship, especially when the child is the grandparent's "namesake." Personal and intimate topics not discussed with parents are taken up freely with grandparents, and grandparents often represent a child's interests at the expense of those of the parent. Also, since older people contribute less to subsistence than do younger adults, they have more time to play with their grandchildren. It is not surprising that children are willing to live with them or with other close relatives, especially during times of conflict with parents. As one young girl explained, "When I was a little girl, I lived with my aunt for weeks, sometimes for months at a time. I didn't cry when I lived with her; she was my second mother."

FIX MY VOICE on the machine so that my words come out clear. I am an old person who has experienced many things and I have much to talk about. I will tell my talk, of the things I have done and the things that my parents and others have done. But don't let the people I live with hear what I say.

Our father's name was Gau and our mother's was Chuko. Of course, when my father married my mother, I wasn't there. But soon after, they gave birth to a son whom they called Dau. Then they gave birth to me, Nisa, and then my younger brother was born, their youngest child who survived, and they named him Kumsa.[1]

I remember when my mother was pregnant with Kumsa. I was still small and I asked, "Mommy, that baby inside you . . . when that baby is born, will it come out from your belly button? Will the baby grow and grow until Daddy breaks open your stomach with a knife and takes my little sibling out?" She said, "No, it won't come out that way. When you give birth, a baby comes from here," and she pointed to her genitals. Then she said, "And after he is born, you can carry your little sibling around." I said, "Yes, I'll carry him!"

Later, I asked, "Won't you help me and let me nurse?" She said, "You can't nurse any longer. If you do, you'll die." I left her and went and played by myself for a while. When I came back, I asked to nurse again but she still wouldn't let me. She took some paste made from the dch'a root and rubbed it on her nipple. When I tasted it, I told her it was bitter.

When mother was pregnant with Kumsa, I was always crying. I *wanted* to nurse! Once, when we were living in the bush and away from other people, I was especially full of tears. I cried all the time. That was when my father said he was going to beat me to death;[2] I was too full of tears and too full of crying. He had a big branch in his hand when he grabbed me, but he didn't hit me; he was only trying to frighten me. I cried out, "Mommy, come help me! Mommy! Come! Help me!" When my mother came, she said, "No,

51

Gau, you are a man. If you hit Nisa you will put sickness into her and she will become very sick. Now, leave her alone. I'll hit her if it's necessary. My arm doesn't have the power to make her sick; your arm, a man's arm, does."

When I finally stopped crying, my throat was full of pain. All the tears had hurt my throat.

Another time, my father took me and left me alone in the bush. We had left one village and were moving to another and had stopped along the way to sleep. As soon as night sat, I started to cry. I cried and cried and cried. My father hit me, but I kept crying. I probably would have cried the whole night, but finally, he got up and said, "I'm taking you and leaving you out in the bush for the hyenas to kill. What kind of child are you? If you nurse your sibling's milk, you'll die!" He picked me up, carried me away from camp and set me down in the bush. He shouted, "Hyenas! There's meat over here . . . Hyenas! Come and take this meat!" Then he turned and started to walk back to the village.

After he left, I was so afraid! I started to run and, crying, I ran past him. Still crying, I ran back to my mother and lay down beside her. I was afraid of the night and of the hyenas, so I lay there quietly. When my father came back, he said, "Today, I'm really going to make you shit!³ You can see your mother's stomach is huge, yet you still want to nurse." I started to cry again and cried and cried; then I was quiet again and lay down. My father said, "Good, lie there quietly. Tomorrow, I'll kill a guinea fowl for you to eat."

The next day, he went hunting and killed a guinea fowl. When he came back, he cooked it for me and I ate and ate and ate. But when I was finished, I said I wanted to take my mother's nipple again. My father grabbed a strap and started to hit me, "Nisa, have you no sense? Can't you understand? Leave your mother's chest alone!" And I began to cry again.

Another time, when we were walking together in the bush, I said, "Mommy . . . carry me!" She said yes, but my father told her not to. He said I was big enough to walk along by myself. Also, my mother was pregnant. He wanted to hit me, but my older brother Dau stopped him, "You've hit her so much, she's skinny! She's so thin, she's only bones. Stop treating her this way!" Then Dau picked me up and carried me on his shoulders.

When mother was pregnant with Kumsa, I was always crying, wasn't I? I would cry for a while, then be quiet and sit around, eating regular food: sweet nin berries and starchy chon and klaru bulbs, foods of the rainy season. One day, after I had eaten and was full, I said, "Mommy, won't you let me have just a little milk? Please, let me nurse." She cried, "Mother!⁴ My breasts are things of shit! Shit! Yes, the milk is like vomit and smells terrible. You can't drink it. If you do, you'll go, 'Whaagh . . . Whaagh . . .' and throw up." I said, "No, I won't throw up, I'll just nurse." But she refused and said, "Tomorrow, Daddy will trap a springhare, just for you to eat." When I heard that, my heart was happy again.

The next day, my father killed a springhare. When I saw him coming home with it, I shouted, "Ho, ho, Daddy! Ho, ho, Daddy's come! Daddy killed a springhare; Daddy's bringing home meat! Now I will eat and won't give any to *her.*" My father cooked the meat and when it was done, I ate and ate and ate. I told her, "You stinged⁵ your milk, so I'll stinge this meat. You think your breasts are such wonderful things? They're not, they're terrible things." She said, "Nisa, please listen to me—my milk is not good for you anymore." I said, "Grandmother! I don't want it anymore! I'll eat meat instead. I'll never have anything to do with your breasts again. I'll just eat the meat Daddy and Dau kill for me."

Mother's stomach grew very large. The first labor pains came at night and stayed with her until dawn. That morning, everyone went gathering. Mother and I stayed behind. We sat together for a while, then I went and played with the other children. Later, I came back and ate the nuts she had cracked for me. She got up and started to get ready. I said, "Mommy, let's go to the water well, I'm thirsty." She said, "Uhn, uhn, I'm going to gather some mongongo nuts." I told the children that I was going and we left; there were no other adults around.

We walked a short way, then she sat down by the base of a large nehn tree, leaned back against it, and little Kumsa was born. At first, I just stood there; then I sat down and watched. I thought, "Is that the way it's done? You just sit like that and that's where the baby comes out? Am I also like that?" Did I have any understanding of things?

After he was born, he lay there, crying. I greeted him, "Ho, ho, my baby brother! Ho, ho, I have a little brother! Some day we'll play together." But my mother said, "What do you think this thing is? Why are you talking to it like that? Now, get up and go back to the village and bring me my digging stick." I said, "What are you going to dig?" She said, "A hole. I'm going to dig a hole so I can bury the baby. Then you, Nisa, will be able to nurse again."[6] I refused. "My baby brother? My little brother? Mommy, he's my *brother!* Pick him up and carry him back to the village. I don't want to nurse!" Then I said, "I'll tell Daddy when he comes home!" She said, "You won't tell him. Now, run back and bring me my digging stick. I'll bury him so you can nurse again. You're much too thin." I didn't want to go and started to cry. I sat there, my tears falling, crying and crying. But she told me to go, saying she wanted my bones to be strong. So, I left and went back to the village, crying as I walked.

I was still crying when I arrived. I went to the hut and got her digging stick. My mother's younger sister had just arrived home from the nut groves. She put the mongongo nuts she had gathered into a pile near her hut and sat down. Then she began roasting them. When she saw me, she said, "Nisa, what's wrong? Where's your mother?" I said, "By the nehn tree way out there. That's where we went together and where she just now gave birth to a baby. She told me to come back and get her digging stick so she could . . . bury him! This is terrible!" and I started to cry again. Then I added, "When I greeted him and called him 'my little brother' she told me not to. What she wants to do is bad . . . that's why I'm crying. Now I have to bring this digging stick to her!"

My mother's sister said, "Oooo . . . people! This Chuko, she's certainly a bad one to be talking like that. And she's out there alone with the baby! No matter what it is—a boy or a girl—she should keep it." I said, "Yes, he's a little boy with a little penis just resting there at the bottom of his stomach." She said, "Mother! Let's go! Let's go and talk to her. When I get there I'll cut his umbilical cord and carry him back."

I left the digging stick behind and we ran to where my mother was still sitting, waiting for me. Perhaps she had already changed her mind, because, when we got there, she said, "Nisa, because you were crying like that, I'll keep the baby and carry him back with me." My aunt went over to Kumsa lying beside my mother and said, "Chuko, were you trying to split your face into pieces?[7] You can see what a big boy you gave birth to, yet you wanted Nisa to bring back your digging stick? You wanted to bury this great big baby? Your own father worked to feed you and keep you alive. This child's father would surely have killed you if you had buried his little boy. You must have no sense, wanting to kill such a nice big baby."

My aunt cut his umbilical cord, wiped him off, put him into her kaross, and carried him back to the village. Mother soon got up and followed, shamed by her sister's talk. Finally, she said, "Can't you understand? Nisa is still a little child. My heart's not happy that she hasn't any milk to drink. Her body is weak. I want her bones to grow strong." But my aunt said, "When Gau hears about this, he'll beat you. A grown woman with one child following after another so nicely, doesn't behave like this." When we arrived back in the village, my mother took the baby and lay down.

Everyone was now coming back from the mongongo groves. After they put down their gatherings, they came to look at Kumsa. The women all said, "Oooh . . . this woman has no sense! She gave birth to such a big baby, yet she was going to kill it!" My mother said, "I wanted his older sister to nurse, that's why I would have done it, and if I had been alone, I would have! I did the wrong thing by not taking my digging stick with me, but others did the wrong thing by tak-

ing him away from me. That's why I'm here with him at all."
The women did not agree. They told my aunt, "You did very
well. You were right to take the baby from Chuko and save
him for his father. Wouldn't Chuko have had to answer to
him if she had killed his baby?"

When the sun was low in the sky, my father came home
from hunting. I greeted him, "Ho, ho, Daddy! Ho, ho,
Daddy's home! There's Daddy!" He came and sat down beside the hut. He asked my mother, "What's wrong? Why are
you lying down? Is something hurting you?" She said, "No,
I'm just lying down." Then he said, "Eh-hey . . . my wife gave
birth? Chuko, it's a boy?" She said, "Yes, a little boy." Then
her sister said, "And a very large baby, too! But Chuko said
she was going to . . ." I interrupted, "*Kill* him!" I rushed on,
"She told me to come back and get her digging stick so she
could kill my baby brother. I started to cry and came back to
the village. But Aunt Koka went back with me and took the
baby away from her." My aunt said, "Yes, I pulled the baby
from his grave and carried him back." Then I said, "There he
is lying over there. Mommy wanted to kill him."

My father said, "Chuko, why did you want to kill my
son? If you had, I would have killed you. I would have struck
you with my spear and killed you. Do you think I wouldn't
do that? I surely would. What was making you feel so much
pain that you would have killed such a large baby? You'll
keep both children, now. Nisa will continue to grow up eating regular food."

After Kumsa was born, I sometimes just played by myself.
I'd take the big kaross and lie down in it. I'd think, "Oh, I'm
a child playing all alone. Where could I possibly go by myself?" Then I'd sit up and say, "Mommy, take my little brother
from your kaross and let me play with him." But whenever
she did, I hit him and made him cry. Even though he was still
a little baby, I hit him. Then my mother would say, "You still
want to nurse, but I won't let you. When Kumsa wants to, I'll
let him. But whenever you want to, I'll cover my breasts with
my hand and you'll feel ashamed."

I wanted the milk she had in her breasts, and when she nursed him, my eyes watched as the milk spilled out. I'd cry all night, cry and cry until dawn broke. Some mornings I just stayed around and my tears fell and I cried and refused all food. That was because I saw him nursing. I saw with my eyes the milk spilling out, the milk *I* wanted. I thought it was mine.

One day, my older brother came back from hunting carrying a duiker he had killed. I was sitting, playing by myself when I saw him, "Mommy! Mommy! Look! Big brother killed a duiker! Look over there, he's killed a duiker." My mother said, "Eh, didn't I tell you this morning that you should stop crying and wait for your older brother to come home? Now, see what he's brought back for you!"

When my brother started to skin it, I watched. "Oooo, a *male* duiker. Mommy . . . look, it's a male." I pointed, "There are its testicles and there's its penis." My older brother said, "Yes, those are its testicles and there's its penis."

After he skinned it, he gave me the feet. I put them in the coals to roast. Then he gave me some meat from the calf and I put that in the coals, too. When it was ready, I ate and ate and ate. Mother told me to give her some, but I refused, "Didn't you stinge your breasts? Didn't I say I wanted to nurse? I'm the only one who's going to eat this meat. I won't give any of it to you!" She said, "The milk you want belongs to your brother. What's making you still want to nurse?" I said, "My big brother killed this duiker. You won't have any of it. Not *you*. He'll cut the rest into strips and hang it to dry for me to eat. You refused to let me nurse so your son could. Now you say I should give you meat?"

Another day, my mother was lying down asleep with Kumsa, and I quietly sneaked up on them. I took Kumsa away from her, put him down on the other side of the hut, and came back and lay down beside her. While she slept, I took her nipple, put it in my mouth and began to nurse. I nursed and nursed and nursed. Maybe she thought it was my little brother. But he was still lying where I left him, while I stole his milk. I had already begun to feel wonderfully full

when she woke up. She saw me and cried, "Where . . . tell
me . . . what did you do with Kumsa? Where is he?" At that
moment, he started to cry. I said, "He's over there."

She grabbed me and pushed me, hard, away from her. I
lay there and cried. She went to Kumsa, picked him up, and
laid him down beside her. She insulted me, cursing my genitals,[8] "Have you gone crazy? Nisa-Big-Genitals, what's the
matter with you? What craziness grabbed you that you took
Kumsa, put him somewhere else, then lay down and nursed?
Nisa-Big-Genitals! You must be crazy! I thought it was Kumsa
nursing!" I lay there, crying. Then I said, "I've already nursed.
I'm full. Let your baby nurse now. Go, feed him. I'm going to
play." I got up and went and played. Later, I came back and
stayed with my mother and her son. We stayed around together the rest of the day.

Later, when my father came back from the bush, she
said, "Do you see what kind of mind your daughter has? Go,
hit her! Hit her after you hear what she's done. Your daughter
almost killed Kumsa! This tiny little baby, this tiny little thing,
she took from beside me and dropped somewhere else. I was
lying down, holding him, and fell asleep. That's when she
took him from me and left him by himself. She came back,
lay down, and started to nurse. Now, hit your daughter!"

I lied, "What? She's lying! Me . . . Daddy, I didn't nurse. I
didn't take Kumsa and leave him by himself. Truly, I didn't.
She's tricking you. She's lying. I didn't nurse. I don't even
want her milk anymore." My father said, "If I ever hear of
this again, I'll beat you! Don't ever do something like that
again!" I said, "Yes, he's my little brother, isn't he? My
brother, my little baby brother, and I _love_ him. I won't do
that again. He can nurse all by himself. Daddy, even if you're
not here, I won't steal mommy's breasts. They belong to my
brother." He said, "Yes, daughter. But if you ever try to nurse
your mother's breasts again, I'll hit you so that it _really_ hurts."
I said, "Eh, from now on, I'm going to go wherever you go.
When you go to the bush, I'll go with you. The two of us will
kill springhare together and you'll trap guinea fowl and you'll

give them all to me."

My father slept beside me that night. When dawn broke, he and my older brother left to go hunting. I watched as they walked off. I thought, "If I stay here, mother won't let me nurse," so I got up and ran after them. But when my brother saw me, he pushed me back toward the village, "Go back and stay in the village. When the sun is hot like this, it could kill you. Why do you want to come with us, anyway?"

This was also when I used to steal food, although it only happened once in a while. Some days I wouldn't steal anything and would just stay around playing, without doing any mischief. But other times, when they left me in the village, I'd steal and ruin[9] their things. That's what they said when they yelled at me and hit me. They said I had no sense.

It happened over all types of food: sweet nin berries or klaru bulbs, other times it was mongongo nuts. I'd think, "Uhn, uhn, they won't give me any of that. But if I steal it, they'll hit me." Sometimes, before my mother went gathering, she'd leave food inside a leather pouch and hang it high on one of the branches inside the hut. If it was klaru, she'd peel off the skins before putting them inside.

But as soon as she left, I'd steal whatever was left in the bag. I'd find the biggest bulbs and take them. I'd hang the bag back on the branch and go sit somewhere to eat. When my mother came back, she'd say, "Oh! Nisa was in here and stole all the bulbs!" She'd hit me and yell, "Don't steal! What's the matter with you that inside you there is so much stealing? Stop taking things! Why are you so full of something like that?"

One day, right after they left, I climbed the tree where she had hung the pouch, took out some bulbs, put the pouch back, and mashed them with water in a mortar. I put the paste in a pot and cooked it. When it was ready, I ate and finished everything I had stolen.

Another time, I took some klaru and kept the bulbs beside me, eating them very slowly. That's when mother came back and caught me. She grabbed me and hit me, "Nisa, stop stealing! Are you the only one who wants to eat klaru? Now, let me take what's left and cook them for all of us to eat. Did you really think you were the only one who was going to eat them all?" I didn't answer and started to cry. She roasted the rest of the klaru and the whole family ate. I sat there, crying. She said, "Oh, this one has no sense, finishing all those klaru like that. Those are the ones I had peeled and had left in the pouch. Has she no sense at all?" I cried, "Mommy, don't talk like that." She wanted to hit me, but my father wouldn't let her.

Another time, I was out gathering with my mother, my father, and my older brother. After a while, I said, "Mommy, give me some klaru." She said, "I still have to peel these. As soon as I do, we'll go back to the village and eat them." I had also been digging klaru to take back to the village, but I ate all I could dig. My mother said, "Are you going to eat all your klaru right now? What will you eat when you get back to the village?" I started to cry. My father told me the same, "Don't eat all your klaru here. Leave them in your pouch and soon your pouch will be full." But I didn't want that, "If I put all my klaru in my pouch, which ones am I going to eat now?"

Later, I sat down in the shade of a tree while they gathered nearby. As soon as they had moved far enough away, I climbed the tree where they had left a pouch hanging, full of klaru, and stole the bulbs. I had my little pouch, the one my father had made me, and as I took the bulbs, I put them in it. I took out more and more and put them all in together. Then I climbed down and sat, waiting for them to return.

They came back, "Nisa, you ate the klaru! What do you have to say for yourself?" I said, "Uhn, uhn, I didn't take them." My mother said, "So, you're afraid of your skin hurting, afraid of being hit?" I said, "Uhn, uhn, I didn't eat those klaru." She said, "You ate them. You certainly did. Now, don't do that again! What's making you keep on stealing?"

My older brother said, "Mother, don't punish her today. You've already hit her too many times. Just leave her alone.

We can see. She says she didn't steal the klaru. Well then, what did eat them? Who else was here?"

I started to cry. Mother broke off a branch and hit me, "Don't steal! Can't you understand! I tell you, but you don't listen. Don't your ears hear when I talk to you?" I said, "Uhn, uhn. Mommy's been making me feel bad for too long now. I'm going to go stay with Grandma. Mommy keeps saying I steal things and hits me so that my skin hurts. I'm going to go stay with Grandma. I'll go where she goes and sleep beside her wherever she sleeps. And when she goes out digging klaru, I'll eat what she brings back."

But when I went to my grandmother, she said, "No, I can't take care of you this time. If you stay with me, you'll be hungry. I'm old and only go gathering one day in many. Most mornings I just stay around. We'll sit together and hunger will kill you. Now, go back and sit beside your mother and father." I said, "No, Daddy will hit me. Mommy will hit me. My skin hurts from being hit. I want to stay with you."

I lived with her for a while. But I was still full of tears. I just cried and cried and cried. I sat with her and no matter if the sun was setting or was high in the sky, I just cried. One month, when the nearly full moon rose just after sunset, I went back to my mother's hut. I said, "Mommy, you hate me. You always hit me. I'm going to stay on with Grandma. You hate me and hit me until I can't stand it any more. I'm tired."

Another time when I went to my grandmother, we lived in another village, nearby. While I was there, my father said to my mother, "Go, go bring Nisa back. Get her so she can be with me. What did she do that you chased her away from here?" When I was told they wanted me to come back I said, "No, I won't go back. I'm not going to do what he said. I don't want to live with Mother. I want to stay with Grandma; my skin still hurts. Today, yes, this very day here, I'm going to just continue to sleep beside Grandma."

So, I stayed with her. Then, one day she said, "I'm going to take you back to your mother and father." She took me to them, saying, "Today, I'm giving Nisa back to you. But isn't there someone here who will take good care of her? You don't just hit and hit a child like this one. She likes food and likes to eat. All of you are lazy. You've just left her so she hasn't grown well. If there were still plenty of food around, I'd continue to take care of her. She'd just continue to grow up beside me. Only after she had grown up, would she leave. Because all of you have killed this child with hunger. With your own fingers you've beaten her, beaten her as though she weren't a Zhun/twa.[10] She was always crying. Look at her now, how small she still is." But my mother said, "No, listen to me. Your little granddaughter . . . whenever she saw food with her eyes, she'd just start crying."

Oh, but my heart was happy! Grandmother was scolding Mother! I held so much happiness in my heart that I laughed and laughed. But when Grandmother went home and left me there I cried and cried. My father yelled at me, but he didn't hit me. His anger usually came out only from his mouth. "You're so senseless! Don't you realize that after you left, everything felt less important? We wanted you to be with us. Yes, even your mother wanted you and missed you. Today, everything will be all right when you stay with us. Your mother will take you where she goes; the two of you will do things together and go gathering together. Why do you refuse to leave your grandmother now?"

But I cried and cried. I didn't want to leave her. "Mommy, let me go back and stay with Grandma, let me follow after her." But my father said, "That's enough. No more talk like that. There's nothing here that will hit you. Now, be quiet." And I was quiet. After that, when my father dug klaru bulbs, I ate them, and when he dug chon bulbs, I ate them. I ate everything they gave me, and I wasn't yelled at any more.

When I was growing up, some days I stayed with my aunt. I lived with her, then went back and lived with my mother. After, I moved on again and lived with my grandmother and stayed with her for a few nights.

They all brought me up. All of them helped. My aunt brought me up; my father and mother brought me up; my grandmother brought me up. But I was very very small. My mother made me stop nursing too early and I was *tiny!* So, even as I am today, although I'm old, I'm still small. Look at my older brother Dau and my younger brother Kumsa and you'll see how big they are. Only I am small.

People failed at bringing me up. I was too difficult for them.

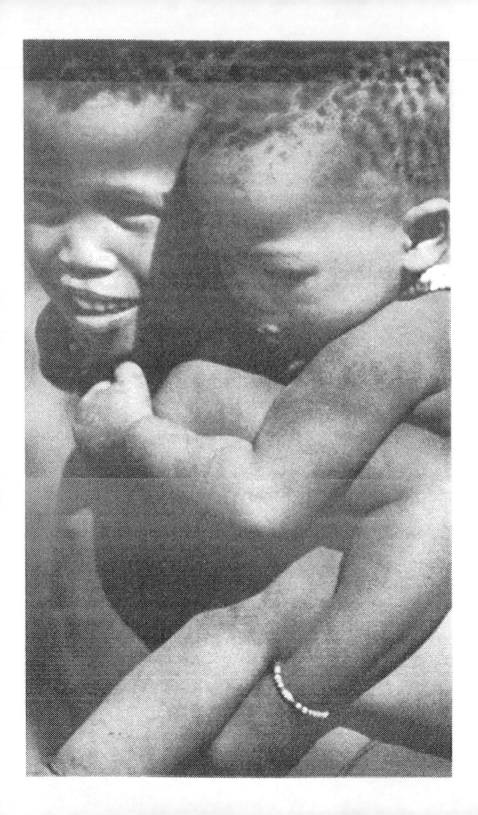

Chapter 2
Family Life

THE ANGER AND RESENTMENT occasioned by the birth of a sibling may be reflected in tensions between adjacent siblings for months or even years. One young girl expressed feelings from her early childhood: "After my sister was born, I remember looking at her and thinking, 'That's not my sister, that's someone else's sister.' I wanted to hit her because everyone kept telling me she *was* my sister. But I just *knew* she wasn't. One day, when she was about a week old, I did hit her. My father punished me, so I didn't do it again. That was bad, of course. But I had no sense at the time."

!Kung children are discouraged from fighting, but anger is recognized as something they ultimately have to learn to handle themselves; children of comparable strength often resolve their own fights before parents become involved. Dealing with anger is difficult for adults as well as for children. Daily tensions often spark conflicts that result in bitter displays of antagonism. Bystanders attempt to quell the truly serious eruptions, but it is not always easy: when arguments arise, everyone is apt to become involved. Physical fights sometimes ensue. Such outbursts are usually followed by personal regret and by attempts to make up for any harm done. Fortunately, most conflicts are resolved before they reach this point, through hours of talk; or, less commonly, by splitting up of the group, either temporarily or permanently.

!Kung siblings are likely to be about four years apart in age—an unusually long birth spacing for a population without birth control. How !Kung women maintain these long intervals between births is a question only now being answered. The !Kung claim to know of plants that cause miscarriage when properly prepared and ingested, but there is no evidence that these are effective—or even that they are used. A taboo against resuming sexual relations is also said to be in effect for about six months after a child's birth, but most couples share their blankets again immediately after a birth and do not abide by this restriction for very long. (Even if they did, it would allow the women to get pregnant soon after the end of the six months, resulting in a birth spacing of two years at most.)

Infanticide has also been suggested as an explanation. Bantu law now prohibits this practice, but even in traditional times it probably occurred only rarely—in cases of congenital deformity, of too short birth spacing, or of twins, regardless of gender. The length of the birth interval could be a life-or-death issue: if a woman had another baby too soon, either the baby or her older child—already the object of great affection—would probably die. Nursing a child requires a large daily intake of calories by the mother. Although the !Kung diet is usually adequate for this, it would be debilitating or even impossible for a woman to produce enough milk for two children. (The milk has been analyzed and found to be nutritionally adequate and almost comparable in composition to samples taken from Western women.) With no other sources of milk available, the older child would have to be weaned onto bush foods, which are rough and difficult to digest. To survive on such foods a child would have to be older than two years—preferably substantially older. (Today cows' milk is available for toddlers, so this problem has largely been eliminated.)

The decision in favor of infanticide was never made lightly or without anguish, but sometimes there was little choice. The woman would probably give birth alone and bury the infant immediately, preferably before it took its first breath. (The traditional !Kung did not consider a child a true person until it was brought back to the village; thus early infanticide was not seen as homicide.) Such cases, however, must have been extremely rare; even stillbirths, only a fraction of which could be concealed infanticide, accounted for only about one percent of births. Thus, only a few women had to face this choice personally and directly.

One likely explanation for the long birth intervals is the !Kung pattern of prolonged nursing. Although solid foods supplement a child's diet as early as six months of age (either premasticated or mashed at this early stage) nursing continues on the average of several times an hour throughout the first few years of a child's life. The constant stimulation of the nipple has been shown to suppress the levels of hormones that promote ovulation, thus making conception unlikely. Another possibility is that the huge calorie expenditure of nursing combined with subsistence-level nutrition does not afford the necessary surplus energy for ovulation to re-establish itself.

Whatever the exact cause, the resulting four-year birth interval is essential to the !Kung way of life. !Kung women are the major providers of child care and carry young children almost everywhere they go—an estimated 1500 miles a year. Women are also the major providers of food and walk between two and twelve miles two or three times a week to go gathering. When they return they carry, along with their child, fifteen to thirty-three pounds of wild vegetables, although loads of forty pounds and more have been recorded. They also make frequent day trips to villages a few miles away and take longer trips when the entire group moves camp or visits people living at distances of up to sixty miles. On these long trips women also carry their few possessions—a mortar and pestle, cooking utensils, water containers, a digging stick, various ornaments and pieces of clothing, as well as water—adding another two to four pounds to their burden.

For women who weigh an average of ninety pounds themselves, maintaining their subsistence activities would be difficult, if not impossible, were the birth interval any shorter. A four-year-old is able to keep pace walking with adults, at least on short trips, or may be willing to stay in the village while her mother goes gathering for the day. A younger child would be more dependent; the mother would have to carry her, as well as the new infant, wherever she went. (Even four years is a compromise, and it is not uncommon to see a woman returning from a gathering expedition loaded with bush foods, a four-year-old—weighing perhaps twenty-eight pounds—astride her shoulder, and an infant—weighing perhaps thirteen pounds—in a sling on her hip.)

Perhaps because they tend to experience only a few menstrual periods between pregnancies, !Kung women consider menstruation "a thing of no account." Although it is occasionally referred to as "having sickness" and although some associated physical discomfort is acknowledged (for example, cramps, breast tenderness, headaches, and backaches), menstruation is not thought to affect women's psychological state. Many !Kung women do believe, however, that if a woman sees traces of menstrual blood on another woman's leg or even is told that another woman has started her period, *she* will begin menstruating as well. (This phenomenon, known as menstrual synchrony, has not been proven to occur anywhere, but it has received some support in American studies.)

!Kung women try to conceal their menstrual blood, but this is not always possible. Leaves, pieces of leather skins, or, more recently, cloth that can be washed and saved are the only articles they have to contain their flow. They are concerned about cleanliness, but water is available only in small quantities during much of the year, making daily bathing difficult. Some women curtail their visiting when the flow is heaviest, but others carry on their normal activities. One women explained, "When I want to visit, I go at night. Then, no one can see if there is blood on my legs." The end of menstruation is followed by bathing, even if water is scarce.

Menstruation is given minimal attention by the !Kung. Women are not set apart and couples do not cease to lie beside each other at night. Sexual activity is expected to come to a halt, but since conception is thought to result from the joining of semen with the last of the menstrual blood, the taboo may give way, especially during the last day or two, if conception is desired.

WE LIVED AND LIVED,[1] and as I kept growing, I started to carry my little brother around on my shoulders. My heart was happy then; I had grown to love him and carried him everywhere. I'd play with him for a while and whenever he would start to cry, I'd take him to Mother so he could nurse. Then I'd take him back with me and we'd play together again.

That was when Kumsa was little. But once he was older and started to talk and then to run around, that's when we were mean to each other and hit and fought all the time. Because that's how children play. One child does mean things and the other children do mean things back. If your father goes out hunting one day, you think, "Won't Daddy bring home meat? Then I can eat it, but I can also *stinge* it!" When your father does come home with meat, you say, "My daddy brought back meat and I won't let you have *any* of it!" The other children say, "How come we play together yet you always treat us so badly?"

When Kumsa was bigger, we were like that all the time. Sometimes we'd hit each other. Other times, I'd grab him and bite him and said, "Oooo . . . what is this thing that has such a horrible face and no brains and is so mean? How come it is so mean to me when I'm not doing anything to it?" Then he'd say, "I'm going to *hit* you! What's protecting you that I shouldn't?" And I'd say, "You're just a baby! I, *I* am the one who's going to hit *you!* Why are you so miserable to me?" I'd insult him and he'd insult me and I'd insult him back. We'd just stay together and play like that.

Once, when our father came back carrying meat, we both called out, "Ho, ho, Daddy! Ho, ho, Daddy!" When I heard him say, "Daddy, Daddy," I said, "Why are you greeting my father? He's *my* father, isn't he? Now, you can only say, 'Oh, hello, Father.'" But he called out, "Ho, ho . . . Daddy!" I yelled, "Be quiet! Why are you saying hello to my father? When I say, 'Daddy . . . Daddy . . .' you be quiet. Only *I* will greet him. Is he your father? I'm going to hit you!" We fought and argued until mother finally stopped us. Then we just sat around while she cooked the meat.

69

She put a few pieces in the coals and the rest she put in the pot. While the meat was cooking, I said, "I'm taking some." She said, "Don't take it from the pot! What do you have there?" I put the piece back and started to cry. Again I said, "I'm taking some." She finally sent me away, "Go, sit somewhere else and wait until the meat is cooked. Do you want to eat it raw?" I sat there, crying. Soon, I went back and this time grabbed meat that was roasting in the coals. She hit my fingers and I sat down and cried again, "How come Kumsa is only a baby and he's sitting there eating and I'm older and am sitting with nothing?" She took a small piece from the pot and gave it to me. I sat there, just starting to eat it, when Kumsa came and grabbed it from me and ran off with it. I jumped up, pounding hard against the sand, and ran after him. I grabbed the meat and bit him, bit him hard. He started to cry and I left him. I sat down again by the fire and ate what was left.

When the meat was done, mother took the pot out of the fire, served my portion, and then served Kumsa's. She said, "Nisa, you and your brother will share this plate and eat together." I refused, "I will not! Kumsa's fingers are dirty. Kumsa has dirty fingers and I won't eat from his plate with him. I'm going to finish this plate myself. Now, serve other meat to your son. Why should Kumsa and I have to eat to-gether?"

We ate separately, but soon Kumsa and I were fighting and arguing again. We had no sense! We always fought with each other. I hated him. And Kumsa? He hated me.

I remember another time with Kumsa. He had a little leather pouch which he hung over his shoulder. One day we followed Mother when she went out gathering klaru bulbs. She had gone first and was soon way ahead of us. We were walking along behind looking for klaru. But one time, when I looked for her, I couldn't see her. I called out, "Mommy!" She didn't answer. I called again, louder, *"Mommy!"* She still didn't answer. I called out again and again and again, but each time it was the same. We didn't know that she wasn't answering because she was hiding near a tree waiting for us. Meanwhile, Kumsa and I followed her tracks, calling out to her. When we came near to where she was hiding, she jumped out suddenly, yelling loudly, "What were the two of you doing? What were you looking for way back there? Why were you staying so far behind? Stay in front of me!" She surprised us! We were so scared, we trembled with fright. She went on, "If you two continue to walk like that, I'll go ahead digging klaru, but when I'm finished, I'll just go home. Then, things of the bush will come and kill you. What's the matter with the two of you that you stay so far behind when I'm gathering?"

We all sat down and rested. Soon, we began to talk again, then, to laugh about things.

After that, we kept up with her. When Kumsa dug up a klaru with a large bulb, he cried out, "Look! Look at mine! Look over here! My klaru is huge!" I said, "Ejaculate on yourself!² You call that a bulb? Why did you call me over to look?" He called out again, "Everyone! Look! Just look at what I have!" Then he came and grabbed one of my bulbs. I yelled, "You're *really* crazy!" and took my digging stick and hit him with it. I said, "Have you no sense? Why did you take my klaru?" We kept walking and soon we returned to the village.

At first, I didn't want to eat any of my klaru and when I saw Kumsa eating his, I said, "Kumsa, give me some. You're not going to refuse me, are you?" He just sat there and ate until he had finished them. I thought, "Ah, I'll just wait until he finishes, because all my klaru are still sitting over there. Later, I'll take them and roast them, but I won't give any to him." That's what I did. I took them out and ate them all by myself.

We lived in that place, eating things. Then we left and went somewhere else.

But life continued and I kept growing up. One day, when I was a little older, I saw something red on my mother's thigh. It was blood. I kept looking at it, looking and looking.

Finally, I said, "Mommy, what . . . how come there's blood there?" She scolded me, "Nisa, are you crazy? You're just a child, yet you stare at other people's genitals? What do you suppose is there.that you are staring like that?" She was menstruating, "seeing the moon."[3] She continued, "Do you already know everything about a woman's genitals that you think you can just stare like that? I'll hit you until you start shitting! I'll tell your father and he'll also hit you. Do you think you can just talk about my genitals like that?"

I was quiet. She got up, then sat down again. I said, "Mommy . . . there's blood . . . there's blood there!" Then in a whisper, I repeated, "Mommy . . . Mommy . . . there's blood there!" She said, "Where is there blood? Don't you know that some day, when you grow up, your genitals will also do that, and you, too, will menstruate? Why are you staring at me like that?" I said, "What? Me? I won't menstruate. I don't have what's needed to do that. I'll *never* menstruate." She said, "Look at yourself. You've got a vagina, right over there, and some day you *will* menstruate. You don't know what you're talking about." Then I said, "Why don't you wipe the blood away. Mommy, take something, some leaves and wipe it away." She wouldn't. Then she slapped my face. I started to cry and cried and cried.

The next day, I said, "Mommy, what's that? Where is that red coming from? Did Daddy strike you with a spear?" She said, "No, your father didn't strike me. This blood, this will also come from your genitals and spill out when you grow up. Someday, that which I see today, you will also see." I said, "Eh . . . really?" She said, "Yes, daughter, really. But I want you to know that when a daughter talks to her mother about seeing her menstrual blood it is an insult. So, don't insult me again by talking about it. Otherwise, I'll tell your father and he'll hit you, hit you very hard." I said, "No, that's not so. Daddy won't hit me *today*. No, he won't hit *me*! *You're* the one with blood. Now, wipe it off, Mommy. Wipe the blood away." But she refused. She wouldn't wipe it off.

A few days later, the moon left her and when I looked at her thighs, I thought, "Eh, hey! Her thighs are clean." I whispered to her, "Mommy . . . Mommy . . . your thighs are so clean! There's no more blood. Mommy, Mommy, there's no more blood on your thighs."

We continued to live and she menstruated again. It came to her when the moon was high in the sky at sunset. Then one moon passed her by and another came and went. Then another, and another; the moons kept passing her by. She was pregnant again.

This is when I was already an older child. My brother Kumsa had also grown, but we still hated each other and treated each other badly. Whenever he wanted to go to mother and nurse, I'd pick him up, carry him into the bush, and drop him there. I'd hit him and say, "Can't you see that Mommy's pregnant?"

It was during one of the early months of her pregnancy that my father became so angry at my mother that he kicked her in the stomach and she almost miscarried. It all started after a few of my father's relatives visited us and stayed for a while.

One of the children who had come with the visitors was Bau, and she and I didn't like each other. We treated each other badly and fought all the time. One day, I went with the other children to play in one of the water pans. I carried my little brother Kumsa and when we got there, set him down to play near the edge of the pan. Then I went and played with the older children, nearby. That's when Bau started to dunk him. She held onto him and pushed him down, again and again, until he almost drowned! When I saw what she had done, I asked "Why were you trying to kill my brother?" I ran and grabbed *her* younger sister and threw *her* into the water. I held her and dunked her and made her swallow a lot of water. I kept dunking her until her stomach was full! And just as my brother almost drowned, her sister almost drowned.

Then, I went to my brother. I rubbed his stomach and helped him throw up all the water he had swallowed. After a while, he was better. Bau helped her sister the same way—

rubbing her stomach until she, too, finally threw up all the water she had swallowed. I said, "Now don't let me see you kill my brother again!"

We stayed near the water pan a little longer. Then, carrying our siblings, we went back to the village. When we got there, our mothers hit us. "Don't ever play at drowning your siblings again! Are the two of you still babies?"

(laughs) Eh, but we really did things when we were small.

There was another incident with Bau. One time, she came with us when I went gathering with my mother and some other women. But no sooner did we start to walk, than she started to cry for her mother. She cried out, "Mommy!" When I heard I said, "Be quiet. What are you yelling for? We're following along with my mommy." We walked along and when we came near to where my mother was gathering, she called out again, "Mom-my! Mommy!" I said, "Have you gone crazy? Bau, be quiet. We're with my mommy now." My mother said, "Leave her be; she's following along with us. She's only asking for her mother. What are you yelling at her for?" We walked along again and dug for more klaru. After a while she did it again, "Mom...my, Mommy!" I shouted, "Be quiet! Your mother took a path that went over there and that's where she's digging klaru. So be quiet and just follow my mother." Then I added, "Also ... any klaru you find, put in my kaross. Give me all the bulbs you dig. Don't save them for your mother to carry." She said, "No! I won't do that! I won't dig klaru for you. Are you a little chief[4] that I should?" I yelled, "I'm going to make you shit! You dig those roots and give them to me and I'll give them to my mommy." She yelled, "Mommy! Nisa's mean!" I said, "I'm going to beat the shit out of you! Have you no sense? You only want to be with your mother. You don't want to be with me." We walked along. The next time she whispered it, "Mommy ..." When I heard, I said, "This time, I'm really going to do it!" I took my digging stick and hit her, again and again. She started to cry. I said, "You've cried enough. Dry your tears and be quiet and just stay with my mommy. We'll keep following her and then later, maybe your mother will join us."

She stopped crying. We walked along and she was quiet. I praised her, "Now that you're not calling for your mother, I like you again." We kept on walking. Finally we arrived home.

But as soon as we arrived in the village, she ran, crying, to her mother, "Mommy . . . Nisa was horrible! I went with Nisa and her mother and Nisa was so mean! See how she hit me, hit my back, hit me all over. That's how awful she was to me!" I cried, "Liar! I wasn't mean to you." (I was lying, of course.) "She's lying. I didn't do any of those things. But because she said that, she won't come gathering with us tomorrow, or ever again! Has she gone crazy?" Bau insulted me, "Death to your genitals! Are *you* crazy? Weren't you the one who asked me to follow you and your mother and . . ."

As she yelled, I just stood there not saying anything. But before she finished, I lunged at her, picked her up and threw her down. I bit her and said, "What's wrong with you? Why did you insult me like that? We're supposed to be friends!" She said, "Liar! You're a baby! That's why you're so full of hate! You're a little child, senseless and full of hate." I said, "I never told you to leave your village and come and live in our village. Why did your mother and father ever bring you here to live with us?" I threatened to bite her again and she ran off toward her parents' hut.

She ran past her parents sitting by the fire outside the hut. I was right behind. I ran between her parents and followed her into the hut. I grabbed her and bit her. Her mother stopped us, saying, "Aie! What sort of child is this? What is she doing? I'm sure her mother didn't tell her to come here and bite my child. Why is she acting so hatefully toward her? When we leave here . . ." I heard her say that and cried, "Yes! When are you leaving? Take your child! Go away! Tomorrow morning would be just fine. Tomorrow, take this miserable child of yours away from here. Just don't let her stay *here* any longer!"

The next morning they were still there. I asked, "Didn't you say you were going to leave? How come you're still sitting around?"

That's when my mother entered the argument. She sup-

ported me, "How come these people living with us are adults,
yet they are being nasty to my daughter? She is only a little
child, so why do they keep yelling at her?"

That was part of the reason behind why my father got so
angry. He told her she shouldn't insult his relatives like that.

The next incident occurred soon after, when my little
brother took one of my father's arrows and hit one of the visiting children with it. Fortunately, the arrow didn't have any
poison on it. I don't remember everything that happened
next, but I do remember my father yelling at my mother in
support of his relatives, "Chuko, you were sitting here, yet
you didn't say anything to your son . . . *our* son . . . and you
didn't even take the arrows away from him? Now he's struck
a child with it!"

That's when he got up and, filled with anger, kicked her.
The blow was aimed higher than where it actually landed—
right on her stomach. Then it was as though he had killed
her; the kick had dropped blood inside her and it started to
come out her genitals and her mouth. I was frightened, "Is
she going to die? Why did my father kill her? Why did he
kick her in the stomach and ruin her pregnancy?" Wasn't I by
then an older child who understood things that were happening? I thought about it, about how she might miscarry and
about how she would surely die. I cried and cried, so much
that my throat was dry.

Others were there, pouring water on her, and all Kumsa
and I could do was stand there and cry. After a while, it was
as though she was alive again, even though the blood was
still spilling. My father washed her feet and gave her water to
drink, trying to help. He also made medicinal cuts on her
lower back. It was only when the sun was low in the sky that
the bleeding finally stopped. When it was all over, we saw
that the blood hadn't come from the baby; it had come from
somewhere else. Eventually she was better and her stomach
continued to grow. The pregnancy had not been ruined.

When my younger brother Kumsa was first born, my
mother said she wanted to kill him, because I was very small

and she wanted me to nurse. Then, before she gave birth to Kxamshe, she said she wanted to kill her, so that Kumsa could nurse. While she was still pregnant, she told people; she even told my father. Everyone refused.

My father said, "I don't understand. Chuko, first you said you wanted to kill Kumsa, and Nisa, a mere child, gave him his life. Today you say you want to kill the child now inside you. So tell me ... do you want to kill me? That must be it, because these children are the children I conceived,[5] yet you want to kill one, then another. What you're saying makes me think you're a bad woman. Why do you talk like that? Are you afraid of having too many children? Or, perhaps, you no longer want me?"

He continued, "When you were a young girl, you wanted me. You grew up inside my hut, beside me, and I helped raise you. When we came to having children, you took care of them very well. Even so, if you kill this child inside you, I will leave you. Aren't there other women to marry?"

Kxamshe stayed in my mother's stomach. When it was time to give birth, it was just the two of us who went. We were living in the bush, just our family; no other women were there. She took me with her when she gave birth. After the baby was born, I said, "Daddy said that if you kill this baby, he'll take me and Kumsa and Dau and leave you." But she said, "Uhn, uhn ... I don't want to kill her. This little girl is too beautiful. See how lovely and fair her skin is?"[6] My heart was happy. She cut the umbilical cord and carried her back to the village. Then she lay down.

My father had been out hunting, and when he came back, mother was lying down in the shade of a temporary shelter nearby. He asked, "Where is your mother?" I said, "She's lying down over there, resting. She gave birth to a little baby with very fair skin." My father went to see her. He asked, "Is it a little boy?" She said, "No, it's a girl."

My father went and cooked the springhare he had brought back with him and poured the gravy for her to drink. That was to give her strength and to help her milk come into her breasts. We slept that night, but her milk didn't come.

The next morning, he went and trapped a guinea fowl, came back and cooked it. She drank the gravy, but her milk still didn't come. Later, he killed and cooked another guinea fowl, and this time, when she drank the broth, the milk finally filled her breasts.

After that, we lived on. Mother stayed inside the hut for a while, and after Kxamshe had grown a little, she carried her wherever she went. Kxamshe had no younger brothers or sisters, because my mother didn't give birth again. Kxamshe just nursed and nursed and grew up. She gave up nursing on her own, while there was still milk in her mother's chest. The milk stayed for a while, then left.

Kxamshe kept on growing, without it. She was very beautiful and she was fair, like a European—that's how light her skin was. And I loved her. She grew and grew and stood tall. She was a young girl, almost a woman. Then, a sickness like malaria came from somewhere and entered her. It was that— the trembling sickness—that killed her and she died.

My mother lived on after that. She menstruated month after month, for a very long time. Then one month came and she didn't menstruate, then another and another. The months just passed her by and she was finished with the moon.

Chapter 3
Life in the Bush

THE NORTHERN FRINGE of the Kalahari Desert is a capricious and demanding environment. Total rainfall of the wet season can vary from as much as forty to as little as five inches from one year to the next. Forty inches fills depressions in the land and forms pools that often remain full for weeks or even months. Travel to distant places is easy, and people are able to disperse in small groups over the area in search of game and other food. Lesser-known plants, seen only once in several years, flourish, but some of the more basic foods may drown. Continuous rains may even cause the fruit of the staple food, the protein-rich mongongo nut, to rot; even worse, rare heavy downpours early in the season may damage the mongongo flowers before they bear fruit.

Five inches of rain, in contrast, is a drought condition, and many of the edible plants gathered by !Kung women may not be found. Severe drought occurs in the Dobe area on the average of one year in four. Knowing where permanent water springs are located, being able to see the shriveled vines that signal large water-storing roots hidden several feet under the ground, remembering the partially enclosed recesses of the thick mongongo and morula tree trunks that hide trapped water, can mean survival. All of this is compounded by the geographical variability of rainfall within one season; one area may receive twice as much as another just a few miles away.

An untrained visitor set down in this sand-and-thorn scrub brush on a typical spring day (September to November), would first look for some shade, and would be grateful to find some where the temperature was only 100°F. The visitor might not see water anywhere, and might find little if anything to eat. Even in the middle of the nut groves, with hundreds of thousands of mongongo nuts lying on the ground, the newcomer might go hungry; it would be necessary to find stones strong enough to crack the quarter-inch shell, then to determine how to hold the nut between the stones and, without smashing a finger, to hit it with just enough power in just the right spot to make it crack along the fault line, releasing the filbert-sized nut inside.

Suppose an animal were sighted and suppose further that the visitor had had the foresight to have fashioned arrowheads from bone remnants, shafts for the arrows from a tall, reed-like grass, poison from the larvae of a certain beetle, a bow from a partly dried green branch, and a string from fibrous plant threads rolled into twine. Even for such a well-prepared visitor, it would take the most extraordinary luck to make a hit without years of training and experience in tracking, stalking, and shooting. And even then, how long might it take for the animal to die? Hours? Days? Would the visitor be able to follow its tracks? To find enough plant food to survive in the meantime?

Even the !Kung average only one kill for every four days of hunting. The hunter must know how to read animal tracks—to know when they were made and what species of animal made them, as well as the animal's age, size, and condition of health. The quarry must not only be tracked but stalked, and the hunter must understand the vagaries of the wind in order to get close enough for a clear shot. If the arrow strikes, he must determine how far the poisoned shaft has entered, how long the animal will take to die, and where it is likely to travel as it dies. If the animal is large, the hunter may go back to the village for the night, and return the next day with others to help. They will pick up the tracks again, find the animal, and, if it is not yet dead, kill it with spears. If already dead, the animal may have attracted lions, leopards, hyenas, jackals, wild dogs, or vultures, separately or in combination, and these will have to be chased away, sometimes at great risk. The carcass will then be butchered and the skin carefully removed to be tanned later and made into clothing or blankets. The liver will be roasted and eaten immediately and the rest of the meat prepared for carrying back. Nothing will be left behind or wasted.

A man's hunting skills and inclinations are fostered early in childhood, often beginning when he is only a toddler. Toy bows and arrows are typically given to small children, usually by children not much older than themselves. Stationary objects are their first targets. Soon moving ones, such as grasshoppers and beetles, are added. As boys get older, they improve their aim by throwing sticks and wooden spears. Their mastery of animal tracks, like their ability to identify the hundreds of plant and animal species in the environment, is a slow process, acquired through practice and observation. Much of the animal lore so necessary to success in the hunt is learned from discussions of present and past hunts. Around the age of twelve boys are given their first quivers—with small bows and arrows—by their fathers, and begin to shoot birds and rabbits. They may also be taught to set snares. The next step is to accompany their fathers, uncles, and older brothers when they go out to hunt.

Hunts are often dangerous. The !Kung face danger courageously, but they do not seek it out or take risks for the sake of proving their courage. Actively avoiding hazardous situations is considered prudent, not cowardly or unmasculine. Young boys, moreover, are not expected to conquer their fear and act like grown men. To unnecessary risks the !Kung say, "But a person could die!"

These attitudes became clear to me as I heard the description of a kill witnessed by Kashe, a boy about twelve years old, and his cousin. Prior to this, the two boys' experience with hunting had been only in play. This time they accompanied their fathers on a real hunt. When they returned, Kashe and his father came to our camp to give us a present of meat from a large gemsbok they had killed. As we celebrated their good fortune (and ours) and talked about the details of the hunt, a broad smile never left Kashe's face. His father reviewed the events— how, after they had struck it with an arrow and had run after it, the gemsbok had finally stood and fought, and how fiercely it had warded off their spears with its long, razor-sharp antlers. Kashe, listening, seemed beside himself with excitement and pride. I asked, "Did you help?" "No," he replied, "I was up in a tree!" His smile became an easy laugh. Puzzled, I asked again, and he repeated that he and his cousin had climbed a tree as soon as the animal had stopped running and had stood its ground. I teased him, saying everyone would have gone hungry if the animal had been left to him and his cousin. He laughed again and said, "Yes, but we were so scared!" There was no hint of embarrassment or of a need to explain what might have been seen, in our culture, as behavior lacking in courage. Nor was there any suggestion that his fear in this situation reflected anything about how he would act when he was fully grown. There would be plenty of time for him to learn to face dangerous animals and to kill them, and there was no doubt in his mind (or his father's, to judge from the expression on *his* face), that he would, one day. When I questioned the father, he beamed, "Up in the tree? Of course. They're only children. They could have gotten hurt."

A boy is likely to kill his first large animal between the ages of fifteen and eighteen. The culture recognizes this event as a milestone and performs two separate ceremonies to celebrate the killing of the first male and the first female animal. Small ritual tattoos are administered and additional small cuts are made to ensure, symbolically, the strength and success of the boy's future as a hunter. Although now considered eligible for marriage, he may not actually marry for as long as ten years. These years will be spent refining his skills and knowledge of the hunt.

By the age of thirty a man enters the most productive period of his hunting career, which is likely to extend for at least fifteen years. During this time, he will walk between 1200 and 2100 miles a year in the pursuit of the fifty-five species of mammals, birds, reptiles, and insects considered edible. He will use various methods to capture animals living above and below the ground, including knocking them down with sticks, snaring them, chasing them with or without dogs, and hunting them in the classic style with poisoned arrows and spears. Relying on his own and other people's knowledge of environmental conditions, he will decide in which direction the hunters should go on a particular day. He may also pay close attention to magical sources—dreams and divination discs—that are thought to provide information on the whereabouts of animals. These sources will also help give him confidence, suggesting as they do that powerful forces of the "otherworld" are behind him. He may hunt alone or with others. When he hunts with others, he will use secret names to refer to animals being pursued, and the hunters will communicate by hand signals and whistles so as not to disturb the game.

If the hunter is successful in killing a large animal, it will be carefully butchered and brought back to the village. There the meat will be distributed according to well-established rules of precedence. Everyone will receive a portion, directly or indirectly. Meat is highly valued—people may speak of "meat hunger" even when other food is abundant—and meat well-laced with fat is especially prized because most desert animals are lean. Since the availability of meat is so uncertain, distributions are emotionally charged events; the size of the portions depends not only on clear issues such as kinship, but on subtle ones such as contribution to the hunt. Matters are further complicated by the tradition that most hunters carry other people's arrows in their quivers alongside their own. The arrow that kills an animal may therefore not belong to the hunter who shot it. According to !Kung custom, the person who owns the arrow is considered the true "owner" of the meat, and the prestigious (and onerous) task of distributing the meat fairly is his (or hers—women sometimes own arrows, as well). Thus the distribution must be handled with great delicacy to insure against insults, real or imagined. Some of the meat may be dried for later consumption, but prodigious amounts will be enthusiastically consumed on the spot. If the hunter is not successful, he may collect some vegetable foods on his way home so as not to come back to the village empty handed.

!Kung men vary widely in their skill at hunting, but different levels of success do not lead to differences in status. Self-deprecation and understatement are rigorously required of the hunter after a successful hunt. This modesty is in evidence from the moment he enters the village to relay his news. Walking silently, he sits down by a fire—his own or someone else's. He greets people and waits. When they ask, he says, "No, I didn't see anything today. At least, nothing worth talking about." The others, well-versed in the rules, press for details: "That nothing you saw . . . did you get close enough to strike it?" Thus the conversation slowly reveals that an eland, a gemsbok, or even a giraffe has been shot. Excitement ripples through the camp as the news spreads; meanwhile, the hunter sits as before, quietly describing the events leading up to the kill. If his demeanor is interpreted as boastful or if his accomplishment is not presented as a mixture of skill and luck, pointed jokes and derision may be used to pressure him back into line. Later, dramatic accounts of the hunt will be given, and other important hunts will be recalled.

The problem for the truly accomplished hunter (or gatherer, musician, healer, and so on) is to perform as well as possible without provoking envy or anger in others. This strain may be decreased by the custom of sharing arrows, which helps to diffuse responsibility for the kill. In addition, a less successful hunter may feel imbued with power when using a more successful hunter's arrows, and this may give him the confidence he needs to succeed. Most hunters also alternate hunting with long periods of inactivity, thereby affording others the opportunity to bring in meat and to receive the praise and attention of the group—for a while.

As he grows older, a hunter starts accompanying younger men on the hunt, helping them to learn the skills and knowledge he has accumulated during his approximately forty years of active experience. By the time he ends his hunting career in his early sixties, he will have killed between 80 and 120 (or more) large game animals as well as hundreds of smaller animals. If he stays in good health, he will eventually shift to setting snares, teaching young boys how to interpret bird and small animal tracks in the bush, and foraging in areas close to the village.

WE LIVED IN THE BUSH and my father set traps
and killed steenbok and duiker and gemsbok
and we lived, eating the animals and foods of
the bush. We collected food, ground it in a
mortar, and ate it. We also ate sweet nin berries and tsin
beans. When I was growing up, there were no cows or goats
and I didn't know who the Hereros were. I had never seen
other peoples and didn't know anything other than life in the
bush. That's where we lived and where we grew up.[1]

Whenever my father killed an animal and I saw him
coming home with meat draped over a stick, balanced on one
shoulder—that's what made me happy. I'd cry out, "Mommy!
Daddy's coming and he's bringing *meat!*" My heart would be
happy when I greeted him, "Ho, ho, Daddy! We're going to
eat meat!"

Or honey. Sometimes he'd go out and come home with
honey. I'd be sitting around with my mother and then see
something coming from way out in the bush. I'd look hard.
Then, "Oooh, Daddy found a beehive! Oh, I'm going to eat
honey! Daddy's come back with honey for us to eat!" And I'd
thank him and call him wonderful names.

Sometimes my mother would be the one to see the
honey. The two of us would be walking around gathering
food and she'd find a beehive deep inside a termite mound
or in a tree. I remember one time when she found it. I
jumped and ran all around and was so excited I couldn't stop
moving. We went to the village to get some containers, then
went back again to the termite mound. I watched as she took
the honey out. Then, we went home.

Long ago, when we were living in the bush, our fathers
brought us plenty of food! And, animals full of fat—that was
especially prized. Whenever my father brought back meat, I'd
greet him, "Ho, ho, Daddy's coming home with meat!" And
felt thankful for everything and there was nothing that made
my heart unhappy.

Except if it was someone else in the village who killed

something and came back carrying it. Then I'd look and think, "Uhn, uhn . . . that one, the people in his hut aren't giving-people. If they have something, they never give it to us. Even when they do, they don't give enough so all of us can eat. They are stingy people." My heart would not be happy at all, because that would mean we would have to ask. So, the next morning we would sit around their hut. If they gave us a large portion, my heart would be happy and I would think, "Yes, these people, their hearts are close to ours. They gave mother and father some of what they had." Then everyone would eat.

But, there is always one hut in the village where the people kill you when it comes to food. I remember when we were living with a group of Zhun/twasi and they were eating meat from an animal they had killed. My father asked for some, but they refused. I sat there, thinking, "I'll just sit here and wait. When Daddy kills an animal, then I'll eat meat." Because my father was a good hunter.

Whenever I saw others coming back to the village with meat, I'd ask, "Daddy, how come you didn't go out hunting and kill something so we would have meat? Those people over there are the only ones who will be eating today." My father would say, "Eh, but my arrows didn't have any fresh poison on them. If they did, then, just as these others went out hunting, I would also have gone hunting and killed something for you and your mother to eat." Then I'd say, "Mm, those others are the only ones who ever hunt."

When we were living in the bush, some people gave and others stinged. But there were always enough people around who shared, people who liked one another, who were happy living together, and who didn't fight. And even if one person did stinge, the other person would just get up and yell about it, whether it was meat or anything else, "What's doing this to you, making you not give us meat?"

When I was growing up, receiving food made my heart happy. There really wasn't anything, other than stingy people, that made me unhappy. I didn't like people who wouldn't give a little of what they had. Then my heart would feel bad and I'd think, "This one, I don't like." Or sometimes I'd say, "As I am, you're a bad person and I'll never give you anything." But other times, I'd just cry. Sometimes I'd cry all night and into the morning. Once, I cried because someone had trapped a very small bird and I didn't get any of it. I wanted it and just sat there, crying and crying. Finally, people told me, "It's just a tiny bird, stop crying over it."

It's the same today. Here I am, long since an adult, yet even now, if a person doesn't give something to me, I won't give anything to that person. If I'm sitting eating, and someone like that comes by, I say, "Uhn, uhn. I'm not going to give any of this to you. When you have food, the things you do with it make me unhappy. If you even once in a while gave me something nice, I would surely give some of this to you." Because people like that are very bad. When they see food in front of them, they just eat it.

I used to watch my father when he left the village early in the morning, his quiver on his shoulder. He'd usually be gone all day. If he shot something, when he came back, he'd say, "Eh, I went out to the bush this morning and first I saw an animal, a giraffe. But I didn't track it well. Then I saw an eland and struck it with my arrow. Let's wait until tomorrow before we go find it." The next day we'd fill our ostrich eggshell containers with water and everyone would go to where the animal had died.

One time, my father went hunting with some other men and they took dogs with them. First they saw a baby wildebeest and killed it. Then, they went after the mother wildebeest, and killed that too. They also killed a warthog.

As they were coming back, I saw them and shouted out, "Ho, ho, Daddy's bringing home meat! Daddy's coming home with meat!" My mother said, "You're talking nonsense. Your father hasn't even come home yet." Then she turned to where I was looking and said, "Eh-hey, daughter! Your father certainly has killed something. He *is* coming with meat."

I remember another time when my father's younger brother traveled from far away to come and live with us. The day before he arrived he killed an eland. He left it in the bush and continued on to our village. When he arrived, only mother and I were there. He greeted us and asked where his brother was. Mother said, "Eh, he went to look at some tracks he had seen near a porcupine hole. He'll be back when the sun sets." We sat together the rest of the day. When the sun was low in the sky, my father came back. My uncle said, "Yesterday, as I was coming here, there was an eland—perhaps it was just a small one—but I spent a long time tracking it and finally killed it in the thicket beyond the dry water pan. Why don't we get the meat and bring it back to the village?" We packed some things, left others hanging in the trees, and went to where the eland had died. It was a huge animal with plenty of fat. We lived there while they skinned the animal and cut the meat into strips to dry. A few days later we started home, the men carrying the meat on sticks[2] and the women carrying it in their karosses.

At first my mother carried me on her shoulder. After a long way, she set me down and I started to cry. She was angry, "You're a big girl. You know how to walk." It was true that I was fairly big by then, but I still wanted to be carried. My older brother said, "Stop yelling at her, she's already crying," and he picked me up and carried me. After a long time walking, he also put me down. Eventually, we arrived back at the village.

We lived, eating meat; lived and lived. Then, it was finished.

My older brother, Dau, was much older than I was. Even when I was born, he already had his own hut and no longer lived with us. Later, he married. But when I was still little, he would go hunting and come home with meat. And just as my father knew how to track and kill animals, my older brother also learned. The memories I have about him aren't unhappy ones—they are the times when my heart felt wonderful.

I used to follow him around wherever he went; I just *loved* him! Sometimes, when he wanted to go hunting, he'd say, "Why don't you just sit in the village? Why are you always following me?" I'd stay home and when he came back with meat, I'd greet him, "Ho, ho ... my big brother's home!"

Sometimes he took me with him, and although I was already fairly big, he'd put me up on his shoulders and carry me. That's part of the reason I followed him around all the time! When he'd see an animal, he'd put me down, track it, and shoot it. If he struck it, we'd return to the village and he would always let me be the first to tell, "My big brother killed a gemsbok!" The next morning, people would go out with him to track it. Sometimes, I was afraid I'd be thirsty and there wouldn't be enough water, so I'd just stay behind.

Sometimes, when I stayed in the village, he'd tell me to set the bird traps. He only told me, never my little brother, because Kumsa always ate the bait, tiny chon or gow bulbs. He loved those little bulbs and just took them away from the birds.

Once, mother went to set some traps not far from the village. After she came back, Kumsa followed her tracks and ate most of the bulbs. When mother went back late in the afternoon, she found a guinea fowl in one of the traps, but the others were empty of both bird and bait.

Another time, Kumsa got his finger caught in one of the traps (as he often did!) and started to cry. I went to him with my older brother. Dau hit him and said, "If you steal the food from the guinea fowl, it won't get caught! Now, stop eating the bulbs! Have you no sense, taking food out of the traps?"

I never did that. I just held the bulbs in my hand and went to the traps. I'd put the bulb in and leave it there for the birds. I'd check the traps later in the day. If a bird was caught, I'd bring it home and my older brother would take the feathers off.

I also set some of my father's traps. I, all by myself. I'd go alone and set them. But my little brother would stay behind, because he really liked those bulbs!

I used to *love* stewed mongongo fruit. If someone was eating some and didn't give any to me, I'd cry and cry until I got some. But once, I had all the fruit soup and mongongo nut meats I wanted, and I had nothing to cry over.

My older brother often went to the mongongo groves

and brought back sacks full of nuts. One time, when he came back, he told my mother, "Here are the nuts. Cook them so you and Nisa can eat. But don't cook so many that you give them away. I'm tired, so listen to what I have to say—I don't want these nuts given away, because I'm giving them all to Nisa. Others will help her cook them so she can drink the fruit soup whenever she wants it. Now, I'm just going to rest until this moon dies. Only then will I go out and collect more nuts." I had all those mongongo nuts to myself and I drank lots of fruit soup and ate lots of cracked nuts.

I also remember the time I got burned. My mother had just come back from digging klaru bulbs, and had put them into a pot to cook into soft porridge. I kept asking, "Mommy, give me some. Why don't you give some to me? Mommy, give me some klaru." Finally, to quiet me, she took some she thought was cool enough from the top of the pot and put it in my hand, but it was still too hot. I dropped it and it landed on my leg. Before I could push it off, it burned me, leaving a large wound. I cried and cried and even after it got dark, I kept on crying. My father said, "Chuko, I've told you again and again, you shouldn't do things that cause Nisa to cry and be full of tears. Why don't you understand? Are you without ears? You keep doing things that make her cry. You, the mother of these little children, can't you understand things?"

People say that salt heals burns, so after they washed it out thoroughly, they crushed some salt into very small pieces and put it on. I wasn't afraid and just let them put it on. Then, I cried and watched as the salt made little bubbles on the wound, "Oh, this salt is terrible ... eeeee ... eeeee ...!" The salt almost killed me. Really, it felt as though it was killing my leg. I almost died from the pain.

The burn lasted a long time and made walking difficult. I couldn't get up easily. When I had to go to the bush[3] I would crawl on my hands. My father blamed my mother, "If you ever do something like that to Nisa again, I, an adult, and her father, will do the same thing to you! I'll take you and throw you into the fire. How could you have almost

killed a child? Now, she can't even walk! I'd like to throw
you into the fire right now. I won't, people say I shouldn't.
But if you ever burn her like that again, I will!" My mother
said, "You're right. If you were to throw me into the fire,
there wouldn't be any wrong done because I was responsible
for your child's getting burned. But she really has no sense.
There's nothing worth anything in her head yet. She has no
sense at all, not even about asking for food to be given to
her."

We lived and lived and after a while the burn healed.

I remember another time, when I was the first one to notice a dead wildebeest, one recently killed by lions, lying in
the bush. Mother and I had gone gathering and were walking
along, she in one direction and I a short distance away. That's
when I saw the wildebeest. I went closer to look but got
scared and ran away. I called, "Mommy! Mommy! Come look
at this! Look at that big black thing lying there." As she came
toward me, I pointed, "There by that tree!" She looked, "Eh!
My daughter! My little Nisa! My little girl! My daughter has
found a wildebeest!" Then she said, "Go back to the village
and tell your father to come." She stayed with the animal
while I ran back, but we had gone deep into the mongongo
groves and soon I got tired. I stopped to rest. Then I got up
and started to run again, following along our tracks, ran and
then rested and then ran until I finally got back to the village.

It was hot and everyone was resting in the shade. My
older brother was the first to see me. "What's the matter?
Dad, look. Nisa's coming back alone. Do you think something
bit mother?"[4] I ran over to them, "No, Mommy hasn't been
bitten . . . but I, I found a wildebeest lying dead in the bush!
We had just left the place where the ground dips down and
where the trees are thick and when we came to the opening
beside the groves, that's where I saw it.[5] I told Mommy to
come look. She stayed there while I ran back here." My father
and my older brother and everyone in the village followed
me. When we arrived, they skinned the animal, cut the meat
into strips and carried it on branches back to the village.

After we came home with the meat, my parents started

to give presents of it to everyone. But I didn't want _any_ of it
given away. I cried, "_I_ was the one who saw it!" Whenever I
saw them give some away, I followed the person to his hut
and took it back, saying, "Did _you_ see the wildebeest?
Mommy and I were together and _I_ was the one who saw it!"
I took the meat away and hung it again on the branch beside
mother's hut. People said, "Oh! This child! Isn't she going to
share what she has? Is she a child who sees something and
doesn't give any of it to others?" But I said, "Did you see it? I
myself saw it with my very own eyes, and this wildebeest is
mine. I'm going to hang it up by my hut so I can eat it _all_."

Later, I went to play. While I was away, mother took the
meat and shared it with everyone. When I came back, I asked
where all the meat had gone because I couldn't see it anywhere.

Mother and I often went to the bush together. The two
of us would walk until we arrived at a place where she collected food. She'd set me down in the shade of a tree and
dig roots or gather nuts nearby.

One time I left the tree and played in the shade of another tree. Hidden in the grass and among the leaves, I saw a
tiny steenbok, one that had just been born. It was lying there,
its little eye staring out at me. I thought, "What should I do?"
I shouted, "Mommy!" I just stood there and it just lay there,
looking at me. Suddenly I knew what to do—I lunged at it
and tried to grab it. But it jumped up and ran away, and I
started to chase it. It was running and I was running and it
was crying as it ran. Finally, I got close enough to put my
foot in its way and it fell down. I grabbed its legs and started
carrying it back. It was crying, "Ehn ... ehn ... ehn ..."

Its mother had been close by, and when she heard it call,
she came running. As soon as I saw her, I started to run
again, still carrying the baby steenbok. I wouldn't give it back
to its mother! As I ran I called out, "Mommy! Come! Help me
with this steenbok! Mommy! The steenbok's mother is coming
for me! Run! Come! Take this steenbok from me." But then
the mother steenbok was no longer following so I took the
baby, held its feet together, and banged it hard against the

sand until I had killed it. Then it no longer was crying; it was dead. I was very happy. My mother came running and I gave it to her to carry.

The two of us spent the rest of the day walking in the bush. While my mother gathered, I sat in the shade of a tree, waiting, and played with the dead steenbok. I picked it up; I tried to make it sit up; I tried to open its eyes; I looked at them. When mother had dug enough sha roots, she came back. We left and returned home.

My father had been out hunting that day and had shot a large steenbok with his arrows. He had skinned it and brought it back hanging on a branch. "Ho, ho, Daddy killed a steenbok!" Then I said, "Mommy! Daddy! I'm not going to share *my* steenbok. Now don't give it to anyone this time. After you cook it, just my little brother and I will eat it, just the two of us."

I remember another time we were traveling. While still on our way, my father and older brother tracked a baby ant-bear, the animal with almost no hair, with skin like human skin and hands like human hands. After they killed it and we ate it, I started to feel sick and threw up. That's when a serious illness entered my body, and I became very sick. My father did a curing trance for me, laying on his hands, and worked with me until I started to feel better. I was still too young to understand that he was curing me, because I still had no sense about those things. All I knew was the feeling of being sick. All I thought was, "Am I going to die from this sickness?" My father worked on me, curing me with his medicinal powers. I started to feel better and soon I was sitting up; then, I was sitting around with other people. Once I was completely better, I started playing again and stopped having thoughts about death.

An older child understand things and knows when someone is curing her. She thinks, "This person is trying to cure me. Perhaps he will make me better because right now, this sickness hurts very badly. Maybe he'll cure me and take the pain out of my body. Then, I'll be better again." I liked when my father cured us, liked when he did something good and helpful. I'd think about how he was making all of us better. If I was sick, I'd feel my body start becoming healthy again; if someone else was sick, I'd sit and sing for my father as he tranced and cured him. An older child understands and thinks about things like that. But a younger one doesn't have those thoughts.

I remember another time when I got sick after eating meat, the time my older brother killed a wildebeest with his poisoned arrows. I was so happy when I saw him coming back, carrying huge pieces of meat, "Ho, ho, my big brother's brought home meat!" I kept thanking him and praising him. And, fat! It was very fat! I was given a big piece and ate it all, especially the fatty parts. I ate and ate and ate, so much, that soon I was in pain. My stomach started to hurt and then I had diarrhea. My insides were too full from all that fat, and my diarrhea was full of fat as well.

Soon I got better, and we just continued to live.

Another time, I broke some ostrich eggshell water containers and my father hit me. I used to put them in my kaross and go to the water well to fill them. But once one fell down and broke, broke into lots of little pieces. When I came back, my father had a branch and said he was going to beat me to death. So ... phfft! I ran away!

But, it happened again. I had taken some ostrich eggshell water containers to the well, and while I was filling one with water, another one fell and ... *bamm!* I said, "Today I won't run. Even if my father kills me, this time I won't run."

My younger brother Kumsa ran off immediately, to tell, "Daddy! Nisa killed another ostrich eggshell!" My father was waiting for me when I returned. He said, "Tell me, what caused that eggshell to break? Aren't you a big girl already? Still, you broke it?" He hit me and I started to cry. Soon he stopped, "All right ... it isn't that important, after all."

But after that, whenever someone said, "Nisa, take the ostrich eggshell containers and fill them with water," I'd refuse. I knew if I broke another one, they'd hit me again.

"Those eggshell containers don't help me at all. I'll just let them sit over there. Otherwise, you'll kill me." Whenever I was thirsty, I took a small can and went to the well to drink. I'd fill the little can with water, cover it with leaves and carry it back. But I wouldn't touch their ostrich eggshell containers. My mother was the only one who brought back water from the well.

A long time passed without my touching those eggshell containers. And we just lived on.

I remember another time when we were traveling from one place to another, and the sun was burning. It was the hot, dry season and there was no water anywhere. The sun was *burning!* Kumsa had already been born and I was still small. We had been walking a long time and then my older brother saw a beehive. We stopped while he and my father chopped open the tree. All of us helped collect the honey. I filled my own little container until it was completely full. We stayed there, eating the honey, and I started to get very thirsty. Carrying my honey and my digging stick, I got up and we continued to walk. The heat was killing us and we were all dying of thirst. I started to cry because I wanted water so badly.

After a while, we sat down again in the shade of a baobab tree. There was no water anywhere. We just sat in the shade like that. Finally, my father said, "Dau, the rest of the family will stay here under this baobab. But you, take the water containers and get us some water. There's a well not too far away." Dau collected the empty ostrich eggshell containers, took the large clay pot, and left. I lay there, dead from thirst. I thought, "If I stay here, I'll surely die of thirst. Why don't I follow my big brother and go drink water with him?" I jumped up and started to run after him. I ran and ran, crying out to him and following his tracks, but he didn't hear me. I kept running, crying and calling out. Finally, he heard something and turned to see what it was. "Oh, no! Nisa's followed me. What can I do with her now that she's here?" He stood, waiting for me to catch up. When I was beside him, he picked me up and carried me high up on his shoulder, and along we went.

The two of us went on together like that. We walked and walked and walked until finally we reached the well. I ran to the water and drank and soon my heart was happy again. We filled the containers and put them in a twine mesh sack that my brother carried on his back. He took me and put me once again on his shoulder.

We started to walk back, Dau carrying the water and carrying me. After a while, he set me down and I ran along beside him. Soon I began to cry. He said, "Nisa, I'm going to hit you! I'm carrying these water containers and they're very heavy. So, just run along beside me and we'll take back this water to our parents. Thirst must have killed them by now. What are you crying about? Have you no sense?" I cried, "No, carry me. Dau, pick me up and carry me on your shoulder." He refused and I ran along beside him, crying, running and crying. After a while he said, "All right, I'll carry you again," and he picked me up. We went a long way before he set me down again. We had gone very far! I ran along with him until I tired again and he carried me again. That's how we were when we arrived at the baobab, where our parents were waiting for us.

They drank the water, drank and drank, more and more. "How well our children have done, bringing us this water! We are alive once again!" We rested in the shade of the baobab. Then we left and traveled to another water hole, and even though it was a long walk, I didn't cry. I just carried my container full of honey and walked. When we finally arrived, we settled there for a while. My heart was happy, eating honey and just living.

Once we went to live near a water hole, but there was no water in it. That was another time we were all thirsty. The only water came from kwa, a large water root. My mother scraped the white pulp into mounds, squeezing out the water for me to drink. She'd say, "Nisa's only a little child, yet she's dying of thirst." Because, although the kwa roots were plentiful, they were also bitter. When I'd drink the juice, I'd cry.

We lived there and after some time passed we saw the rain clouds. One came near, but just hung in the sky. It stayed hanging, just like that. Then another day, more rain clouds came over and they, too, just stood. Then the rain started to spill itself and it came pouring down.

The rainy season had finally come. The sun rose and set and the rain spilled itself. It fell and kept falling. It fell tirelessly, without ceasing. Soon the water pans were full. And my heart! My heart within me was happy. We lived and ate meat and mongongo nuts and more meat and it was all delicious.

My heart was so happy I moved about like a little dog, wagging my tail and running around. Really! I was so happy, I shouted out what I saw: "The rainy season has come today! Yea! Yea!"

There were caterpillars to eat, those little things that crawl along going, "Mmm . . . mmmm . . . mmmm . . ." And people dug roots and collected food and brought home more and more food. There was plenty of meat and people kept bringing more back, hanging on sticks, and they hung it up in the trees where we were camped. My heart was bursting and I ate lots of food and my tail kept wagging, wagging about like a little dog. And I'd laugh with my little tail, laugh a little donkey's laugh, a tiny thing that is. I'd wag my tail one way and the other, shouting, "Today I'm going to eat caterpillars . . . cat—er—pillars!" Some people gave me meat broth to drink and others prepared the skins of caterpillars and roasted them for me to eat and I ate and ate and ate! Then I lay down to sleep.

But that night, after everyone was dead asleep, I urinated right in my sleeping place. In the morning, when the others got up, I just lay there, lay there in the same place where I had urinated. The sun rose and was already high in the sky, and I was still lying there. I was afraid of people shaming me. Mother said, "Why is Nisa acting like this, refusing to leave her blankets when the sun is sitting up in the sky? Oh . . . she probably wet herself!"

When I did get up, I stood looking at my little pubic apron. *Wet!* "Ooh! I peed on myself!" And my heart felt miserable. I thought "I've peed on myself and now everyone's going to laugh at me." I asked one of my friends, "How come, after I ate all those caterpillars, when I went to sleep I peed in my bed?" Then I thought, "When this day finishes, I'm going to lie down separate from the others. If I wet my bed again, won't Mother and Father hit me?"

I remember one time, when my friends and I found a snapping turtle. We had been swimming and splashing around in a water pan. We started to play with the turtle—picking it up and throwing it back and forth to one another. But on my turn, the turtle bit my finger. I screamed, but it didn't let go. I shook my hand and cried, "Mommy! My hand! Do something about my finger! Keya! Noni! Come, help me! You're all without brains! Come here and help me! I've been bitten!"

I beat my hand against the sand, but the turtle wouldn't let go. I kept looking at it holding onto my hand and kept crying out for help. I pulled at it with my other hand and finally it dropped to the sand. My finger was throbbing, "Pow ... pow ... pow ... pow." I sat down to rest while the others killed it. I sat there, staring at my finger. It hurt; it burned! The other children started a trance dance for me. They made believe they were curing me and layed on hands. They danced around, and tried to make my finger better. The boys went into trance and tried to pull the sickness and pain out of my hand. When the sun was late in the sky, we returned to the village, carrying the turtle to be cooked and eaten.

When we arrived, my mother asked, "What happened? What bit you?" I said, "A turtle. This turtle. We were playing with it and throwing it around. When I tried to grab it, it bit me, bit me very hard."

After that, I was afraid of turtles and wouldn't touch them. When the other children threw them around, I just stood and watched. I really had no sense when I was young! Even a bad thing like that, I had just touched. I hadn't been afraid and just picked up that turtle. Then it bit me. Even today, my hand is ugly in that very spot. Do you think that when you are a child you have any sense?

I remember another time when I had been walking with my friends in the bush. Our families were moving from one camp to another and my friends and I were walking ahead of the adults, riding on top of each other, making believe we were donkeys. That's when my friend Besa saw a wildebeest lying dead on the ground; then he saw another and then another; they had all been recently killed by lions. We ran back on our tracks, crying out, "We saw three dead wildebeests, killed by lions!" The adults said, "Ho, ho, our children . . . our wonderful children . . . our wonderful, wonderful children!"

We went back to where the wildebeests were, set up camp, and lived there for a while. The first day, the animals were skinned, water was found, and meat was eaten. The next day, the women went for more water and returned. We ate meat and lay down to sleep. That was the night that the lions came back, came back to eat the animals they had killed—they had eaten only one of the three wildebeests.

The lions came near our camp and stayed just outside the circle of firelight. We could see their eyes shining out of the darkness of the surrounding bush. One pair of eyes were in one place, another pair of eyes were in another place, and there were others. They were many; they wanted to kill us.

My father entered a medicinal trance. While his body tranced, his spirit flew to the spirit world, to talk to the gods. Together, the spirits sent the lions away, because soon they left and went to another water hole far away. When my father came out of the trance, he returned to us. Then we all slept.

Another day, when I was already fairly big, I went with some of my friends and with my younger brother away from the village and into the bush. While we were walking I saw the tracks of a baby kudu in the sand. I called out, "Hey, Everyone! Come here! Come look at these kudu tracks." The others came over and we all looked at them.

We started to follow the tracks and walked and walked and after a while, we saw the little kudu lying quietly in the grass, dead asleep. I jumped up and tried to grab it. It cried out, "Ehnnn ... ehnnn ..." I hadn't really caught it well and it freed itself and ran away. We all ran, chasing after it, and we ran and ran. But I ran so fast that they all dropped behind and then I was alone, chasing it, running as fast as I could. Finally, I was able to grab it. I jumped on it and killed it. Then I picked it up by the legs and carried it back on my shoulders. I was breathing very hard, "Whew ... whew ... whew!"

When I came to where the rest of them were, my older cousin said, "My cousin, my little cousin ... she killed a kudu! What have the rest of us been doing? We men here ... how come we didn't kill it but this young girl with so much 'run' in her killed it?"

I gave the animal to my cousin and he carried it. On the way back, one of the other girls spotted a small steenbok and she and her older brother ran after it. They chased it and finally her brother killed it. That day we brought a lot of meat back with us to the village and everyone had plenty to eat.

Was my childhood a happy one? By the time I had grown and was a young girl, I knew that my heart was usually happy. But when I was a small child, I wasn't aware enough of things to be able to think about whether I was happy or sad.

Chapter 4
Discovering Sex

THE !KUNG HAVE little privacy, either in the village or within the family dwelling. Parents and children sleep together, sharing their blankets, in small one-room huts that have no dividers or private sections. Adults try to keep children from noticing their sexual activity, but arranging meetings in the bush is difficult and young children often insist on accompanying their mothers wherever they go. The alternative is to wait until the children are asleep, and try to be discreet. But children, especially older ones, are curious, and a modest effort to stay awake (while feigning sleep) may enable them to observe their parents' lovemaking. Parents encourage older children, especially those in their early teens, to sleep elsewhere; often the children themselves initiate this transition, building huts to sleep in alone or with other adolescents. Occasionally they may choose to live with their grandparents for a while.

This early sexual awareness and curiosity flourish in the unrestricted free time that makes up much of the !Kung child's day. !Kung children have no schools, nor are they expected to contribute to subsistence, to care for younger children, or, except for occasionally collecting water, to help out much around the village. It is only in their mid-teens that girls—married or unmarried—begin to accompany their mothers regularly on gathering expeditions and to collect wood and water and that boys begin to go with their fathers on hunting trips.

Most parents prefer to leave all but the youngest children in the village while they gather: food collection is more efficient that way, and distances traveled can be greater. Also, most children want to stay at home with the other children: playing with friends is highly preferable to the stressful travel and long hours often involved in gathering. This is especially true in the hot, dry months of summer, when the sand burns the feet and water en route is available only in limited quantities carried in ostrich eggshell water containers. When children do accompany adults, they contribute almost nothing to the task at hand. Instead they spend their time eating—food given them and food they forage for themselves—and playing in the bush. Since women gather only about three days a week, there is usually someone either resting or working in the village who can supervise the children left behind.

One woman described it this way, "If you force a child to go gathering with you, she cries and makes it impossible to accomplish anything. If you leave her behind, she won't cry and you can come home with a lot." But in answer to my next question, she explained, "When I sit in the village and my children are playing around me, I don't worry; I just watch what they do. When I leave them behind and go gathering, I worry that they won't be well taken care of, especially if the only person in the village is there because she isn't feeling well."

In most societies around the world older children and young teenagers make substantial contributions to the economy, and their lack of such responsibility in !Kung life is striking. It reflects the stability and security of the !Kung subsistence base, and it seems to indicate that gathering and hunting, even in this marginal environment, is not a terribly arduous way of life: if the adult work load were too great, the !Kung would need only to tap the store of energy sitting idle in their young people. (In fact, teenagers often spend less time helping out than younger children do.)

Village life gives children a secure and socially rich environment in which to play. A village averages about thirty people—relatives, friends, and visitors, all of whom the child knows—and most activities take place outside, beside the fire that defines each family's living space. Children have easy access to the entire village area and alternate between visiting at people's huts and playing in the large communal space, denuded of shrubs and grass, within the circle of huts that forms the perimeter of the village. Sometimes they play in the bush just beyond this circle, but even then adults are usually near enough to respond to any trouble. Cases of children getting lost in the bush around the village or while out gathering are extremely rare, and the children are always found quickly.

Although a watchful surveillance is always kept, adults rarely interfere in children's play, nor do they offer frequent suggestions. They do occasionally mediate fights, especially between children of unequal size, and they generally try to prevent children from getting hurt. The greatest danger in an otherwise fairly harmless village environment is fire, and burns—minor and severe—occur with an unsettling frequency. Despite parental admonishments, children are often seen picking up coals (and quickly dropping them again) or running from one fire to the next with burning branches or weeds. They also handle knives (double-edged, long and sharp) with what appears a casual abandon; yet cuts are rare. Poisoned arrows and spears, the most dangerous of the ordinary objects in the village, are carefully hung out of children's reach. Owning little, the !Kung do not have to worry much about protecting their possessions from children's harm (or vice versa), and children can safely roam throughout the village.

Because of the small number of families, village play groups are typically made up of only a few children of various ages—whoever happens to be living in the village at a given time. These groups, which may range in age from infants to young teens, usually stay around the village in the vicinity of adults or set up their own "villages" a few hundred yards away—within earshot, but not within view. Many of their games are imitations of adult activities: hunting, gathering, singing and trancing, playing house, and playing at parenthood and marriage. (Little children, carried about by older children, often become the "sons and daughters" of these "mothers and fathers.") Occasionally their imitations become reality—foraging roots and berries in the area just beyond the village, or even catching or trapping small animals and birds. Because little formal teaching is done—observation and practice are the basis of all learning—it is in these groups that children acquire many of the skills that will make them productive adults.

The nomadic travels of families have important effects on a child's play group. Its composition may vary from week to week, but the greatest influence on its size is the variation by season. In winter, when people congregate in large numbers near the few permanent springs, there are many children to play with. In summer, when the rains fill the land with standing water, people disperse—to visit relatives in distant villages or to live near food and game resources. A handful of families may travel together, or perhaps only one or two. This is a difficult adjustment for many children, and the return to the permanent springs is usually anticipated with enthusiasm.

!Kung girls and boys play together and share most games. Most cultures, including our own, consider some activities appropriate for girls and others for boys, and encourage the two sexes to play separately from an early age. Our derisive terms "tomboy" and "sissy" seem to have no counterparts in !Kung vocabulary. !Kung children are not segregated by sex, neither sex is trained to be submissive or fierce, and neither sex is restrained from expressing the full breadth of emotion that seems inherent in the human spirit. Although boys and girls both engage in roughhousing, imitation of adult aggressive behavior is rarely seen, and the elaborate preparations for learning to fight found among boys in many societies do not occupy the time of !Kung boys. Because the !Kung impose no responsibilities on their children, place no value on virginity, and do not require that the female body be covered or hidden, girls are as free and unfettered as boys.

Most childhood games involve little or no competition. Children play beside one another, sharing activities, but group rules are rarely established. Each child attempts, through repetition, to become more accomplished, not to defeat or outshine someone else. It is likely that the small number of children playing together and the lack of others the same age against whom to judge themselves encourage this attitude. But !Kung adults also actively avoid competition and the ranking of individuals into hierarchies. In fact, the cultural constraint against drawing sharp differentiations among people leads the !Kung to shun such determinations as winner, prettiest, and most successful, or even best dancer, hunter, healer, musician, or bead-maker. People are aware, of course, of the often impressive talents of others around them, and they derive great benefit from those talents; but it is considered extremely bad manners to call attention to them.

A closer look does reveal subtle distinctions in the kinds of activities engaged in by the two sexes. A study of !Kung children at play showed that boys were more physically aggressive than girls and that girls interacted with adults other than their mothers more than boys did. But, in contrast to studies of children's play in other societies, !Kung girls and boys were found to be equally active, equally capable of sustaining attention to tasks, and equal in the amount of time they spent playing with objects. Also, !Kung children showed no preference for playing only with children of their own sex.

!Kung children are essentially left to their own devices Far from leading to boredom, this freedom results in inventive and energetic play, which characterizes much of their day. Although this play includes many different games and activities, sexual play is what many adults remember most vividly. The amount of such play varies from one group to another, but experimentation of some kind seems universal. Sexual play of younger children begins with boys playing together and girls playing together, and then changes to boys and girls playing with each other, with the boys as the usual—sometimes aggressive—initiators. The play of older children often involves some genital contact, but actual sexual intercourse does not seem to occur until years later, and some girls who marry young reach marriage without having experienced it.

Adults do not approve of sexual play among children and adolescents, but they do little to keep it from happening. They remember such play from their own childhood and, although they usually deny it, they know that their children are playing that way too. As long as the sexual play takes place out of the adults' view, children are not actively prevented from engaging in it. If they are caught, they are scolded and told to "play nicely," but that is all. Children know they will not be intruded on in their play villages, and when they play "marriage" they feel quite grown up and far away from their parents—at least until they need food, or water, or the help of an adult to settle a fight.

Thus, life for the !Kung child appears generally hospitable, but for the nearly fifty-fifty chance of dying before reaching adulthood. All !Kung children live under this threat of disease and death, not only for themselves but also for their siblings. Even their parents are more vulnerable than are adults in cultures like our own, and many later-born !Kung children lose one or both parents before reaching maturity.

I AM AN OLD WOMAN and know about things, because whenever I hear people talking, I listen.[1] I'm going to tell you a story I heard my grandmother tell my mother about our mythical past, a story about the Beginning, when people still didn't know about sex, when they didn't know how to have sexual intercourse.

A very very long time ago, there were two women who built some huts; they were the only two living in their village. Elsewhere were two men who also were just living in their village. The two women lived in one place and the two men lived in another.

One day the men discovered the women's village. The next day while the sun was low in the morning sky, they left their village and went with the idea of stealing the two women. But when they arrived, the women weren't there— they had gone out collecting food and nuts. Later, when the women returned home, they put down the day's gatherings and sat down. Only then did they see the two men. One said, "What? Where am I that there are also men there? My thoughts tell me we live in a place where there are no men. Are there really men here?"

Because these women were going to teach the men

about sex. It was still early and the women just stayed around and ate. But when night came and sat, one of the men went over to one woman and the other man went over to the other woman. The two couples lay there for a long time. Then, one of the men wanted to have sex, so he got up and tried to have sex in the woman's mouth. She said, "No, not like that." He tried the woman's eyes. She said, "No, not like that." Next he tried her ear. "No, not like that." Then, her nostrils. "No, not like that, that's not how you have sex. Look, there's a vagina over here, right between my legs. Now, with my mouth, I eat. With my eyes, I look for things. With my ears, I listen. And with my nose, I breathe. So, how come my vagina is sitting right here, yet you don't try that? All you've been trying to do is to have sex with my face?" That's when he took his penis and pushed it into her vagina, and that's how they finally had sex—then, and during the rest of the night.

When dawn broke, the two men left in search of other people to tell, "Last night we found out how to have sex. There's something called a vagina and that's where you do it." When the other people heard, they and everyone else started having sex as well.

At night, when a child lies beside her mother,[2] in front, and her father lies down behind and her mother and father make love,[3] the child watches. Her parents don't worry about[4] her, a small child, and her father just has sex with her mother. Because, even if the child sees, even if she hears her parents doing their work at night, she is unaware of what it *is* her parents are doing; she is still young, without sense. She just watches and doesn't have any thoughts about it.

Perhaps this is the way the child eventually learns, because as she gets older, she begins to understand that her mother and father are making love. At first she thinks, "So, that's another thing people do with their genitals." Then if the child is a little boy, he'll take the little girl, or perhaps his sister, and do the same thing to her; he'll teach himself.[5] He'll make believe he's having sex with her as he saw his mother and father do. And once he's learned it, he'll try to play that way with everyone.

As children get older, they start to become more aware of their sexual feelings. If, while they are sleeping in their parents' hut, they haven't fallen asleep and their parents start to make love ... if they are just lying there, hearing everything, *then* they feel pain. They might think, "All right, so mother and father are just doing their work." But even so, when they hear, they start to get sexually aroused. Because older children are almost like adults and their sexual feelings are very strong; if they just hear other people making love, they get excited. So they just lie there, until dawn breaks. But when morning comes and they join the other children at play, they tell how they heard their parents doing their work the night before. Then, if the child is a little boy, when he sees a girl, he'll play sexually with her.

That's what an older child does. He waits until he is with a little girl and lies down with her. He takes some saliva, rubs it on her genitals, gets on top and pokes around with his semi-erection, as though he were actually having intercourse, but he is not. Because even though young boys can get hard, they don't really enter little girls. Nor do they yet know about ejaculation. Only when a boy is almost a young man does he start to have sex like an adult.

At first, girls refuse that kind of play—they say all that poking around hurts. But when they are a little older, they agree to it and eventually, even like it.

When I was still small, the work between a man and a woman, the work of living and lying down together, the work the adults took care of and enjoyed, like dancing, the work of a man lying on top of a woman, of rising and falling and rising and falling over her, that work I didn't understand. At first, I thought, "Eh, hey ... so that is something people do." And I thought it was the same thing the children did to me when we played.

It was only when I was older that I became aware of

what my father and mother were actually doing when they
lay down together like that. She would lie down, then they
would lie down together, and then . . . their work would
begin. That's when I thought, "When people do that, is the
woman being killed? Perhaps something terrible is happening,
where one person is killing the other. Is Daddy's work going
to kill Mommy?"

Because at night, my father would lie with my mother.
Sometimes, I still wouldn't have fallen asleep. I'd just be lying
there in front of her and my father would be lying down behind her and I would watch. At first it didn't make me unhappy. But once I was older I started to think, "Why doesn't
my father care that I might still be up? I'm fairly old now,
why isn't he being more respectful of me? Adults should be
concerned about others. Can't they see I'm not sleeping? Why
is he lying with her?" I would lie there, thinking those
thoughts. Or, other thoughts, "How come Mother and Father
don't care? I'm already very grown up. They shouldn't have
sex when someone hasn't begun to sleep. They should wait;
then they could do it." And eventually, others: "No, today I
won't just lie here, I'll go and sleep in another hut. My father
obviously isn't thinking about me; his heart just goes ahead
and does its work. I don't agree to that and I won't sleep in
their hut. What value would continuing to sleep there have
for me now?"

That's when I found a little hut, just for myself, and
started to sleep there. They continued to do their things,
alone in their hut, I suppose. That was their work. But why
hadn't they been more concerned about me?

A child who is nursing has no awareness of things. Milk,
that's all she knows. Otherwise, she has no sense. Even when
she learns to sit, she still doesn't think about anything because her intelligence hasn't come to her yet. Where could
she be taking her thoughts from? The only thought is nursing.

But when she grows and is bigger and begins to walk,
she has many thoughts. She sits and starts to think about

things, and to think about her work—sexual play. Because when children play, that is what they do. Little boys play at sex and teach themselves, just as baby roosters teach themselves. Little girls also learn it with one another in the same way.

At first, boys play that play with other boys—poking their genitals around one another's behinds—and girls play that play with little girls. Later, if a boy sees a little girl by herself, he takes her and "has sex" with her. That's how little boys and little girls learn.

Little boys are the first to know the sweetness of sexual games. That's why they do that when they play. Yes. A girl, while she is still young, doesn't know about sex. Her thoughts don't really understand. But a little boy has a penis and perhaps, while he is still inside his mother's belly, he already knows about sex. Because boys know how to do things with their genitals, they know how to move them up and down. They just take little girls, push them down and have sex with them. Even if the girls and boys are just playing, they do that.

When girls are alone, they sometimes play sexually together. But when boys are there, they don't, because the boys are there to play that way with them. Girls can only touch genitals together; that's not really much help. Boys are the ones with hardness, with penises; boys have their spears. Girls have no spears, they have nothing; only softness. They don't have anything that moves around like a penis. So when girls are alone and take one another, they don't do it very well. No, a little boy is best; he does it right.

When I was a small child, I played at nothing things. I had no understanding of things around me and didn't know about sexual play. Even if we were just girls playing, we played nicely. Because there is good play and bad play. Bad play is when you touch each other's genitals; good play is when you don't.

But when I was older, I had some sense, and with that sense came the awareness of sex. That was still before the little girls and little boys actually knew what kind of play "playing sex" was; we just talked about it. The boys would ask each other, "When you play at sex, what do you do?" and they would ask us. We would say, "We don't know how to play that kind of play. You're the ones always talking about it. But we, we don't know. Anyway, however you play it, we won't do it. Why can't we just play?" That's when the boys would say, "Isn't having sex what playing is all about?" They would say, "You girls don't know anything, so look, first we'll play together, then we'll get married, and then we'll touch each other's genitals and have sex." The girls always refused, "Playing that way is very bad. Why do you keep saying we should do it when we don't want to?"

Eventually my girlfriends started to play sexually with each other. They'd put saliva in their hands, rub it onto their genitals, and touch genitals together. I didn't know how to do it and just sat, refusing. They'd ask, "How come you don't play with us?" And I'd say, "If I did, my genitals would smell terrible. You put saliva on them and I don't like that." I'd wait around, and when they started to play nicely again, I'd join them and we'd play and play and play.

Not long after, some of the girls started playing that kind of play with little boys. They learned about it long before I did; they taught themselves and didn't cry. I refused for a very long time before I learned. I didn't know what it was, and I cried whenever the boys asked. They'd say, "How come you always cry when we play?" I'd say, "Because you say we should play sexually, that's why." Other times I'd say, "I'm going to tell Mommy you said we should do that." Because I didn't want to play bad play and stayed with the other girls who cried. We stayed together and refused together.

But we did watch. We watched the others to see what they were actually doing. Even so, whenever we saw them playing that way, we cried. Only after we had seen it over and over again and felt we understood—when we felt we knew exactly what they were doing—only then did we stop being so afraid. Finally, we agreed. That's when I thought, "So, when you're a child, touching each other's genitals must be the way you play." Because after watching the others, I started to play that way myself. Eventually, I liked it.

Because children, their hearts just like one another. They play together like that. That's how they grow up.

And that's how we grew up. We would leave our parents' village and set up a small, "grown-up" village of our own nearby. We played at gathering food from the bush, at bringing it back and eating it. Then we "married" and played sexually together. We played like that all day.

If one of our fathers had killed an animal, we would go back to the village to get some meat, take a little can or a pot and, our hearts happy, bring it to our little village. We would spend the rest of the day living in our village. One boy would sit with one girl and another boy with another girl. We would sit there, cooking meat and giving presents of it to one another, just like adults. When the meat was finished, one of the children would go get more, bring it back, cook it and serve it again. Only when the sun stood late in the sky would we return to our parents' village to stay. But even there, we would just continue to play.

When I was older, I began to fear that adults would see what kind of play we were playing, and I learned to sit around like them. Before that, the adults would sometimes yell at us—especially if we were playing sexually in the heart of a group of people. Because little children aren't afraid of adults. Even if they are right in their midst, they just play sexual games. They have no fear; they have no sense. They don't think that people might see and yell at them.

Some days, I stayed in the adult village with my younger brother. Other days, I joined the children. We would play ordinary play for a while. Then they would want to take me. Sometimes when I refused, they threw me down and held me, then pulled off my leather apron and had sex with me. It hurt! Is a penis not like a bone? They'd poke it around and the hurt was like it was killing me. I'd cry and cry and cry. I was still a child and didn't know any of its sweetness.

But other times I'd agree. That's how we lived, sometimes

playing ordinary play, other times playing the play of lying down together.

The boys would sometimes accuse us of being unfaithful. They would say, "People tell us that you like other men." We'd say, "No, we don't like other men. What's wrong with you that you think that?" They'd leave and say, "Let's leave the women by themselves." Other times, they'd say, "No, these women are doing bad things, they have lovers. Today, we're going to hit them, hit them so they won't make love to other men."

One time I went with a friend back to the village to get some blankets. When we came back, we covered ourselves and lay down. The boys came and lay down with us. Later, I told the adults, "Everybody! Everybody! We were playing today and the boys 'screwed'[6] us." The older people said, "If the boys try to touch your genitals, leave them and play only with the girls. Let the boys play by themselves." I said, "But even when we play alone, they sneak up on us and chase us. Then they play with us and ruin our genitals." (That's what we called it.) The adults said we should tell the boys to leave us alone, that we should only play nice games. They said it was wrong for us to play with our genitals.

Later, I thought that I shouldn't have told. Why had I? The adults only yelled at me. So after that, I didn't say anything. We just played and played and I never said anything again.

Another time the boys asked us to play and I said, "Keya and I are going to go off and play by ourselves. You want to play sexually. Go play your play. But we won't. You want us to do something bad." The boys said, "That's not why! You're going off together so you can *screw!*" We said, "Not true. Do we have penises to have sex with each other with? Can two vaginas screw?" The boys said, "You're always playing sexually together. That's why you refuse us." We said, "All of you are crazy. Go play your play. We're going to stay by ourselves." They threw sticks at us as we walked away. We yelled back, "You're not having us . . . too bad!"

Later, we returned. We asked, "How come you left us? Aren't we playing together anymore?" They said, "What? *You're* the ones who left us. You were afraid we would play sexually with you. That's why you left. Right?" We said, "Yes, because touching each other's genitals is bad. That's what our mothers told us." The boys said, "Your mothers were fooling you. So let's make believe we're lovers and that we have to sneak away to the bush to meet. Except Nisa, because whenever we play like that, she goes and tells."

Keya and I built some little huts and played together while the others played inside their huts. After a while, we sneaked up on them. We yelled out suddenly, "Aie! Look what they're doing!" One of the boys said, "The two of you are going to be shitting pretty soon. That Nisa, she has no brains. She's like a baby—no thoughts! What's the idea of sneaking up on us like that?" We cried, "You're screwing!! You're screwing!!! You'd like to screw us too, but we refuse! Sex is *bad* and makes your genitals smell rotten."

We stayed there playing like that. Later, we returned to the adult village. There the boys said "Come on . . . everyone . . . let's go back to *our* village and play." We took our blankets and things there. Keya and I entered our hut. The others, with husbands, were in their huts. We visited each other, just like adults.

Two boys came over to us, "Let's lie down and do our work as the others are doing." We said, "When you do that work, how do you do it? What work are you talking about." They yelled, "Our work is—*screw! screw* . . . We'll show you. We'll be your lovers because we already have wives in the other huts over there. We'll come and do what lovers do, then go back to them." We said, "So that's what you're talking about? You've come here to make love to us? Well, the answer is *no*. We are two women who have no husbands and you two are married. Since we have no husbands, we'll follow you back to your village and eat meat and food there. We'll stay and all of us will just live together." The boys refused, "No, what we'll do is this. My brother and I will go out to the bush, find things to eat, and bring them to you. Then we'll be your lovers. After that, you can visit our wives. Later, we'll even come back and ask you to be their co-wives." We said, "Look, we're just children. Let's just play nicely. That's all we want to do." We joined the others and just played other kinds of play.

Eventually, Keya and I had boyfriends and learned. Keya was with Besa, and I was with Tikay. The two of them taught us about men, and once we knew it, we played that way every day. We'd build little huts and have sex there. That was when I realized that playing like that was a good thing. I thought, "How come this thing is so nice, yet I refused it? The other children knew about it but I had no sense. Finally, I have learned and now I know that when you are a child, this is something you do. You teach it to yourself." At the time, I still didn't understand about sexual pleasure—I just liked what Tikay did and I liked playing that play.

After Tikay taught me, I really liked him! When we played, the children said I should play with other boys, but I refused. I only wanted Tikay. I said, "Me? I won't take a horrible man. I won't go off with someone who's ugly." They teased Tikay, "Hey ... Tikay ... you're the only one Nisa wants! She refuses the rest of us!" But Tikay said, "That's all right. I'll play with her."

Once Tikay tore off my pubic apron and threw it up in a tree where it just stayed, hanging. He wanted to have sex with me, but I didn't want to. He grabbed me and I fought with him; he grabbed my chest and grabbed all over my body. Even though I still had no breasts, he kept grabbing and holding on to me. I said, "Are my genitals supposed to be having sex? No, I haven't even started to develop yet. You're the one with the penis, but me, I have no genitals to have sex with. Because just as you *have* a penis, I *don't* have a vagina! When God made your penis and put it there, God didn't make a vagina to put there for me. I have no vagina at all. My genital area is bare. So how can you have sex with something that's not there?" He said, "I'll have sex with you! You're lying! Aren't we friends? Aren't we the same age?

You're a child and I'm a child. Why are you saying things like that to me?"

He came and grabbed me again. I refused and started to cry. That's when he tore off my pubic apron and threw it up in a tree. I shouted, "I don't care! Feel bad! You won't have sex with me!" I stood there crying, covering my genitals with my hands because there was nothing else covering me. I left them playing in the bush and ran alone back to the village. Mother gave me another pubic apron and soon I went and joined them again.

After a while, everyone left to play in a large water pan. I said, "Tikay, climb up and get me my pubic apron." He refused. I asked him again, and again he refused. Finally I asked my cousin, who went up and brought it down. I put it on, on top of the one my mother gave me, and wore both of them.

Some days all the girls refused the boys and went off together and played. Sometimes Nai and I married. I really liked her—she was beautiful! Other times I married Kunla and we played together. Sometimes we even refused to be with the other girls and Kunla and I went off together and played, sometimes sexually, other times not. We used to make believe we were giving birth to children and took turns being the baby. We'd play alone that way until the boys sneaked up on us and separated us. Then each of us would take our husband and our hearts would continue to be happy.

When there was a lot of rain and the water pans were full, we played in the water. One day, while we were splashing around in a large pan of rain water, the boys said they wanted to have sex with the girls, right in the middle of the water. I told Tikay, "No, if you do, you'll kill us. The water will come into our nostrils and we'll drown. We'll gasp until we die, so don't try it here." Then I bit him, "Anyway, you're dumb! Do my genitals belong to you? What makes you think you can have me now?"

When we left, we went back to play in the bush, in our little village. We entered our huts and stayed there, playing. The boys pretended they were men, that they were tracking an animal and that they struck it with their poisoned arrows. They took some leaves and hung them over a stick, carrying them as though they were strips of meat. The girls stayed in the village, and when the boys came back, we pretended we were living there and eating—until all the meat was gone. On the next hunt, the boys took the girls and we followed along. After we found another animal and killed it, we all carried the meat back: the girls, in their karosses, and the boys, hanging it on sticks. We played in the bush like that, pretending we were living there, getting water and eating meat.

One time we all left and moved to the East,[7] near the Hereros. The first time I saw cows' milk, I wouldn't drink it. I just sat there, looking at it, and refused. I was afraid of the Hereros, and ran away whenever a Herero man or woman came near. I soon learned not to run away, but I was still afraid of them, and when the children played, I wouldn't play sexually with them; I'd just get up and leave if they tried to touch me.

While we were still there, Tikay started playing with one of the young Herero girls. He told me to find another boyfriend. I didn't want to and just stayed by myself. "I don't want another boyfriend. I'll stay alone in the single-women's hut. If I don't want to play sexually, what difference does it make? The rest of you, just marry without me." Because I really liked Tikay and wanted him to play with me, not with the other girl. I wanted to be the only one.

Tikay made me one of his two wives. My hut stood in one spot and the young Herero girl's hut stood in another. Tikay would lie down with me for a while, then go and lie down with her. But she was just as jealous of me as I was of her. She'd say, "How come your boyfriend doesn't lie down with you, but only lies down with me?" That really wasn't true. Tikay acted just like a grown man with two wives: he'd stay with me a few days, then go to the Herero girl's hut for a few days.

Until one morning, I said, "In the beginning, you had only me. Now, you have set someone else beside me. I don't want to do co-wives anymore. We'll have to separate." He said, "Haven't I been treating you well? Don't you know how to *do* co-wives?" I said, "No. When you are children, you don't play at having co-wives. One girl should play with one boy and other girls with other boys. I told you I didn't want to play sexually at the start, but you said we were only playing. Now, if we're only playing, how can you want me to have a co-wife?"

But I really liked him!

I met Tikay again, quite recently, and there we were, two adults. Even then he said, "Nisa, when we were children I taught you about men. Now that I'm a grown man, why don't I lie down with you again, the way we did long ago?"

While we lived in the East, I played with the children I had played with for years. But then my family left and went to live near my mother's sister at the Chotana water hole. But once there, I wouldn't play; I just stayed with the adults and thought about my friends in the East. I said, "I miss the children I used to play with. Mommy, didn't you say we were going to go back East? Mommy ... Daddy ... let's go back there again." But they said, "What would we be wanting there?" I said, "I want to be with the children I played with. Where we're living now, I don't see any children." They said, "Right over there ... just go over there and you'll find children to play with—your aunts and nieces and cousins.[8] Play with them." I said, "Not true, there aren't children here. Let's go back East. I don't want to play with my cousins." I started to cry. I missed my friends and cried and cried. My parents told me I must surely be crazy not to want to play with my cousins.

But I could see them as I sat there. I watched them playing and thought, "Those children over there ... no, I won't go over to them." One day my cousin Tasa came over to me, "Nisa, come play with me." I said, "I don't want to." She said, "Let's go play in the pan and swim in the water." "I don't want to swim." I sat there, refusing everything she suggested. Finally, she pulled me up, took me with her, and we went off together. Later we joined the other children and played with them. We just played nice play: going to the water pan, swimming around, going back to the village, going back to play in the water again. On the way we sometimes collected na and nin berries to bring back. We played one game for awhile, went back to the village, and then played something else.

A child has no sense and just tries to do as the adults do. That's why, even with my cousins, we eventually played sexually together. Whenever my cousin Tuma wanted to play that way with the girls, we'd be mean to him. Then he'd be mean back to us. He'd hit us and make us cry. I'd say, "Leave us alone. My boyfriend is no longer with me and I won't have sex with anyone else. My boyfriend is in the East."

You see, I, too, was senseless and didn't understand anything—I thought there was only one boy who was mine and that there wasn't anyone else.

I said, "My husband is in the East. Besides, there are only ugly men here and I won't have any of them. My husband is handsome and isn't like the men here, who are so very ugly. My husband is beautiful. The rest of you here are awful!" Then I said, "Anyway, you, Tuma, you've got an *enormous* penis! I don't want to be with someone like that!" He said, "We're going to play and have sex with Big-Vagina over there." He meant me. "Big-Vagina! Aren't you also Nisa, the crazy one?" "How come you're insulting *me?*" I said, "Tuma, your penis is so big, you'll never have sex with me! You'll always feel ashamed because you want me!"

We started to fight. I bit him and he hit me. I said, "You won't have me! Think about that! If you try, I'll tell my mother and she'll scare the shit out of you, you Big-Penis!" He said, "You think I want to have sex with Nisa-Big-Vagina? Is there anyone who thinks her genitals are good?" I said, "Feel bad! You're the one who wants me! Why don't you have sex with someone else? If you came to me, what could I possibly learn from you?" He said, "You think your genitals are so great, don't you? Well, they're not and you're ridiculous!" I said, "What? There's not a female around here with the name Nisa who would have sex with such a large penis as yours. If you want sex so badly, why don't you have it with your little sister? Isn't that something children do? When we lived in the East, Besa used to play that way with his sister. So, go have sex with her. If you won't, why do you say you will with me?" He said, "Nisa-Big-Vagina! Who taught you to talk like that? Have sex with my sister? Don't you know you're not supposed to do that?" I said, "Feel bad! Because that's just what you want to do! You with the big penis, go have sex with your sister!"

Tuma's sister said, "Nisa, you're crazy! What are you telling him that for?" I said, "You're the one who's crazy, not me. Now go tell him to come to you. Tuma, go, screw your sister. She'll be your girlfriend." As Tasa and I started to play, I said to her, "Now, don't *you* have sex with him. If you did, he'd tear open your genitals."

We all lay down. Tasa and I lay together and Tuma and his sister lay under some blankets together. The blankets started to move. We watched. I whispered to Tasa, "Look! Do you see that?" We were quiet. Suddenly, we screamed very loud, "Are you crazy? Screwing your sister? Oooh! Big-Penis is screwing his sister! We're going to *tell!*" Tuma yelled back, "I swear ... if you tell, I'll take my father's poison arrows and kill the two of you." We said, "Em—bar—rassed!!! We've caught you. You're not supposed to screw your sister, don't you know? You have no brains in your head. Now, leave her alone." He said, "I'll keep doing just what I'm doing. What thoughts should I be thinking that would make me be afraid of her?" We said, "Well, *our* siblings are respectful of us. They never do what you're doing. But that's because you're stupid."

A few months later, we left Chotana and went back to live again at our old water hole. All my friends were there, and when I saw them I was happy again. We played and played and danced and sang, played music and sang and danced, and my heart was happy to be with the children I liked.

We used to make believe about everything. We made believe we cooked food and took it out of the fire. We had trance dances and sang and danced and danced and sang and the boys cured us. They went, "Xai—i! Kow-a-di-li!" They cured us and we sang and danced and danced, danced all day.

Sometimes we played with the children from another village; sometimes we just played by ourselves. Other times, the other children came and found us playing and went back with us to our little village. They'd greet us just as adults do, "How are all of you?" And we'd answer, "Eh, we're just fine." We'd stay around together and then they'd say they were going back to their village and were going to play at making a trance dance. So we'd go with them and dance and sing. Sometimes the sun set while we were there, but even though it was dark, we just stayed in the center of the village and played. We'd sometimes stay into the night, dancing and singing, and only leave when it was time to go home to sleep.

Chapter 5
Trial Marriages

YOUNG WOMEN are not considered truly adult or expected to assume full responsibility for themselves or for others until they reach their late teens, have menstruated and married, and are likely soon to become mothers. Although in recent years girls have been marrying around the age of sixteen and a half—also the average age of first menstruation—previous generations sometimes married as early as ten or twelve years of age. Boys, in contrast, are usually not considered eligible for marriage until they are between twenty and thirty, and then only after they have demonstrated their ability to provide for a family by killing a large animal. Men, therefore, are often ten or more years older than their wives. No matter how early a girl marries, sexual relations are not expected to begin until she shows signs of sexual maturity—culturally recognized as the time around the first menstruation. These early marriages are unstable and often brief in duration, and a girl may enter several of them before she starts having children, usually with one life-long partner.

Parents and other close relatives arrange first marriages and, if the children are still young, subsequent ones as well. Trips will be made to visit potential spouses residing within a wide geographical area, to ensure parents the broadest possible choice. But low population density often limits this number, and when rules of appropriateness and eligibility are applied, the choices are narrowed even further. The !Kung adhere to the nearly universal taboo of prohibiting marriage between closely related kin, but in contrast to many other gathering and hunting societies, they also forbid marriage between first cousins. In addition, they discourage marriage to anyone having the same name as one's father, one's mother, one's sibling, or, as might be the case in later marriages, one's child.

In choosing a son-in-law, parents consider age (the man should not be too many years older than their daughter), marital status (an unmarried man is preferable to one already married and seeking a second wife), hunting ability, and willingness to accept the responsibilities of family life. A cooperative, generous, and unaggressive nature is looked for, as well. Or, an appropriate prospect might be the son of a close family friend or someone with access to an area with coveted vegetable, game, or water resources. A first wife, meanwhile, should be young, industrious, agreeable, and capable of bearing children. I asked one man who was in his early forties and looking for a second wife, "Would you marry a woman smarter than you?" He answered without hesitation, "Of course. If I married her, she would teach me to be smart, too."

Once the two sets of parents agree, the marriage is likely to take place even if the girl has to be pressured into accepting it. Resistance to marriage is typical of young girls, and is usually interpreted as being directed at marriage itself, rather than at a specific man. After marriage, the husband usually joins his wife at her parents' village, because girls are not expected to leave their mothers while they are still young. Essentially informal, this "bride service" is one of the major inducements for marrying daughters off so young: the husband helps to provide meat for the girl and her family. Her parents can also watch how he behaves toward their daughter and themselves and can represent her interests in times of conflict. Marriage also expands the parents' social world, giving them close ties to their son-in-law's family, as expressed through gift exchange, visiting, and the sharing of mutual concerns. It also ensures each family access to the resources and village life of the other in times of scarcity. Since the availability of edible plants can vary significantly from one area to another and rainfall often does the same, this access may be lifesaving, even if the two areas are only a few miles apart.

The girl's parents may encourage the couple to remain with them by making life as pleasant as possible for their son-in-law. Many men do take up long-term residence, staying from three to ten years, on average, or sometimes for life. This arrangement affords the girl's parents additional economic support, as well as the comfort of having their children and grandchildren around them. For these reasons, the husband's family may compete for the couple's attention, and many younger couples divide their time between the two families before settling in (more or less) with one.

If a girl is determined that she will never feel any affection for her husband she can insist on ending the marriage. She may try to elicit support from influential members of her family, or she may make life so unpleasant for her husband that he simply leaves. When she is older, she may decide for herself whom she wants to marry, and hope that the adults will accept her choice. If she becomes pregnant, she is likely to marry the father of the child, whatever objections are raised by others. (Such independently formed attachments usually involve men who are much younger than ones chosen by parents and much closer geographically.)

The early years of many marriages are stressful ones for both partners, especially when they differ widely in age. Although getting married does not suddenly fill a girl's life with responsibility, she is expected to sleep in the same hut with a man ten years older than herself, a man she may not know very well. In addition, she is expected gradually to assume some of the burden of maintaining her household—while her unmarried peers are still essentially carefree.

The groom, meanwhile, is usually fully grown and sexually mature. Marrying a young girl means he has to wait, sometimes for as long as five years, while his wife slowly develops. Living with her in her parents' village, he is expected to help her father hunt and bring back food. He may also have to endure her indifference or even rejection. Although these circumstances are far from ideal, many young men are willing to accept them. Because some older men are married to two women, young marriageable girls are at a premium. If a young man wants to be assured of having a wife sooner rather than later, and a young woman rather than an older widow or divorcee, he has little choice. The girl's parents can exercise a good deal of control over him, but, to be sure, they do not want to drive him away. Despite his willingness to cooperate and despite his patience, however, it is not likely that this first marriage will last.

The marriage ceremony is quite modest, although negotiations and gift exchange are typically begun long before the actual marriage takes place. A hut is built for the couple by members of both families, and is set apart from the rest of the village. As sunset approaches, friends bring the couple to the hut. The bride, with head covered, is carried and laid down inside; the groom, walking, is led to the hut and sits beside the door. Coals from the fires of both families are brought to start the new fire in front of the marriage hut. Their friends stay with them, singing, playing, and joking. The couple stay apart from each other, maintaining a respectful reserve, and do not join in the festivities. After everyone leaves, they spend their first night together in the hut. The next morning, oil is ceremonially rubbed on both of them—each by the other's mother. Because sleeping next to a strange man can be frightening for the girl, an older woman, usually a close relative, sometimes accompanies the girl and sleeps beside her in the marriage hut until she begins to adjust to her new status.

Most !Kung experience one long-term marriage, although most are also married more than once. Dissolution of marriages by divorce is quite common. It usually occurs during the first few years of a marriage, before the couple has had children, and is usually initiated by the woman. No formalities or legal procedures are necessary, but emotions often run high. Arguments for and against termination may go on for days or even weeks, as everyone in the village expresses a point of view. Eventually, a decision is made, and if the choice is separation, it ends there. Since no dowry or bride-price is involved in getting married, there is nothing to be repaid when getting divorced. (Gifts are exchanged during the marriage ceremony, but this is primarily to celebrate the occasion.) Only a minimal investment in hut sites or living compounds is made, so it is easy for one of the spouses simply to move away. In addition, all goods are owned individually, not jointly, thus eliminating possible disputes over the division of property. Whether the couple has ever engaged in sexual relations does not become an issue. No premium is placed on virginity—indeed, I could not find a word for virginity in the !Kung language. The divorced girl or woman simply re-enters the category of highly desirable potential wives, to be sought after by eligible men. Both divorced partners are likely to marry again within a year. If children are involved they usually remain in the custody of the mother.

Women do not give up their friendships with other women when they marry. Friendship is highly valued by the !Kung; their word ≠dara, meaning friend, agemate, or peer, describes this relationship, which goes beyond kinship and name-relations. If girls who have grown up together remain in the same village after marriage, their relationships are not likely to change immediately, since little pressure is exerted on young brides to assume wifely roles. As they mature and have families, they will continue to cooperate in work and in leisure. An active exchange of gifts—typical of the network of exchange maintained by all !Kung adults with various others—will formalize and strengthen their ties. As their children grow older, they may even support each other's exploration of the spiritual realms of trancing and curing. Unless one of the women moves away, this friendship is likely to last throughout their lives. So, too, may the relationships between co-wives in successful polygynous marriages be sustained over years. Although sexual jealousy and rivalry try these relationships, strong and loyal bonds of friendship between the women often form and last for many years.

WHEN ADULTS TALKED TO ME, I listened. When I was still a young girl with no breasts, they told me that when a young woman grows up, her parents give her a husband and she continues to grow up next to him.[1]

When they first talked to me about it, I said, "What kind of thing am I that I should take a husband? When I grow up, I won't marry. I'll just lie by myself. If I married, what would I be doing it for?"

My father said, "You don't know what you're saying. I, I am your father and am old; your mother is old, too. When you marry, you will gather food and give it to your husband to eat. He also will do things for you. If you refuse, who will give you food? Who will give you things to wear?"

I said, "There's no question about it, I won't take a husband. Why should I? As I am now, I'm still a child and won't marry." I said to my mother, "You say you have a man for me to marry? Why don't you take him and set him beside Daddy? You marry him and let them be co-husbands.[2] What have I done that you're telling me I should marry?"

My mother said, "Nonsense. When I tell you I'm going to give you a husband, why do you say you want me to marry him? Why are you talking to me like this?"

I said, "Because I'm only a child. When I grow up and you tell me to take a husband, I'll agree. But I haven't passed through my childhood yet and I won't marry!"

A long time passed before my mother talked about it again. "Nisa, I want to give you a husband. Who shall it be?" I knew there was another man she wanted me to marry. I said, "I won't marry him." I almost added, "You marry him and set him beside Daddy," but I stopped. This time I was ashamed of myself and didn't say anything more. I thought, "Why am I not agreeing with her? When I speak like that, am I not shitting on her?"

We continued to live after that and just kept on living. It wasn't until a very long time had passed that they talked about it again.

I've had many husbands—Bo, Tsaa, Tashay, Besa, and another Bo. They all married me. Have men not liked me?

When I still had no breasts, when my genitals still weren't developed, when my chest was without anything on it, that was when a man named Bo came from a distant area and people started talking about marriage. Was I not almost a young woman?

One day, my parents and his parents began building our marriage hut. The day we were married, they carried me to it and set me down inside. I cried and cried and cried. Later, I ran back to my parents' hut, lay down beside my little brother, and slept, a deep sleep like death.

The next night, Nukha, an older woman, took me into the hut and stayed with me. She lay down between Bo and myself, because young girls who are still children are afraid of their husbands. So, it is our custom for an older woman to come into the young girl's hut to teach her not to be afraid. The woman is supposed to help the girl learn to like her husband. Once the couple is living nicely together and getting along, the older woman leaves them beside each other.

That's what Nukha was supposed to do. Even the people who saw her come into the hut with me thought she would lay me down and that once I fell asleep, she would leave and go home to her husband.

But Nukha had within her clever deceit. My heart refused Bo because I was a child, but Nukha, she liked him. That was why, when she laid me down in the hut with my husband, she was also laying me down with her lover. She put me in front and Bo was behind. We stayed like that for a very long time. As soon as I was asleep, they started to make love. But as Bo made love to Nukha, they knocked into me. I kept waking up as they bumped me, again and again.

I thought, "I'm just a child. I don't understand about such things. What are people doing when they move around like that? How come Nukha took me into my marriage hut and laid me down beside my husband, but when I started to cry, she changed places with me and lay down next to him? Is he hers? How come he belongs to her yet Mommy and Daddy said I should marry him?"

I lay there, thinking my thoughts. Before dawn broke, Nukha got up and went back to her husband. I lay there, sleeping, and when it started getting light, I went back to my mother's hut.

The next night, when darkness sat, Nukha came for me again. I cried, "He's your man! Yesterday you took me and brought me inside the hut, but after we all lay there, he was with you! Why are you now bringing me to someone who is yours?" She said, "That's not true, he's not mine. He's *your* husband. Now, go to your hut and sit there. Later, we'll lie down."

She brought me to the hut, but once inside, I cried and cried and cried. I was still crying when Nukha lay down with us. After we had been lying there for a very long time, Bo started to make love to her again. I thought, "What is this? What am I? Am I supposed to watch this? Don't they see me? Do they think I'm only a baby?" Later, I got up and told them I had to urinate. I passed by them and went to lie down in mother's hut and stayed there until morning broke.

That day, I went gathering with my mother and father. As we were collecting mongongo nuts and klaru roots, my mother said, "Nisa, as you are, you're already a young woman. Yet, when you go into your marriage hut to lie down, you get up, come back, and lie down with me. Do you think I have married you? No, I'm the one who gave birth to you. Now, take this man as your husband, this strong man who will get food, for you and for me to eat. Is your father the only one who can find food? A husband kills things and gives them to you; a husband works on things that become your things; a husband gets meat that is food for you to eat. Now, you have a husband, Bo; he has married you."

I said, "Mommy, let me stay with you. When night sits, let me sleep next to you. What have you done to me that I'm only a child, yet the first husband you give me belongs to Nukha?" My mother said, "Why are you saying that? Nukha's husband is not your husband. Her husband sits elsewhere, in another hut."

I said, "Well . . . the other night when she took me and put me into the hut, she laid me down in front of her; Bo slept behind. But later, they woke me up, moving around the way they did. It was the same last night. Again, I slept in front and Bo behind and again, they kept bumping into me. I'm not sure exactly what they were doing, but that's why tonight, when night sits, I want to stay with you and sleep next to you. Don't take me over there again."

My mother said, "Yo! My daughter! They were moving about?" I said. "Mm. They woke me while I was sleeping. That's why I got up and came back to you." She said, "Yo! How horny that Bo is! He's screwing Nukha! You are going to leave that man, that's the only thing I will agree to now."

My father said, "I don't like what you've told us. You're only a child, Nisa, and adults are the ones responsible for arranging your marriage. But when an adult gives a husband and that husband makes love to someone else, then that adult hasn't done well. I understand what you have told us and I say that Bo has deceived me. Therefore, when Nukha comes for you tonight, I will refuse to let you go. I will say, 'My daughter won't go into her marriage hut because you, Nukha, you have already taken him for a husband.' "

We continued to talk on our way back. When we arrived at the village, I sat down with my parents. Bo walked over to our marriage hut, then Nukha went over to him. I sat and watched as they talked. I thought, "Those two, they were screwing! That's why they kept bumping into me!"

I sat with Mother and Father while we ate. When evening came, Nukha walked over to us. "Nisa, come, let me take you to your hut." I said, "I won't go." She said, "Get up. Let me take you over there. It's your hut. How come you're already married but today you won't make your hut your home?"

That's when my mother, drinking anger, went over to Nukha and said, "As I'm standing here, I want you to tell me something. Nisa is a child who fears her husband. Yet, when you took her to her hut, you and her husband had sex together. Don't you know her husband should be trying to help bring her up? But that isn't something either of you are thinking about!"

Nukha didn't say anything, but the fire in my mother's words burned. My mother began to yell, cursing her, "Horny, that's what you are! You're no longer going to take Nisa to her husband. And, if you ever have sex with him again, I'll crack your face open. You horny woman! You'd screw your own father!"

That's when my father said, "No, don't do all the talking. You're a woman yet, how come you didn't ask me? I am a man and I will do the talking now. You, you just listen to what I say. Nisa is my child. I also gave birth to her. Now, you are a woman and will be quiet because I am a man."

Then he said, "Nukha, I'm going to tell you something. I am Gau and today I'm going to pull my talk from inside myself and give it to you. We came together here for this marriage, but now something very bad has happened, something I do not agree to at all. Nisa is no longer going to go from here, where I am sitting, to that hut over there, that hut which you have already made your own. She is no longer going to look for anything for herself near that hut."

He continued, "Because, when I agree to give a man to my daughter, then he is only for my daughter. Nisa is a child and her husband isn't there for two to share. So go, take that man, he's already yours. Today my daughter will sit with me; she will sit here and sleep here. Tomorrow I will take her and we will move away. What you have already done to this marriage is the way it will remain."

Nukha didn't say anything. She left and went to the hut without me. Bo said, "Where's Nisa? Why are you empty, returning here alone?" Nukha said, "Nisa's father refused to let her go. She told him that you had made love to me and that's what he just now told me. I don't know what to do about this, but I won't go back to their hut again." Bo said, "I have no use for that kind of talk. Get the girl and come back with her." She said, "I'm not going to Gau's hut. We're fin-

ished with that talk now. And when I say I'm finished, I'm
saying I won't go back there again."

She left and walked over to her own hut. When her husband saw her, he said, "So, you and Bo are lovers! Nisa said
that when you took her to Bo, that the two of you . . . how
exactly *did* Bo reward you for your help?" But Nukha said,
"No, I don't like Bo and he's not my lover. Nisa is just a child
and it is just a child's talk she is talking."

Bo walked over to us. He tried to talk but my father said,
"You, be quiet. I'm the one who's going to talk about this."
So Bo didn't say anything more, and my father talked until it
was finished.

The next morning, very early, my father, mother, and
aunt packed our things and we all left. We slept in the mongongo groves that night and traveled on until we reached another water hole where we continued to live.

We lived and lived and nothing more happened for a
while. After a long time had passed, Bo strung together some
trade beads made of wood, put them into a sack with food,
and traveled the long distance to the water hole where we
were living.

It was late afternoon; the sun had almost left the sky. I
had been out gathering with my mother, and we were coming back from the bush. We arrived in the village and my
mother saw them, "Eh-hey, Bo's over there. What's he doing
here? I long ago refused him. I didn't ask him to come back. I
wonder what he thinks he's going to take away from here?"

We put down our gatherings and sat. We greeted Bo and
his relatives—his mother, his aunt, Nukha, and Nukha's
mother. Bo's mother said, "We have come because we want
to take Nisa back with us." Bo said, "I'm again asking for
your child. I want to take her back with me."

My father said, "No, I only just took her from you. That
was the end. I won't take her and then give her again. Maybe
you didn't hear me the first time? I already told you that I refused. Bo is Nukha's husband and my daughter won't be with

him again. An adult woman does not make love to the man who marries Nisa."

Then he said, "Today, Nisa will just continue to live with us. Some day, another man will come and marry her. If she stays healthy and her eyes stand strong, if God doesn't kill her and she doesn't die, if God stands beside her and helps, then we will find another man to give to her."

That night, when darkness set, we all slept. I slept beside mother. When morning broke, Bo took Nukha, her mother, and the others and they left. I stayed behind. They were gone, finally gone.

We continued to stay at that water hole, eating things, doing things, and just living. No one talked further about giving me another husband, and we just lived and lived and lived.

I had refused Bo, but Tsaa, my next husband, I liked. When I married him, my breasts were just beginning to develop.

A long time after Bo and I separated, after many seasons had passed, my family and I moved to another water hole. One day, my father left to visit people living at another water hole to exchange gifts of hxaro with them. That's where he saw Tsaa.

When he came back, he said to my mother, "While I was away, I saw a young man. I stood and watched him. Chuko, I'd like your daughter to marry him." My mother asked, "Who is he?" My father said, "Tsaa, the son my relative Bau gave birth to. Tsaa asked me if he could marry Nisa." My mother said, "I've been refusing a second marriage for a long time. But now, I'll agree. We'll take her to him so he can marry her. After he marries her we will see whether or not he takes care of her well. After all, she is still a child."

The next morning we left for their village. That night we slept along the way. The next morning we left again and walked, a very long way, gathering and eating. We walked that day and slept that night. The next morning we left and walked again, walked and walked and walked. Finally, we arrived at their village. We slept there that night, and the next morning when we woke we stayed there.

That morning, Tsaa's mother and father came to where my parents were sitting. My father said, "Here I am, today, having brought you your future daughter. We have journeyed far to come to you." His father said, "You have done well. I'd like to take your daughter and give her to my son. I haven't wanted to give any other girl to him. I wanted to give him a girl who belongs to my own people, to the daughter of one of my relatives. Nisa is the one I want to give to my son." Everyone agreed to the marriage, including me.

We slept that night, and the next morning they started to build the marriage hut. That night they took me and put me inside the hut. Then they took Tsaa and put him inside. We were in the hut, just the two of us.

The next morning, they rubbed marriage oil first on me and then on Tsaa. I gave presents of beads to him and he gave other presents of beads to me.

We lived together a long time, and I began to like him. But then, he started to want me sexually. He didn't really bother me about it, not so that we argued, but I refused. I thought, "Oh, I'm still a child. Why do I have to have a husband?" And, "I have no breasts and my genitals haven't begun to develop. What does this person think my genitals can possibly have for him?"

I remember one night we were sitting around the fire, eating a large duiker he had caught in one of his traps. He had given it to my mother and father. They cooked it and we all ate. We lay down. Soon I got up and sat by the fire. I sat, looking at Tsaa's back, at scars he had from where he had been burned, years before. I thought, "This person, his back is ruined. Why was I given a man whose back has died?" Later, I got up, went into the hut again and lay down.

Another night, I left him in the hut by himself, and lay down beside my mother. The next night I went back to our hut. Some nights I would sleep in my mother's hut and others, in our hut. That's what finally ended the marriage.

One morning, when I woke in my mother's hut, I stayed

there. Tsaa said, "This girl is already a young woman, so what is she doing? I've taken her as my wife, but she just leaves me and sleeps with the adults. When, if ever, will the two of us really start living together? She doesn't like me. That's why I'm going to leave her." My father said, "Why are you going to leave her? Her thoughts are still those of a child."

But by then, my heart had changed and I no longer liked him. Once my breasts started to develop, I refused him completely.

One day, he left and went to a nearby village where an animal had been killed to ask his older brother for some meat. When he came back, he set the meat down. But after, he didn't sit; he just lay down.

I had been roasting some tsin beans. I peeled the skins, and when they were clean, I set them down beside him. He didn't want any. I thought, "Isn't it to your husband that you're supposed to give things? Isn't this the man I married? Why did he marry me if he refuses to take food I prepare for him?"

My father asked, "Nisa, won't you give me some of the gemsbok meat Tsaa was carrying when he came back?" I asked Tsaa, "Give me some meat so I can roast it." But he refused. I asked him again and again he refused. Then my father asked, "Won't you give me some meat that I can cook for you and Nisa?" He refused my father, too.

Tsaa got up, took the meat from where he had set it down, and put it all up in a tree. Although there was a lot, he put it all in the tree.

My father watched. Then he said, "Eh! It really isn't important that you refused to give meat to my daughter. You have married her and she is your wife, so even if you refuse to give something to her, it doesn't mean very much. But I, I am her father, and me you don't refuse. Because when you do that, you make me feel very bad." He continued, "Therefore, as you are now here, tonight you may lie here and sleep in your hut. But tomorrow, when you wake, you will take all your things—don't leave anything here—and you will go away. If you ever come back, don't let me see you with my daughter!"

Then Tsaa said, "It doesn't matter, after all. Because me, I haven't married. I have no wife. This girl has made me weary. I've given her many beads and the meat I've brought back has been plentiful. But the way she is with me defeats me. So, as I am now, I will sleep here tonight, and tomorrow I will take my things and go back to my older brother's village. Then he and I will travel together to our parents' village."

My father said, "Yes, that's the way it will be, so go along your way." Tsaa said, "Eh, but if I go, I'm going to take every last one of my things back from my wife." My father said, "Eh, very good. You take your things. Even the presents we've given each other, I'll give those back to you as well. Anything that is yours that any of us have taken . . . take them all!"

I collected the things he had given me and gave them to him. My father did the same. Tsaa lay down and slept, slept without giving any meat to any of us, slept without even cooking it for himself. The next morning, at dawn, he gathered his things, took others from my mother, put them into a large bundle, and left.

When he arrived where his older brother was living, his brother asked, "Where's your wife? Yesterday you were here alone. Today you were going to come back with her. Will she join you another day?" Tsaa said, "My wife . . . her parents spoke awful things to me. Her father yelled at me about the meat. I told him I wanted to take his daughter with me to come live here, but he refused."

They traveled the distance to their parents' village. When they arrived, Tsaa told them, "My wife's father forced me to leave. He chased me away." His parents said, "When he forced you to leave, what was in his mind. What did he say?" Tsaa said, "Her father chased me because . . . first my wife asked me for meat to roast and eat, but I didn't give her any. I told her I wanted to wait until the morning, that I would cook it then. Her father also asked me for meat to cook for himself and for me. I told him I didn't want to cook the meat yet, that I wanted to wait. When my father-in-law heard that, he told me that I should keep the meat, just as it was, that I should sleep that night, but that in the morning, I should pack my things and come back to you. I stinged him, he said.

That's why I took my things and am here, now. Is there anything more for you to ask?"

They slept that night. The next morning they packed the rest of the meat, left their village and traveled to us.

The whole family arrived—Tsaa, his mother and father, his brother, even his older sister. His father said, "We have come to talk. We haven't come for any other purpose. I am Tsaa's father and have come here to talk to my in-laws. You, my son's father-in-law, are you going to take away your child after you yourself got up and gave her to him in marriage? What has my son done that today you have chased him away? What have you done that my son is no longer sitting beside your daughter?"

My father said, "I am an old person and my heart is not strong. My heart is slight. If I have a son-in-law, when he has food, I expect him to set it beside me. I will prepare it because I know how. Then I will give it to him and to my daughter and they will give me some so I can eat. I am an old person and my heart has little strength."

Then he said, "Today, this marriage is dead. Once before Nisa married a man and he was a bad one. I dropped him. Now, today, another man has married her and he is also bad. So, get up, have your son get up and leave with you. Go back with the things you have brought. Find another woman for your son to marry. My daughter will just lie by herself and that is all there is to say. She is no longer married to your son."

That was all. They stayed for a while longer, then they packed their things and left. I stayed behind with my family. My heart was happy. Was I not still a young girl? I didn't know much about things and was just happy. I'd sit by my hut and watch as the younger children played. My breasts were developing and I no longer played with them. I'd sit there and think about how adult I was, how I was almost a woman.

After I married and left my first husband and after I married and left my second husband, that was when I started with Kantla. His heart went out to me and mine went out to him. He was and always has been one of the important men in my life. Even when my breasts were just starting to develop, he was already mine.

But I wouldn't marry him. He was already married to Bey, the woman he's still married to today. She was young and I was young and Kantla wanted to be married to both of us, two young children. But I refused. Bey agreed to it and told Kantla, "My friend Nisa, I like her. We will both be married to her."

But I didn't want to. I did stay with them for a while, but I cried the whole time. Finally, I ran away from their village. When dawn was beginning to break, I ran away and returned to my parents' village where I stayed.

Another day, Bey and Kantla came for me and took me back to their village. They took me from my mother's hut and brought me, crying, into their hut. Bey told me, "We two are friends. Now sit here; the two of us will sit here together. Are you saying I will do something bad to you? I won't hurt you. We are children and we will finish our childhoods together. This man, Kantla, he will bring us up—together. He will bring both of us up inside one hut. Why do you refuse me?"

I said, "I'm not refusing you; I like you. I'm refusing that man. You are Bey and I like you. We are friends. We will continue to play together as always. It's the man I refuse."

She said, "No, you're refusing me. My friend, I beg you. Sit here and be quiet and we will all lie down together. You will lie in front of me and Kantla, he will lie down behind me. All of us will be here together."

I listened to what she said and was quiet. But after we all lay down, I thought, "How can I possibly sleep? No, I'm going to run away." I waited until they were both sleeping. I got up, very slowly, and quietly took one of the blankets from them. I tiptoed around them, ever so carefully, and sneaked away. As soon as I was far from the hut, I started to run. It was the middle of the night and it was dark. I ran and ran until I arrived at my parents' village. I lay down beside my mother.

Soon after, Bey woke up. "What? My husband . . . where did Nisa go?" Kantla said, "Do I know? She was sleeping in front of you. Weren't you watching her?"

They talked about me until dawn broke. When morning came, the two of them, along with Kantla's mother and father, arrived at our camp. They went over to my mother and asked, "Did Nisa come back to you? We followed her tracks here. Did you see her come back?" My parents said, "Yes, she's a bad one and it's bad that she returned here. She's just gone to the well to get water."

We stayed around my parents' village until the sun was late in the afternoon sky. Then they took me back with them again. That night, I lay down in their hut. This time, I was in front of Kantla. We all slept. But when dawn was just beginning to break, I ran away again. The next morning, Kantla came after me, alone. When he arrived at my parents' village he said, "This woman . . . my heart really likes her and I want to bring her up beside Bey. But I'm afraid that one night when she runs away, something might kill her before she reaches your village. So, take care of her for me. As I stand here now, I'm going to return to my village. Tomorrow, we will go elsewhere. Take good care of her and give her to me as my wife another day."

He left. My heart was happy. I thought, "Very good. I will just stay here."

Months later they came back. I was returning from digging klaru bulbs and picking sweet nin berries with my mother. We were heavy with food. On our way back, we stopped at the water well. I took some water for myself and gave some to mother. We drank and sat down.

That's when Bey and Kantla saw us. Bey called out, "My co-wife! My co-wife! Have you married yet?" I said, "No, I've refused to. I still haven't taken myself in marriage." Then my mother said, "No, she hasn't married yet. The only one who is talking about marriage now is a Herero."[3] Bey said, "No! I will steal her away and we will have her in our marriage once again."

We left the well and returned to my parents' village. I

didn't sleep beside Bey and Kantla that night. When dawn broke, they said they were going to take me back with them. I refused, "What are you going to do if I don't want to be married? The Herero has even offered me cows, but I won't marry him either."

Then I was by myself again. Bey and her husband left and I just sat by myself.

Chapter 6
Marriage

MARRIAGE AND FIRST MENSTRUATION are two of the milestones of women's lives that are formally recognized and celebrated by the !Kung (a first animal kill and initiation are comparable occasions for men). The ceremonial aspects of these events may require that the participants assume a demeanor of restraint, respect, and even silence. Variously translated as "awe," "fear," and "respect," the !Kung term *kua* describes both the feelings and the actions associated with ritual events, as well as with nonritual events involving intense emotions. When marriage is being considered for a girl, when she first menstruates, or when she finds herself alone with the man she has just married, kua describes the way she is expected to act and, most likely, to feel. If she knows her husband well or if they have been lovers, she will still probably feel kua during the marriage negotiations, during the marriage ceremony, and for a considerable time afterward. Even if she is eager to marry her prospective spouse, a young girl may hide her willingness or feign distress; this is appropriate and almost expected behavior.

For some, however, reluctance is genuine, especially when the man is much older or a virtual stranger. Although sexual knowledge is each !Kung woman's legacy from the sexual play of childhood, most young girls see a world of difference between playing with boys their own age and having sex with their husbands—grown men. A girl's first experience of adult sex is, therefore, often traumatic. Sexual relations may be postponed for years, but once a girl shows clear signs of sexual development she is generally pressured to accept her husband's sexual advances.

The !Kung generally express, rather than suppress, strong emotions, so an unhappy young wife is free to act out her displeasure. If her distress becomes too great, however, and the marriage is still not terminated, she may take more dramatic action. At the most extreme, she may threaten her own life. Such threats are rare, and no actual suicides are known to have resulted—but they remain one of the most compelling ways the !Kung (mostly women) call attention to their feelings and win group support for their cause. The threat, or attempt, may involve eating poison from the shafts of poisoned arrows. This may cause nausea or temporary illness, but it is unlikely to do serious damage. Self-stabbing with these arrows is potentially harmful and immediately involves others in an attempt to extract the poison by sucking and blood-letting of the wound. Even in these cases, however, women may protect themselves by choosing aged arrows with less potent poison.

Running away to the bush is another drastic measure. If a woman leaves at sunset, the villagers will search but are unlikely to find her; tracks are nearly impossible to follow at night. Only a very strong motivation would make a woman willing to spend the night alone in the bush—without fire, food, or blankets, and exposed to possible attack by lions, leopards, or hyenas. Nevertheless, women do occasionally risk it, and, as with threats of suicide, there are no known recent incidents in which they have been harmed. The woman is usually found when the search resumes the following morning. By then, she is likely to be willing to return, having made everyone aware of the strength of her feelings.

People usually view such actions with tolerance, especially if the woman is still young. If she is recently married, they know she may be confused: she may actually dislike the man, as she claims, or she may simply be chafing against the reality of growing up. She may not be quite ready to accept sexual commitment nd adult responsibility. As she grows older, however, her rejection of these inevitable steps forward will be less indulged, and she will experience increased pressure to conform.

A girl's first menstruation is celebrated in a ritual performed by adult women, somewhat reminiscent of the marriage ceremony. The girl has been instructed ahead of time to sit and cover herself, and not to speak or move, when she notices her first menstrual blood. This behavior is easily interpreted by other women, who find her and carry her to the village. There, she is "made beautiful," bedecked with ornaments, rubbed with oil, and brought into a hut built for the ceremony.

The occasion is festive for all participants except the girl herself. While women dance and sing outside her hut in bawdy, high-spirited displays of femininity, including baring their buttocks, she lies inside, with her head covered, eating and talking as little as possible. Men should not see her face, "Because it could hurt them in the hunt." First menstruation is believed to engage powerful spiritual forces identical to those involved in trance medicine. It must be approached properly and handled respectfully. One woman remarked, "If a man sees a girl's face during the ceremony and women find out, they'll take everything away from her that they had given her, even cut off her hair. Then they'll tell her the ceremony is over." Thus !Kung men never see the girl as she lies inside the hut. But the hut is within the limits of the village. Sitting slightly apart, the men watch closely and comment exuberantly on the actions of the women. (This is a contrast to the male initiation ceremony which takes place entirely in secret, far away from where women can see or hear.)

The ceremony lasts for three or four days, ending with the end of the menstrual flow. The girl is then washed, rubbed with herbs, and brought out of the hut. Although subject to certain food taboos, she resumes her normal activities. But her manner is expected to remain reserved and restrained (*kua*) until after she experiences her second menstrual period and the second menstrual dance is performed.

Menstruation does not mark entrance into adulthood for !Kung girls as it does for girls in many other cultures. If the girl is married, her mother and in-laws still contribute substantially to her household economy, while she herself may continue to spend much time playing with friends. It does indicate, however, that the last stages of carefree adolescence and youthful irresponsibility have arrived. If sexual relations have been postponed they are likely to be inaugurated at this time, despite any resistance the girl may still offer. Others around her will no longer support her refusals, nor is her husband likely to abstain from "taking what is his" any longer. When the young woman has her first child, usually between the ages of eighteen and twenty, she will be considered—finally—adult.

Even before motherhood comes, the girl may begin to view marriage in a more positive light. She will identify with and enjoy its privileges, such as the meat, beads, and other presents given her by her husband and his family. Her fear of her husband gradually lessens, and may be transformed into feelings of love. This transition is difficult, but for many women, the years after the onset of menstruation and before the birth of their first child are happy and even romantic ones.

The average age of first menstruation for !Kung girls is 16½, quite late compared to the United States, where in the 1970s it was about age 12½. But in most nonindustrialized populations of the world menstruation begins substantially later than it does for us, and even our own grandmothers and great-grandmothers experienced it late. !Kung girls also tend to be infertile for almost two years after the onset of menstruation. Referred to as "adolescent infertility," this delayed reproductive functioning occurs in many human populations, making pregnancy unlikely for from one to three years after first menstruation.

The benefits of late maturity for !Kung girls, with their early and frequent sex play, are evident. The dangers of childbirth, great enough for the !Kung generally, would probably be even greater for teenage mothers. Then too, mothers who were little more than children themselves might not have the emotional maturity to care for infants as responsibly as older women do. With infant and child mortality as high as they are, even a slight departure from optimal conditions of care would probably result in higher mortality. If the !Kung are any example, the human reproductive system seems designed for motherhood during the twenties and thirties. Since the trend toward earlier menstruation seems to be a fairly recent phenomenon, it is possible that the reproductive pattern found among the !Kung is the one that has been typical for most of the several hundred thousand years since human beings evolved.

L ONG AGO, my parents traveled far, to a distant water hole. There we met Old Kantla and his son Tashay, who had also come to live near the well.[1] One day soon after we had arrived, I went with my friend Nukha to get water at the well. That's when Tashay saw me. He thought, "That woman . . . that's the young woman I'm going to marry." He called Nukha over to him and asked, "Nukha, that young woman, that beautiful young woman . . . what is her name?" Nukha told him, "Her name is Nisa." He said, "Mmm . . . that young woman . . . I'm going to tell my mother and father about her. I'm going to ask them if I can marry her."

Nukha came back and we finished filling the water containers. We left and walked the long way back to our village. When Nukha saw my mother, she said, "Nisa and I were getting water and while we were there, some other people came to the well and began filling their water containers. That's when a young man saw Nisa and said he would ask his parents to ask for her in marriage."

I didn't say anything. Because when you are a child and someone wants to marry you, you don't talk. But when they first talked about it, my heart didn't agree. Later, I did agree, just a little; he was, after all, very handsome.

The next night there was a dance at our village. We were already singing and dancing when Tashay and his family came. They joined us and we danced and sang into the night. I was sitting with Nukha when Tashay came over to me. He touched my hand. I said, "What? What is the matter with this person? What is he doing? This person . . . how come I was just sitting here and he came and took hold of me?" Nukha said, "That's your husband ... your husband has taken hold of you. Is that not so?" I said, "Won't he take you? You're older. Let him marry you." But she said, "He's my uncle. I won't marry my uncle. Anyway, he, himself, wants to marry you."

Later his mother and father went to my mother and father. His father said, "We came here and joined the dance, but now that the dancing is finished, I've come to speak to you, to Gau and Chuko. Give me your child, the one you both gave birth to. Give her to me and I will give her to my son. Yesterday, while he was at the well, he saw your child. When he returned, he told me that in the name of what he felt, I should today ask for her. Then I can give her to him. He said he wants to marry her."

My mother said, "Eh, but I didn't give birth to a woman, I gave birth to a child. She doesn't think about marriage, she just doesn't think about the inside of a marriage hut." Then my father said, "Eh, it's true. The child I gave birth to is still a child. She doesn't think about her marriage hut. When she marries a man, she just drops him. Then she gets up, marries another, and drops him, too. She's already refused two men."

My father continued, "There is even another man, Dem, his hut stands over there. He is also asking to marry her. Dem's first wife wants Nisa to sit beside her as a co-wife. She goes out and collects food for Nisa. When she comes back, she gives Nisa food to cook so Nisa can give it to her husband. But when the woman unties the ends of her kaross and leaves it full of food beside Nisa, Nisa throws the food down, ruins it in the sand and kicks the kaross away. When I see that, I say that perhaps Nisa is not yet a woman."

Tashay's father answered, "I have listened to what you have said. That, of course, is the way of a child; it is a child's custom to do that. When she first marries, she stays with her husband for a while, then she refuses him. Then she goes to another. But one day, she stays with one man. That is also a child's way."

They talked about the marriage and agreed to it. I was in my aunt's hut and couldn't see them, but I could hear their voices. Later, I went and joined them in my father's hut. When I got there, Tashay was looking at me. I sat down and he just kept looking at me.

When Tashay's mother saw me, she said, "Ohhh! How beautiful this person is! You are certainly a young woman already. Why do they say that you don't want to get married?" Tashay said, "Yes, there she is. I want you to give me the one who just arrived."

The day of the wedding, everyone was there. All of Tashay's friends were sitting around, laughing and laughing. His younger brother said, "Tashay, you're too old. Get out of the way so I can marry her. Give her to me." And his nephew said, "Uncle, you're already old. Now, let *me* marry her." They were all sitting around, talking like that. They all wanted me.

I went to my mother's hut and sat there. I was wearing lots of beads and my hair was completely covered and full with ornaments.

That night there was another dance. We danced, and some people fell asleep and others kept dancing. In the early morning, Tashay and his relatives went back to their camp; we went into our huts to sleep. When morning was late in the sky, they came back. They stayed around and then his parents said, "Because we are only staying a short while—tomorrow, let's start building the marriage hut."

The next day they started. There were lots of people there—Tashay's mother, my mother, and my aunt worked on the hut; everyone else sat around, talking. Late in the day, the young men went and brought Tashay to the finished hut. They set him down beside it and stayed there with him, sitting around the fire.

I was still at my mother's hut. I heard them tell two of my friends to go and bring me to the hut. I thought, "Oohh ... I'll run away." When they came for me, they couldn't find me. They said, "Where did Nisa go? Did she run away? It's getting dark. Doesn't she know that things may bite and kill her?" My father said, "Go tell Nisa that if this is what she's going to do, I'll hit her and she won't run away again. What made her want to run away, anyway?"

I was already far off in the bush. They came looking for me. I heard them calling, "Nisa . . . Nisa . . ." I sat down at the base of a tree. Then I heard Nukha, "Nisa . . . Nisao . . . my friend . . . a hyena's out there . . . things will bite and kill you . . . come back . . . Nisa . . . Nisao . . ."

When Nukha finally saw me, I started to run. She ran after me, chasing me and finally caught me. She called out to the others, "Hey! Nisa's here! Everyone, come! Help me! Take Nisa, she's here!"

They came and brought me back. Then they laid me down inside the hut. I cried and cried. People told me, "A man is not something that kills you; he is someone who marries you, who becomes like your father or your older brother. He kills animals and gives you things to eat. Even tomorrow, while you are crying, Tashay may kill an animal. But when he returns, he won't give you any meat; only he will eat. Beads, too. He will get beads but he won't give them to you. Why are you so afraid of your husband and what are you crying about?"

I listened and was quiet. Later, we went to sleep. Tashay lay down beside the opening of the hut, near the fire, and I lay down inside; he thought I might try and run away again. He covered himself with a blanket and slept.

While it was dark, I woke up. I sat up. I thought, "How am I going to jump over him? How can I get out and go to mother's hut to sleep beside her?" I looked at him sleeping. Then came other thoughts, other thoughts in the middle of the night, "Eh . . . this person has just married me . . ." and I lay down again. But I kept thinking, "Why did people give me this man in marriage? The older people say he is a good person, yet . . ."

I lay there and didn't move. The rain came beating down. It fell steadily and kept falling. Finally, I slept. Much later dawn broke.

In the morning, Tashay got up and sat by the fire. I was so frightened I just lay there, waiting for him to leave. When he went to urinate, I went and sat down inside my mother's hut.

That day, all his relatives came to our new hut—his mother, his father, his brothers . . . everyone! They all came. They said, "Go tell Nisa she should come and her in-laws will put the marriage oil on her. Can you see her sitting over there? Why isn't she coming so we can put the oil on her in her new hut?"

I refused to go. They kept calling for me until finally, my older brother said, "Uhn uhn. Nisa, if you act like this, I'll hit you. Now, get up and go over there. Sit over there so they can put the oil on you."

I still refused and just sat there. My older brother grabbed a switch from a nearby tree and started coming toward me. I got up. I was afraid. I followed him to where the others were sitting. Tashay's mother rubbed the oil on me and my aunt rubbed it on Tashay.

Then they left and it was just Tashay and me.

We began to live together, but I ran away, again and again. A part of my heart kept thinking, "How come I'm a child and have taken another husband?"

One night, I ran away and slept in the bush, the far away bush. We had been lying together inside the hut, sleeping. But I woke up and quietly tiptoed around his feet and then, very quickly, ran off. I went far, very far, past the mongongo groves near where we were living. It was very dark and I had no fire. I lay down beside the base of a tree and slept.

Dawn broke. People started to look for me and then saw my tracks. They followed them past the mongongo groves and came to where I had slept that night. But I had already left and was digging sha roots in the shade of some trees far away. They came closer. Nukha rushed ahead and, following my tracks, found me. She said that she had come alone looking for me and that the others were elsewhere. She said that we should stay together and dig roots together. I thanked her and told her she was a good friend.

We dug sha roots, and after a while she said, "Let's sit in

the shade of that tree. After we rest awhile, we'll dig more roots. I'll stay with you the rest of the day, but when the sun is late in the sky, I'll leave you and return to the village. You can stay alone in the bush again. Tomorrow, I'll roast some of the roots and come back and give them to you to eat." I praised her, "My friend! You are very kind. But when you return to the village, don't tell them you saw me."

We sat in the shade together, resting. Then I looked around and saw the others approaching. I said, "Nukha, people are coming! You lied to me. You said they were in the village, but they're already here. I can't leave now. I'll just have to sit here with you."

The others found us sitting in the shade, full with the sha roots we had dug. They sat down with us. They were many—my older brother, my father, and Tashay. My father said, "What's the matter with you, leaving in the middle of the night like that, running away and sleeping among things of the night? If a lion had seen you, it would have killed you. Or a hyena. Or wild dogs. Any one of them would have killed you. What's the matter with you? Who is responsible for this? You are. You're the one trying to kill yourself."

I said, "Yes, if I want to sleep among the things of the night, what am I taking with me that belongs to any of you? I didn't take anything. I just left and slept by myself. Even if my heart desired it right now, I'd go as far as I wanted. Because that *is* what I want to do, to go far away. If I go back and stay with you, you'll just find me another husband. But everything that I am at this moment refuses one."

My older brother said, "Why should a husband be refused? Isn't a husband like a father? He helps you live and he gives you food. If you refuse to marry, where do you think you'll find food to eat?" I cried, "As I am now, if you take me and bring me back to the village, I will take a poison arrow and kill myself. I don't want to be married!"

My older brother answered, "If you say you are going to stick yourself with a poison arrow, then I'll beat you until you understand what a poison arrow is and what you think you are going to do with it. You're insulting your very self. You are a person, a woman, and you aren't alive to talk like that; you are alive to play and to be happy."

He continued, "Look at your friends, all of them are married. Even Nukha, who is sitting with you, has taken herself in marriage. Why don't you think about how you and Nukha will be married and have homes? Why should your friend have a home and not you?"

I said, "This friend of mine may have taken a husband, but she is certainly older than I am. She is already a grown woman. But me, I'm a child and don't know what I would do with a husband."

He said, "Mm ... put the roots in your kaross and let's go, because the person who sits here *is* your husband and he isn't anyone else's. He is the man we gave you. You will grow up with him, lie down with him, and give birth to children with him."

We all got up and returned to the village. I didn't go to my hut but went to my mother's hut, put down the sha roots, and stayed there. Tashay went and sat by our hut. After a while he called to me, "Nisa ... Nisa ..." I thought, "What does he want?" and went over to him. He gave me some roots he had dug. I took a few and gave them to my mother; I took the others and went back to our hut and stayed there. In the late afternoon, when dusk was falling and the red sky began to stand, I started roasting food by the fire outside our hut. I took the food out of the coals and set it aside. Then I took some and gave it to Tashay. When they had cooled, we ate them—together.

That Zhun/twa, that Tashay, he really caused me pain.

Soon after we were married, he took me from my parents' village to live at his parents' village. At first my family came and lived with us, but then one day they left, left me with Tashay and his parents. That's when I started to cry. Tashay said, "Before your mother left, you weren't crying. Why didn't you tell me you wanted to go with them? We could have followed along." I said, "I was afraid of you. That's why I didn't tell you."

But I still wanted to be with my mother, so later that day, I ran away. I ran as fast as I could until I finally caught up with them. When my mother saw me she said, "Someday a hyena is going to kill this child in the bush. She's followed us. Here she is!" I walked with them back to their village and lived with them a while.

A long time passed. One day Tashay left and came to us. When I saw him, I started to cry. He said, "Get up. We're going back." I said, "Why does this person keep following me? Do I own him that he follows me everywhere?" My father said, "You're crazy. A woman follows her husband when he comes for her. What are you just sitting here for?"

Tashay took me with him and I didn't really refuse. We continued to live at his village and then we all went and lived at another water hole. By then, I knew that I was no longer living with my mother. I had left my family to follow my husband.

We lived and lived and then, one day, my heart started to throb and my head hurt; I was very sick. My father came to visit and went into a medicinal trance to try and cure me. When I was better, he left and I stayed behind.

After Tashay and I had been living together for a long time, we started to like each other with our hearts and began living nicely together. It was really only after we had lived together for a long time that he touched my genitals. By then, my breasts were already big.

We were staying in my parents' village the night he first had sex with me and I didn't really refuse. I agreed, just a little, and he lay with me. But the next morning, I was sore. I took some leaves and wound them around my waist, but I continued to feel pain. I thought, "Ooo . . . what has he done to my insides that they feel this way?"

I went over to my mother and said, "That person, last night . . . I'm only a child, but last night he had sex with me. Move over and let me eat with you. We'll eat and then we'll move away. Mother . . . mother . . ."

My mother turned to my father and said, "Get up, get a

switch and hit this child. She's ruining us. Get up and find something to hit her with." I thought, "What? Did I say something wrong?"

My father went to find a switch. I got up and ran to my aunt's hut. I sat there and thought, "What was so bad? How come I talked about something yet ... is that something so terrible?"

My father said to my aunt, "Tell Nisa to come back here so I can beat her. The things this young girl talks about could crack open the insides of her ears."[2]

My mother said, "This child, her talk is terrible. As I am now, I would stick myself with a poison arrow; but my skin itself fears and that's why I won't do it. But if she continues to talk like that, I will!"

They wanted me to like my husband and not to refuse him. My mother told me that when a man sleeps with his wife, she doesn't tell; it's a private thing.

I got up and walked away from them. I was trembling, "Ehn ... nn ... nn ..." I looked at my genitals and thought, "Oh, this person ... yesterday he took me and now my genitals are ruined!" I took some water and washed my genitals, washed and washed.

Because, when my genitals first started to develop,[3] I was afraid. I'd look at them and cry and think something was wrong with them. But people told me, "Nothing's wrong. That's what you yourself are like."

I also thought that an older person, an adult like my husband, would tear me apart, that his penis would be so big that he would hurt me. Because I hadn't known older men. I had only played sex play with little boys. Then, when Tashay did sleep with me and it hurt, that's when I refused. That's also when I told. But people didn't yell at him, they only yelled at me, and I was ashamed.

That evening, we lay down again. But this time, before he came in, I took a leather strap, held my leather apron tightly against my legs, tied the strap around my genitals, and then tied it to the hut's frame. I was afraid he'd tear me open and I didn't want him to take me again.

The two of us lay there and after a long time, he touched me. When he touched my stomach, he felt the leather strap. He felt around to see what it was. He said, "What is this woman doing? Last night she lay with me so nicely when I came to her. Why has she tied her genitals up this way? What is she refusing to give me?"

He sat me up and said, "Nisa . . . Nisa . . . what happened? Why are you doing this?" I didn't answer. He said, "What are you so afraid of that you had to tie up your genitals?" I said, "Uhn, uhn. I'm not afraid of anything." He said, "No, now tell me. In the name of what you did, I'm asking you."

Then he said, "What do you think you're doing when you do something like this? When you lie down with me, a Zhun/twa like yourself, it's as though you were lying with another, a stranger. We are both Zhun/twasi, yet you tied yourself up!"

I said, "I refuse to lie down with anyone who wants to take my genitals. Last night you had sex with me and today my insides hurt. That's why I've tied myself up and that's why you won't take me again."

He said, "Untie the strap. Do you see me as someone who kills people? Am I going to eat you? No, I'm not going to kill you, but I have married you and want to make love to you. Do you think I married you thinking I wouldn't make love to you? Did you think we would just live beside each other? Do you know any man who has married a woman and who just lives beside her without having sex with her?"

I said, "I don't care. I don't want sex. Today my insides hurt and I refuse." He said, "Mm, today you will just lie there, but tomorrow, I will take you. If you refuse, I'll pry your legs open and take you by force."

He untied the strap and said, "If this is what use you put this to, I'm going to destroy it." He took his knife and cut it into small pieces. Then he put me down beside him. He didn't touch me; he knew I was afraid. Then we went to sleep.

The next day we got up, did things and ate things. When

we returned to our hut that night, we lay down again. That's when he forced himself on me. He held my legs and I struggled against him. But I knew he would have sex with me and I thought, "This isn't helping me at all. This man, if he takes me by force, he'll really hurt me. So I'll just lie here, lie still and let him look for the food he wants. But I still don't know what kind of food I have because even if he eats he won't be full."[4]

So I stopped fighting and just lay there. He did his work and that time it didn't hurt so much. Then he lay down and slept.

After that, we just lived. I began to like him and he didn't bother me again, he didn't try to have sex with me. Many months passed—those of the rainy season, those of the winter season, and those of the hot season. He just left me alone and I grew up and started to understand about things. Because before that, I hadn't really known about men.

But I started to learn. People told me, "A man is someone who has sex with you. He doesn't marry you and just keep you there, like a string of beads. No, a man marries you and makes love to you." They told me more, "A man, when he marries you, he doesn't marry you for your face, he doesn't marry you for your beauty, he marries you so he can have sex with you."

And more. My mother told me, "When a woman marries a man, he doesn't just touch her body, he touches her genitals and has sex with her." And my aunt, "A man marries you and has sex with you. Why are you holding that back from him? What's the matter with your genitals, the ones right there?" And even Tashay talked about it. I used to watch other couples who were together and he'd say, "The old people told you that people make love to one another, didn't they? That's what people do, they make love."

I listened to what everyone said and then I understood, my thoughts finally understood.

We were living in his parents' village again when my breasts began to swell. They grew bigger and bigger and then they were huge. I thought, "Why are my breasts hurting me?" Because they were tender and painful.

Some days, I would tell Tashay that I wanted to go gathering with the other women. But often, he refused, "We two, just the two of us will go about together." He'd refuse to let me go. He was jealous; he said that when I followed along with the women, a man might come and make love to me.

He didn't want me to leave him, and we were always together: when he went to gather food, it was the two of us that went; when we went to get water, it was the two of us that went. Even to collect firewood, that's the way we went—together.

One day, my breasts felt especially sore and painful. Earlier that morning, the women had said, "Tashay, won't you lend Nisa to us so we can take her gathering? You take the springhare hook and go with your younger brother Twi to look for springhare. Nisa will go with us to gather things and to collect dcha fruits; we'll go to the well before we return."

Tashay refused, "Nisa's not going to do that. She's going to go with Twi and me. I'll take them both with me. If you find food that Nisa would have gathered, collect it for yourself. Nisa will go kill springhare with us and help carry back the meat."

I was unhappy. I wanted to go with the women, but I followed along instead with the two men. There wasn't another woman, only the two of them and myself. We walked for a long time and then came to a springhare burrow. They trapped the animal and killed it. They gave it to me and I carried it in my kaross. We walked and walked and walked. They were a little ahead of me. I was walking behind and stopped to urinate. I saw something red. I thought, "Is it the urine that's red or am I menstruating?" I took something and wiped my genitals. I looked at it, "Oh, I'm menstruating! I have followed along with the men and now I'm menstruating, way out here! What am I going to do?"

Because when you first menstruate, you don't tell anyone. A child who begins to menstruate isn't supposed to talk. I was stunned. I started to shake; I was trembling. I took my digging stick and threw it aside, because whatever a young girl was supposed to do, that's what I did. I took off my kaross and lay down on a part of it and covered myself with the rest.

My heart was miserable. I thought how I was still a child and how I didn't want to menstruate yet. I don't know why I was so afraid. Perhaps, of the days of hunger during the menstrual ceremony; I really don't know.

Tashay and his brother had walked on ahead and had reached the next group of trees. Tashay called to me, "Nisa ... he—ey! Nisa ... he—ey!"[5] But I didn't call back. I was silent.

Tashay said to his brother, "Twi, Nisa's breasts are very big. Maybe she has begun to menstruate. Or, maybe she just ran away, following those other people whose tracks we passed. Go look for her. Call out to her and see if you can find her tracks. If she ran away with those other people, just leave her. But if she started to menstruate, come back to me."

Twi followed back along their tracks, calling out to me as he went. I lay still. When he came near to where I was lying, he saw the digging stick. He acted respectfully, as custom dictates, because a man isn't supposed to be there when a woman first menstruates. He stood there, then took the digging stick back to Tashay.

He said, "Here's your wife's digging stick. Just this morning Mother said, 'Your wife's a child. Now leave her and let the women take her with them.' But you refused to let her go. Now, she has begun the moon. I found her lying down at the base of a tree."

Tashay walked and walked, following the tracks, until he saw me lying there. He thought, "Oh, there's my wife. She has started to menstruate, but there are no other women around!" He stayed with me while Twi went to bring back the others. He told them, "Tashay and I went with Nisa today and while she was way out in the bush, she started to menstruate. We two men didn't know what to do."

All the women came to me. They took their beads and ornaments and tied them in my hair; they rubbed oil on my skin. Then Tashay's younger sister, my friend, picked me up and carried me back to the village. They made a place for me to lie down, then made the hut. After they put grass on it, they laid me down inside and started to dance and sing. I lay there and listened. They sang like this:

Ouh -- eh ---- ouh, ouh - eh, ouh - eh, eh - hi -- hi.

They sang and talked and danced and danced. I thought, "Mm . . . I don't see my mother . . . I'm living with Tashay's people . . ." Then I thought, "When am I going to be like the others again. I'm feeling terrible. When are they going to give me food to eat?"

Because they didn't give me much food to eat or water to drink. I just got up in the morning and stayed there, resting in the hut. I hardly ate or drank. I just lay there. I started getting thin, thin to death. The third day, my husband said, "What is this? My wife is only a child. It was days ago that she started to menstruate but she has hardly eaten food or drunk water. Why is that?"

He got up and went out to get some food. He dug for sha roots and cooked a springhare. He roasted and peeled the roots and gave them to his younger sister and said, "Go, give this to my wife. A child doesn't live for days with hunger." She came and gave it to me and I ate, but only very little. Wouldn't my stomach have hurt otherwise? I ate just a little and gave the rest to the others. His sister also gave me water to drink.

They danced every day until it was finished. Then they washed me, and we continued to live.

One day, soon after that, Tashay asked, "Do you want to go to your mother's?" I said yes, so we traveled the long distance to my mother's village. I was, of course, very beautiful then, young and beautiful. Not drawn and lined like a horse's face, as I am now.

When we finally arrived at my mother's village, my mother saw me. She asked, "What young woman has just arrived and is sitting over there? Whose daughter is that?" My father said, "It's Nisa and her husband." My mother cried out, "My daughter ... little Nisa ... my daughter ... my little Nisa!"

I sat at a distance from her hut, by another hut, out of respect and due to custom. My husband got up and went and sat with them. Then my mother and my aunt came and brought me back to their hut. My mother asked, "The way you are sitting ... the way you are acting ... because you were sitting over there by that hut, does that mean you started to menstruate?" I said, "Mm."[6] She cried, "Oh, my daughter! Is it right for a little girl like yourself to have menstruated for the first time in someone else's village, without your relatives? Could they possibly have taken care of you well?"

I stayed with her for a while. Tashay left me there and I just stayed with my mother. I thought, "Today, I'm happy. I've come to my mother and I'm happy. All the time I was living at Tashay's village, I wasn't. But now I am."

Tashay left me to spend time with my mother for a while. Then he came back and brought me again to his village. We lived on and then I menstruated again. Both of my ceremonial months occurred in Tashay's village and not in my mother's. The women danced for me again during the days of the flow, and then it was over. I left the hut and the women washed me.

We continued to live and it was as if I was already an adult. Because, beginning to menstruate makes you think about things. Only then did I bring myself to understand, only then did I begin to be a woman.

When Tashay wanted to lie with me, I no longer refused. We just had sex together, one day and then another. In the morning, I'd get up and sit beside our hut and I wouldn't tell.

I'd think, "My husband is indeed my husband now. What people told me, that my husband is mine, is true."

We lived and lived, the two of us, together, and after a while I started to really like him and then, to love him. I had finally grown up and had learned how to love.[7] I thought, "A man has sex with you. Yes, that's what a man does. I had thought that perhaps he didn't."

We lived on and I loved him and he loved me. I loved him the way a young adult knows how to love; I just _loved_ him. Whenever he went away and I stayed behind, I'd miss him. I'd think, "Oh, when is my husband ever coming home? How come he's been gone so long?" I'd miss him and want him. When he'd come back my heart would be happy, "Eh, hey! My husband left and once again has come back."

We lived and when he wanted me, I didn't refuse; he just lay with me. I thought, "Why had I been so concerned about my genitals? They aren't that important, after all. So why was I refusing them?"

I thought that and gave myself to him, gave and gave. We lay with each other and my breasts were very large. I was becoming a woman.

Chapter 7
Wives and Co- Wives

ONCE A MARRIAGE has survived a few years beyond the young wife's first menstruation, the relationship between the spouses becomes more pleasant and more equal. Communication is open, and opinions on all subjects are easily shared. The more mature a woman becomes and the more children she has, the more likely it is that her personal talents and attributes will find expression. If she is strong, intelligent, and inclined to leader ship, she is also likely to exert a substantial influence on group life. Other strong women in the village will serve as role models.

Equality between the sexes is probably greater among gatherers and hunters, including the !Kung, than in most other societies around the world. Despite the prominence of !Kung women, however, men generally have the edge. One reflection of their dominance is the pressure they can exert on their wives to accept other women as co-wives in marriage. Polygynous marriage is something many men want and about 5 percent have at any one time. The advantages for the man are obvious: he gains a new sexual partner, he is likely to have additional children, and he adds a substantial new provider of food to his family. The usual advantages of obtaining a first wife also apply: he gains recognition and status in the community, and he extends his social and political influence to include his new in-laws, their village, and their foraging grounds. Therefore, if a man has proved himself to be a good hunter and if life has treated him and his first family well, he may seriously think about taking a second wife. If his first wife has a younger, unmarried sister, she will be a likely choice. The wife of a deceased brother is another logical candidate.

Most women, however, do not want to become involved in such relationships. Many become furious when their husbands suggest it. They claim that sexual jealousy, rivalry, subtle (and not so subtle) favoritism, and disputes over chores and other responsibilities make the polygynous life a very unpleasant one. Co-wives either share the same hut or have separate huts only a few feet apart; either way, each woman's life with the husband is carried on in full view of the other. If the second wife is neither a close relative nor a friend, this enforced intimacy is even harder to tolerate.

Sisters are more likely to remain at peace with each other, so the !Kung say, because they are already used to living in close contact and cooperation. For co-wives who get along, the arrangement does offer benefits: constant companionship, someone to share chores and child care, someone to take over in the event of illness or disability, and a possible ally in struggles with the husband. The outcome of such marriages is largely dependent not only on the strong consent but on the personalities of the women involved. If they are compatible and work well together, they may even form intensely loyal bonds.

One woman who was very close to her sister argued that the polygynous life was preferable to the monogamous one: "I love my sister. If she hadn't married my husband, she would have married someone else and I probably wouldn't see her very often." This woman, however, had married first and was well aware of the advantage this circumstance offered her: "I am in the stronger position because I am older and because I married our husband first. Even if I had had no children it would have been this way. Because now, if I want, I can tell my sister to get water, but she never tells that to me. Sometimes, she goes gathering without me. But I never go without her." In answer to another question she said, "Yes, if she had married our husband first, it would have been the reverse."

Although many polygynous marriages actually last a long

time, the delicate balance sometimes gives way to bitter argument and conflict. Fights between co-wives, even between sisters, are fairly common. When co-wives have agreed to the marriage half-heartedly, their motivation to make it work is not usually great enough to stand up to the strains. If the senior wife decides to make life unbearable for her co-wife and their husband, she is likely to succeed in forcing the newcomer to leave.

Many men, no matter how prominent, would not entertain the notion of entering such a marriage, especially with two young wives. Polygynous marriages are difficult to manage, both economically and socially; food and material goods, as well as attention and sexual favors, must be meted out more or less equally to prevent jealousy. The tensions characteristic of any marriage involve, in this case, three people instead of two, three relationships instead of one. Men say, "There is never any peace in a household with two women in it," and this observation is usually correct.

The woman who was so pleased with her own polygynous marriage was less optimistic when asked whether a similar arrangement would suit her two daughters when the time came for them to marry. She responded, "I would refuse for either of them to be a co-wife with a cousin, because only sisters get along in this situation. But even sisters beat each other on the head. My sister and I, of course, don't—we no longer have our mother and father, and we depend on each other. But if my two daughters married one man? It wouldn't work. They *would* fight."

Unlike many other problems in !Kung life, most of those arising from polygynous marriages are seen as being brought on by the people themselves rather than by an uncaring or vengeful God. Telling stories of the complications resulting from these three-way matches is an endless source of amusement for the 95 percent of the !Kung who live monogamously—and more stably—married.

WHEN A MAN MARRIES one woman, then marries another and sets her down beside the first so there are three of them together, at night, the husband changes from one wife to another. First he has sex with the older wife, then with the younger. But when he goes to the younger wife, the older one is jealous and grabs him and bites him. The two women start to fight and bite each other. The older woman goes to the fire and throws burning wood at them, yelling, "What told you that when I, your first wife, am lying here that you should go and sleep with another woman? Don't I have a vagina? So why do you just leave it and go without having sex with me? Instead you go and have sex with that young girl!" Sometimes, they fight like that all night, until dawn breaks.

A co-wife is truly a terrible thing!

My father never really had two wives, only once—for two nights. All my father had told my mother was that he and his brother were going to go and sleep at another village and exchange presents. What he didn't tell her was that he was also going to get Saglai, another wife.

The two men left together, and when they arrived at the other village, they exchanged presents and slept. The next day my father took Saglai with him, and when the sun was low in the afternoon sky they arrived back in our village.

My mother, my aunt, and I had been gathering mongongo nuts that day in the nearby nut groves. On our way back, we stopped at the well. That's where my aunt saw Saglai's footprints in the sand; my aunt had known her and recognized her tracks.[1] She said, "Chuko, here's where a woman sat and here's where your husband sat." My mother said, "Oh? What did Gau do over there? Didn't he say he was going to ask for some presents of beads? Yet you say he came back with a woman?" My mother was very angry.

We walked back, carrying the mongongo nuts with us to the village. When my mother saw my father, she was drinking anger. She punched him with her fists and said, "Is this your _true_ wife sitting by the hut? Why didn't you tell me you were going away to get another wife, to get Saglai with the big vagina; Saglai, the woman for the cold." My mother insulted her until Saglai was so afraid of her that she wouldn't enter the hut. When night sat, she just slept outside.

The next morning, my father, still fearful of my mother, was quiet. His younger brother said, "Why don't you tell your wife that you'll leave Saglai? When we were still at her village, I told you not to take her right away. You even told me that when you came home, Chuko would object. But you said you would tell her that you had already married Saglai and were giving Saglai to her as another wife. Yet, you didn't tell her that. When Chuko spoke as she did, you should have told her that Saglai was going to sleep inside the hut. You shouldn't have let her sleep outside." My father said, "This is defeating me. Chuko keeps yelling at us and insulting us. She told Saglai to sleep outside the hut. How could I possibly have brought her inside the hut after that?"

My mother told my father, "If I myself had said to you, 'Gau, as I am, I'm getting old and walking slowly. So, go, get yourself another wife and bring her here. She will get water and give it to me and get firewood that we can use and sit beside.' If I had taken you and had said that, then you, having listened to me, could have taken another wife. But you acted deceitfully and forced something on me, and that's why I am making you feel ashamed."

We slept that night. The next morning, when the rooster first crowed, Saglai got up and went back to her village—alone. She was in our village for two nights and the next morning, she left.

My uncle told my father, "Get up. Follow her tracks and take her back to her village. My father said, "I'm not going to. I went and got her and brought her here, but Chuko refused her. Why should I follow after her now?" His younger brother said, "What? You don't know? If, while on her way from here, Saglai comes upon something and it kills her, or even if she arrives safely in her village, her relatives will come here and ask about your responsibility in having taken her and having married her." My father said, "I'm not going to follow

her. She is an adult and she just left. What would I be doing
if I started to cry over that?"

My grandfather Tuka, my father's father, he married many
women! First he married one, then another, and then another.[2] He would go to his first wife, then to his second wife,
and then to his third. One slept alone and the other two
shared a hut together. He'd live with the two of them for a
while, then stay with the other one, then go back to the two
of them and live with them again.

Sometimes, when he was sleeping in the hut with his two
wives, he'd get up very quietly to go to his third wife. His
first wife, the oldest, would yell, "Tuka, what are you looking
for over there?" Because she was very jealous. So Tuka would
leave his third wife and lie down beside his first wife again.
He'd lie there, waiting for her to go to sleep. When she
started sleeping, he'd get up and look at her. He'd whisper,
"Are you going to be getting up again?" If she didn't answer,
he'd go over to his third wife and they'd stay together the
rest of the night. When the rooster first crowed, he'd go back
to the other hut. His first wife would ask, "Where did you
go?" And he'd say, "Uhn uhn. I just went to urinate."

But one night, after he had been with his first wife and
had left her to go to his third wife, his first wife woke and
said, "Tuka, what are you doing up and about? Why aren't
you sleeping? What are you looking for in the middle of the
night?"

That's when he said, "My wife, as I am, I am also married
to others. What do you think I have married them for? I married them and I want to make love to them. I also will make
love to you. Are you the only one who has something for
me? All women have it. Are you saying that if I am married
to another woman, I shouldn't sleep with her? That I should
only sleep with you? Your talk is nonsense!"

I did it once. Before I had children with Tashay, he
brought another wife into our marriage. I was still a young

girl and his other wife, Tiknay, was also a young girl. He married both of us and brought us up together.[3]

When he first asked me, I refused. He kept asking me. Again and again and again. Finally, I said, "All right, go ahead, marry her and bring her here." But when he came with her, I didn't want her there; I wouldn't even greet her.

The three of us lived together for less than a year. During that time, I wouldn't let Tashay near me and I wouldn't let him have sex with me. I said he would give me her dirtiness; that he would come to me with her vaginal wetness and give it to me. I didn't want any of that.

We fought a lot, especially at night. In the middle of the night, when everyone else was dead asleep, Tashay would make love to her, but while they were having sex they'd bump into me and push against me. I'd wake up. One time, I thought, "What's pushing me around like this and not letting me sleep?" I got up, grabbed their blanket and threw it out toward the fire. I yelled, "Get up, both of you! Go to the bush and screw! Let me lie here and sleep!" Tiknay got up and we started to fight. We fought until Tashay separated us. Later, we all lay down and tried to sleep.

The next morning, I grabbed a knife and tried to stab Tashay with it. Tiknay pulled it away from me. That's when my heart rose into my words, "Tiknay, get out of here! Get up and go back to your village! How come there are so many men but you didn't marry any of them? Why did you marry my husband?"

Tiknay said, "That's not the way it was—your husband brought me here. I didn't come myself." I said, "I don't care how you came here. There are lots of other men and I have no need to share my husband with you! Is he the only one with a penis? Don't all men have penises? With this one, am I supposed to have it and then you're also supposed to have it? Now, get up and go back to your village!"

Finally, I chased her away and she went back to her parents. Only after she was gone did I let Tashay touch me again; only after I had chased her away did we start to live with each other again and make love together.

175

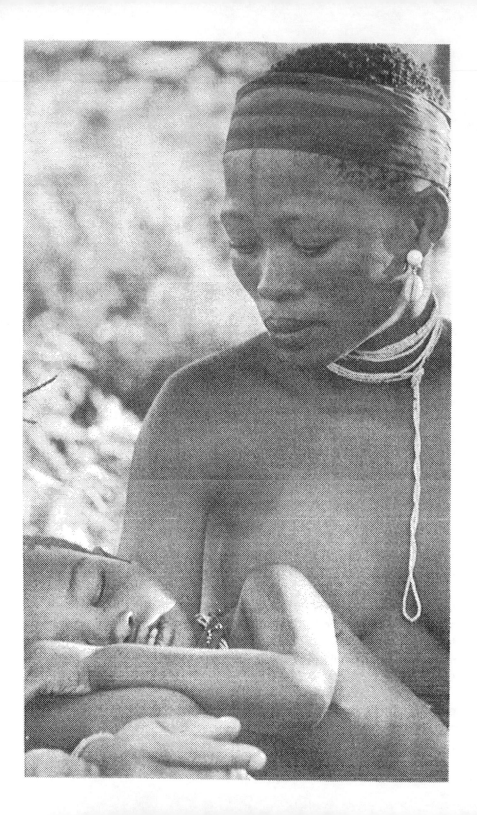

Chapter 8
First Birth

TO SIT IN FRONT of your hut, pound mongongo nuts, cook meat in your fire, feed your older children and nurse your youngest, talk and laugh with visiting relatives, play music or participate in a trance dance if one should begin, or just to sit alone with your husband after everyone has left, after your children are comfortably asleep—that is the way a woman's life should be. But this !Kung ideal of fulfillment can be achieved only after a number of less comfortable stages have been passed. For girls, social recognition and adult status come with motherhood—after a girl has confronted the often frightening events of pregnancy and childbirth.

The !Kung recognize that pregnancy—which they sometimes refer to as "when a child hits fists inside the womb"—results from sexual intercourse, and they understand menstruation to show that conception has not occurred. They believe, however, that conception takes place at the end of the menses, when semen joins with the last of the menstrual blood. They have a somewhat more accurate idea of the duration of pregnancy: if a husband has had a long absence at around the time conception must have occurred, he will be likely to challenge his wife as to the paternity of the child.

!Kung women anticipate their periods by the phases of the moon; if a moon comes and goes without the expected onset of menstruation, they begin to suspect pregnancy. If other signs are there as well—a darkening of the areola around the nipple, an unexplained dislike for certain foods, a tendency to nausea and vomiting, a craving for meat, and any unusual emotionality—the suspicion strengthens. When a second and third moon have passed, probability turns to certainty. Although others may already suspect it, a woman will not speak openly about it until after the next moon passes—in adherence, perhaps, to the general expectation of humility whenever the enviable happens. This silence may also protect the woman psychologically in case of spontaneous miscarriage, which is more likely to occur in the first months of pregnancy.

The !Kung claim to know a number of ways to "ruin" or terminate a pregnancy. A woman is said to be declaring her desire to abort if she cooks food at someone else's fire or if she has sex with a man other than the one whose child she carries. Other alternatives are physical agents such as riding a horse or donkey and chemical ones made from plants. It is not clear how widespread the use of herbal remedies is or whether they are effective. In any case, a woman will resort to them only when she thinks that conditions for the unborn child's survival—uncertain at best—are worse than usual.

Once the pregnancy is known to the group, others offer help—by carrying an older child, by giving food, or by assisting with chores. Still, the woman is not viewed as in need of protection, nor is she expected to cease her normal activities. She continues to travel the usual distances to gather food and is apt to return with her usual load. If she doesn't feel well, she will rest until she feels better. But many women maintain their normal work routines until the day they give birth. Pregnancy is thought of as a given; it is "women's work."

Emotions, however, tend to undermine the equanimity women try to maintain. Many !Kung women experience extreme mood fluctuations during pregnancy. This moodiness, seen as normal, is accepted and easily tolerated, but it is not encouraged. One woman, pregnant with her third child, explained, "Some women get angry, but I don't. Those who do are bad. I just sit quietly." She said that her mother had told her that women who scream during pregnancy are more likely to have difficult births or even to die. That was presumably part of her reason for be-having sedately—or for believing she should. She fell far short of this goal, as revealed in an interview with her mother-in-law, who said, "Last week my daughter-in-law became so enraged that she ran away from the village and slept in the bush. The next morning everyone went looking for her, and when they found her, she was alone. She hadn't even made a fire for herself. She had been upset and jealous, and had accused her husband of having an affair with another woman. But it wasn't true. It was just the baby inside making her so angry."

Most !Kung love children, and the ideal is to have many. But !Kung women know intimately the physical cost of pregnancy, as well as the work and responsibility that having many children entails. One woman, pregnant too soon with her fourth child, expressed her unhappiness this way: "Having too many children makes you skinny because they are too hard to carry."

Children are valued, however, for their ability to make life more enjoyable. One !Kung man, whose wife was reaching menopause without ever having children, said, "I want children very badly. When you go out hunting and come back, they run to your side and sit beside you. They say, 'Daddy . . . give me some meat!' Just having them there makes you happy." He voiced a widespread !Kung attitude when he added, "I'm look-ing for another wife to give me children. I don't want someone else's child. I'd refuse if someone offered me one. I want my own."

Pregnant women face childbirth with no medical facilities and with no traditional midwives or other birth specialists to call upon. The prospect of giving birth is often frightening, especially for women pregnant for the first time; they are the ones most likely to experience complications or to die. The overall death rate in childbirth (two maternal deaths out of five hundred births recorded), however, is fairly low—certainly not unusual for cul-tures without modern medical care. It has been suggested that this incidence might be higher were it not for !Kung women's rather stoical attitude toward childbirth: by striving to give birth alone or with minimal assistance, they lower the risk of infection.

Although solitary childbirth is the stated cultural ideal, other women often help, especially with a first birth. A young woman may prefer to have her mother or other close female relatives with her, but if she is living with her husband's family, she will receive assistance from his female relatives. Even with others present, however, the woman herself is considered responsible—except on the rare occasions when God capriciously intervenes—for the progress of labor and delivery. An uncomplicated delivery is said to reflect her full acceptance of childbearing: she sits quietly, she does not scream or cry out for help, and she stays in control throughout the labor. A difficult delivery, by contrast, shows her ambivalence about the birth, and may even be seen as a rejection of the child.

Fear of childbirth is thought to be dangerous, causing tension that makes delivery more difficult. It brings on an even greater danger, however: God, interpreting a woman's apprehension as indicating that the child is not wanted, may kill the child and "take it back to the spirit world." In such cases, the mother may also be taken away. So strong is the !Kung belief in the necessity for facing childbirth bravely that women who prove cowardly may be privately ridiculed, while those who give birth "properly" may be used as models for young girls, who will be encouraged to observe their births.

A fifteen-year-old girl who had not yet begun to menstruate responded to my question about childbirth this way: "People tell me that I am female and that I will marry and give birth to a child one day. They also say that giving birth is like something that kills. Those who fear, die and are buried. Those who don't fear, live. A woman who isn't afraid sits quietly; she doesn't walk around or even brush the flies off her face. If she does, others will say that she is afraid and will laugh at her. Her husband will yell at her, too; he will search for a wife who isn't afraid, and their marriage will die. When I look at everything people have told me, I say that childbirth is about death—and that makes me afraid. Am I not afraid of dying?" This, despite the fact that she did not personally know of anyone who had died in childbirth.

When complications do occur, the father, who otherwise remains absent from the birth scene, may tie a medicinal string around the mother's chest—a measure thought to help speed delivery. Alternatively, medicine men may enter trance to per-suade the spirits to abandon their evil designs on the mother or the child.

A !Kung woman will have, on average, four or five live births during her reproductive life. With each successive birth, she is more likely to attain the ideal of delivering alone. Without tell-ing anyone, she walks a few hundred yards from the village, pre-pares a cushion of leaves, and gives birth to her child. Accompa-nied or not, most births occur close enough to the village so that others can hear the baby's first cries. This signals the woman's female relatives and friends that the child has been born and that the mother may welcome assistance in delivering the after-birth, cutting the umbilical cord, and wiping the baby clean. Perhaps carrying the baby for her, other women will accompany her back to the village. Only the most experienced and deter-mined women insist on being alone during these last stages.

Although most !Kung women aspire to this ideal, those who actually meet it may be admonished by their closest relatives. One woman was criticized for having exposed herself to danger when she came back with her baby after giving birth alone and at night. She had not asked anyone for help, even after the baby was born. When scolded, she merely said, "Am I not a woman who had a job to do? I went and did it, that's all."

Once back in the village, the mother will lie down and rest. The child will not be given the first milk—the colostrum—that fills the mother's breasts; and if there are no other lactating women to help nurse the child, it may go two or three days without being fed. (Newborn infants have special fat stores that enable them to generate warmth even without food.) Circum-stances of group life permitting, the mother may remain in the village for a number of days after the birth of the child. Although there is no recognized "lying-in" period, she will also minimize her daily activities until she feels strong enough to resume them. Because of the excellent physical condition resulting from the nomadic gathering life, for most women this recovery period is brief.

Soon after the child is brought back to the village, she is given the name of a close living relative, usually that of a grandparent, aunt, or uncle, according to well-established rules of precedence. The relationship that ensues between the child and the "namesake" is likely to be important in both their lives. Since the !Kung recognize the mother's relationship to the child as undeniable, they believe that the first few children born to a couple should be named after members of the father's family. This helps guarantee their connection to the child through the "name relationship." After the father's family has been assigned a few namesakes, later names will be distributed more evenly.

The birth of her first child marks a woman's full entry into adulthood. The firstborn is seen as distinct from subsequent children; a unique expression—literally, "the one from the middle of my forehead"—exists to describe this child. In addition, the terms of address for the parents change as they begin to be referred to by their relationship to the child—"Nai's father," or "Kumsa's mother"—instead of by their own names. These designations may change with subsequent births.

With this entrance into the adult world, the young woman becomes the focus of loving attention from family, friends, and in-laws. She may feel that she has proven herself by having faced the ordeal of childbirth and, in most cases, by having produced a healthy child. She will also have stabilized her marriage; there are few divorces after the birth of the first child. Caring for her infant is the most important responsibility she has yet had, and child care is likely to be a central preoccupation for the rest of her life.

But to have children is to risk losing them. Nearly 20 percent of !Kung children die within their first year, and only 54 percent of those born live to marry. The death of one's children is thus a fairly common experience for the !Kung; but its frequency does not seem to make the resulting pain any less profound. Forced to recognize the tenuousness of their children's lives, the !Kung nevertheless do not hold back on nurturance or love.

WHEN YOU ARE STILL YOUNG, your husband touches your genitals to help make them grow and he has sex with you.[1] Once you are older, you think, "Aren't my genitals beautiful now?" That's also the time when your husband has sex with you frequently. Then, you get pregnant. Your husband may continue to have sex with you during the first few months of your pregnancy, maybe the first two, or he may have sex with you all the months of your pregnancy.

Just after you give birth, however, he won't have sex with you for a while; he's afraid of the blood that's healing. He may wait several months, until the child has started to grow. But most women only wait a month or so after they give birth. That's when they share their blankets with their husbands again.

Listen. When a child has only one month and is learning to laugh, some women start having sex again. The Tswanas and Hereros don't do it like that;[2] they are different people. We have much lighter skin and we have different ways. With us, even if the child hasn't started to sit up, the father may start to have sex with his wife. That's how the woman can get pregnant with another even if the first child is still small.

I watched as my mother gave birth to my younger brother. She didn't fear or cry out; she had courage. She told me, "Nisa, when you grow up, one day you will be pregnant and will give birth to a child. Childbirth is something that is very painful and the pain feels like it is killing you. But don't be afraid. If you fear, your insides may tear and you may die. If you are afraid and cry out, if you throw yourself down in the sand again and again, it will hurt the baby. Then the baby will try to push out through your anus. If this happens, you will die.

"But if you don't fear and sit quietly, sit just the right way, the child will come out from your vagina and live; and you will, too."

I wasn't afraid when I saw my mother give birth, and because of that, when I gave birth, I went alone. I just sat there until the birth was over. Only then did people come to me.

They said I was without sense. Why hadn't I told them before I left, so they could have gone with me? I said, "I have no need to give birth and have everyone look at my genitals." But they said, "That's not good. Look here, one day you may be pregnant and God may refuse to let the baby go; God may not let the baby be born. Then the childbirth will be difficult and you will feel much pain. Next time, tell others so they can help you, so the child will come out quickly."

But I refused, "God is taking care of me. Even if I'm in pain, as you say, God will be with me. Because I will be sitting where God will have set me down. God makes the labor of childbirth hurt and will have been the one to have set me down to give birth. God will take care of me and I won't ask everyone else for help. No, I will always give birth by myself. When you hear the child crying, then you can come to me."

Because a woman who is afraid and cries, that woman gives birth to a baby that dies. The bones of her legs can kill the child. Or the woman herself may not survive; the flesh inside may tear and she may die.

When a baby is still inside you, before you give birth, you have many thoughts. You think, "The day I give birth, will I be courageous? Will I be afraid? Will I live? The day I feel the pains will my heart be strong enough to withstand it?"

Sometimes your heart is filled with rage. You think, "What am I going to do about this?" But another part of your heart says, "My pregnancy is going very well and maybe I'll give birth very well. One day I will feel it moving, because I am a woman and not a man; one day I will feel the labor."

Other times your heart is miserable. You think, "A baby isn't itself a painful thing. Why should a painless thing hurt so much when it comes from your insides, hurt like a sickness, hurt with such a big pain?"

You live and live and listen to yourself. You watch as your body changes. One day you feel the baby moving, rising high inside you. Another day you feel it elsewhere. You live, feeling the baby as it does things.

You soon start to feel the movements more often—near

your back and everywhere. Then it moves to where it is
going to be born. That's when it first hurts; that's when the
two of you meet up against each other. You struggle with
each other, and the baby grabs at your heart. Your heart
throbs; the strength of the pain grabs your heart away from
you.

Then the pains start to come, again and again. There's
hurt and pain and it comes like it's fire! Again and again it
comes, then it rests. It's quiet, lying still. Then it rises again,
jabbing and hurting, bigger and bigger, coming over and over
again. There's another rest; even if it's already pushing out, it
just rests. But it rises again and there's more pain and pushing
and it starts to come out from the mouth of your stomach.
It's on its way out. Another quiet and another rise. Then a
pain like fire is at the lips of your vagina and the head and
the hair on the head start pushing through. Those are the
things that hurt; not the body, that doesn't hurt at all. Then
more quiet and more pushing. With the next rise, it pushes
against and rushes out.

That's the birth of a baby.

Babies, yes ... the day your baby is about to be born,
that day your heart is miserable. But once it is lying on the
sand, a baby is a wonderful thing. Your heart is very happy
because you love children. You and your child talk together,
even if it is just tiny.

But their anger at birth[3] and the pain ... that's something
I have no use for!

A woman is strong. But the woman who gives birth to
twins, that woman's heart is especially strong; that woman,
her heart stands up.

A woman I know did that—gave birth to two children in
one day. Two of them! First the pain of one rises inside you,
then the pain of the other. That's when a woman's heart may
leave her,[4] especially if her heart is weak. Then she cries
when the first one is born and cries when the second one is
born. I don't know myself, but to have the anger of two children! What do you do but die of the pain?

Another woman I know gave birth to a very small baby. I

wasn't sure if it was a miscarriage or not, or how she was able to give birth to such a tiny thing. The woman took the baby from where she had given birth and carried it back to the village. When she got there, she lay down and covered it with blankets.

The old people said, "Can it possibly live? No, even if people take care of it well, it will die. Because this little thing was born too soon. If it lives, it will only be because God wants it to."

I went to visit her with my mother. The woman told her, "I just now gave birth, but my belly isn't well. Why should it hurt me now?" People started to cure her and laid hands on her stomach where the sickness had entered her blood. They tried to help, laying on their hands where the blood was hurting her, but she died. The day she gave birth was the very day that she died.

People said, "Oh, what caused that to happen to her? She gave birth well; even though the childbirth hurt, she wasn't afraid. So what killed her?" Her husband said, "Now that this has happened, I'll take the child, lay it down beside my wife and kill it." But people said, "What! You won't do that. Instead, there is an unmarried woman you have had as a lover. She knows you and has made love to you. She will carry the child, care for the child, and bring it up."

The woman took the child and carried it. She and the father of the child were lovers for a while, then they married. They brought the child up and it grew and grew.

Then it died.

After I had menstruated for a long time, I was truly an adult. One of my breasts began to droop and the other stood out. That's when I became pregnant with my very first child. I lived and watched as my stomach grew.

I was angry and cried a lot. My heart was full of rage and felt pain, but I didn't know why. Whenever I ate meat, I threw up, and whenever I ate sweet berries, I threw up. But when I ate water root or pounded gwia leaves or do roots, I didn't throw up.

I asked the old people, "Why do I throw up when I eat meat?" That was when my stomach was still small. They said, "Your nipples are dark, you must be pregnant." Even Tashay's mother told me, "If you are throwing up like this, it means you have a little thing inside your stomach." I said, "But my husband has been away. What little thing could I possibly have inside me?"

Because, when I first became pregnant, Tashay was living in a village in the East, working for the Tswanas. I had been living by myself and had learned about having lovers. When Tashay went away, they came and slept with me.

After Tashay and I had lived together and he had taught me about men, Kantla, the one who had wanted to marry me and had me live with him and his first wife, taught me about lovers. When Kantla heard that I had taken myself a husband, he came and said, "What talk is this? When I left you with your parents, I told them that you were still mine. I told them they should take good care of you and then give you to me in marriage. Why have they given you to another man?"

That's when he started as my lover. Tashay was the only one I had known before that. But when I was an adult, Kantla came and taught me. Tashay didn't find out about him, because he only came to me when Tashay was away. Kantla had sense.

But Twi, Tashay's younger brother and my next lover, didn't; he had no brains at all. When he started with me, I was already a grown woman and knew about men. But even when I was in my hut, he would just come inside and stay with me. When Tashay came home, he'd find the two of us sitting together, talking. Do you say a man has intelligence? Well, that man didn't.

Twi would wait until Tashay went somewhere before he came and slept with me. One night, I said, "Your older brother may be coming back tonight. So just stay with me a short while, then go and stay by your hut." He slept with me and then left. I lay by myself until dawn broke. His brother didn't come back.

The next morning Twi asked, "Didn't you say my brother

was coming back. Why isn't he with you today? Were you just chasing me away?" I said, "No, I was afraid. I'm afraid of your older brother. If he catches us, he'll kill me. The two of you share the same mother and father so he won't kill you. But me, I'm an outsider and he'll kill me." He said, "Nonsense, he won't kill you. At worst, he'll hit you and leave it at that." I said, "No, he already told me what he would do."

Later that afternoon, Twi and I were sitting together inside the hut, resting and talking. That's when Tashay came back. He called for me and then for his brother. Twi got up and went to him. Tashay said, "Go get me some water that we can drink together." Twi went for the water and came back.

I was trembling. Soon I left the hut and went and joined them. We sat in the shade together. Everyone must have been off gathering because the village was deserted. We were the only ones there. We sat around until the others came back. I kept waiting for Tashay to ask me what Twi and I were doing inside the hut together. But he didn't ask. That was good; I thought, "God, now don't take hold of this man's mouth and have him ask me."

But in the evening, when the two of us were inside the hut, he asked, "Why is it that every time I go away for a few days, when I come back I always see you and Twi together inside the hut? Always, there the two of you are, resting together. What do you two concern yourselves with?"

I said, "Twi and I aren't concerning ourselves with anything. Isn't he my brother-in-law? Am I not only a child? What would he be doing with me? When you aren't here, we just stay together and talk about things. What do you think he's doing to me?"

He said, "All right, but another day ... another time when I go away, I'll come back at night and we'll see." I said, "Fine, even if you come at night, you won't see anything."

We lived and lived, and then one day he went away. He said, "Today I'm going away and will be gone for a few months." He was deceiving me; he went and stayed in a nearby village. He stayed there all day.

Later that day, Twi came to me. I said, "Your brother

once said he would go away, but that he would come back
in the night. Now don't let him catch us. You're a man and
will be able to run away. But me, he'll beat me and kill me."
Twi said, "If that's what might happen, I won't stay the night.
We'll spend some time together, we'll talk, and then I'll go
back to sleep in my own hut."

When night sat, Twi came back. We talked and talked,
did our work, and when we were finished, he left and lay
down in his own hut.

Very late that night, Tashay walked back to our village.
He walked quietly up to the hut, entered slowly, and sat
down. He touched around, first in front of me and then behind. He didn't feel anyone else there. Then he lay down. He
called my name, "Nisao . . ." I said, "Eh?" Then I asked, "Why
were you feeling around me like that? What were you search-
ing for? Didn't I tell you that even if you came at night you
wouldn't find me with anyone? That you wouldn't catch me
doing anything? I'm still a child and don't have lovers. A
woman only has them when she is fully grown. But today I
am learning from you that you think a child has lovers. The
old people have told me differently. Even my mother told me
that you don't have lovers when you are a child."

He said, "All right, I've seen what I wanted tonight. I
won't come again at night. I'll just stay around and see what
happens." After that, he had to stop accusing me; he hadn't
seen anything.

We lived on. Twi and I continued to steal away together.
The only way we ever met was in the bush. Then, after a
long time passed, Tashay went away to work for the Tswanas
again.

It was after he left that I became pregnant. At first, I
didn't know it. If I had, I would have tried to ruin the pregnancy. Then, when Tashay came back, I would have been
without it; I would have been just myself. But I was very
young. I didn't know that a root existed that would ruin the
pregnancy. I was still a child, was I not? I also didn't know
that if I slept with another man, that might also ruin it. I
didn't know. I just let my stomach sit there and grow.

One morning Twi came to me and we went off together.

I said, "Twi, you've made me pregnant. I'm a child and you made me pregnant." He said, "What's wrong with that? If you're pregnant, why not?" I said, "My husband is away. When he comes back, he'll kill me."

We stayed together that day and later returned to the village. I tried to eat, but I threw up. People saw me and knew.

My stomach grew bigger and then it was standing out. My heart began to change. I didn't want Twi and I missed Tashay. I wondered when he would come back.

Then, one night, while everyone was talking, the sound of a truck broke through the night. A Tswana had bought a truck and my husband had gotten a ride back with him. I asked, "Is the truck sounding a white person's truck?" People said, "Probably not. It's probably your husband coming with the truck the Tswana bought." I thought, "What am I going to do about my stomach? What can I hide it with?" Another woman said, "Oh, Nisa! What are you going to do with your stomach?" Again I thought, "What can I do to make it go away so when my husband comes back there won't be anything there?"

The truck kept coming closer and closer. When it arrived, I heard my husband call for me. I thought, "What should I do?" I took one blanket, then another, and covered myself. I sat down in the dark so he wouldn't be able to see me well. He called to me again and said, "Nisa, come here. Let me take a look at you."

Oooh! I was frightened! I went to where he was and sat down, covering my stomach so he couldn't see. He asked, "Have you been well?" I said, "Mm, I've been fine." He said, "Has anything given you trouble? Have you been sick?" I said, "Nothing's been bothering me."

We sat together. He asked, "What have you been eating that you look so full?" I said, "I've been eating lots of food and meat." He didn't say anything more. Later, we put the blankets down and lay down together. He was lying next to me, behind, and I was in front. He put his arms around me and one of his hands touched my stomach. He moved his hand around. Then he stopped. He moved his hand around again, touching all over, and then stopped. He said, "Nisa, what's inside your stomach that just kicked me?" I thought, "What should I tell him? Why can't this baby lie still? Why did it have to kick him!" He said, "I asked you what's moving around inside your stomach?" I said, "Sickness, maybe. Maybe I'm sick. My stomach is upset and inside, it is pushing about."

We went to sleep. The next morning we got up and sat together. I forgot and had only a small piece of cloth covering my stomach. He looked at me, looked and looked and looked. He said, "Your eyes look white, just like when a woman is pregnant. I know you are, so tell me who did it to you. Where is he?" I said, "You're wrong, I'm not pregnant." He said, "Yesterday I was willing to believe that you had been eating a lot. But today I see that your stomach is very big. Now tell me, who made you pregnant?"

I said, "Someone else didn't make me pregnant. The menstrual blood that I had when you were still here, that blood you cut off before you left. You, yourself, cut me from the moon. After you left, I stopped menstruating. That's when I finished with it. The pregnancy is yours. After you left, it just grew. I am a child and couldn't have known about having a lover."

He said, "Eh . . . is that the truth?" I said, "It's the truth. Am I not still a child? It was the month you left that cut me from my menstrual cycle." He said, "Eh, that's all, then. Perhaps you have been good and perhaps you haven't." I said, "You yourself conceived this child. There's no reason for you to talk against it and say it isn't your child. No, without doubt, I conceived this child before you left."

My stomach grew larger and I became angry. I yelled at Tashay and bit him. I said, "Let's go to my mother so she can help me give birth to my child." But he refused to let me go or to bring me to her; he said I should give birth in his mother's village. Because after we married, we went and stayed with Tashay and his relatives. Mother was far away. I had left her and was living where Tashay's people lived. That was where Tashay took me. That was also where I got pregnant and where I gave birth.

While I was pregnant, I'd think, "Here I am, just a child.

The old people tell me that childbirth is something that hurts and that after I have lived with being pregnant, the child will start to move. It will change position and I will cry." But I thought, "No, I won't cry. If I do, people will laugh at me and say I was afraid. I won't cry." Then I thought, "Uhn, uhn. I'll surely cry. Everyone says that childbirth is painful. I know what I'll do! When I'm near the end of my pregnancy, I'll go to the white people and give myself to them. They'll open the mouth of my stomach and take the baby out. That way it won't hurt." Then I thought, "No, even if the pain feels as though I will surely die, I'll just sit there and feel it. Then my child will be born."

A few days before I gave birth, we went to live in a bush camp so the men could hunt. There were very few of us: Tashay, myself, his grandmother, and his grandfather.

One day Tashay and I were walking in the bush together, playing around and grabbing each other. I felt the first pains; they came in my lower back. I thought, "What's making my back and stomach hurt like this?" I told Tashay to stop grabbing me and we walked on. After a while we sat down again and he started to play with me again—pushing my clothes from my stomach and saying, "My wife! How come you're naked today?" I said, "What are you talking about? Something's hurting me!"

We spent the rest of the day digging sha roots and walking about. My stomach was huge and stood far out. The pains in my lower back came again. I thought, "Am I going to give birth today? I'm only a child. How am I going to give birth? Will I be afraid?"

We slept that night and morning broke. We slept another night and another morning broke. The baby was still with me; its time was ready but it didn't want to leave. I started to worry that it might make me sick.

The next night we slept where we had camped the previous few nights. Tashay brought some firewood and made a fire. I sat there. I started to feel the baby again and the hurt. I thought, "Is this what the older people told me about? Is this what they meant when they said a baby hurts?" Because,

Mother! Even though I had seen others, when I gave birth for the first time, I didn't really know what a baby did or how much it hurt or how it actually got born. The only pain I myself had known before that was the pain of being sick.

I sat there and started to cry. I thought, "No, I won't cry. Me, I'm not going to cry." So I just sat there, thinking my thoughts. When the pains came again, they hurt for a while and then were quiet. They came and they went. I thought, "This really hurts! Hey ... hey ... everyone ... how come my stomach hurts so much?" But I didn't say anything.

Later that night, the pains came again. I thought, "Why should this hurt so much? If only I were with my mother, then I would be able to cry. But I'm living with other people and I won't cry. If I do, they'll laugh at me and say, 'How come you're already a young woman, yet, when you feel the labor, you start to cry?' Later they'll laugh and say I cried during childbirth."

I tried to stay away from them, just so I wouldn't cry.

We all lay down to sleep that night, but when dawn was just breaking—the time when the rooster first crows—I woke up. It was hurting again. I thought, "Is it sickness that's hurting me or is it the baby?" Because I didn't really understand. I was in pain and wasn't sure what I was supposed to do. I thought, "People told me that a baby hurts your insides like when you're sick."

I lay there and felt the pains as they came, over and over again. Then I felt something wet, the beginning of the childbirth. I thought, "Eh hey, maybe it is the child." I got up, took a blanket and covered Tashay with it; he was still sleeping. Then I took another blanket and my smaller duiker skin covering and I left. Was I not the only one? The only other woman was Tashay's grandmother, and she was asleep in her hut. So, just as I was, I left.

I walked a short distance from the village and sat down beside a tree. I sat there and waited; she wasn't ready to be born. I lay down, but she still didn't come out. I sat up again. I leaned against the tree and began to feel the labor. The pains came over and over, again and again. It felt as though

the baby was trying to jump right out! Then the pains
stopped. I said, "Why doesn't it hurry up and come out? Why
doesn't it come out so I can rest? What does it want inside
me that it just stays in there? Won't God help me to have it
come out quickly?"

As I said that, the baby started to be born. I thought, "I
won't cry out. I'll just sit here. Look, it's already being born
and I'll be fine." But it really hurt! I cried out, but only to
myself. I thought, "Oh, I almost cried out in my in-laws' village." Then I thought, "Has my child already been born?" Because I wasn't really sure; I thought I might only have been
sick. That's why I hadn't told anyone when I left the village.

After she was born, I sat there; I didn't know what to do.
I had no sense. She lay there, moving her arms about, trying
to suck on her fingers. She started to cry. I just sat there,
looking at her. I thought, "Is this my child? Who gave birth
to this child?" Then I thought, "A big thing like that? How
could it possibly have come out from my genitals?" I sat
there and looked at her, looked and looked and looked.

The cold started to grab me. I covered her with my
duiker skin that had been covering my stomach and pulled
the larger kaross over myself. Soon, the afterbirth came down
and I buried it. I started to shiver. I just sat there, trembling
with the cold. I still hadn't tied the umbilical cord. I looked
at her and thought, "She's no longer crying. I'll leave her here
and go to the village to bring back some coals for a fire."

I left her, covered with leather skins. (What did I know
about how to do things?) I took a small skin covering, tied it
around my stomach, and went back to the village. While I
was on the way, she started to cry, then she stopped. I was
rushing and was out of breath. Wasn't my genital area hurting? I told myself to run, but my judgment was gone; my
senses had left me.

My heart was pounding and throbbing when I arrived. I
sat down by the fire outside my hut to rest and to warm myself. Tashay woke up. He saw me with my little stomach, and
he saw the blood on my legs. He asked how I was. I told him
everything was all right. He asked, "Where is that which I

thought I heard crying?" I told him the baby was lying covered where I had given birth. He asked if it was a boy. I said
she was a girl. He said, "Oh! Does a little girl like you give
birth to a baby all alone? There wasn't even another woman
to help!"

He called to his grandmother, still asleep, and yelled,
"What happened to you that you, a woman, stayed here
while a little girl went out by herself to give birth? What if
the childbirth had killed her? Would you have just left her
there for her mother to help, her mother who isn't even here?
You don't know that the pain of childbirth is fire and that a
child's birth is like an anger so great that it sometimes kills?
Yet, you didn't help! She's just a little girl. She could have
been so afraid that the childbirth might have killed her or the
child. You, an adult, what were you asking of her?"

Just then, the baby started to cry. I was afraid that maybe
a jackal had come and hurt her. I grabbed some burning
wood and ran back to her. I made a fire and sat. Tashay continued to yell, "Find her. Go over there and cut the baby's
umbilical cord. What happened to you that you let my wife
give birth by herself?"

His grandmother got up and followed Tashay to where I
was sitting with the baby. She arrived and called out softly to
me, "My daughter-in-law . . . my daughter-in-law . . ." She
talked to the infant and greeted her with lovely names. She
cut her umbilical cord, picked her up, and carried her as we
all walked back to the village. Then they laid me down inside
the hut.

That day, my husband went gathering and came back
with sha roots and mongongo nuts, which he cracked for me
to eat. But my insides were still sore and I was in pain. He
went out again and killed a springhare. When he came back,
he cooked it and I drank the gravy. That was supposed to
help the milk come into my breasts, but my milk didn't come
down.

We lived in the bush and there was no one else to help
feed her. She just lay there and didn't eat for three nights.
Then milk started to fill one breast, and the same night the

other one filled. I spilled out the colostrum, the bad thing, and when my chest filled with good milk, she nursed and nursed and nursed. When she was full, she went to sleep.

We continued to live. When the others went out gathering, she and I would lie together in the hut. I would look at her, look and look. I'd think, "Oh, what a tiny thing is filling my lap!" and she'd suck on her fingers. It was the two of us, together.

I'd look at her and say, "My little sister ... my little sister!" She would burble, "Oh-oh ... oh-oh ... oh-oh ..." Did I really understand? Finally my husband told me, "No, you yourself gave birth to this little baby, now call her, 'My daughter.' Don't greet[5] her as your younger sister. The two of us gave birth to her; she is the baby we both conceived. When she grows up she'll greet me and say, 'Daddy' and she'll greet you and say, 'Mommy.' She's a little girl and you'll say, 'My daughter.'" Even my mother-in-law said, "When your child laughs with you, how can you not greet her and say, 'My daughter'?"

Soon after, I left the hut and carried her about. I'd take her with me and we'd go gathering together. She would cry, and after a while I'd return and sit around the village with the others.

When she started to laugh, they took me to my mother. When my mother saw me, she said, "When did you give birth to this baby? Take care of her so she grows well." We lived with my mother for a long time and the child grew. Little Chuko—she was very beautiful! And light-skinned. I'd look at her and think, "My lover conceived a beautiful baby!" She'd crawl around and try to get up; soon, she was able to stand.

But as she grew, she didn't look like my husband, she looked like Twi: her face was his face and her mouth was his mouth. When I looked at her, I knew she was the child of my lover. Even Tashay said she was Twi's child. He said her face was like Twi's and he could also tell by the eyes. He said, "This child is Twi's. You said that I was the one who cut you from your menstrual cycles, that I was the one who made you pregnant, but just look at the child you are holding in your lap. The child sitting there looks just like my younger brother."

I said, "Yes, Twi is your brother, your very close relative. Chuko looks just like your family. But it wasn't because he and I were lovers that she was conceived." Tashay said, "I don't need revenge. My younger brother conceived her. He will help take care of her."

But God refused. God didn't watch over her well and killed her, because she was my lover's child. She grew and grew until she was just starting to walk. That's when a sickness entered her chest. A few days later, she died.

It happened after we moved back to where Tashay's family was living. One day, on our way to the bush, we stopped to visit in a nearby village. I sat down with the baby among a group of women and men who were sitting around. The women asked me to take her out from my sling so they could look at her and admire her. They held her up and praised her, "Oh, what a beautiful child! What a lovely, wonderful child! Tashay truly has a lovely daughter!"

Tashay came over and told me that we were leaving, "Get up, let's go. What are you looking for around here that you're still sitting around?" He walked away. The women were still playing with Chuko, calling her lovely names and talking to her. Tashay came back again and looked around. Were there not many men there? He looked around and said, "What's the matter with Nisa that I already told her we were leaving, yet she is still lying around here, letting others play with the baby? Why isn't she getting up and coming with me? I told her she should only enter where the people were sitting to ask for water and that we would then leave."

I picked up Chuko, put her in the sling, and got up. As I passed him, Tashay yelled at me and accused me of not wanting to leave with him. He was very jealous. He grabbed a branch and started to hit me, on my hand and on my back, close to where my daughter was nestled. People quickly pulled him away saying, "What are you doing? Your wife is carrying a child. Are you just going to kill it? Even if you are jealous, do you hit a child with her mother? Why didn't you make sure your child was somewhere else before you started to hit Nisa? How could you hit a baby with her mother?"

Chuko was crying. All the anger had frightened her and she started to tremble. She shook and cried and wouldn't stop. That's when the sickness grabbed her, the sickness that eventually killed her. It entered her chest and finished her, as fast as a whip.

Later that day, we left and went somewhere else to live. Once there, Tashay said we should go together to gather mongongo nuts in the groves nearby. We went and started to collect the nuts, but while we were there, Chuko started to cry. It was the same sickness that had taken her before, that had entered her when she was afraid and trembling. I sang to her and walked with her, but she cried and cried; she wouldn't stop. Tashay took her but she kept on crying, crying and crying. He carried her on his back and we started to walk. Finally, she slept. But it wasn't real sleep, it was the sickness that affected her eyes.

I thought, "My child ... today my child is no longer nursing." I took her from Tashay and carried her. When she woke, I put my breast in her mouth, but she refused and nursed very very little. We went on like that, carrying mongongos, until we finally arrived at the village.

I told everyone, "My child is sick. This very beautiful child of mine, she's sick. While we were in the nut groves, she started to cry. She cried then as she is crying now. My milk she nursed only very little. Even now, when she nurses, I can hardly feel it. My heart is truly miserable."

They performed a curing ceremony for her. The medicine men tranced and tranced and tried to cure her. One of them said, "It's the branch with which her father hit you. That branch made her tremble and the sickness was able to grab her." We prayed for her as the others tried to cure her, but we couldn't reach her. They tranced, but she couldn't hear their efforts. She couldn't get better because God said that her father had refused her.

Children don't survive with me. She slept that night and when morning came, she died.

When she died, I looked around for a quiver and yelled at Tashay. I said I wanted to stick him with an arrow, "You killed my child! You said you hadn't given birth to her, that she wasn't yours. You said she was like someone else, like your brother. But the very branch with which you hit me was the branch that killed her. You all along refused that child in your heart and now you have killed her!"

Then I said, "You haven't treated me well and now maybe I should kill myself. You want me to give birth to a baby that's yours, but you've killed my child. You never even let me go to give birth with my mother or near my relatives. I gave birth with your people.

"You've just given me ruin. You destroy me every day. Now you have destroyed my child, my very first born child."

He said, "No. She was both of ours; we both conceived and gave birth to her. It was God who took the child from us and killed her."

My heart pained and I started to cry. My breasts were full of milk, and it spilled out. It was only because my heart was so full of pain that I spoke to my husband like that. But my heart did not leave; my heart stayed there with him.

We lived there for a while, then moved on. Soon I became pregnant with another, with another little girl.

Chapter 9
Motherhood
and Loss

IN MANY WAYS, gathering and hunting afford the !Kung a moderately healthy and safe existence. Their diet is adequate in
quantity and rich in nutritional quality. Daily subsistence activities require vigorous exercise, and adults, even in middle age, are
usually lean and muscular and in excellent physical condition.
They are also free of certain diseases that may be related to diet
or to stress.

Nevertheless, the overall health level of the !Kung is not
good. Although the relatively high altitude (3300 feet above sea
level) and dry climate prevent some of the infectious diseases of
tropical Africa from penetrating the Dobe area, the major cause
of death to the !Kung of all ages is infectious and parasitic disease. Influenza, pneumonia, bronchitis, gastroenteritis, rheumatic fever, and tuberculosis are prevalent; malaria is common
during the rainy season. In recent years, gonorrhea has also become widespread. A significant number of adults die in the
prime of life; infants and children are even more vulnerable to
disease and death.

The !Kung believe that when a person dies the worldly body
is left behind, while the spiritual body and soul join the world of
the ancestral spirits—a place in the heavens similar in many ways
to the world of humans on earth. Other spirits and gods also live
there, including the two most prominent !Kung gods: the Great
God, creator of the universe, usually seen as the purveyor of

good; and the Lesser God, under his command, who brings mostly misfortune and death.

When people get sick and die, the spirit world is seen as the underlying cause. Human actions can occasionally influence the spirits, and people may even share some of the responsibility for the death of someone who has been neglected or mistreated. But most often the actions of the spirits are unrelated to those of humans: the most cooperative and well-loved person is just as likely as one less generous and well-meaning to meet with misfortune or to die of illness. The !Kung see the treacherous nature of the Lesser God and of some of the other spirits as responsible for initiating these evil deeds. The lesser spirits, sometimes vengeful but often only cavalier, can often be convinced to let a person live. Mediating between the spirit and human worlds is the role of traditional !Kung healers. The success of a cure depends on the healer's arguments and the spirits' obstinacy.

!Kung culture encourages strong bonds between parents and children, and between spouses. Husbands and wives sleep beside each other, eat together, share food, and cooperate in family chores such as cooking and getting firewood. They often accompany each other on gathering trips or during hunts. All in all, they are together a great deal. Husband, wife, and children form the basic living unit, with a variable number of other people joining from each spouse's extended family. Adults remain closely attached to their parents; in contrast to our own society, in which such closeness is often viewed as unhealthy, the !Kung consider these feelings natural and express them freely.

When any member of such a close group dies, a major adjustment is required for everyone remaining. Some of the social networks in the group will have led through the deceased, and the death may cause the group to split up. Those who remain have to learn to live without a person they had relied on for meat or other food, for knowledge and experience, for healing power, or simply for love and companionship.

!Kung women are more likely than men to be widowed, since women tend to be about ten years younger than their husbands and since men are more vulnerable to disease. Young widows are likely to marry again and to resume family life with a new husband. Many older women also marry again; if other men are not available they may join a sister or other close female relative as a co-wife. Some older women choose not to marry, preferring to live in a separate hut in the same village as their grown children.

The !Kung, like many other peoples, encourage mourning that is intense but not prolonged. When a person dies, friends and relatives living elsewhere try to gather for the funeral or come later to see where the death and burial took place. Funerals are the time for all to grieve. Public mourning continues for a number of days. Women cry and wail; men sit and talk, although sometimes they, too, cry. The deceased is buried near the village in a hole dug in the ground or bored deep into one of the towering, hard-earth termite mounds found scattered throughout the desert.

Other customs set the death apart. If a child dies, other children are not allowed to see the body; the !Kung believe this could make a healthy child sick. After any death and burial, the village is abandoned and a new one erected nearby; the traditional huts can be built in a matter of hours, and a new village can go up in a few days.

The grief of those closest to the deceased, even if extreme, finds acceptance and support from many others around. Eventually, however, the mourner is encouraged to re-enter the mainstream of life: a widow or widower is likely to remarry; a mother who has lost an infant is likely to become pregnant again; and a person who has lost a mother, father, or sibling may move to a village where other close kin live.

The !Kung live in familiarity with death, but from the viewpoint of the individual, the death of an important person in one's life is anything but commonplace. A young girl's response to my question about her younger sister's death years before showed how profoundly disturbing this event had been for her: "God is one who doesn't help, first giving a child, then killing it. It makes me angry. I want to know why God chose a small child to kill and not someone older, like me. When my sister died, I was miserable. My heart ached and I wouldn't talk to people. I really loved her."

Another woman described her younger brother's sudden change in behavior after their mother's death. The brother was married to a woman he had loved so greatly that he had persuaded two reluctant families to allow their wedding. But when his mother died he turned angry and sullen. He began drinking beer at a nearby Herero cattle farm instead of hunting or foraging as he had done before. When he returned home, he often accused his wife of infidelity, and in a drunken state he even beat her. His sister attributed this change of character to his mourning for their seventy-two-year-old mother, who had died six months earlier after a long illness. No one condoned his extreme behavior, but neither did anyone doubt or belittle the attachment he had felt for his mother or the pain he experienced upon her death.

The dead are not entirely lost to the living; their spirits are believed to intervene from time to time in the lives of family members who survive them. One woman described the way her long-dead father saved her sister's child: "Yesterday, my younger sister gave birth to her baby, but when it was born, its eyes wouldn't open and it wasn't breathing. Only the slightest pulse was in his heart. I tried to revive him in every way I could, but nothing seemed to work. That's when I started to pray to the spirits of my father and grandfather, asking them to let the child live. I kept rubbing his face, head, and back with water. Eventually, he opened his eyes and started to cry. He's been fine ever since." She continued her story. "Last night there was a medicine dance and one of the healers in trance saw what had happened. He told me, 'It was because you called out to your father that the child was saved. The other ancestral spirits wanted to take the child, but your call to your father helped all of us—by yelling, he prevented them from taking the baby.' Yesterday, I was miserable, afraid that my sister's baby was not going to live. Today, my heart is overjoyed." She paused, then added emphatically, "Yesterday, my father really helped me!"

Another story was told by an older man about an incident that had occurred twenty years earlier. He had been very sick and, he claimed, very close to death. While in semidelirium, he was visited by the spirit of a brother who had recently died. His brother was angry at him for being sick and scolded him, telling him he was *not* to die. He said, "Now, get up from your sickbed and have an old person sing you the gemsbok medicine song, the one that is no longer sung. Learn it and you will get better." The man, who had not been able to move for days, rose and went to the old people. He told them about the visitation, and they revived the song, which had been in disuse for many years. Not long after, the man regained his strength. Twenty years later, he was a powerful healer, and he believed that only the gemsbok song enabled him to continue to tap his healing powers. Looking back, he felt that if not for this visitation, he would have followed his brother in death. It was as though he had needed his brother's permission to remain alive after the brother died.

WHEN I GAVE BIRTH to Chuko, I was still a young girl and hadn't given birth before.[1] Her birth caused me pain that was almost unbearable. My genitals were still very narrow and the pain was very great. I was larger when I gave birth to my second child. But for all, the pain of childbirth was always the same; even a small easing wasn't to be had.

Children—the first birth is painful, the second birth is painful, and the third birth is painful. There isn't a child whose birth is painless. It hurts like a terrible sickness.

Little Chuko was the first of my children to die. She died before I was pregnant with the other. After she died, I cried and cried, and after a few moons, I stopped mourning.

Then I became pregnant with Nai. The day I gave birth to her, the sun was burning hot. I had gone with the others to the nut groves. When the sun was at its hottest, when it was killing us, we sat down to rest in the shade of the nut trees. After a while, I said, "I don't want to rest now. I'm going to look for water roots." I left, and that's when the labor pains started. I thought, "Eh-hey, am I going to give birth now? I'll just go to that open, grassy area over there where I'll also be able to find more water roots."

I walked a little farther, dug some roots, and set them in a pile. When the pains became sharp, I sat down. No one was with me. Soon little Nai was born. I cut her umbilical cord and picked her up. I collected the pile of roots and walked back to the others. Everyone was lying in the shade, sleeping. I sat down. Soon, Nai started to cry. The women woke, startled. "What baby is crying? Where is that crying coming from?" Then, "Oh, Tashay's wife has given birth ... Nisa has given birth! How well she has done!" They praised Nai and they praised me, calling our names in affectionate greetings.

We stayed there, drinking water from the water roots, because there were many more where I had found them. And we just continued to live there for a time.

Nai grew and I had her with me. But the next time I became pregnant, it ended in a miscarriage. Tashay conceived the child, but he went away soon after that and Twi and I became lovers again. One month passed me by, then the next came and hung there and I saw as my body changed. The next month Tashay came back. When he saw that I was pregnant, he was furious, "What happened this time? You weren't pregnant when I left; you had only just finished menstruating. How is it that today I find you with a stomach again?" I said, "My husband, don't speak like that. It was the month that we were last together that is growing inside me and is the stomach you now see me with. Who do you think I'm having this child with?" He said, "I left you many months ago, but today, as you are, your months are very few. I don't know who has made you full like this; I only know that many months have passed since I went away."

This time, he talked about it incessantly. He asked me about it every night, and every morning, when dawn broke, he talked about it again. When he went away on short trips he would ask as soon as he came back, "Another man made love to you while I was gone, the same one who made you pregnant. Who is it?" I thought, "What does this man want me to do? Should I kill myself with a poison arrow?" Then he'd say, "All right ... you take care of Nai and I'll go about doing things. But if I ever see someone with you, I'll leave you. If I don't, I'll kill you. Because you're a horny one! You're so young, yet all you want is sex!"

I said, "Don't you think I know about you and your older brother's wife? As long as your brother is around, you're afraid and you stay with me in our hut. But as soon as he packs his blankets and goes hunting, you get up after you think I'm asleep and lie down with her. I've sat up and not been able to see you beside me—yet, I haven't said anything. I haven't followed you. I haven't sneaked up on you, watched, and then returned. Do you think that's because I was afraid? I wasn't afraid. I just left the two of you alone. Even in the morning, I never said anything. You'd come to me and I'd prepare food for you to eat." Then I said, "But it is true, beyond doubt, that you two are lovers."

I continued, "Now you say that one of your relatives has given me this baby. You yourself did it. Do you think if a man makes love to a woman, he doesn't set her with a baby? Now, don't let my ears hear any more of this talk!" He yelled, "If you sit there and continue to speak those thoughts, I'll cut your stomach open and the child will come out!"

I thought about it. He most certainly knew about Twi. I thought, "All right, I'll start cooking my food at other people's fires. The older people say that that makes you abort. From now on, whenever I have sha roots to roast, I'll roast them there, or mongongo nuts. I'll roast all my food at other fires; I'll no longer cook at my own."

That's what I did. I went around to all the different fires, roasting my food. I thought, "This man might hurt me because of this pregnancy and because of his younger brother. He asks and asks and asks; he is wearing me out."

Not long after, my stomach rose up in pain. It felt like fire. Tashay looked at me and said, "What's hurting you today that you're like this?" I said, "Nothing is hurting me." We sat together. Later, I lay down to rest. He said, "Why are you lying down while the sun is out? What is it?" I said, "I just want to lie down. Nothing is bothering me." Early that evening, Tashay built a fire and cooked some dried gemsbok meat. He pounded it, served it, and we ate. He said, "Nisa,

what is it? Even though you have been eating, when I look at
your eyes, it is like they are sick." I didn't want to tell him
what it was and said my back was hurting me. We ate and
then lay down to sleep.

I slept a long time. Just before dawn was about to break,
I got up and left the village; I carried little Nai with me because she woke and refused to stay behind. I sat in the bush
and started to miscarry. I thought, "It's just as I thought it
would be. If a man says things like what Tashay has said, this
is what you have to do." I sat there and soon it came down. I
didn't see a baby, just blood. I broke off a branch, dug a big
hole, and buried it—the blood with the little thing inside. I
thought, "Mm, it is finished. My husband wanted me to do
this, didn't he?" My heart was miserable, "Oh, my husband
has ruined this lovely baby for me." But that was only part of
the reason I miscarried. It was also because Twi and I had
slept together. My insides refused when I made love to him,
refused a different man from the baby's father. That also
ruined the pregnancy.

I returned to the village, took Nai from my kaross, and
lay down beside the fire outside the hut. I didn't go inside,
but just lay there until morning broke. While I was sleeping
Tashay woke and looked at me; he lay down beside me.
When it was light, he asked, "Nisa, my wife. Tell me what
happened yesterday. Even today, the way your eyes are . . .
are you missing your lover Twi? If not, what are you pining
about?" I said, "No, I'm not thinking about him. I'm sick."

But when I got up and he saw me standing, he said, "Is
this the way my wife is now?" I said, "Yes, that which I was
carrying yesterday, I carried until sunset and it was with me
while I slept. But during the night, I got up and it left me; it
has been ruined." He said, "Your pregnancy has been ruined?
What ruined it?" I said, "You . . . yes. As the person whose
hut I am in, you told me that my stomach was someone
else's and that you didn't want me anymore. Me, the woman
from inside your hut." He said, "In the name of that, you
dropped it?"

I didn't answer.

The one who came next, I called Bau. That was a very good pregnancy. I menstruated a number of times and then I stopped; I just lived with the small thing growing inside me. Much later, it started to move. It would move and then be quiet. It grew very nicely. Then, one day, while we were traveling, I gave birth beside a female acacia tree.

Bau was growing. She'd crawl around and play; she'd crawl and sit and then crawl again. She hadn't started to walk and was about the same age as my firstborn when she died. The sickness came from her little chest and it killed her. The medicine men tried to cure her, but they said the sickness was coming from a bird, one that hovers in the air, one that comes from the heavens and is sent by God. The spirit of the bird entered her and killed her.[2]

When I gave birth to Kxau, my lastborn, we were living in a Tswana village where Isak, the Tswana headman, lived.[3] I was truly an adult by then and knew about giving birth.

It was raining very hard when I left the village, but I felt the pains and knew it was time. I got up and just as I am now, went out alone and fixed myself a grassy place to sit. I sat there while the pains came, again and again; then they were quiet. There was more pain and more quiet. Then, the strongest pain came and my body started to shake. Oh, but that hurt! Other women may cry, but I didn't; I just sat there, my body trembling. Especially when the head started to come out, uhn, uhn . . . I felt my heart throbbing and cried out. After Kxau was born, people in the village heard him cry and came running. They cut his umbilical cord, picked him up, and we returned to the village.

I have always refused to give birth with anyone there. I have always wanted to go alone. Because, although people try to help you by holding and touching your stomach, they make it hurt more. I didn't want them to kill me with any more pain. That's why I always went by myself. When I gave birth to Kxau, I did it very well. Only after did they come to me.

It was while we were visiting in the Tswana village and just after Kxau was born that Tashay died.[4] When the moon first struck and was standing in the early evening sky, he got sick. He was sick for only a few days, not even a month; after that, his nights were very few.

The day I gave birth to Kxau, we slept. The next day we lay down and rested; the next night and the next and the next, we also slept. But it was just that many days after Kxau was born that the sickness entered Tashay's chest; it touched him in the night, entering his body. It struck him just once.

The next morning he woke and was in pain. That day, people tried to cure him. He slept that night. The next day the medicine men tried to cure him again, but they couldn't see what was causing the sickness. He slept that night, and the next day it was the same. The sickness was hurting him; it was hard for him to breathe and he was throwing up blood. The next night we slept beside each other, but soon after the rooster of the early dawn called for the first time, and when the edge of morning was beginning to break in the East, he died.

I couldn't hear him breathing. I touched him, again and again and again, but there was no breath. I called out, "Tashay ... Tashay ... Tashay ..." but he didn't answer. I called again, "Tashay!" And again. And again. But he was silent. I took my hand and felt him; he still wasn't breathing. I felt his heart, but it wasn't beating. I said, "Oh, my husband ... has he already died? My husband, whom I lay beside and slept beside, even this very night ... is he dead? Just now we were sleeping beside each other and now he is dead!"

I lay there and thought, "Why did this happen? The two of us gave so much to each other and lived together so happily. Now I am alone, without a husband. I am already a widow. Why did God trick me and take my husband? God is stingy! He just takes them from you. God's heart is truly far from people."

I picked up my infant son, and that was when my crying

began. I sat there and cried and cried and cried. People heard me and came to me. They sat with me and the other women started to cry, too. After a long time, they said, "You have children to take care of, don't lie beside your husband any longer. Your husband is dead; it's over. To lie down beside him won't give him back life. Now, take your children with you and lie down over here. Cover your husband; he will just stay over there. Wanting him is no longer good, because he is dead. You can't have him as a person any longer; he has left. So cover him up and let him lie there. Then, cover your children and lie down with them over here."

I listened to them and made a bed of blankets outside our hut. The others went and covered Tashay as he lay there. The next morning, the Tswana headman said, "Oh! One of my Zhun/twasi died a terrible death. Why did this happen to him? There is no other like him. The two of us were living beside each other, yet his death was already upon us." Then he said, "Now, the rest of you, dig a hole in that termite mound, take his body and bury it there, bury this Zhun/twa of mine. My eyes no longer want to see him because his death is so painful to me." The men dug the hole and buried him.

Then I was without my husband and my heart was miserable. Every night I missed him and every night I cried, "I am without the man I married." I thought, "Where will I see the food that will help my children grow? Who is going to help me raise this newborn? My older brother and my younger brother are far away. Who is going to help me now?" Because Kxau had only just been born; he was so small he almost didn't exist. Then I said, "Everyday food will do it. I will start today to gather the food that will bring them up," and I went out and brought back what I could.

But whenever I looked at my children, I saw that they looked just like Tashay. I thought, "Why is it that other women's husbands haven't died? So many people are here, young women like myself, whose husbands live. Why my husband? Why the man I married? Why, while we were still lying together and having children together, did he die?" I felt the pain and cried and cried and cried.

The Tswana headman finally said, "This Nisa ... this Nisa is mourning for her husband, but what good is it going to do?" He asked me, "What are you going to do now?" I said, "I'll just stay here until I see someone who will tell Mother to come for me. Today I'm without anyone here who is mine. When I think about what my husband was to me, I see that he was like a father. Now that he has died, I'm without a home. Today I'd like to go back to where my mother and father are living." The headman said, "Fine, I'll ask others who are going near there to take you along."

There was another reason I wanted to leave. After Tashay died and the news reached his parents, they came to me. When they arrived they asked, "What killed our son?" I said, "Death itself killed him. It was God. Are you saying something else did? The only thing was God." When they heard, they started to cry. Later, they said they wanted to take me back to live in their village, that they would take care of me. But I didn't want to go, "Today, I'll go to my mother's. I won't live in someone else's village again. Before, I lived with my husband in your village, but now that he is dead, I don't want to live there anymore. If I did, you would start hating me and would yell at me all the time."

It would have happened that way, too. Because, very shortly after that, Tashay's relatives started saying that I had killed Tashay. They had known about Kantla and they also heard that Kantla wanted to marry me now that Tashay was dead. That was why they began saying that Kantla's spirit had killed Tashay.[5] When I heard about it, I thought, "Eh, there is no longer anything in Tashay's village that can help me live. God has just killed my husband, yet his people say I have done what God himself has done. I won't go back to their village. I'll go to where my family is, live there, and lie down there. I won't go where my in-laws will accuse me of having killed my husband. If I lived there, they would eventually kill me."

So, I didn't go with them; I went and lived with my parents. I lived there and mourned—for the months of the hot dry season—and spilled out my heart. I opened my heart until finally, I was able to stop mourning.

I lived in my parents' village for a long time and my children continued to grow. When I gathered food, they ate, and when I saw honey, they also ate. My brothers were living there, too, and they also helped. Whenever they saw honey or hunted game, my children ate. Even my mother gathered food for them.

Soon, Kxau started to crawl; he picked up one leg, set it on the ground, pulled out the other, set it on the ground, and then fell down. I watched and thought, "Oh! My breasts are making my child grow strong."

And I just lived on in their village.

Chapter 10

Change

THE INITIAL TSWANA AND HERERO settlements in the Dobe area were probably tolerated by the !Kung mostly because it was easier to accommodate than to fight. But it is likely that there was some positive !Kung response to their presence as well. Fixed villages with permanent food resources were as dramatic a contrast to nomadic bush life, as the tall, heavy-set, Christian, Bantu-speaking people were to the !Kung. The relative ease of Tswana and Herero life—drinking milk, tending gardens, raising domestic animals for meat and trade, and wearing colorful clothes (Herero women wear dresses sewn from more than twelve yards of cloth, fashioned after nineteenth-century missionary dress)—must also have seemed appealing. Their stable, settled villages, with sturdy huts set slightly apart from the animal corrals, were also a kind of insurance for the !Kung against occasional scarcity of bush foods. When necessary, the !Kung could exchange their labor for milk and perhaps grain—assuming, of course, that the Bantu-speakers had enough to spare. (There were also years in which crop failure forced them to depend on the !Kung knowledge of bush foods.)

But the disadvantages to the !Kung were also clear. Springs became contaminated by the cattle and goats watered nearby. The concentration of animals, animal droppings, and gourds of fresh and cultured milk brought swarms of flies. Venereal disease and other human diseases, more common in the Tswana and

Herero because of their contact with large population centers, spread to the !Kung—some perhaps for the first time. The herds of cattle and goats frightened the game and denuded the region of grass, roots, berries, and other wild plants, which both the !Kung and the animals they hunted relied upon. Thorn bushes were the only plants that could survive the roving herds, and they did—in abundance. The herds grazed farther and farther from the permanent waterholes, encroaching steadily on the lands where the !Kung still gathered and hunted.

As Tswana and Herero village sites expanded to encompass more of the traditional !Kung waterholes, maintaining the !Kung way of life became increasingly difficult. Asking for handouts from their richer neighbors became not only acceptable but necessary. Except for !Kung girls who married into Tswana or Herero families, many !Kung who lived in and around the settled villages were essentially beggars or were in positions of servitude, working long hours for little direct compensation. !Kung men and women who had once provided meat and vegetable foods for their families, and who had conducted their lives with independence and dignity, were now living in low-status positions in relation to people who treated them as inferior. Given the psychological effects of such a change in circumstances, it is not surprising that drinking the home-brew sold in the villages became an appealing pastime for many of the !Kung. Many others, however, were able to adapt and even to benefit from the Tswana and Herero settlements. When standing water was scarce, they would exchange their labor for milk. But when the rains came, they would leave the villages, following the lure of plentiful bush foods in distant areas, or of abundant meat from large animal kills. Visiting people far away and the excitement of moving to new, clean places also enticed many !Kung away from the bustle of the cattle posts.

Tribal politics in the Dobe area became official in 1948, when the Tswana tribal administration appointed its first legal representative, Isak Utugile, as the regional headman. Before that, conflicts within or among !Kung, Tswana and Herero groups had gone unregulated. Part !Kung himself and a fluent speaker of all three languages, Isak mediated conflicts of all kinds: accusations of cattle theft, exploitation of !Kung hired help, adultery, physical fights, even murder. He pronounced judgments based on tribal law and meted out punishments, including jail sentences, when necessary. He was also often consulted about marriages and divorces. Highly respected by all groups, he promoted an atmosphere of fair treatment for the !Kung, those who worked for the others and those who did not. He held office until 1973, when poor health forced him to resign in favor of another headman.

Although a few !Kung families lived apart from settlements as late as the 1960s, subsisting primarily on bush foods, the unquestionable trend has been toward sedentary village life. Each year finds more !Kung tending their own or other people's goat and cattle herds, clearing and planting garden plots, raising chickens, and selling crafts, to earn the money to purchase grains, sugar, and salt. They are also using more traded and store-bought goods—pots, pans, dishes, silverware, kerosene, lamps and candles, colorful cloth and manufactured clothing, blankets, shoes, flashlights, and occasionally even a radio. !Kung hut style is also changing: huts are now being built to last, with sturdy frames, mud-base plaster walls, and separate thatched roofs—replicas of Bantu huts. Perhaps more significantly, individual compounds are, for the first time, being demarcated within the larger village area.

Inevitably, there have been changes in daily life. Girls and boys who would have been playing or learning to gather or hunt now care for herds of goats. Adults are also busy with the tasks of the settled villages: elaborate thorn-bush fences have to be erected and repaired to protect gardens; planting and weeding have to be done; new huts, often requiring a week's work, have to be built, plastered, and maintained; dishes have to be washed; clothing and blankets need sewing, washing, and mending; and some of the new foods need long preparation times.

The pattern of child care has also been affected. Women who live more sedentary lives have shorter birth spacing between children. One explanation for this change may be the availability of cows' and goats' milk and its effect on nursing patterns. Or perhaps women are better fed and less active, making it easier to begin and maintain pregnancy. In any case, with two children to carry, the women are less likely to go gathering; they become more dependent on the new food sources, animal husbandry and agriculture. Having more children to care for and more household chores than before, !Kung women may actually be providing less food for their families than they used to. This trend, along with !Kung men's increasing participation in tribal politics, may jeopardize the influence and the relatively high status !Kung women have traditionally enjoyed.

The same may be true of the older !Kung. Once they were looked up to as the repositories of traditional culture. But how will their skills and knowledge apply to the concerns of their grandchildren, who are going to school, milking cows, herding goats and donkeys, and even learning to bore wells and use dynamite? What happens to the once-respected "owners" of land areas and food resources in a world where land is controlled by government land boards, who allocate parcels to applicants with large herds of cattle and the sophistication to fill out complex legal forms? Despite these questions, some signs are positive. The relatively sedentary life of herding and farming is easier on old people: excursions to the bush are less frequent; older children, left behind in the village to tend the herds, are able to care for older adults as well; and donkeys, carrying back food from distant areas, make excursions more efficient and of shorter duration.

The !Kung have managed to respond to many of the changes in their way of life with flexibility and humor, if not always with enthusiasm. They understand that adopting new ways is their best chance for survival. They have therefore begun to work within the country's legal system to secure rights to their traditional lands. With the support of the Botswana government and the Kalahari People's Fund, the !Kung are receiving guidance in digging and dynamiting wells, without which gaining title to their land would be impossible. School fees are also being paid for !Kung children—who are willing and able to go to school. Clinics are making an impact on mortality. Agricultural and veterinary specialists are advising the !Kung on working the land and tending domestic animals, and government buyers are encouraging the manufacture of traditional crafts for sale. The hope is that the transition to a new economy will be achieved without sacrificing the richness of traditional !Kung culture.

This hope may yet be realized. !Kung women living in sedentary villages continue to gather bush foods occasionally, keeping their diet more varied than that of their Bantu-speaking neighbors. They say, "Milk and food from the garden are village foods. Even if we have enough in the village, we still go to the bush to get *our* food; our hearts yearn for the taste of it." Although donkeys rather than men and women are now carrying sacks of mongongo nuts back from the nut groves, this nutritious food continues to be an important part of the !Kung diet. !Kung children who are going to school and learning the values of modern culture are still being exposed to many of the traditions of their parents and grandparents, with whom they spend much time. Many of the traditional hunting and tracking skills are also being maintained, although in an altered form: unrivaled masters of the hunt, !Kung men are being employed by the Tswana and Herero to hunt with them or for them, with rifles and on horseback.

Another encouraging trend is the flourishing of both the ceremonial trance dance, and the women's drum dance in the sedentary villages. Now that they are less mobile, people seem more inclined to expend energy on all night dances; the larger number of people also creates an exciting and festive atmosphere. The faith the Tswana and Herero express in the power of !Kung medicine has helped maintain its prestige. The non-!Kung village people often attend the dances, where they are ritually cured along with everyone else. They also employ !Kung healers in times of illness. Their support lends added dignity to !Kung spiritual accomplishments in the context of culture contact and change.

WHILE I WAS LIVING in my parents' village and after some time had passed, my cousin told me her husband wanted me to be his second wife. But I didn't like him. Even if he hadn't been married, I would have refused. I asked, "What is it I have that you want? Isn't the food I have just like the food you already have? What kind of marriage do you want?" He said, "I want you as my second wife." I said, "No, that I refuse. A co-wife, an older woman, would kill me." His wife said, "Not so! I won't kill you. My husband will marry you and you will be just like a younger sister to me; we'll sit together and do things together."

I said, "No, I won't do that. If he marries me and the two of us do things together, won't there be a time when he will want me and will refuse you, when he will start to yell at you? Living that way, won't you feel pain? You'll feel it, don't you see? One day your husband will make love to me and will refuse you. Then, while we are lying down inside the hut, you'll get up and pretend to stoke the fire . . . but you'll take the coals and burn us with them!"

She said, "You're wrong. Our people are related and I want us to sit together inside one hut. And even when my husband goes to you, I won't yell. I'll just continue to like both of you completely." I said, "No, all my heart refuses. I have children and won't enter a hut with another woman as a co-wife. If I did, I would never get any sleep. I'm a grown woman. Does someone like myself enter another woman's hut? No, I will lie by myself. The man I married has recently died and I don't want to marry again. When I do, I'll find a man who kills animals just for me. I'll share with you then; even beads, we can continue to exchange. But why should we sit together inside one hut?"

My mother agreed, "Yes, what Nisa says is true. I, her mother, I also refuse a marriage for her with more than one woman because a marriage that has co-wives is a difficult one. Even older people who have that kind of marriage, find it hard. When the younger wife goes to the older wife for food, the older one sometimes refuses. When their husband comes back with meat, the younger wife has to sit there, waiting until the first wife gives it to her, and that I don't like." She continued, "You say you want to take Nisa and put her inside your hut. But Nisa has children to take care of. What if you don't live together well and if you argue with each other? Then you'll say that Nisa is bad and you'll go around saying bad things about her."

My cousin's husband asked, "What is this all about? My wife says she wants her younger cousin to be her co-wife, yet you refuse to part with her. Would you rather someone else married her?" My mother said, "Yes, someone who will get food and give it to her to eat. Because you, even if you had something, you'd be afraid not to give it to your first wife and you wouldn't give any to Nisa. She'd have to sit and wait for her cousin to give her some. Only then would she eat. I want her to marry a man where she is the only one. When her husband comes home with food, he will give it to her and she will feed her children. But a co-wife . . . uhn, uhn . . . Nisa would be waiting for food and her children would be crying. In the name of all that, I refuse."

My cousin said, "Why do you say I wouldn't give meat to my younger wife or that I would sit and eat it myself while the children cried? I would help take care of them, help bring them up. Wouldn't I also be their mother?"

I continued to refuse, and eventually I left and went back to live in the Tswana village.[1] Months passed and my cousin and her husband came for me once again. I told them, "Zhun/twasi! I still refuse! What can I tell you that you want to hear? My husband has died and I want to sit and take care of myself. The pain I feel, that pain I will just sit with and feel. I get my own food, I prepare my own food, and I eat my own food. I don't ask you or others for your food or meat. I collect enough for myself."

They left and went back to their village, and I continued to live.

It was while I was living in the Tswana village that Besa first came to me.[2] Besa, the one with the huge behind. He's married to someone else today, but he wasn't married at the time. We had not been lovers, nor had he entered my hut while Tashay was still alive. It was only after Tashay died that he came to me and said, "Today I want to love this woman, to sleep with her and to marry her."

At first I refused, "My husband has just now died. I'm not marrying another man. If I did, what would I be doing?" But the Tswana headman told me, "Marry Besa and let him help bring up your children." I said, "Have I not been bringing them up? Have my breasts not been feeding them? Has my food not also been feeding them? What could Besa do to help?" He said, "You're not seeing clearly if you refuse. I think you should marry him." I said, "I don't like him. His stomach is too big and his behind is too big. Even me, my behind may be big, but my stomach is not like his and I won't marry him."

I built my own hut and lived there. Soon after, Besa entered it as my lover.

Kantla, the man who first taught me about lovers, still wanted to marry me and have me be a co-wife with Bey, his first wife, as he had wanted before I married Tashay. He told the headman, "I'm going to marry this woman because I have already slept beside her and have given her things. What are you talking about when you say you will give her to Besa? Give her to me and let me marry her." Kantla even told Besa, "You're not going to marry Nisa. I'm an older person, truly I am. And I say that I will have her. Why are you saying we two should share her?" They almost fought, but I said, "No, I'm not going to marry Kantla, and Besa will not marry me, either. The two of you will just be my lovers."

But my heart wanted Kantla; I loved him very much. My heart was huge toward him and only small toward Besa. I thought, "Why don't I marry Kantla? Besa's ways aren't good, after all. When Besa says we should lie down together, I'll tell him he's not the one I want. I'll tell him to leave so Kantla can marry me." Because this time, I no longer refused to be Bey's co-wife. Years before when they had wanted me to, she and I were still children. When Kantla wanted us both then, I refused. But after Tashay died, I was willing to think about it again.

Not long after, Kantla left Bey in their village and built a small hut for himself in my village. Then, we were all living there—Besa, Kantla, and me. Besa slept in one hut and Kantla and I in another. Besa asked, "How is it that the two of us came here to be with this woman, yet you're the only one who sleeps beside her?" Kantla said, "Because she's my woman. Besa, this woman is mine." Then he said, "See here, when Nisa's husband died, her in-laws almost killed me. They said that my spirit had killed their son and they would, in turn, kill me. They accused me and their words rose all around me. Then it passed. Now all that is finished and I'm going to marry her, not you. And where I have been lying down, I will continue to lie, and where you have been lying down, you will also continue to lie."

That night, we slept. The next morning, Besa left and Kantla stayed. Because Kantla and I, our hearts were very big toward each other.

There were other men in my life at that time as well. One was Tsaa. One time, I was sitting with Tsaa by my hut; little Kxau was resting on my lap, nursing. Kantla came by and he and Tsaa started to argue. Kantla yelled at him and became so angry, he grabbed some coals from the fire and threw them all around. I jumped up, grabbing Kxau from my lap, and handed him to Tsaa; I brushed the coals from around me. Then we sat down again.

Another time, after Besa came back, he asked, "How come you and Tsaa always sit together? Even yesterday, I saw the two of you together." He accused me of being with other men and started to hit me. Doesn't a man who is your lover sometimes do that? He hit me on my back and it started to swell. The headman finally stopped him, "You're going to beat Nisa to death! You're not even married to her, so stop hitting her. What are you doing this for? How is it helping her?" Then he said, "It's true that Nisa's husband has recently died, but I don't like that she isn't marrying again, that she just meets different lovers like this." Because Besa had been

entering my hut for a long time by then, and the headman
said we should marry.

When my father heard that Besa wanted to marry me, he
almost killed him. My father left his village and came to me
with my mother and my cousin. Besa and I were inside my
hut when they arrived. My father came right into the hut,
pulled out a spear (that man was really senseless!) and said,
"Is this bad thing going to marry my daughter? Get up and
leave!" I got up, grabbed the spear from him, and said,
"Don't you see I have my children with me? What anger do
you have toward the man I am with?"

He said, "I don't like Besa and you won't marry him.
Your husband just died and instead of staying with us, you
came back to live in the Tswana village. Now you're saying
you're going to give yourself a husband? No, come with me
and let me give you a husband. What are you doing, deciding
this yourself?"

Then he said to Besa, "And you, you're not going to
marry her, because her husband has just died. What are you
pestering her for? Why didn't you ask for her in marriage instead of just living with her like this?" Besa said, "I am going
to marry your daughter. Why shouldn't I? Even if you want to
kill me ... if you do, I can't do anything about that, but if
you don't, I'm going to marry her. I will marry her and take
care of her children."

Because Besa, his heart was very big toward me. But even
then, my heart was small toward him, even when we first
lived together. My heart never cried for him; it was really only
a small part that went out to him. So I answered, "I myself
will take care of my children and bring them up on the food
I gather. My relatives will bring me meat and my father will
give me food. That's how they will be brought up. Now that
their father has died, why should I take another man to help
raise them?" Besa said, "Nonsense. Your relatives may be
here, but I will also help bring up your children."

My father said, "I don't like you, Besa. I want my daughter to come with me. I'll find her a man who lives in the
bush and who knows the bush. I don't want her to marry a

man from the villages." My mother agreed. When they left, they took me with them and Besa stayed behind.

When I went back again to the Tswana village to live, Besa was waiting for me. My heart still didn't agree to him much, but I let him enter my hut and lie with me. I thought about how he had hit me and how I didn't like being with a man like that. I thought, "I'll have many lovers. Later, Besa and I will separate."

But, while Besa and I were living together, everyone said I should marry him. Finally, I agreed. I thought, "Eh, yes. Today I will marry him because I can see he will treat me well." The Tswana headman said, "Besa, now that you've entered Nisa's hut, you must take good care of her and her children. You've bothered her and persisted so long, she finally has agreed to you. So, take good care of her."

That's when I married him. Kantla had given up by then and my parents finally agreed. Even my feelings had changed when I married him, and I had learned to love him with a large part of my heart. We lived together for many years and shared many rainy seasons. We went about and did things together. Sometimes we went to the bush and he'd shoot an animal, perhaps a gemsbok. The next morning we would track it, cut up the meat, and bring it back to the village. Another time he'd kill something else, perhaps a steenbok. Or, an eland. Then people would go with us to the kill site, cut up the meat, and help carry it back. We'd have lots of meat to eat and my heart would be happy.

Besa also helped me bring up Kxau. Because when Tashay died, Kxau was still pink and hadn't grown up, even a little. Once Kxau was older, he called Besa his father. His older sister didn't. Nai had known her father; he had helped her bones get strong and helped bring her up. That's why a part of her heart refused to call Besa Father and instead called him Uncle. That's also why she often spent long stretches of time living with my brothers and their families.

Whenever Nai heard Kxau call Besa Father, she would say, "Have you no brains? Besa isn't your father. He's just someone who married Mother. Ask and she'll tell you that your father died and that Besa came along after and married her. So, why are you calling someone Father who isn't? Call him Uncle the way I do."

Once Kxau was older, he asked, "He isn't our father? Then how come he yells at Mommy so much?"

Besa and I did argue a lot, usually about sex. He was just like a young man, almost a child, who lies with his wife day after day after day. Don't her genitals get sore after a while?

Every night Besa wanted me and every night he would make love to me. That Besa, something was wrong with his brain! I thought, "No, this man is a bad one. What kind of man has sex like this? Perhaps he thinks I am something other than a wife?" I said, "Besa, don't you know that you married me, that I am the woman inside your hut? Why don't you have sex with me once, then go and have sex with someone else?"

He said, "What? Are you telling me to sleep with someone else? You're my wife." I said, "Yes, because I don't like the way you are. In one night, you want sex too many times. Perhaps you aren't well. You're just like a rooster. The way a rooster always wants sex with a chicken, that's the way you are with a woman. You may hurt me yet this way."

He said, "You must have other men. That's why you are refusing me and are telling me these things." I said, "No, that's not it. Now, listen to me. A woman's genitals are part of a woman's body. It's not a separate thing that you can have sex with all the time. At night, once is good; once is enough and then you go to sleep. Another night, you have sex again and that's good too. But as you would have it, in one night you'd screw a woman to death! That's why I ask you—where are you going to find all the sex you want?"

We argued like that all the time. He even wanted to bring me to the Tswana headman, but I refused. That man, he wanted sex more than anything else! After a while, I realized I didn't like his ways. That's when I thought, "Perhaps I will leave him. Perhaps I'll find another man and see what he is like."

I didn't leave him, not for many years. But I did have lovers and so did he. Because, as I am Nisa, my lovers have been many. At that time, there was Tsaa and Nanau. One day Tsaa would make love to me, another day Nanau. They were jealous of each other, and once Tsaa even went to Besa and told him that Nanau and I were lovers. Besa said, "What can I do about it?"

Another time, I went from the village to get firewood. Nanau followed my tracks and found me where I was collecting wood. We lay down together. Besa had also left the village to look for some of the Tswana cows that had wandered off. As he was walking about, he saw my tracks in the sand and followed them. He also saw how Nanau's tracks joined mine and he followed those as well.

Nanau and I had finished making love. We were sitting very close to each other, talking together beside a tree. From near by, we heard, "Where has Nisa gone? Her powder smells so sweetly over here . . ." My heart started to pound. "That's Besa talking!" I whispered. Nanau and I moved farther apart and just sat there, waiting. Soon, Besa came and stood beside us. He spoke my name and he spoke Nanau's name. Then he said, "Didn't you tell me you weren't going to have any more lovers?" I said, "Yes, that's what I said." He said, "Then who are you sitting with?" I said, "Nanau." He said, "What were you doing?" I said, "We were making love." Because there was no way to deny it; there was nothing more to be afraid of. I had been found out; I was already dead. Besa said, "Let's go back to the village."

We all went back together. Nanau and I were trembling with fear. When we got there, Besa went to the Tswana headman. He said, "Nisa and Nanau were just making love to each other." The headman called us to him. I was shaking. He asked Nanau, "What were you two doing? Did Besa see you?" He said, "Mm, yes." Then he asked me, "Nisa, did Besa catch you?" I said, "Mm, he caught us." He said our punishment would be beatings.

I refused. "No, I won't be hit. I'm a woman and don't

want to be beaten. If you hit me on my back, I'll feel pain for
a long time. Instead, do this: get a gun and shoot a bullet
into me. Because if you hit me, you'll make my heart rise up
in anger."

They left me and Nanau was the only one beaten. He lay
down and the headman hit him four times. Then we all left
and went home. My heart was miserable and I thought about
how Besa had been the cause of Nanau's being hit.

Not long after, I went to visit my mother at her village
and stayed there for a few nights. Nanau followed me and
lived with me there. Besa must have suspected something,
because while I was still away he cut a thin branch and set it
aside to become hard and dry. Then he waited for me to return. The day I came home, we just slept. The next night it
was the same. But the next morning, he said, "Today, your
blood is already on my hands."

I had gone to milk the Tswanas' cows, and when I came
back I poured it into the milk gourds. That's when Besa came
to me, grabbed the gourds from my hands, and started to hit
me. He yelled, "I'm going to beat the beauty out of you. You
think you are so beautiful, that you are a beautiful woman
and that I am an ugly man. Well, today I'm going to destroy
all that beauty." I said, "I don't care. I'm not afraid."

He sat down. Then he left to do some work for the headman. When he finished, he came back again, grabbed my
arm, and hit me—my back, my body, all over. He hit me until
my back started to swell again and it stood out, as before.
The headman said, "Enough! You'll kill her. Nisa's not a donkey, yet you've been hitting her since you rose this morning.
Now the sun is late in the sky. That's enough! You'll beat her
to death."

He stopped hitting me. My back kept swelling and I
started to cry. I cried and cried and couldn't stop the tears or
the pain. Later, I moved out of Besa's hut and lived in an
empty hut in the village. Besa lived alone in ours. When he
would come back from the well with water, he would bring it
to me, but I'd refuse, "I won't drink water you bring." When
he poured out milk for me, I said, "I won't drink milk you

bring, either." I refused to take anything from him and only drank the milk others gave me.

My back soon started to heal, although it continued to hurt. But even then, I let Tsaa lie down beside me. I thought, "I'm really stubborn! I've been beaten because of this, yet here I am still doing it and I won't stop." Tsaa would lie with me at night and leave only when it started to get light.

It was only after my back healed completely that I went back to Besa and lived in our hut again.

When I was a young woman, I had many lovers, but Tsaa was truly one of my important loves. We were together for a long time, but we ended when he left me for another woman. He had so many women! He wasn't afraid of anyone, not even of me.

It happened the night a group of us went to a dance in another village. We had planned to sleep there when the dance was over. But that night, Tsaa stayed with another woman, even though I was there. He didn't fear me; he didn't care that I would see. He just lay down with her.

The next morning I said, "So, this is how you do things? You don't care who sees you?" He said, "Don't you have another man, your husband? That's why I didn't think about you and stayed with this other woman." I said, "Oh, that's how it is? Hasn't she also a husband? She does. But today, you have slept with her in front of me to show me that she is important and that I am not. I'm just a worthless thing to you, so you took her instead." Then I said, "Since this is how it is, you and I are finished. You and she can be lovers. I won't share you with her."

We separated and the two of them remained lovers for a long time. But I was jealous; my lower lip was in a pout all the time. Tsaa asked me, "Why are you pouting like that?" I said, "Because you really made me feel pain."

We lived and I continued to feel bad. Another time, Tsaa asked, "Nisa, won't you pour me a little water to drink?" I said, "No, because after you drink it, you'll say the water I have is not good. Go and ask your other woman for some."

He came again and asked me to pour some water so he could wash. I said, "No, if I pour any water, I'll pour it for my husband. I won't pour anything for you." I was jealous and miserable, and my pout was covering my whole face.

Sometime later, the woman's husband came back from where he had been. I thought, "Wonderful! Now Tsaa will get his! Now Tsaa won't have what he wants. Let him drink sand! He thought I wasn't good enough, so let him drink sand and feel humbled!"

Tsaa was afraid of the woman's husband and that's why he came back to me, asking to lie down beside me. I looked at him and said, "*You* sleep with *me*? You, Tsaa, you want to sleep with me today? Never! We've separated and now we're finished."

We continued to live and soon Tsaa left and went to live in the East.

After that, a man named Kashe spoke to me about being his lover. Some time later, I agreed. Once, when Besa went away for a few nights, I went to my mother's village to stay. Kashe followed me there. But one night, while we were lying together, Besa came and sneaked up on the hut in the middle of the night. I heard something. I whispered, "Kashe, I think Besa's out there." I heard something again. Then, I saw him. I tapped my fingers lightly against Kashe's skin, quietly trying to wake him, "Besa's here . . . Kashe . . . Besa's here." Kashe woke, "Besa? He won't do anything to me. I'm not afraid of him." I said, "Are you crazy?" I started to shake and whispered to him, but he was still full of sleep and wouldn't listen. I pushed him, again and again, saying, "Get up. Go and sit over there. Are you senseless?" But he said, "I'm not getting up. I'm going to lie here and see what Besa's going to do."

Besa saw he wasn't afraid. He said, "Is this what he wants? He wants to insult me again and wait to see what I will do? He wants to humiliate me further?" Besa lunged at him, about to hit, but Kashe jumped up and ran outside the hut. Besa followed, chasing him. Then he pulled out a knife.

By then, everyone was up. My mother started to scream, "Don't use the knife . . . don't use the knife . . ." Finally, Besa came back and set the knife down. He yelled at my mother, "What's wrong with you? Here you are, living right where your daughter is living, yet men just come into her hut and make love to her. And you, you don't even chase them away!"

Mother yelled back, "Are you stupid? Does a mother police her daughter? Am I here to spy on her? I wouldn't do that. Does your mother or father police you?" He said, "Every time she comes to visit you, she meets her lovers. Whenever she comes here, she brings along a man she wants to make love to." My mother said, "Lies! Nisa doesn't bring men here with her. They come themselves, looking for her; they come on their own, following her. Anyway, why are you talking to *me* about it? You've seen for yourself; you came upon Kashe just now, yet you aren't going to do anything about it anyway."

After that Kashe stayed away. Besa went back to our village while I stayed on in my mother's village. But a few days later Kashe came back. My father was sitting with a group of people when he saw Kashe enter the village. He said, "What? Kashe's here again?" Then he said, "Kashe, I don't want you to come here again, not after what happened the night Besa caught you. Because, although he didn't kill you that time, the next time he sees you, he will kill my daughter. So, I don't want you around here anymore. Leave right now. Go back to your village."

Kashe just sat there. My father said, "You're someone with no sense!" He grabbed a walking stick and hit Kashe in the stomach with it. Kashe bent over in pain, holding his arms where he was hit. My younger brother yelled at my father, "What are you doing? You told him to leave, now let him go. If you kill him, what excuse will you have?"

My father said, "I don't want to kill him. But my heart . . . my heart has no need for the things this young man does. My heart doesn't like any of this. He's come back today and will be responsible for killing your sister; her husband will kill her this time. That's why he has to leave; I hit him so he would go."

Soon, Kashe got up. He left and returned to his village.

Not long after that, Kashe and I separated and Besa and I continued to sit together.

A long time passed. One day, Kantla came back and said he would take me to my mother's village. I was very happy and left with him. I left Besa behind and he didn't say anything. Because Besa was afraid of Kantla.

Yes, afraid. I guess you haven't seen that yet, when one person is that afraid of another. Besa was beside himself with fear of Kantla because Kantla is a person with truly fierce anger.

That wasn't the first time, either. Soon after Besa and I married, Besa and Kantla both worked for a few days in another village. When they came back, they came together, riding donkeys. Besa walked over to my hut and was about to come in, when Kantla said, "No, you lie over there. I'm going in." Besa said, "What? You're going to take my wife, the woman I asked for and married? You're going to go in and lie with her while I lie in the bush? Is that what you're saying? Well, that's not going to happen." But Kantla refused and came into the hut and lay down. Besa was the one to lie down by the fire.

The next morning Besa was jealous and angry. Kantla said to him, "Go get the donkeys so we can leave." Besa refused. Kantla said, "Stop refusing. Go and get them." Besa still refused. Kantla said, "All right, then I'm going to take Nisa home with me and tell Bey that she'll be sharing our hut with us again."

And that's what he did. He took me to his village. Bey was away, and only when she came back did I return; only then did Besa and I start living together again.

There was one other man I was with at that time—Kantla's younger brother Dem. He spoke to me and eventually I agreed. One time when I went to visit my mother, he followed me there and we lived together.

His older brother Kantla must have heard about us, because he came looking for us. The day he arrived Dem and I were washing at the well. Kantla didn't see me and asked my mother where I was. She told him I was at the well. When he came to where Dem and I were sitting, he and his brother started to shout and yell at each other. Kantla accused me of sleeping with his brother; he was beside himself with jealousy. During the argument, Kantla grabbed my arm and pulled me toward him. Dem grabbed my other arm and pulled me back toward him. They were pulling me apart! I cried out, "You're going to break my arms! Help! Mother! They're going to pull my arms until they break!"

My mother heard and ran to where we were. She yelled, "What's the matter with the two of you? Have you no sense? Can't you see you'll break her arms? You're going to kill her. And she's carrying a small baby! You'll break both of them in two!" Kantla said, "All right, but Dem is a child without enough sense to know he can't have a woman as his lover who is also my lover. Is he trying to humiliate me? Why is he taking her and sitting with her? Who does he think he's doing this to? Does he think we are equals? Does he think he can share a woman with his older brother?"

Dem said, "This woman does not belong to you; she is not your wife. Both of us are stealing with her. You are having an affair with her and I am having an affair with her. You can't act as though you are her husband because Besa is the one married to her."

We all returned to the village. Soon Kantla left and Dem and I stayed there together. My arms hurt and were sore from having been pulled apart. We lived together a while longer, then I returned to my own village to live.

Besa didn't know about any of this until someone told him. He asked me, "So, you not only have Kantla, you have his younger brother as well?" I said, "Dem isn't my lover and Kantla—you knew about him from the time we married. You even knew about Tsaa. When you married me, you knew these other men had been with me before you and that they would continue to stay with me. You knew that, but you married me anyway. But Dem, he isn't my lover."

Besa was angry, "No, you . . . you aren't a woman, maybe that's what it is. Maybe you're a man, because you act like one—one lover and another and another. What kind of woman are you, acting like this? Is your mind crazy that it has you do this?" I said, "Besa, you listen to me. It's because I refuse you. I don't want you. Even when I married you, I did it only because everyone insisted I should. I was afraid to say no, so I married you. You have no right to accuse me with your jealousy. If you do, I'll just leave you. I didn't want to marry you in the beginning, and even now, only a small part of my heart goes out to you. It is not a full heart you have from me. So, just leave me alone with my lovers. And if you think someone might be my lover, tell yourself he is. Even so, what will you do?"

Then I said, "Anyway, you and Twah have been lovers for years; you even have a child with her. But I haven't said anything; I haven't been jealous. So why are you accusing me? You have your own heart with your lovers and I have my heart with my lovers. Even so, your thoughts always speak of jealousy, but mine don't."

He said, "Why do you talk like that, saying you take care of your heart while I take care of mine? When people marry . . . when I married you, your heart became mine and my heart became yours. I don't want you telling me now that your heart belongs only to you and mine, only to me. I don't understand what's making you say this."

I said, "Because I don't want it that way. I don't want my heart to be yours, or yours to be mine. If it were like that, your jealousy would become so great that you would kill me with it; you'd beat me because of it. Therefore, the way it has been, is the way it will be."

Besa was furious. He yelled, "You aren't a woman . . . you have no respect for me! You'd do anything in front of me. You act as though I am nothing you have to bother about! Yet, I don't ever hit you." I yelled, "Go ahead! Hit me! It won't make a difference."

We began to fight and it was then that I got the scar you see here, the one high up on my thigh. Besa threatened me and came at me with a knife. I grabbed it away from him and yelled, "What's making you so crazy that you want to kill me? Are you mourning for my genitals? Is that why you want to kill me?" Besa's father said, "Have you gone crazy, wanting to kill a woman? A woman has no strength; you don't kill a woman."

The blood was flowing from my wound and my leg started to swell. I was sick for days and days and then it started to get better. I said, "Besa, you almost killed me that time. I'm going back to my mother's." But he refused, "You're not going anywhere. The two of us are just going to sit beside each other right here. The way we are now sitting is the way we'll continue to sit." Even his father said, "No, you almost killed your wife, now take her back to her mother's village. How can you want to kill her and then want to be with her right after that?"

But Besa refused, and we just continued to live.

Chapter 11

Women and Men

THE POSITION OF WOMEN in !Kung society has been of great interest to anthropologists and others trying to understand the variation in women's roles and status found in the world's cultures. Despite the substantial differences in how women live and what they do, one generalization can be made: in the overwhelming majority of societies, women have a lower status than men—by their own accounts and by observation of the culture as a whole—and their activities are less highly valued than men's activities. Margaret Mead recognized this in 1949 when she wrote, "In every known society, the males' need for achievement can be recognized. Men may cook or weave or dress dolls or hunt hummingbirds, but if such activities are appropriate occupations for men, then the whole society, men and women alike, votes them important. When the same occupations are performed by women, they are regarded as less important."

In relation to this pattern, the !Kung are something of an anomaly. Here, in a society of ancient traditions, men and women live together in a nonexploitative manner, displaying a striking degree of equality between the sexes—perhaps a lesson for our own society. !Kung men, however, do seem to have the upper hand. They more often hold positions of influence—as spokespeople for the group or as healers—and their somewhat greater authority over many areas of !Kung life is acknowledged by men and women alike. A close look at this balance is not of merely academic interest. Other contemporary gathering and hunting societies have a similar high level of equality between the sexes—higher, at least, than that of most agricultural or herding societies. This observation has led to the suggestion that the relations between the sexes that prevailed during the majority of human prehistory were comparable to those seen among the !Kung today. Perhaps the extremes of subordination of women by men found in many of today's more socioeconomically "advanced" cultures are only a relatively recent aberration in our long human calendar.

!Kung women assume roles of great practical importance, both in the family and in the economy. They have maximum influence over decisions affecting their children for years, starting with birth. !Kung men are usually discouraged from being present at a birth, and women have complete control over the process, including the decision for or against infanticide. The sex of the child seems to have no influence over this decision, and the !Kung express no preference for either sex before the child's birth.

Mothers are responsible for close to 90 percent of child care, but the public nature of village life—the fact that most activities take place outside and in groups rather than behind closed doors—eases this burden and frees women for other pursuits as well. Mothers are rarely alone and children rarely lack playmates. The isolated mother burdened with bored small children is not a scene that has parallels in !Kung daily life. Older children can be left behind in the village with other adults while their mothers go gathering, so women with large families are able to make as much of an economic contribution as those with small families.

!Kung fathers have been shown to provide more care for infants and young children than fathers in many societies, even though they spend much less time in contact with children than mothers do. !Kung children seem to be very comfortable with either parent, and are frequently seen touching, sitting with, or talking with their fathers. The father is not set up as an authority whose wrath must be feared; both parents guide their children, and a father's word seems to carry about the same weight as a mother's. Children probably misbehave equally with both, but parents avoid direct confrontations and physical punishment.

The lack of privacy in !Kung life also protects women from being battered by their husbands, and children from being abused by either parent. Arguments between husbands and wives occur within sight of their neighbors. If a fight becomes physical, other people are always there and ready to intervene.

In some cultures, a mother's influence is thought to pose a threat to her son's masculinity or ability to attain full male status, and boys are separated from their mothers to counteract this feminizing influence. The !Kung, in contrast, allow both boys and girls to sleep in their parents' hut, often beside their mothers, for so many years that the child is usually the one who decides to sleep elsewhere. The only time !Kung boys are deliberately isolated from women is for a few weeks between the ages of fifteen and twenty, when they participate in Choma, the male initiation ceremony. During this intense and rigorous ritual the initiates experience hunger, cold, thirst, and the extreme fatigue that comes from continuous dancing. It takes place over a period of six weeks and is considered sacred time, when the ritual knowledge of male matters is passed from one generation to the next.

When Choma is over, however, boys resume village life as before—eating, sleeping and working amid the typical absence of segregation by sex. Village space is basically communal, and no one is denied access to any of it. Although there are certain prohibitions against women's touching men's arrows, especially while menstruating, and to engaging in sex during the height of the menstrual flow, these prohibitions do not extend to sleeping beside each other during the same time. Some men say it is bad to have sexual intercourse before a hunt, but this seems to be related as much to ideas about their own strength as to fear of being polluted by women. Also, menstruating and pregnant women and women with newborn infants are not isolated from the rest of the community as they so often are in other cultures. Thus the few taboos that do exist in !Kung life do not exclude women from the highly valued social, political, or economic life of the community. Women are not considered a threat to the ability of !Kung men to maintain their male identities and functions.

!Kung women's influence increases as their children grow older. (A barren woman is not ostracized or looked down upon, although, having missed out on a major part of life, she may be pitied.) When daughters or sons reach marriageable age, mothers play a major role in deciding whom they will marry and when. The choice of a spouse has a far-reaching impact on the family's social and economic life, and often on that of the entire group. Marriage ties together a couple's families in intimate rounds of visiting, mutual obligations, and gift exchange, and sometimes even in the establishment of permanent living arrangements. After marriage a couple is as likely to live near the wife's family as near the husband's. This fact further assures daughters the same loving treatment as sons, since both are equally likely to enhance their family's standing in the community.

Parents often arrange marriages for their daughters, usually with adult men while the girls are still in their early teens. These marriages, not surprisingly, are quite unstable. The husband may not live up to his in-laws' expectations, or he may not have the patience to wait for his wife, who may be uncooperative and rejecting, to grow up. Usually, however, it is the girl who initiates divorce in these early marriages, which are otherwise essentially unequal relationships. The man is physically larger and stronger; although the girl is protected by her family, the threat of his exercising his will or power against her—especially in sex—is always there. Later marriages are generally more equal, especially those in which the couple are close in age. (In the 20 percent of marriages in which the husband is younger than his wife, the wife's influence is often greater than his.) The control !Kung women retain over this part of their lives is a marked contrast to other cultures where girls have no choice but to comply with the wishes of their parents and husbands.

!Kung women are recognized by men and women alike as the primary economic providers of the group. They gather vegetable foods from the wild about three days a week, providing the majority of the daily diet of their families and other dependents.

Their economic activity is an autonomous undertaking. Men do not regulate women's schedules, do not tell them which foods to gather or where to go, and do not control the distribution of gathered foods. Women tell their husbands when they plan to be gone for the day, but this is as much a courtesy as a potential restraint, and it is what men usually do as well. If a husband were to forbid his wife to go, saying that there were chores to be done near the village or that they should go visiting together, she would probably listen to him. But men cannot afford to restrain their wives much, since they also depend on the women's efforts for food.

Although women occasionally gather alone, most prefer the company of others, for social reasons as well as for safety. Even the few miles between villages should preferably be traveled in groups. Fear of occasional predators, strangers, or even encounters with familiar men who might suggest romance, make solitary travel a moderately anxiety-provoking experience. If a male prerogative were in need of justification, the argument that !Kung women should have men's protection while traveling in the bush or between villages could gain a foothold. !Kung men do not exploit this possibility, however; women travel up to five miles away from camp, into the uninhabited wilderness, unprotected by men or their weapons. Loud talking creates a noisy enough progression as women advance from one gathering location to another so that large animals avoid them, and poisonous snakes are killed easily enough with digging sticks.

The only significant difference in mobility between !Kung men and women is in overnight absences. Women usually return to the village at the end of a day of gathering. If an overnight gathering trip seems necessary, the entire group will move. In contrast, while hunting, men are often away from camp for a few days at a time (although they prefer not to be). A male bias may underlie this difference, but it is not difficult to postulate more practical reasons. Success in the hunt is unpredictable, and it often takes several days to make a kill. With gathering, by contrast, one day or even part of a day is usually enough time to collect as much as can be carried home. Also, women are responsible for the care of the children, and overnight trips would involve either coping with children in an unfamiliar and perhaps dangerous area or leaving them behind in someone else's care.

As a subsistence strategy, gathering for a living is quite satisfying. It can be energetically engaged in, no matter what the size of a woman's family. The schedule is flexible, the pace is self-determined, and the work is accomplished in the company of others. Although each woman basically gathers for herself, this does not isolate her from other women. Women present choice findings to each other as offerings of good will and solidarity. The work is challenging: each expedition taps a woman's ability to discern, among the more than two hundred plants known by name and in the general tangle of vegetation, which plants are edible, which are ripe for harvesting, and which are most worthy of her efforts. It is also efficient: a day's work is usually enough to feed a family for a few days. Unlike !Kung hunters, !Kung gatherers have the solid assurance that when their families are hungry they will be able to find food—an assurance that fills them with pride. As one woman explained, "I like to gather. If I just sit, my children have nothing to eat. If I gather, my children are full." Finally, although gathering requires considerable stamina, the four days a week that women are not gathering afford them abundant time for visiting and for leisure.

When a woman returns to the village, she determines how much of her gatherings, if any, will be given away, and to whom. She sets aside piles of food for those she feels inclined to give to, and places the rest in the back of her hut or beside her family's fire. The food she and her family eat that night, the next day, and perhaps even the next, will consist primarily of the things she has brought home. From start to finish, her labor and its product remain under her own control.

Another indication of the high standing of !Kung women is their relationship to the gift-giving network called _hxaro_. All !Kung adults (and some children) are part of this network; each has a discrete number of partners with whom certain goods are exchanged. Women's participation in hxaro is basically the same as that of men, with no significant difference in the number of exchange partners or in the quality or quantity of exchanges.

In addition, core membership in a band, as well as "ownership" of water holes and other resources, is inherited through women as well as men. No male prerogative can be exercised in relation to this important source of influence in !Kung society.

This picture of !Kung women's lives might seem to challenge Margaret Mead's observation about the universality of the male bias. Unfortunately, though, the !Kung are not the exception they at first appear to be. !Kung women do have a formidable degree of autonomy, but !Kung men enjoy certain distinct advantages—in the way the culture values their activities, both economic and spiritual, and in their somewhat greater influence over decisions affecting the life of the group.

Meat, the economic contribution of men, is considered more valuable than gathered foods. Most gathered foods, except the mongongo nut, are described as "things comparable to nothing," while meat is so highly valued that it is often used as a synonym for "food." Squeals of delighted children may greet women as they return from gathering, but when men walk into the village balancing meat on sticks held high on their shoulders, everyone celebrates, young and old alike. It may even precipitate a trance dance. The one thing women can bring in that causes a comparable reaction is honey, but the finding of honey is a much rarer event and one that men are usually enlisted to help with. !Kung women may control the distribution of their gathered products, but the distribution of meat, while more constrained by formal rules, involves men in a wider sphere of influence.

!Kung men also provide women with their basic gathering kit and other implements: tanned skins to make carrying devices (infant slings, karosses, clothing, and pouches), digging sticks, mortars and pestles, sinew for mending and for stringing and sewing beads and ornaments, and shoes. These items are durable, however, and women assume their maintenance and upkeep. In contrast, women provide none of the articles associated with hunting. In fact, the opposite is true: women are prohibited from handling hunting equipment and from participating in the hunt, especially during menstruation—although this taboo seems to have few practical consequences.

The economic picture becomes more complex when hunting and gathering activities are looked at more closely. Animal

protein is not brought into the village only by men. Women collect lizards, snakes, tortoises' and birds' eggs, and insects and caterpillars, as well as occasional small or immature mammals.
They also provide men with crucial information on animal tracks
and animal movement that they observe while they travel in the
bush. But !Kung women cannot be considered hunters in any serious way. The one prominent exception I heard about was a
middle-aged woman who allegedly craved meat so intensely and
was so tired of complaining that her husband was lazy that she
decided to go out and hunt for herself. I was, unfortunately,
never able to meet her. Those who knew her (including men)
said that she was a fairly proficient hunter, but it was clear that
she was considered eccentric and was in no way seen as a model
for other women to emulate. She earned far less respect for her
accomplishments than a man would have, as was evident from
the snickering that accompanied discussions about her. No one
actually said that what she was doing was wrong, but it was repeatedly pointed out that she was the *only* one. She was, however, considered accountable for her actions primarily in relation
to herself, rather than in relation to her husband; her behavior
was not seen as emphasizing his shortcomings or publicly emas-
culating him. This would probably not have been the case in
many other societies, including our own.

!Kung men have an easier relationship to gathering than
!Kung women have to hunting. No social prohibitions comparable to the taboo against menstruating women's touching arrows
implicate men as a negative influence on the success of women
gatherers; nor are men's efforts at gathering seen as unusual, out
of character, or even worthy of comment. (This is in contrast to
many cultures in which men feel ashamed of performing tasks
usually associated with women.) Men's knowledge about plants
is comparable to that of women, and gathering is something men
do whenever they want to. Men can account for as much as 20
percent of all foods gathered.

The male prerogative is more clearly exhibited in !Kung spiritual life, the central expression of which is the traditional medicine dance (described in Chapter 13), in which healers tap their

healing power by entering trance. Most healers are men. An occasional woman has mastered the art of healing, especially in the context of the women's drum dance, but women most often use their healing skill in response to the need of a close family member and not in a ritual setting. The status and respect that go with being a healer are, therefore, only minimally available to women; unquestionably, men have traditionally dominated this realm of !Kung life.

Perhaps the most crucial aspect of the balance of power is the process of leadership and decisionmaking. Determining how the !Kung actually make important decisions is quite difficult. With no formal leaders or hierarchies, and no political or legal institutions to convey authority, decisions are made on the basis of group consensus Each group has individuals whose opinions carry more weight than those of others—because of age, of having ancestors who have lived in the area longer, or of personal attributes such as intelligence, knowledge, or charisma. These people tend to be more prominent in group discussions, to make their opinions known and their suggestions clear, and to articulate the consensus once it is determined. Despite their lack of formal authority, they function very much as group leaders.

!Kung men occupy these positions more frequently than women do, although older women, especially those with large extended families, occasionally assume such roles. Men are also generally more vocal in group discussions. As contact with other cultures increases, and as the demand for spokespeople to represent the group thus intensifies, !Kung men are stepping forward more prominently. They are the ones who learn foreign languages, who attend government meetings, and who speak out on behalf of the regional !Kung communities.

Further evidence of male bias can be found: it is men who initiate sex, for example, and male initiation rites are secret while female initiation rites are public. !Kung women themselves refer to, and do not seem to reject, male dominance. The fact that this bias exists is important and should not be minimized—but it should also not be exaggerated.

!Kung culture downplays many of the attitudes that encourage male dominance in other societies. Competition, ranking of individuals, boastfulness, and self-aggrandizement are all discouraged. Formalized aggression of any kind—in most cultures the province of men—is absent, and preparations for fighting do not occupy men's time or boys' education. Wealth differentials are also minimized, by sharing food and possessions and by giving presents. The division of labor by sex is not rigidly defined. Village life is so intimate that a division between domestic and public life—an apt distinction for many other cultures—is largely meaningless for the !Kung, a fact that helps to promote sexual equality.

All in all, !Kung women maintain a status that is higher than that of women in many agricultural and industrial societies around the world. They exercise a striking degree of autonomy and of influence over their own and their children's lives. Brought up to respect their own importance in community life, !Kung women become multifaceted adults, and are likely to be competent and assertive as well as nurturant and cooperative.

AFTER BESA and I had lived together for a long time, he went to visit some people in the East. While there, he found work with a Tswana cattle herder. When he came back, he told me to pack; he wanted me to go and live with him there. So we left and took the long trip to Old Debe's village, a Zhun/twa village near a Tswana and European settlement. We lived there together for a long time.[1]

While we were there, my father died. My older brother, my younger brother, and my mother were with him when he died, but I wasn't; I was living where Besa had taken me. Others carried the news to me. They said that Dau had tried to cure my father, laying on hands and working hard to make him better. But God refused and Dau wasn't able to see what was causing the illness so he could heal him. Dau said, "God is refusing to give up my father."

I heard and said, "Eh, then today I'm going to see where he died." Besa and I and my children, along with a few others, left to take the long journey west. We walked the first day and slept that night. The next morning we started out and slept again that night; we slept another night on the road, as well. As we walked, I cried and thought, "Why couldn't I have been with him when he died?" I cried as we walked, one day and the next and the next.

The sun was so hot, it was burning; it was killing us. One day we rested such a long time, I thought, "Is the sun going to stop me from seeing where my father died?" When it was cooler, we started walking again and slept on the road again that night.

We arrived at the village late in the afternoon. My younger brother, Kumsa, was the first to see us. When he saw me, he came and hugged me. We started to cry and cried together for a long time. Finally, our older brother stopped us, "That's enough for now. Your tears won't make our father alive again."

We stopped crying and we all sat down. My mother was also with us. Although my father never took her back again after the time she ran away with her lover, she returned

247

and lived near him until he died. And even though she slept alone, she still loved him.

Later, my mother and I sat together and cried together.

We stayed there for a while, then Besa and I went back again to live in the East where he had been working for the Europeans. A very long time passed. Then, my brother sent word that my mother was dying. Once again we made the journey to my family and when we arrived I saw her: she was still alive.

We stayed there and lived there. One day, a group of people were going to the bush to live. I said, "Mother, come with us. I'll take care of you and you can help me with my children." We traveled that day and slept that night; we traveled another day and slept another night. But the next night, the sickness that had been inside her grabbed her again and this time, held on. It was just as it had been with my father. The next day, she coughed up blood. I thought, "Oh, why is blood coming out like that? Is this what is going to kill her? Is this the way she's going to die? What is this sickness going to do? She's coughing blood ... she's already dead!" Then I thought, "If only Dau were here, he would be able to cure her. He would trance for her every day." But he and my younger brother had stayed behind. Besa was with us, but he didn't have the power to cure people. There were others with us as well, but they didn't help.

We slept again that night. The next morning, the others left, as is our custom, and then it was only me, my children, my husband, and my mother; we were the only ones who remained. But her life was really over by then, even though she was still alive.

I went to get her some water and when I came back, she said, "Nisa ... Nisa ... I am an old person and today, my heart ... today you and I will stay together for a while longer; we will continue to sit beside each other. But later, when the sun stands over there in the afternoon sky and when the new slim moon first strikes, I will leave you. We will separate then and I will go away."

I asked, "Mother, what are you saying?" She said, "Yes, that's what I'm saying. I am an old person. Don't deceive yourself; I am dying. When the sun moves to that spot in the sky, that will be our final separation. We will no longer be together after that. So, take good care of your children."

I said, "Why are you talking like this? If you die as you say, because that's what you're telling me, who are you going to leave in your place?" She said, "Yes, I am leaving you. Your husband will take care of you now. Besa will be with you and your children."

We remained together the rest of the day as the sun crawled slowly across the sky. When it reached the spot she had spoken of, she said—just like a person in good health— "Mm, now ... be well, all of you," and then she died.

That night I slept alone and cried and cried and cried. None of my family was with me[2] and I just cried the entire night. When morning came, Besa dug a grave and buried her. I said, "Let's pull our things together and go back to the village. I want to tell Dau and Kumsa that our mother has died."

We walked that day and slept that night. We walked the next day and stopped again that night. The next morning, we met my brother Kumsa. Someone had told him that his mother was sick. When he heard, he took his bow and quiver and came looking for us. He left when the sun just rose and started walking toward us, even as we were walking toward him. We met when the sun was overhead. He stood and looked at me. Then he said, "Here you are, Nisa, with your son and your daughter and your husband. But Mother isn't with you ..."

I sat down and started to cry. He said, "Mother must have died because you're crying like this," and he started to cry, too. Besa said, "Yes, your sister left your mother behind. Two days ago was when your mother and sister separated. That is where we are coming from now. Your sister is here and will tell you about it. You will be together to share your mourning for your mother. That will be good."

We stayed there and cried and cried. Later, Kumsa took

my little son and carried him on his shoulders. I carried my daughter and we walked until we arrived back at the village. My older brother came with his wife, and when he saw us he, too, started to cry.

After that, we lived together for a while. I lived and cried, lived and cried. My mother had been so beautiful . . . her face, so lovely. When she died, she caused me great pain. Only after a long time was I quiet again.

Before we returned to the East, I went with Besa to visit his family. While I was there, I became very sick. It came from having carried my mother. Because when she was sick, I carried her around on my back. After she died, my back started to hurt in the very place I had carried her. One of God's spiritual arrows must have struck me there and found its way into my chest.

I was sick for a long time and then blood started to come out of my mouth. My younger brother (he really loves me!) was visiting me at the time. When he saw how I was, he left to tell his older brother, "Nisa's dying the same way our mother died. I've come to tell you to come back with me and heal her." My older brother listened and the two of them traveled to where I was. They came when the sun was high in the afternoon sky. Dau started to trance for me. He laid on hands, healing me with his touch. He worked on me for a long time. Soon, I was able to sleep; then, the blood stopped coming from my chest and later, even if I coughed, there wasn't any more blood.

We stayed there for a few more days. Then, Dau said, "Now I'm going to take Nisa with me to my village." Besa agreed and we all left together. We stayed at my brother's village until I was completely better.

Besa and I eventually moved back East again. But after we had lived together for a long time, we no longer were getting along. One day I asked, "Besa, won't you take me back to my family's village so I can live there?" He said, "I'm no longer interested in you." I said, "What's wrong? Why do you feel that way?" But then I said, "Eh, if that's how it is, it doesn't matter."

I was working for a European woman at the time, and when I told her what Besa was saying to me, she told him, "Listen to me. You're going to chase your wife away. If you continue to speak to her like this, she'll be gone. Today, I'm pregnant. Why don't you just let her be and have her sit beside you. When I give birth, she will work for me and help me with the baby."

That's what we did. We continued to live together until she gave birth. After, I helped wash the baby's clothes and helped with other chores. I worked for her for a long time.

One day, Besa broke into a little box I had and stole the money she had paid me with. He took it and went to drink beer. I went to the European woman and told her Besa had taken five Rand[3] from me and had left with it. I asked her to help me get it back. We went to the Tswana hut where everyone was drinking and went to the door. The European woman walked in, kicked over a bucket and the beer spilled out. She kicked over another and another and the beer was spilling everywhere. The Tswanas left. She turned to Besa and said, "Why are you treating this young Zhun/twa woman like this? Stop treating her this way." She told him to give her the money and when he gave it to her, she gave it to me. I went and put the money in the box, then took it and left it in her kitchen where it stayed.

Later Besa said, "Why did you tell on me? I'm going to beat you." I said, "Go ahead. Hit me. I don't care. I won't stop you."

Soon after that, I became pregnant with Besa's child. But when it was still very tiny, when I was still carrying it way inside, he left me. I don't know what it was that made him want to leave. Did he have a lover? I don't know. He said he was afraid of a sore I had on my face where a bug had bitten me. It had become swollen, and eventually the Europeans helped to heal it. Whatever it was, his heart had changed toward me and although my heart still liked him, he only liked me a very little then. That's why he left.

It happened the day he finished working for the Europeans. He came back when the sun was low in the sky and said, "Tomorrow, I'm going to visit my younger brother. I have finished my work and have been paid. I'm going, but you'll stay here. Later, Old Debe and his wife can take you back to your brothers' village." I said, "If you are leaving, won't I go with you?" He said, "No, you won't go with me." I said, "Why are you saying you'll go without me? If I go with you and give birth there, it will be good. Don't leave me here. Let me go with you and give birth in your brother's village." But he said, "No, Old Debe will bring you back to your family."

When I saw Old Debe, he asked me what was wrong. I said, "What is Besa doing to me? If he doesn't want me, why doesn't he just end it completely? I've seen for a long time that he doesn't want me." I thought, "Besa ... he took me to this faraway village, got me pregnant, and now, is he just going to drop me in this foreign place where none of my people live?"

Later, I said to Besa, "Why did you take me from my people? My brothers are still alive, yet you won't take me to them. You say someone else will. But, why should someone else, a near stranger, take me to my family after you've given me this stomach. I say you should take me to them, take me there and say, 'Here is your sister. Today I am separating from her.' Instead, you're saying you'll just leave me here, with these strangers? I followed you here, to where you were working, because you wanted me to. Now you're just going to leave me? Why are you doing this? Can there be any good in it?"

I continued, "You're the one who came here to work. Yet, you have no money and have no blankets. But when you had no more work and no more money, I worked. I alone, a woman. I entered the work of the European and I alone bought us blankets and a trunk. I alone bought all those things and you covered yourself with my blankets. When you weren't working, you asked people to give you things. How can you leave me here in this foreign place after all that?" He answered, "What work could I have done when there wasn't any to be had?"

I said, "It doesn't matter, because I can see that you will only be here for a few more nights, then you will go. I know that now. But, if you leave me like this today, then tomorrow, after you have gone and have lived with your brother, if you ever decide to come to where I am living, I will refuse you and will no longer be your wife. Because you are leaving me when I am pregnant."

The next morning, early, he tied up his things and left. He packed everything from inside the hut, including all our blankets, and went to his brother's village to live. I thought, "Eh, it doesn't matter, after all. I'll just sit here and let him go." He left me with nothing; the people in the village had to give me blankets to sleep with.

Besa, that man is very bad. He left me hanging like that.

Once he left, I saw that I would be staying there for a while. I thought, "Today I'm no longer going to refuse other men, but will just be with them. Then, maybe I will miscarry. Because this is Besa's child and didn't he leave it and go? I won't refuse other men and will just have them. I will drop this pregnancy; then I will go home."

That's when Numshe entered the hut with me. He spoke to me and I agreed. People said, "Yes, she will enter the hut with him. But when he tastes her,[4] the pregnancy will be ruined." Old Debe's wife said, "That won't be so bad. If her pregnancy is ruined, it won't be a bad thing. Because Besa dropped her. Therefore, I will sit here and take care of her. Later, I will bring her to her family."

I lived there for a long time. I lived alone and worked for the Europeans. Then one day, just as my heart had said, my body felt like fire and my stomach was in great pain. I told Old Debe's wife, "Eh-hey, today I'm sick." She asked, "Where does it hurt? Do you want some water? Where is the sickness hurting you." I said, "My whole body hurts, it isn't just my stomach." I lay there and felt the pains, rising again and again and again. I thought, "That man certainly has made me feel bad; even today, I'm lying here in great pain."

She looked at my stomach and saw how it was standing out. She said, "Oh, my child. Are you going to drop your pregnancy? What is going to happen? Will you be able to give birth to this child or will it be a miscarriage? Here, there are just the two of us; I don't see anyone who will bring more help to you. If you miscarry, it will be only us two." I said, "Yes, that's fine. If I drop this pregnancy, it will be good. I want to drop it, then I can leave. Because my husband certainly doesn't want it."

We stayed together all day. When the sun was late in the sky, I told her it was time and we went together to the bush. I sat down and soon the baby was born. It was already big, with a head and arms and a little penis; but it was born dead. Perhaps my heart had ruined my pregnancy. I cried, "This man almost ruined me, did he not?" Debe's wife said, "Yes, he destroyed this baby, this baby which came from God. But if God hadn't been here helping you, you also would have died. Because when a child dies in a woman's stomach, it can kill the woman. But God . . . God gave you something beautiful in giving you this baby and although it had death in it, you yourself are alive." We left and walked back to the village. Then I lay down.

After that, I just continued to live there. One day I saw people visiting from Besa's village. I told them to tell him that our marriage had ended. I said, "Tell him that he shouldn't think, even with a part of his heart, that he still has a wife here or that when we meet another time in my village that he might still want me." That's what I said and that's what I thought.

Because he left me there to die.

Soon after, a man named Twi saw me and said, "Did your husband leave you?" I said, "Yes, he left me long ago." He asked, "Then won't you stay with me?" I refused the first time he asked as well as the second and the third. But when

he asked the next time, I agreed and we started to live together. I continued to work for the European woman until my
work was finished and she told me I could go home. She
gave us food for our trip and then all of us—Old Debe, his
wife, Twi, and me—traveled the long distance back to where
my family was living.

Twi and I lived together in my brothers' village for a long
time. Then, one day, Besa came from wherever he had been
and said, "Nisa, I've come to take you back with me." I said,
"What? What am I like today? Did I suddenly become beautiful? The way I used to be is the way I am now; the way I
used to be is what you left behind when you dropped me. So
what are you saying? First you drop me in the heart of where
the white people live, then you come back and say I should
once again be with you?" He said, "Yes, we will pick up our
marriage again."

I was stunned! I said, "What are you talking about? This
man, Twi, helped bring me back. He's the man who will
marry me. You're the one who left me." We talked until he
could say nothing more; he was humbled. Finally he said,
"You're shit! That's what you are." I said, "I'm shit you say?
That's what you thought about me long ago, and I knew it.
That's why I told you while we were still living in the East
that I wanted you to take me back to my family so we could
end our marriage here. But today, I came here myself and you
only came afterward. Now I refuse to have anything more to
do with you."

That's when Besa brought us to the Tswana headman to
ask for a tribal hearing. Once it started, the headman looked
at everything. He asked me, "Among all the women who live
here, among all those you see sitting around, do you see one
who lives with two men?" I said, "No, the women who sit
here . . . not one lives with two men; not one among them
would I be able to find. I, alone, have two. But it was because this man, Besa, mistreated and hurt me. That's why I
took this other man, Twi, who treats me well, who does
things for me and gives me things to eat." Then I said, "He is
also the man I want to marry; I want to drop the other one.

255

Because Besa has no sense. He left me while I was pregnant and the pregnancy almost killed me. This other one is the one I want to marry."

We talked a long time. Finally, the headman told Besa, "I have questioned Nisa about what happened and she has tied you up with her talk; her talk has defeated you, without doubt. Because what she has said about her pregnancy is serious. Therefore, today she and Twi will continue to stay together. After more time passes, I will ask all of you to come back again." Later, Twi and I left and went back to my brothers' village to sleep.

The next day, my older brother saw a honey cache while walking in the bush. He came to tell us and take us back there with him; we planned to stay the night in the bush. We arrived and spent the rest of the day collecting honey. When we finished, we walked toward where we were planning to camp. That's when I saw Besa's tracks in the sand. I said, "Everyone! Come here! Besa's tracks are here! Has anyone seen them elsewhere?" One of the men said, "Nonsense! Would you know his tracks ..." I interrupted, "My husband ... the man who married me ... I _know_ his tracks." The man's wife came to look, "Yes, those are Besa's tracks; his wife really did see them.

The next morning, Besa walked into the camp. Besa and Twi started to fight. My older brother yelled, "Do you two want to kill Nisa? Today she is not taking another husband. Today she's just going to lie by herself." I agreed, "Eh, I don't want to marry again now."

Twi and I continued to live together after that. But later we separated. My older brother caused it, because he wanted Besa to be with me again. He liked him and didn't like Twi. That's why he forced Twi to leave. When Twi saw how much anger both Dau and Besa felt toward him, he became afraid, and finally he left.

I saw what my brother had done and was miserable; I had really liked Twi. I said, "So, this is what you wanted? Fine, but now that you have chased Twi away, I'll have nothing at all to do with Besa." That's when I began to refuse

Besa completely. Besa went to the headman and said, "Nisa refuses to be with me." The headman said, "Nisa's been refusing you for a long time. What legal grounds could I possibly find for you now?"

After more time passed, a man who had been my lover years before, started with me again. Soon we were very much in love. He was so handsome! His nose . . . his eyes . . . everything was so beautiful! His skin was light and his nose was lovely. I really loved that man, even when I first saw him.

We lived together for a while, but then he died. I was miserable, "My lover has died. Where am I going to find another like him—another as beautiful, another as good, another with a European nose and with such lovely light skin? Now he's dead. Where will I ever find another like him?"

My heart was miserable and I mourned for him. I exhausted myself with mourning and only when it was finished did I feel better again.

After years of living and having everything that happened to me happen, that's when I started with Bo, the next important man in my life and the one I am married to today.

Besa and I lived separately, but he still wanted me and stayed near me. That man, he didn't hear; he didn't understand. He was without ears, because he still said, "This woman here, Nisa, I won't be finished with her."

People told Bo, "You're going to die. This man, Besa, he's going to kill you. Now, leave Nisa." But Bo refused, "Me . . . I won't go to another hut. I'll just stay with Nisa and even if Besa tries to kill me, I'll still be here and won't leave."

At first, Bo and I sneaked off together, but Besa suspected us; he was very jealous. He accused me all the time. Even when I just went to urinate, he'd say that I had been with Bo. Or when I went for water, he'd say, "Did you just meet your lover?" But I'd say, "What makes you think you can talk to me like that?" He'd say, "Nisa, are you not still my wife? Why aren't we living together? What are you doing?" I'd say, "Don't you have other women or are they refusing you, too? You have others so why are you asking me about what I'm doing?"

One night, Bo and I were lying down inside my hut and as I looked out through the latched-branch door, I saw someone moving about. It was Besa; I was able to see his face. He wanted to catch us, hoping I would feel some remorse and perhaps return to him.

I said, "What? Besa's here! Bo ... Bo ... Besa's standing out there." Bo got up; Besa came and stood by the door. I got up and that's when Besa came in and grabbed me. He held onto me and threatened to throw me into the fire. I cursed him as he held me, "Besa-Big-Testicles! Long-Penis! First you left me and drank of women's genitals elsewhere. Now you come back, see me, and say I am your wife?" He pushed me toward the fire, but I twisted my body so I didn't land in it. Then he went after Bo. Bo is weaker and older than Besa, so Besa was able to grab him, pull him outside the hut, and throw him down. He bit him on the shoulder. Bo yelled out in pain.

My younger brother woke and ran to us, yelling, "Curses to your genitals!" He grabbed them and separated them. Bo cursed Besa. Besa cursed Bo, "Curses on your penis!" He yelled, "I'm going to kill you Bo, then Nisa will suffer! If I don't kill you, then maybe I'll kill her so that you will feel pain! Because what you have that is so full of pleasure, I also have. So why does her heart want you and refuse me?"

I yelled at him, "That's not it! It's you! It's who you are and the way you think! This one, Bo, his ways are good and his thoughts are good. But you, your ways are foul. Look, you just bit Bo; that, too, is part of your ways. You also left me to die. And death, that's something I'm afraid of. That's why you no longer have a hold over me. Today I have another who will take care of me well. I'm no longer married to you, Besa. I want my husband to be Bo."

Besa kept bothering me and hanging around me. He'd ask, "Why won't you come to me? Come to me, I'm a man. Why are you afraid of me?" I wouldn't answer. Once Bo answered, "I don't understand why, if you *are* a man, you keep pestering this woman? Is what you're doing going to do any good? Because I won't leave her. And even though you bit me and your marks are on me, you're the one who is going to move out of the way, not me. I intend to marry her."

Another time I told Bo, "Don't be afraid of Besa. You and I will marry; I'm not going to stay married to him. Don't let him frighten you. Because even if he comes here with arrows, he won't do anything with them." Bo said, "Even if he did, what good would that do? I am also a man and am a master of arrows. The two of us would just strike each other. That's why I keep telling him to let you go; I am the man you are with now."

The next time, Besa came with his quiver full of arrows, saying, "I'm going to get Nisa and bring her back with me." He left with another man and came to me at my village. When he arrived, the sun was high in the sky. I was resting. He said, "Nisa, come, let's go." I said, "What? Is your penis not well? Is it horny?"

People heard us fighting and soon everyone was there, my younger and older brothers as well. Besa and I kept arguing and fighting until, in a rage, I screamed, "All right! Today I'm no longer afraid!" and I pulled off all the skins that were covering me—first one, then another, and finally the leather apron that covered my genitals. I pulled them all off and laid them down on the ground. I cried, "There! There's my vagina! Look, Besa, look at me! This is what you want!"

The man he had come with said, "This woman, her heart is truly far from you. Besa, look. Nisa refuses you totally, with all her heart. She refuses to have sex with you. Your relationship with her is finished. See. She took off her clothes, put them down, and with her genitals is showing everyone how she feels about you. She doesn't want you, Besa. If I were you, I'd finish with her today." Besa finally said, "Eh, you're right. Now I am finished with her."

The two of them left. I took my leather apron, put it on, took the rest of my things and put them on.

Mother! That was just what I did.

Besa tried one last time. He went to the headman again,

and when he came back he told me, "The headman wants to see you." I thought, "If he wants to see me, I won't refuse."

When I arrived, the headman said, "Besa says he still wants to continue your marriage." I said, "Continue our marriage? Why? Am I so stupid that I don't know my name? Would I stay in a marriage with a man who left me hanging in a foreign place? If Old Debe and his wife hadn't been there, I would have truly lost my way. Me, stay married to Besa? I can't make myself think of it."

I turned to Besa, "Isn't that what I told you when we were still in the East?" Besa said, "Mm, that's what you said." I said, "And, when you left, didn't I tell you that you were leaving me pregnant with your baby. Didn't I also tell you that?" He said, "Yes, that's what you said." I said, "And didn't I say that I wanted to go with you, that I wanted you to help make our pregnancy grow strong? Didn't I say that and didn't you refuse?" He said, "Yes, you said that." Then I said, "Mm. Therefore, that marriage you say today, in the lap of the headman, should be continued, that marriage no longer exists. Because I am Nisa and today, when I look at you, all I want to do is to throw up. Vomit is the only thing left in my heart for you now. As we sit together here and I see your face, that is all that rises within and grabs me."

The headman laughed, shook his head and said, "Nisa is impossible!" Then he said, "Besa, you had better listen to her. Do you hear what she is saying? She says that you left her while she was pregnant, that she miscarried and was miserable. Today she will no longer take you for her husband." Besa said, "That's because she's with Bo now and doesn't want to leave him. But I still want her and want to continue our marriage."

I said, "What? Besa, can't you see me? Can't you see that I have really found another man? Did you think, perhaps, that I was too old and wouldn't find someone else?" The headman laughed again. "Yes, I am a woman. And that which you have, a penis, I also have something of equal worth. Like the penis of a chief . . . yes, something of a chief is what I have. And its worth is like money. Therefore, the person who drinks from it ... it's like he's getting money from me. But not you, because when you had it, you just left it to ruin."

The headman said, "Nisa is crazy; her talk is truly crazy now." Then he said, "The two of you sleep tonight and give your thoughts over to this. Nisa, think about all of it again. Tomorrow, I want both of you to come back."

Besa went and lay down. I went and lay down and thought about everything. In the morning, I went to the headman. I felt ashamed by my talk of the night before. I sat there quietly. The headman said, "Nisa, Besa says you should stay married to him." I answered, "Why should he stay married to me when yesterday I held his baby in my stomach and he dropped me. Even God doesn't want me to marry a man who leaves me, a man who takes my blankets when I have small children beside me, a man who forces other people to give me blankets to cover my children with. Tell him to find another woman to marry."

The headman turned to Besa, "Nisa has explained herself. There's nothing more I can see to say. Even you, you can hear that she has defeated you. So, leave Nisa and as I am headman, today your marriage to her is ended. She can now marry Bo."[5]

Besa went to the headman one more time. When he tried to discuss it again, saying, "Please, help me. Give Nisa back to me," the headman said, "Haven't you already talked to me about this? You talked and talked, and the words entered my ears. Are you saying that I have not already decided on this? That I am not an important person? That I am a worthless thing that you do not have to listen to? There is no reason to give Nisa back to you."

I was so thankful when I heard his words. My heart filled with happiness.

Bo and I married soon after that.[6] We lived together, sat together, and did things together. Our hearts loved each other very much and our marriage was very very strong.

Besa also married again not long after—this time to a woman much younger than me. One day he came to me and said, "Look how wrong you were to have refused me! Perhaps you thought you were the only woman. But you, Nisa, today you are old and you yourself can see that I have married a young woman, one who is beautiful!"

I said, "Good! I told you that if we separated, you'd find a young woman to marry and to sleep with. That is fine with me because there is nothing I want from you. But you know, of course, that just like me, another day she too will be old."

We lived on, but not long after, Besa came back. He said that his young wife was troubled and that he wanted me again. I refused and even told Bo about it. Bo asked me why I refused. I said, "Because I don't want him." But what he says about his wife is true. She has a terrible sickness, a type of madness. God gave it to her. She was such a beautiful woman, too. But no longer. I wonder why such a young woman has to have something like that . . .

Even today, whenever Besa sees me, he argues with me and says he still wants me. I say, "Look, we've separated. Now leave me alone." I even sometimes refuse him food. Bo tells me I shouldn't refuse, but I'm afraid he will bother me more if I give anything to him. Because his heart still cries for me.

Sometimes I do give him things to eat and he also gives things to me. Once I saw him in my village. He came over to me and said, "Nisa, give me some water to drink." I washed out a cup and poured him some water. He drank it and said, "Now, give me some tobacco." I took out some tobacco and gave it to him. Then he said, "Nisa, you really are adult; you know how to work. Today, I am married to a woman but my heart doesn't agree to her much. But you . . . you are one who makes me feel pain. Because you left me and married another man. I also married, but have made myself weary by having married something bad. You, you have hands that work and do things. With you, I could eat. You would get water for me to wash with. Today, I'm really in pain."

I said, "Why are you thinking about our dead marriage? Of course, we were married once, but we have gone our different ways. Now, I no longer want you. After all that happened when you took me East—living there, working there, my father dying, my mother dying, and all the misery you caused me—you say we should live together once again?"

He said that I wasn't telling it as it happened.

One day, he told me he wanted to take me from Bo. I said, "What? Tell me, Besa, what has been talking to you that you are saying this again?" He said, "All right, then have me as your lover. Won't you help my heart out?" I said, "Aren't there many men who could be my lover? Why should I agree to you?" He said, "Look here, Nisa ... I'm a person who helped bring up your children, the children you and your husband gave birth to. You became pregnant again with my child and that was good. You held it inside you and lived with it until God came and killed it. That's why your heart is talking this way and refusing me."

I told him he was wrong. But he was right, too. Because, after Besa, I never had any more children. He took that away from me. With Tashay, I had children, but Besa, he ruined me. Even the one time I did conceive, I miscarried. That's because of what he did to me; that's what everyone says

Chapter 12
Taking Lovers

WHEN THE GODS GAVE PEOPLE SEX, say the !Kung, they gave us a wonderful thing. Sex is often referred to as food: just as people cannot survive without eating, the !Kung say, hunger for sex can cause people to die. For a population whose food resources are unpredictable and of constant concern, this analogy is significant indeed.

Talk about sex seems to be of almost equal importance. When women are in the village or out gathering, or when men and women are together, they spend hours recounting details of sexual exploits. Joking about all aspects of sexual experience is commonplace except between people who maintain "respect" relationships and are forbidden to make sexual references in each other's presence. Those in "joking" relationships often exchange uproariously funny insults referring to each other's genitals or sexual behavior: "Your penis is huge!" "Your testicles hang down to your knees and smell!" "Your labia are long, dark, and ugly!" "Screw sand!" "Ejaculate on yourself!" (Most sexual expressions can be employed both in jokes and when serious insults are intended; the context determines how they are received.) Descriptive gestures are likely to accompany insults made in jest. Some exchanges even attract an enthusiastic audience. Onlookers cheer as men pretend to grab each other's testicles and throw them into the air, to be left hanging in the trees. Lurid details of what vultures or other creatures will do to them become part of the general entertainment.

The !Kung sometimes use sexual joking in a deliberate way to dispel tension. While I was in the field, a man was trying to rout a spitting cobra from the grass thatching of a hut. He apparently came too close, and the snake shot venom into his eyes. Water was brought to wash out the poison; then there was nothing to do but wait until his vision, which had become blurred, would return. During the next half-hour, while everyone sat and watched, two men began describing the incident in an especially graphic and dramatic way, to distract the man and to help keep up his spirits. Telling and retelling the story, their hand gestures became exaggerated and increasingly suggestive. The last depictions of the snake rising up and spitting were blatantly (and hilariously) pornographic. Laughter started to sweep through the group. The injured man, still nursing his eyes, was unable to resist the energy of the moment and joined in. As others followed, the remaining tension dissolved in the high-spirited, infectious repartee. (A few days later the man's vision had returned almost to normal.)

Not everything about sex, of course, is amenable to light talking and joking. Sex is also recognized as tapping some of the most intense and potentially explosive of human emotions—especially where extramarital attractions are concerned. In such cases, sex is considered outright dangerous: many affairs that become known lead to violence, which, in the past, sometimes resulted in death. Except for those who intend to goad their spouses, therefore, people who participate in such relationships are extremely careful and discreet.

Love exists in !Kung marriages and is expressed in a variety of ways: couples make a point of going off alone to gather and hunt, sometimes for days at a time; make presents for one another; and assist in each other's daily chores. Women readily acknowledge their intense emotional involvements with their husbands. Nevertheless, quite early on in marriage, many women start having lovers. Affairs are often long-term, from a few months to a few years, and some continue throughout a lifetime.

There is some question as to whether extramarital relationships were common in traditional !Kung life, or whether the phe-

nomenon results from the influence of Herero and Tswana settlements. Considerable disagreement exists on this question
even among the !Kung. But infidelity is frequent in !Kung oral
history and myth, and it was acknowledged and talked about in
the early 1950s when the Marshall family studied a group of traditional !Kung living in Nyae Nyae, thirty miles west of Dobe. It
is therefore not likely to be of recent origin.

The best insurance against complications arising from love
affairs is not to be found out. Great care must be taken to arrange
meetings at safe times and places, away from the eyes of others.
First-person testimony from those who "see with their own eyes"
is taken very seriously, but those who know may choose to remain silent. Those who tell what they know may become central
figures in fights that ensue; they may even be held partially responsible for the outcome.

It is also important to maintain some emotional restraint in
relation to a lover. One's spouse must always come first, no matter how romantic and exciting an affair may be. The slightest indication of infidelity—the rejection of a husband's sexual advances, being unusually argumentative or angry, or spending too
much time away from the village—can easily provoke angry accusations and jealousy. But controlling these feelings can be difficult, especially when a new lover becomes a central preoccupation (at least temporarily). In rare instances, long-term marriages
are actually terminated when feelings between lovers become
very strong. At other times (also rare), it is because the woman is
pregnant: if the husband has been away, it is clear who the father
is. In such cases, the lovers may try to dissolve their prior relationships and marry each other. Even if violence does not occur,
the emotional cost for everyone involved makes this situation
decidedly not preferred.

To succeed at and to benefit from extramarital affairs, one
must accept that one's feelings for one's husband—"the important one," "the one from inside the hut"—and for one's lover—
"the little one," "the one from the bush"—are necessarily different. One is rich, warm and secure. The other is passionate and
exciting, although often fleeting and undependable. Some !Kung
women (and men) think it ideal to have both. The appeal of affairs, they say, is not merely sexual; secret glances, stolen kisses,

and brief encounters make for a more complex enticement. Often described as thrilling adventures, these relationships are one of the subjects women spend much time discussing among themselves.

Partly because of the lack of privacy in !Kung life, actual extramarital sexual encounters seem to be infrequent. Also, not all !Kung adults have affairs: some are deterred by the danger of discovery, others by fear of venereal disease, which is recent in the area.

For others, however, love affairs have great appeal. I talked with a young man who was the lover of a woman I had been interviewing. It took place a few days after the lovers had exchanged gifts—a candid acknowledgment of their bond—in my presence.

There was little activity in the camp that day until late afternoon, when squeals and shouts of excitement brought me out of my hut. A young couple, recently married, were playing chase, running after each other. As I stood watching, I noticed the young man sitting in the shade of a tree, also watching. I said, "They're very much in love, aren't they?" He answered, "Yes, they are." After a pause, he added, "For now." I asked him to explain, and he said, "When two people are first together, their hearts are on fire and their passion is very great. After a while, the fire cools and that's how it stays." I asked him to explain further. "They continue to love each other, but it's in a different way—warm and dependable." Seeing my questioning expression, he continued, "Look, after you marry, you sit together by your hut, cooking food and giving it to each other—just as you did when you were growing up in your parents' home. Your wife becomes like your mother and you, her father." How long did this take? "It varies among couples. A few months, usually; sometimes longer. But it always happens." Was it also true for a lover? "No," he explained, "feelings for a lover stay intense much longer, sometimes for years." What did he feel for the woman I had been interviewing—hadn't they been lovers for a long time?

As soon as I mentioned her name, his manner changed and a smile crossed his face. He described what an exceptional and beautiful woman she was and how deeply he loved her, "With a burning heart." He confirmed what she had already told me—that they often fantasized about running away together. I asked, "What would it be like?" A dreamy look came over his face, then he smiled again and said, "The first few months would be wonderful!"

Since such affairs are not openly condoned, it is most important that a lover have "sense"—that he be discreet and play by the rules. He should also show his affection—by arranging rendezvous, by being faithful, and by giving gifts. Gift exchange between lovers is quite common, although by no means necessary. (The man usually gives presents to the woman, although the exchange often works in both directions.) A man, to be considered attractive, should have a slim, strong body with a small behind and stomach, but men of different appearances also attract women as wives and lovers. Another requirement is that a man be a capable lover: he should be concerned about the woman's pleasure, be small to moderate in genital size, and have a "strong back" (that is, be virile). If there is sufficient time, he should also be willing to engage in additional acts of sexual intercourse to ensure that the woman's "work" is "finished" and that she is satisfied.

Most !Kung are proud of bearing and possess a self-confidence that seems to be the natural outcome of the way they grow up. One clear instance of this is the social environment in which young girls make the transition from childhood to adulthood. The small size of villages means that girls approaching puberty have few, if any, peers to compare themselves to. Thus they do not develop to maturity in a context of intense comparison and competition. Each young girl is likely to be the center of attention for a number of years. As a girl begins to mature, the men of the village offer running commentaries on the changes in her body—obvious in a culture where the breasts are not covered—and joke about wanting to marry her or to run away with her. Some may seriously propose that she marry them as a second wife. It is unlikely that the attention will have to be shared.

This experience seems to inspire self-esteem. One day I noticed a twelve-year-old girl, whose breasts had just started to develop, looking into the small mirror beside the driver's window of our Land Rover. She looked intently at her face, then, on tip-toe, examined her breasts and as much of her body as she could see, then went to her face again. She stepped back to see more, moved in again for a closer look. She was a lovely girl, although not outstanding in any way except by being in the full health and beauty of youth. She saw me watching. I teased in the !Kung manner I had by then thoroughly learned, "So ugly! How is such a young girl already so ugly?" She laughed. I asked, "You don't agree?" She beamed, "No, not at all. I'm beautiful!" She continued to look at herself. I said, "Beautiful? Perhaps my eyes have become broken with age that I can't see where it is?" She said, "Everywhere—my face, my body. There's no ugliness at all." These remarks were said easily, with a broad smile, but without arrogance. The pleasure she felt in her changing body was as evident as the absence of conflict about it.

The self-possession !Kung women gain in childhood and young adulthood continues throughout life. In contrast to the experience of many women in our own culture, this feeling is not worn down by cultural ideals of "perfect" beauty to which women are constantly comparing themselves. Differences in innate physical attractiveness are generally recognized by the !Kung, and some individuals are acknowledged as being particularly good-looking or beautiful, but the culture does not elaborate much on these differences. The opportunity to make oneself attractive is available to everyone: one simply dons one's best clothes—a traditional leather kaross with beaded designs or, more recently, a brightly colored cloth dress—after washing and oiling one's face and body and applying cosmetics made from wild plants.

Except for those who are sick, "too thin" or very old, most women think of themselves as attractive. The phrase most often heard to describe their sense of self-esteem can be translated as "I have work," "I am productive," or even, "I have worth." Having lovers, therefore, is an option most !Kung women feel is available to them, although not all choose it. As for attracting a husband and marrying, that goal is achieved by all !Kung women without exception.

MARJORIE, those people who tell you that when people live in the bush they don't have lovers, or that people only learned about it recently from the blacks, they are deceiving you. They are giving you lies and are trying to fool you with their cleverness. But I, I am like your mother and don't offer you deceit; only the truth is what I give you. I am an old woman and when I see what other people tell you, I can see through them. Because affairs—one married person making love to another not her husband—is something that even people from long ago knew. Even my father's father's father's father knew. There have also always been fights where poison arrows are shot and people are killed because of that. Having affairs is one of the things God gave us.

I have told you about my lovers, but I haven't finished telling you about all of them, because they are as many as my fingers and toes.[1] Some have died and others are still alive. Me, I'm a bad one. I'm not like you who have no lovers. Because, when you are a woman, you don't just sit still and do nothing—you have lovers. You don't just sit with the man of your hut, with just one man. One man can give you very little. One man gives you only one kind of food to eat. But when you have lovers, one brings you something and another brings you something else. One comes at night with meat, another with money, another with beads. Your husband also does things and gives them to you.

But sitting with just one man? We don't do that. Does one man have enough thoughts for you?

There are many kinds of work a woman has to do, and she should have lovers wherever she goes. If she goes somewhere to visit and is alone, then someone there will give her beads, someone else will give her meat, and someone else will give her other food. When she returns to her village, she will have been well taken care of.

Even if she goes with her husband, she should still have a few lovers. Because each one gives her something. She gathers from one man one thing, from another man something else, and from another, yet something else. It is as though her genitals were worth money— Pounds! Rands! Shillings (laughs)! She collects her gatherings from each different place until she has filled her kaross with beads and pubic aprons and money.

When she returns home, she confides in her friends, "One of my lovers gave me this, another gave me that, and another gave me this . . ." Her friends say, "Oh, the place you went has such wonderful lovers. They treated you very well." She says, "Listen, if all of you are as beautiful as I think you are and if you also went there, the men would see you and like you, too. Then just as they treated me, they would also treat you."

It's the same when a woman remains home. One day when she and her husband are living as usual, her husband says, "I'm going away for a few days." She stays behind, and that's when she sees her lovers. If one of her lovers lives in a village nearby and an animal is killed, he'll cut some meat and bring it to her. It will be beautiful meat, full of juice and fat. He'll sit with her, cooking it until the broth is rich and heavy. She will drink it and her heart will be happy. She'll think, "Oh, my husband has just left and here I am, drinking this wonderful broth."

Another day, perhaps he comes to her and they sleep together. He asks, "When is your husband coming back?" She says, "Not for a while. My leg hasn't started to shake," meaning her husband isn't coming home yet. They make love, and when the rooster crows before dawn breaks, he leaves.

Another day, perhaps he comes again. The two of them lie down together and he asks, "I'd really like to stay with you the rest of the night. The last time I came to you, I left right after we made love. Now, today . . . what is your leg telling you?" She says, "This morning as I was sitting around, my thighs started to tremble, ever so slightly. Perhaps my husband will come back later. Perhaps he will come in the middle of the night. I don't know when he planned to come back. But my leg was shaking, so it may be tonight." Her lover says, "All right, I will only lie with you a short time. Then I will leave."

The two of them lie together and then separate. He leaves, and soon after, her husband comes back. The next morning, when she is about doing things, perhaps getting water at the well, her lover meets her and asks if her husband came back. She says, "Yes, he arrived soon after you left. Didn't I tell you that my leg was trembling in the morning? It was a true warning." Her lover says, "Now that your husband is here, my heart feels pain! It really hurts! Later, when the sun is low in the sky and after you've finished your work, let's meet somewhere." She says, "Fine, but only if my work is finished. I have a lot of things to do. After I finish with the water, I have to do things for my husband, because he has just now come back. Only much later, when the sun is near to setting, will I be able to leave his work and meet you."

The next day, she and her husband stay together. She works for him, washing and cooking. She thinks, "My lover told me we will meet again today." She spends the whole day doing the things she has to do. She works so hard that the time she was supposed to meet him passes. She works until she goes to sleep. She thinks, "Oh, when my lover sees me tomorrow, he's going to be angry!" She's afraid. Then she thinks, "There's no reason for him to be angry. I didn't meet him because I was working for my husband."

The next day, as she is filling her water containers at the well, her lover sees her and says, "What did I tell you the other day? Didn't I say we would meet?" She says, "I told you I had all my husband's work to do—washing and cooking. When he told me to get firewood, he also wanted me to do other things when I came back. He had me work very hard and I wasn't even aware of when it was time to meet you. That's why I worked past it." Her lover is angry and says, "If it was because of your husband, that's all right. But if you do it again, I'll beat you! What's the matter with your genitals? Are they too old to care?" She says, "What did I do that I should be hit? I was doing things for my husband."

After that, she lives as usual. She continues to work for her husband and works hard. Then, one day, she says, "I'm going to look for some firewood. Why don't you watch the pot of food that's cooking?" She leaves and walks far from the village, looking for wood. She meets her lover, lies down with him, and makes love. She leaves and returns to the village, carrying firewood. Her heart is happy because she's been with her lover and her husband doesn't know. And she lives on like that.

For another woman, it may be different. Her lover may have been away. But when he comes back and she sees him, her heart knows that he is around once again. She lives, waiting until she has a chance to be alone with him. When they meet, he says, "Perhaps you didn't think about me?" He asks, "As you were living, day after day, did you ever think about me?" She says, "What? I thought about you often. What could have stopped me? What could I have been doing that I wouldn't? Am I not a person?" Because when you are human, you think about each other.

He says, "I thought maybe you had forgotten." She says, "No, I thought about you often and with strength." He says, "Mm, that's why I came to talk to you, to see what you were thinking." She says, "And how do you feel now that you have seen?" He says, "You ... you really made me miserable! The month I left, my heart pained for you and wanted you very much." She says, "It's been the same with me. I also wanted you and my heart also pained for you."

They wait until her husband goes away and meet far from the village. Then they do their work.

Sometimes, a woman may even meet her lover at night, after she and her husband have gone to sleep. Her lover will have already told her to meet him that night. When he arrives in the village, he goes to one of her friends and tells the friend to wake her up. The friend goes to the hut and whispers, "Your person is here. Get up and go to him." She thinks, "Oh! What shall I do with my husband? How can I do this?" She wakes her husband and says, "I'm going to visit the

hut where all the people are talking. I'll come back later and
lie down." She and her lover meet and do their work. When
they are finished and her lover leaves, she sits and talks with
the others. Then she goes back and lies down beside her husband.

Yes, women have cleverness!

Even my mother had lovers. I'd be with her when she
met them. But my father, if he had them, I didn't know. Because he didn't take me around with him; I only followed the
women. So, even if he had lovers, I never saw anything. But
the women ... when I was a child, I knew all of their
lovers—even my mother's and my aunt's.

I remember, when I was still small, seeing my mother
with one man. He met her, took her, and made love to her. I
sat nearby and waited. When she came back carrying firewood, I thought, "I'm going to tell!" Then I thought, "Should
I tell Daddy or shouldn't I?" But when we arrived back at the
village, I didn't say anything. I thought if I told, my father
would kill my mother.

Except Toma, he was the only one I told about. That was
after my younger sister, Kxamshe, died and my mother's older
sister came from the East to take us back with her. I was still
very young, without breasts, when we went to live with her
there. It was soon after that, that Toma, her sister's husband,
started with my mother. Much later, he even took her away
from my father; he tricked her into leaving with him. I
watched it happen. He told her, "I want to make love to you
and take you away with me. I want to marry a new woman."

When they first became lovers, my father didn't know
about it. They would meet in the bush. Mother would set me
down and go off, nearby, with him. I'd sit and wait. Sometimes, I'd stand there and cry. Once I said, very loudly,
"When Daddy comes back, I'm going to tell. Mommy, now
you tell that person to stop ruining you. Tell him we have to
go. I'll tell Daddy he had sex with you!" When my mother
came back, she said, "You must understand that if you tell
your father, he'll kill me. Now don't tell or you won't see me

275

any more." I listened to what she said, and when we returned I didn't say anything.

But the time I did tell, they had kept me waiting for a very long time. I was tired and unhappy. I thought, "I want to go home. What's the matter with this man that he's not letting us go home? How come someone else is with Mother, anyway? When Daddy comes back from the bush, I'm going to tell him."

When we returned, that's just what I did. I said, "Daddy, when Mommy and I went for firewood, Toma was there. He took Mommy away from me and went and had sex with her. I just sat there and waited."

My parents started to fight and my father hit my mother. I thought, "Why did I tell? Mommy's going to die. I did a bad thing, telling; I'll never do that again. Even if I see her with a man, I'll just sit there. I won't tell again."

Sometimes Toma stayed with us when my father was away hunting and we'd all lie down together. My heart would be miserable and I'd think, "What is this?" But when my father came home, I wouldn't say anything.

It was like that for a long time. Then came the fighting. I remember one time, my father yelled at my mother, "Chuko, I'm going to kill you with poison arrows and then kill Toma the same way. What kind of thing is he² that he isn't staying with his wife and taking care of her, or that he took you and isn't giving you back? What do you possess that no one else has?"

Later, he yelled at Toma, "When something happens that defeats me, I do something. I am a person of the bush, unlike you who are a person of the villages; I will just grab you and kill you. Then I'll go back to the bush with my children. Now take your own wife again and leave here; I'll stay with the woman I've been married to."

Other days, it was my brothers who fought with Toma. When my older brother stopped, my younger brother started. Was he not fairly old by then? Kumsa would say, "Give my mother back to my father. What makes you think you can just take us to the East and turn my mother away from my father?"

One time Kumsa grabbed him and threw him down on the ground. They fought until people separated them. Another time Kumsa screamed at my mother, "Get up and go over to my father! Why are you sitting with this other person? What are you looking for? If you don't go over to Father, I'll kill you." Then he said, "What are you doing? Why did you start up with your sister's husband and why do you now refuse to leave him? How come you like this old Zhun/twa, anyway?"

He grabbed something and hit her. He yelled at her, and kept insulting her until people took him away. They said, "Your mother has no sense, now leave her alone. Your mother is a woman. If you keep hitting her like that you'll kill her. This other one, he's a man, fight with him." Then they said, "What is Toma doing, anyway? His first wife, an older woman, is still alive. When she dies, he won't go and bury her. All he's set on doing is taking your mother away from your father. So stop hitting her; he's the one—go, fight with him."

Kumsa went over to Toma and they started to fight. When it was over, we kept on living.

Until one day, Toma took my mother and they left. Earlier, there had been a lot of fighting. My older brother had yelled at my mother and had hit her, "You're going to drop ·Father? You're going to leave him and go off with Toma? What about your youngest son who has been sitting around, day after day from sunrise to sunset, crying? How can you drop your children and not take care of them?"

But they left. Toma tricked my mother away from my father. I thought, "Mommy is wrong, dropping my father and marrying another man."

Kumsa and I cried and cried. We just stayed with my father and cried.

Not long after, my father followed them to their village. When he saw my mother, he said, "Chuko, what are you doing? Why aren't you sitting with me? The two of us could still be beside each other."

Again, there was a lot of fighting. My mother's older sister said, "Chuko, go back with your husband and take care of your children. Why have you hung yourself on top of my husband, going wherever he goes, like this?"

My mother left with us that time, leaving Toma behind. She had come back again, had come back to me.

We lived and lived, a very long time. Then, one day, Toma came again. I thought, "Is this the way the two of them are going to live with my mother?"

Again my father tried to keep my mother, but it was no use. My father yelled at them, insulted them, and fought with them. He even bit my mother's hand while they were fighting. I said, "If you keep on like this, when you're finished, you'll have killed her. Let her go."

Finally, he did; he gave up and left my mother for Toma to have. He thought, "Eh-hey, so this is what this man is like? Then I, I will leave this woman. I'll give her to him and will find a young girl to marry." He told them, "All right, take that thing of yours and do whatever you like with her." Toma had succeeded in winning my mother again, so my father just dropped the whole thing. He finally let Toma have her.

Soon after, my father took me, Kumsa, and Dau with him and we went away; Toma and my mother stayed in the East. We went to one village where we stayed for a while, then to another. We lived and lived, and after more time passed, my father left us in the care of others, saying he wanted to get some of his things, elsewhere. When he came back, he brought an older woman with him. She was his new wife. Then he took us and we went to live in her village.

Toma's first wife didn't marry again. And just as the others had said, she lived for a while and then she died, somewhere else. She had refused to have my mother as a co-wife, so she left them and went away. When she died, Toma wasn't with her; he was with my mother. He didn't even go to see where she was buried.

We lived and lived, staying with our father, growing up beside him. Then one day, Toma died and my mother came back to us, came back to where we were living. My brothers and I were happy that he had died. We praised God and said that he had done well by us.

But my father refused her. She had wanted my father to sleep beside her again. But he said she had refused him and now he didn't want her: "I won't have you because you already left me. And even though your husband is dead, I won't marry you and have you with me. Today you will just sleep by yourself. If you marry again, it will be no concern of mine. Because, after you left, I married and today I have another wife. Did you think you were the only woman? Today you will lie separately, because that which used to be ours, our marriage, no longer exists."

Then he said, "But the children we gave birth to, they will just live between the two of us, because they are both of ours. And we will live as before. We can continue to exchange presents and do hxaro. If you have beads, you can give them to me and I will give something else back to you. There's no problem with that. Or food. If I prepare something or if you gather, you'll give me and I'll give you. Even the woman I married, my wife, she will give you food and meat to eat and beads to have."

He continued, "We've had our children together—those who didn't live are dead and those who did live are here with us now. But you pulled apart the bonds of marriage that were between us. So today, you will lie separately from me. And whatever happens will happen. Until God kills us, or until he kills you or me, this is the way we will continue to live."

After that, my mother just stayed with us. She lived in her hut and my father and his wife lived in theirs. Nothing more happened. Kumsa, Dau, and I would sit for a while by our father's fire, then get up and sit at our mother's fire. We'd eat with her, then go back to our father and eat with him.

And we just continued to live.

I like having lovers, but their ways are to ruin my heart and to spill semen all over me.

There was one man I once had as my lover, and after we had made love he went and told his wife. The next time we were together, he told her again. That's when his wife came looking for me, and when she found me she started yelling. I thought, "What kind of man is this? When he steals with a woman, he tells his wife?" I told her, "Your husband is lying. We aren't lovers." But I was angry, "If that's the reason you've come to me, it makes me want to kill you. Even though you are a large woman and I am tiny, as I am. Your husband is crazy, saying something like that, because he and I haven't made love."

The next time I saw him, I said, "You're the one who wanted me and spoke to me about love. I didn't come to you. I am a woman; you are a man and you yourself came to me. Only then did I agree to you. So, what did you see that you went and told your wife? If that's how you want it, I'll go and tell my husband. Is there no sense in your head that you told her?"

But after that, whenever his wife saw me, she would come to wherever I was sitting and start yelling at me. I'd yell back at her. One day, I finally said, "My heart is fed up with our fighting all the time. Every day you come and insult me; every day I listen to your remarks. So, today, I'm going to tell you: your husband is and always will be my lover. That should keep you quiet. Now, what are you going to do to me? I'd like to see. Probably nothing."

There were others sitting around in the shade of the tree, including my husband. The next time she started in again, insulting and cursing me, I didn't say anything. I thought, "This woman . . . I'm going to get her today!" She kept on insulting me; still, I didn't answer. But when she came over and stood very close to me shouting, I said, "By my own mother! How I would love to hit you and leave you hanging over there!" I started to laugh. Then I asked, "What do you think you can possibly take away from me by insulting me this way?" Then added, "But, since this is how you've come to me, I think there's going to be a fight."

I pulled off my bracelets and hit her, hit her in the stomach, and she fell down. She got up and came at me, but I hit her again and again she fell. When she got up and came at me again, I called her name and said, "This time, I'll kill you." I started to laugh again, "I'll kill you, so you'd better go and sit down. If you come back, I'll hit you so hard that it will leave you dead. You'd better go and sit down."

One of the women grabbed her and sat her down. I was furious! I continued to yell at her, then jumped up and bit her hand. She yelled out, "Ouw! Nisa bit me ... Nisa bit me ..." I said, "I'd like to beat you until you shit! Do you think because I'm so small I can't fight? I can fight, even against someone big like you. My bones, my very bones here will grab you and make you shit! Am I the child of your mother's relatives that I shouldn't answer your insults? I am of one family and you are of another. Your husband is yours and my husband is mine."

Finally, the elders said, "Talk of having affairs is bad talk. This has to stop now." We listened and stopped. She and her husband went back to their village. After that, he and I were no longer lovers. I saw what a bad one he was and how he caused people to want to kill each other. He had no sense at all.

He wasn't like other men.

Sometimes the women talk. After a woman has been with her lover, she says, "That one, my lover, he came to me last night." Her friend says, "He came and slept with you?" The first woman answers, "Yes, he lay with me and had sex with me until morning broke. Then we separated and he left." Her friend says, "Uhn, uhn ... last night, when darkness just started to sit and everyone was talking and then went to sleep, my lover also came to me and had sex with me. But it was just one time. After, we lay beside one another and fell asleep. I don't really understand what happened. Perhaps it was the way we were sleeping, but he didn't have sex with me again. Now I don't know. Perhaps he doesn't really like me or why did he come to me at all?" The first woman says, "Mine wasn't like that. Mine had sex with me until we separated and we both went to sleep. He wants me to meet him tonight in another hut and make love again."

Women talk to each other about men and enjoy their talk. One woman asks, "What about that man over there ... what's he like?" Another woman says, "Mm ... that one over there? His penis is huge! His penis is so big he almost killed me with pain. If he comes to me again, I'll refuse. He really hurts!"

Women talk in other ways, too. One woman may say, "What's happening to me? Are my genitals already old? Because even if a man sleeps with me, I can't seem to find any excitement within myself. Am I so old that my genitals are exhausted? It was like that for him, as well. We didn't find any pleasure in each other."

Sometimes that happens when a woman is too wide and the man is too small for her. Then she can't hold him well. The man just moves about inside, but she is too big. Although he may be virile, they do not have good sex together. After, the man says, "It's all right. It's really not that important."

The next morning, the woman asks her friends, "What am I going to do? My friends, my genitals have become old. The man who lay beside me last night broke the dawn open having sex with me, but he didn't receive any pleasure."

Even the man, he will tell other men, "That woman there, she killed all the strength I had. She's too big; her insides are stretched. Last night I slept with her and even though I made love all night, I didn't feel any pleasure. She's so wide, she's like a Herero's mouth! I just flounced around inside, but I couldn't feel anything. I don't know what it was like for her, but today my back hurts and I'm exhausted. Today, I won't be going back to her."

Zhun/twa women also tell each other about their problems with men and their complaints. A woman may tell about her husband and about how he hasn't satisfied her. She'll tell what she said to him, "What's happening to us? You, my own husband, sleep with me and finish your work. But when you stop and leave me, I haven't finished mine.[3] Why should it be like this when we're married? When you sleep with me and finish your work, my work should also be finished. Don't you know you'll make me sick? We have to make love so that we both finish." Her friend says, "By the time you start to feel pleasure, your husband has finished? Why does he leave you before you feel any real pleasure?" Women sometimes talk that way about their husbands, but not usually about their lovers. Because lovers know how to satisfy. When a woman is with a lover, he usually does very well.

Those are the things Zhun/twa women talk to each other about. Don't all women ask each other about those things?

There are many different kinds of lovers. Some men have small penises and some, their penises are large. Other men, their penises are full with lots of semen. A man like that doesn't do very well because when he has sex he spills his wetness over everything. You think, "This man's semen is so plentiful he's ruining my clothing. This is the first time I've slept with him, yet why does he have so much semen?" After that, you refuse to see him again and you find another man, a man whose semen is small. That's a good man to have as your lover.

If a man's penis is too big, it also isn't good. A man like that makes your genitals hurt. You think, "No, his penis is so big he'll kill me and cause sickness to enter my insides."

A man with a small penis is the best kind. A man like that doesn't make you sick.

Most men have strength in their backs and many, when they are old, still have sexual vigor. Those men, even if they aren't aroused at first, when you touch them, their penises become strong and you help them inside. But there are others whose penises stay soft. Their hearts desire you, but their penises are dead. When you lie down with a man like that, although he tries, he never really becomes erect and doesn't enter you well. Even when he does, it is only a little and he finishes very quickly. A man like that, his back has no strength. It happens to young men as well as to old. Their penises are soft, like cloth.

When a man is with a woman who agrees to be with him and his penis stays soft, he thinks, "What's doing this to me?" He touches himself, "What's happening to me?" He touches himself again, "What am I going to do?" The woman asks, "What's wrong? Don't you want me? What is it doing ... let me feel ... what? Has your penis died?" They both touch it and try to have sex, but the spilling of semen is all that happens. It never really becomes erect because, although the woman was excited, the man wasn't. The woman finally says, "We've been lovers for a long time and have had this chance to be together again. But even though we tried to make it work, your penis refused. I don't understand why. Our hearts made love well but your penis didn't do any work and didn't help me at all. You'd better leave now, because you've made me feel very bad."

I was once with a young man like that. He's given birth to a number of children since then. That really surprised me! What was he able to make his wife pregnant with? Perhaps he took some medicine to strengthen his back. Because, before he married her, he was soft as cloth. We were lying down together and my genitals were right there. But no matter how we tried (and we tried!), it refused. I asked, "What's the matter? What's your penis doing? Doesn't it want something to eat?" We kept trying but nothing happened. I said, "Uhn, uhn. I thought when I agreed to you, that perhaps you were a man with strength. But ... is this the way you are?" He said, "I don't know what's happening. Why is my penis refusing?" I said, "If we stay here any longer, my husband will find us. If you had had the strength, we would already have finished. But, without strength, how can you be of any help to me?" He finally did it, but he finished immediately.

The next day, he went to his friends, "Hey, all of you. I'm feeling very bad. Even if I speak to a woman and she agrees, when I go to her, I can't sleep with her. I try to make it erect, but it refuses. I beg you, give me some medicine so I can help myself. My back has no more strength. Won't you help me?"

He explained, "Yesterday, the woman I asked was willing. She is truly beautiful! But when I went to her, we just touched bodies. I couldn't make love to her. My heart wanted to sleep with her, but my penis refused. But I really like her and want to go back to her. My friends, won't you give me medicine? I like women the same as the rest of you, but you're all having sex and I'm not!"

A man asks his friends things like that. His friends ask, "If she's as beautiful as you say, why couldn't you have sex with her? We also visited women in that village yesterday. But we had sex with them; we didn't just play."

The man says, "I beg you, won't you please help? This woman is so beautiful! When I look at her face, it's so lovely! I like her so much. Yet, when we lay down, I couldn't do it. Me, a man, I couldn't do it. Today I feel terrible. In the name of all this, I'm asking for some medicine to take this very day. If I had had strength in my back yesterday, I would have stayed beside her, a woman that beautiful, and had sex with her until dawn."

One of the men gives him medicine. He drinks it and it makes his penis strong and hard again. After, he lies with women very well.

A man who is strong, a man with a strong back . . . his penis is *hard!* He becomes very erect. When a man like that speaks to a woman, speaks to her from his heart . . . when a man like that speaks about his heart and looks right at her standing near her hut . . . it is already becoming erect! That man is one with a strong back. That man, when he talks to a woman about making love, it just rises.

The woman thinks, "I see that what his heart is saying his penis is also saying. I'd like to be with this one," and she agrees. Then, just as you and I are inside this hut together, Marjorie, the two of them go alone inside a hut where he takes her and has sex with her.

When two people make love, the woman moves and the man moves. When they share desire for each other and they both work hard, that's when both become full with pleasure. But if the woman doesn't really want the man and only he works, they enjoy each other only very little.

Sometimes the woman finishes first and the man, after. Sometimes they finish together. Both ways are equally good. The only way it is bad is when the woman hasn't finished and the man has. That sometimes happens when a man is sleeping with a woman for the first time. She is so pleasurable and so good ... she's like sugar. Or honey! That's why, when he is just getting started, he is already finished. The woman, still holding full with excitement, thinks, "This man has just made love to me and has finished his work. But I haven't finished mine. Why is he leaving me like this?" They lie around together for a while. When he becomes aroused, he goes to her again. She thinks, "Yes, I'll be able to finish now." They start to make love again and this time, he goes for a long time, a very long time. Perhaps she finishes first and he is the only one to continue, or perhaps, when he is full, she is also full. Then they go to sleep.

Other times, it's the woman's heart that hasn't fully agreed. If she feels no desire, if her heart hasn't risen and only the man's has and he makes love to her, she thinks, "Even though he is making love to me, my heart isn't rising. Why is this happening?" When the man finishes, she doesn't. But then her heart changes. Her heart rises and the next time he comes to her, they both finish. I mean even if her heart hadn't wanted it at first. Because a woman's sexual desire is always with her and even if she doesn't want a certain man, she still feels her desire inside. That's why there are no medicines to make women want men as there are to make men want women: it comes directly from inside a woman's heart.

But there is medicine that a woman can take to make men like her. It is sweet smelling, and when she rubs it on, her husband and other men will want her. Men have one, too. If a man rubs this medicine on, it changes a woman's heart toward him. When he lies down with her, she will like him and they won't refuse each other's wanting.

All women know sexual pleasure. Some women, those who really like sex, if they haven't finished and the man has, will wait until the man has rested, then get up and make love to him. Because she wants to finish, too. She'll have sex with the man until she is also satisfied. Otherwise she could get sick. Because, if a woman doesn't finish her work, sickness can enter her back.

Only rarely, if a woman is really frustrated, will she touch herself. Adult men also touch themselves, either in the bush or sometimes, even in their huts. But only if they are refused by women.

Women don't take men's genitals into their mouths nor do men kiss women's genitals. Men only kiss women's mouths. Because a woman's genitals could burn a man's mouth. So he just kisses her mouth and when he gets hard he lies with her.

When little girls play sexually together, they don't know about what their genitals can do; they just make believe they are having sex. But adults know, adults know how to touch a woman's genitals just right. When a man lies with a woman, he touches her genitals,[4] and has sex with her, and touches her genitals, and has sex with her. That's how he finishes and how she also finishes.

Yes, knowing how is very important!

Sex with a lover a woman really likes is very pleasurable. So is sex with her husband, the man of her house. The pleasure they both give is equal. Except if a woman has pulled her heart away from her lover, then there is little pleasure with him.

When a woman has a lover, her heart goes out to him and also to her husband. Her heart feels strong toward both men. But if her heart is small for the important man and big for the other one, if her heart feels passion only for her lover and is cold toward her husband, that is very bad. Her husband will know and will want to kill her and the lover.

A woman has to want her husband and her lover equally; that is when it is good.

Women are strong; women are important. Zhun/twa men say that women are the chiefs, the rich ones, the wise ones. Because women possess something very important, something that enables men to live: their genitals.

A woman can bring a man life, even if he is almost dead. She can give him sex and make him alive again. If she were to refuse, he would die! If there were no women around, their semen would kill men. Did you know that? If there were only men, they would all die. Women make it possible for them to live. Women have something so good that if a man takes it and moves about inside it, he climaxes and is sustained.

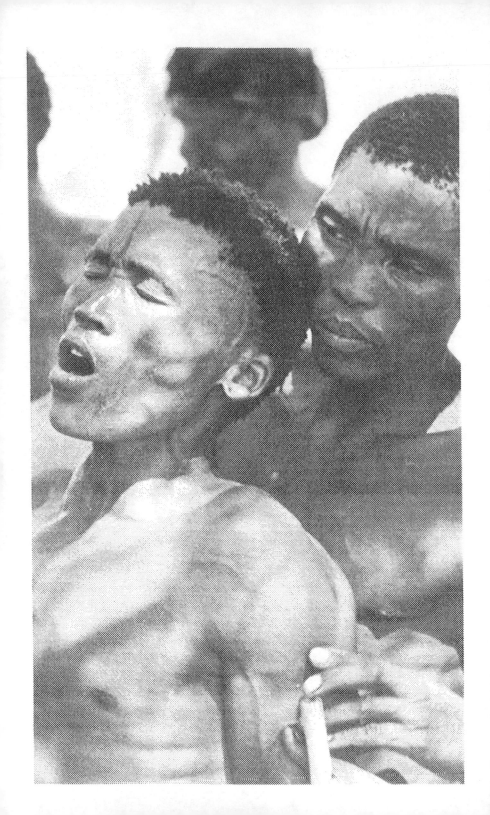

Chapter 13
A Healing Ritual

THE REALM OF THE SPIRITUAL infuses all aspects of !Kung physical and social life, and is seen as a fundamental determinant in the delicate balance between life and death, sickness and health, rain and drought, abundance and scarcity. This realm is dominated by one major god in command of an entourage of lesser gods. Both the greater and lesser deities are modeled on humans, and their characteristics reflect the multitude of possibilities inherent in the human spirit. Sometimes they are kind, humane, and generous; at other times, whimsical, vindictive, or cruel. Their often erratic behavior is thought responsible for the unpredictability of human life and death.

One way the spirits affect humans is by shooting them with invisible arrows carrying disease, death, or misfortune. If the arrows can be warded off, illness will not take hold. If illness has already penetrated, the arrows must be removed to enable the sick person to recover. An ancestral spirit may exercise this power against the living if a person is not being treated well by others. If people argue with her frequently, if her husband shows how little he values her by carrying on blatant affairs, or if people refuse to cooperate or share with her, the spirit may conclude that no one cares whether or not she remains alive and may "take her into the sky."

Interceding with the spirits and drawing out their invisible arrows is the task of !Kung healers, men and women who possess the powerful healing force called *n/um*. N/um generally remains dormant in a healer until an effort is made to activate it. Although an occasional healer can accomplish this through solo singing or instrumental playing, the usual way of activating n/um is through the medicinal curing ceremony or trance dance. To the sound of undulating melodies sung by women, the healers dance around and around the fire, sometimes for hours. The music, the strenuous dancing, the smoke, the heat of the fire, and the healers' intense concentration cause their n/um to heat up. When it comes to a boil, trance is achieved.

At this moment the n/um becomes available as a powerful healing force, to serve the entire community. In trance, a healer lays hands on and ritually cures everyone sitting around the fire. His hands flutter lightly beside each person's head or chest or wherever illness is evident; his body trembles; his breathing becomes deep and coarse; and he becomes coated with a thick sweat—also considered to be embued with power. Whatever "badness" is discovered in the person is drawn into the healer's own body and met by the n/um coursing up his spinal column. The healer gives a mounting cry that culminates in a soul-wrenching shriek as the illness is catapulted out of his body and into the air.

While in trance, many healers see various gods and spirits sitting just outside the circle of firelight, enjoying the spectacle of the dance. Sometimes the spirits are recognizable—departed relatives and friends—at other times they are "just people." Whoever these beings are, healers in trance usually blame them for whatever misfortune is being experienced by the community. They are barraged by hurled objects, shouted at, and aggressively warned not to take any of the living back with them to the village of the spirits.

To cure a very serious illness, the most experienced healers may be called upon, for only they have enough knowledge to undertake the dangerous spiritual exploration that may be necessary to effect a cure. When they are in a trance, their souls are said to leave their bodies and to travel to the spirit world to discover the cause of the illness or the problem. An ancestral spirit or a god is usually found responsible and asked to reconsider. If the healer is persuasive and the spirit agrees, the sick person recovers. If the spirit is elusive or unsympathetic, a cure is not achieved. The healer may go to the principal god, but even this does not always work. As one healer put it, "Sometimes, when you speak with God, he says, 'I want this person to die and won't help you make him better.' At other times, God helps; the next morning, someone who has been lying on the ground, seriously ill, gets up and walks again."

These journeys are considered dangerous because while the healer's soul is absent his body is in "half-death." Akin to loss of consciousness, this state has been observed and verified by medical and scientific investigators. The power of other healers' n/um is all that is thought to protect the healer in this state from actual death. He receives lavish attention and care—his body is vigorously massaged, his skin is rubbed with sweat, and hands are laid on him. Only when consciousness returns—the signal that his soul has been reunited with his body—do the other healers cease their efforts.

The underlying causes of illness that healers discover while in trance seem to reflect an understanding of the role psychological factors may play in disease. The analysis a !Kung healer offered of a young woman's bout with malaria, for example, illustrated his awareness that her father's recent death might have been affecting her health. The healer's soul made a journey to the world of the dead to find out why the woman was sick. He found the spirit of the woman's father sitting on the ground with the spirit of his daughter in his arms. He was holding her tenderly, rocking her and singing to her. The healer asked why his daughter was with him in the world of the dead and not in the land of the living. Her father explained that he had been desolate without her in the spirit world. He had brought her there so he could be with her again. The healer defended the daughter's right—and obligation—to remain alive: "Your daughter has so much work still to do in life—having children, providing for family and relatives, helping with grandchildren." After an impassioned debate, the healer convinced the spirit to give his daughter time to experience what life had still to offer and to grow old: "Then she'll join you." As the father reluctantly agreed, he loosened his grip on the young woman and her spirit returned to her body. A cure was thus effected, and her health restored.

N/um reflects the basically egalitarian nature of !Kung life. It is not reserved for a privileged few: nearly half the men and a third of the women have it. There is enough for everyone; it is infinitely divisible; and all can strive for it. Almost anyone who is willing to go through the rigors of apprenticeship can attain it. Not everyone wants to, however. Many apprentices become afraid or lack ambition and drop out. Others—though few in number—try but do not succeed. Although one can often strengthen one's n/um by working at it, its limit is said to be determined by God.

The usual way a young man receives n/um is from an experienced healer, often a close male relative, during the ceremonial medicine dance. The apprentice follows the healer around—dancing alone or with his arms wrapped tightly around the healer's waist—hour after hour, with only short rests, often from dusk until dawn. Each time the healer's trance state swells with sufficient intensity and power, he rubs the apprentice's body with his sweat, lays on hands, and snaps his fingers repeatedly against the apprentice's waist to shoot spiritual arrows—through which n/um is said to be transferred—into him. This process may be repeated several times during the night and may continue for a number of months or years—however long it takes the novice (typically in his late teens or early twenties) to become accomplished.

This apprenticeship involves a profound dependency on the teacher, which seems to help the novice drop his defenses, thereby making possible an altered state of consciousness—or, as the !Kung would view it, a heightened spiritual reality. The beginner often experiences extreme fluctuations in his emotional state as he learns to trance. At one moment, he may grab burning coals, throw himself into the fire, or run out into the bush and the night. He may cry, or rage against the group, or throw coals or hot sand at people, or break things around him. The next moment may find him whining plaintively, like a small child, begging for water or food; given it, he may spit it out on the ground. If the trance becomes too powerful, he may even be overcome and enter half-death, falling violently to the ground.

These actions do not really alarm others around him. Women sitting by the fire prevent him from burning himself and men run after him to bring him back from the bush. The other healers, especially his teacher, are responsible for ensuring that his soul returns to his body after he enters half-death and for helping him to learn to control the trance. Only when trance energy is harnessed can it be used for social good. Younger men, most dramatic and extreme in trance, are therefore usually less powerful as healers than are older men who have mastered the great forces released in trance.

One older man put it this way, "My n/um is so strong I can talk to people or even get up and put wood on the fire when I'm in trance." Healers like this one can also usually enter trance easily, almost at will, and depend minimally on external stimulation. For others, however, the weakening of the body that accompanies aging is reflected in a similar weakening of spiritual power.

Toma, another powerful healer, told me how he had received his n/um. His father was an experienced and highly respected healer. When Toma, his oldest son, was a teenager, he started to teach him n/um. Late one night, not long after his spiritual education had begun, Toma had what he described as a visitation: while he was asleep, God took him from his hut and sat with him because "He wanted to meet me." Frightened, Toma started to cry. His mother woke and found him sitting outside his hut alone in the dark. The next time Toma's father entered a trance, God explained that he wanted to help give the boy n/um.

Some time later, again at night, God came to Toma and placed a small tortoise in his hand. In his sleep, Toma buried it under a tree. The next morning he woke with a vague recollection of the encounter. When he went to verify what he remembered, he found the tortoise buried deep in the sand—in the very spot revealed to him in his "dream." He took the tortoise to his father, who cooked it and ate it.

The next night God came again and asked, "Where is the

tortoise I gave you?" Toma said, "I gave it to my father and he ate it." God was enraged. He said, "I'm going to kill him." The next morning, Toma's father was ill, so ill that it was "as though he were dead." His mother, who had also received n/um from his father, entered a trance to pull the sickness out. God came to her and said, "Toma is the only one who can help your husband now. Tell your son to go to his father, to sit beside him, and to hold him. Tell Toma to stay this way until his father's health returns." Toma sat all day with his arms wrapped tightly around his father. They sat and sat and sat. When the sun was near setting, Toma's father opened his eyes. By evening, he was better.

That night God came to Toma again and said, "Does your father have so little sense that he ate something given by God? Tell him, if he ever does that again, I will really kill him." That was the turning point in Toma's relationship with his father—and with God. After that, Toma's n/um was greater than his father's. As Toma put it, "My father did the wrong thing."

Despite the serious and dramatic nature of n/um, the atmosphere of a ceremonial medicine dance is anything but reverential. It is an important social gathering, a time of general excitement and festivity, a time for people to ensure their safety, to suspend conflicts, and to act out and verify the common bond that unites them. People talk, joke, flirt, and comment on everything that happens. Dances are rarely planned, except in cases of serious illness, and most often occur spontaneously: after the first rains of the season, after a large animal has been killed, or perhaps after children have staged a mock trance dance of their own, tantalizing everyone with their high spirits. Although the healers and apprentices are the central characters, a dance could never be sustained without the active participation of others. Everyone who wants to can join. In the winter months, when people congregate near the permanent springs, dances attract large numbers of participants. Healers report a deepening of their trance states when many men enter trance at the same dance. They believe their n/um to be more powerful at such times, as well.

Women, too, are likely to sing and clap more enthusiastically when a chorus of rich voices is available to give the all-enveloping sound they strive for. Men who are not themselves healers impress the gathering with fancy dance steps and elaborate rhythms, sounded out by the dance rattles around their legs, or even with sheer flirtatious appeal. Babies, in slings astride their mothers' hips, variably sleep and wake, as the women improvise melodies with endless variations or, moved by a handsome dancer or just by the spirit of the moment, get up and dance a few turns around the dance circle. As the dance moves deeper into the night, some participants retire to nearby fires, to sleep or to rest. Before dawn, intense trancing is likely to start up again, lasting until sunrise.

!Kung women constitute the chorus at these ceremonial dances. Their singing and clapping are essential to the dance, influencing the strength of n/um a healer will be able to summon forth. They also play a fundamental role in protecting those in trance from hurting themselves in and around the fire. Some wives hold or massage their husbands' bodies until the men regain control of their trance states. One or two women, experienced healers themselves, may also lay on hands and cure, side-by-side with male healers. Nevertheless, trance is available primarily to men, and the purpose of a ceremonial medicine dance is to make trance possible. It is men who assume the responsibility for the general well-being of the community.

There is another dance, however, in which women become more actively involved with n/um and with the associated spiritual exploration. The women's dance or drum dance seems to be of fairly recent origin in the Dobe area, although it probably came into existence at least one hundred years ago. The presence of a male drummer beating out distinctive rhythms sets this dance apart from the ceremonial medicine dance. So, too, does the semicircle of women standing, instead of sitting, who sing and clap songs of a distinct melody and cadence. The most striking difference is that women are the predominant participants—in singing, in clapping, in dancing, and in entering trance. The drum dance has been occurring with increasing frequency, and is beginning to assume a distinct role in the religious life of the community. Although some men do not bother to attend, others are drawn to it and sit watching.

Nevertheless, the central psychic experience of the two dances seems to be comparable. As the women dance in place, within the half-circle of women singing and clapping, those who possess n/um become affected by the beat of the drum, by the heat of their dancing, and by the fire. The intense inward concentration typical of men entering trance is also evident in the women as their n/um starts to heat toward boiling. When trance is achieved, however, its physical manifestation is somewhat different: the woman stands in place while a rapid vibration, similar to a shimmy, engulfs her body from head to foot, especially accentuated in the lower torso. Experienced trancers are able to sustain this movement for long periods of time; less experienced ones often become overwhelmed or frightened and sit down to calm themselves. Women who are determined to explore the full force of the trance state often face the same difficulties men do in handling the intensity of feelings released in trance. They may lose control and run off into the bush, or tease themselves and others with fire, or fling themselves violently to the ground.

About one third of !Kung women are capable of entering trance, but only a small number of these learn to lay on hands and cure—without doubt, the most prestigious activity in !Kung spiritual life. The remainder do not channel their n/um into helping others, but seem to view the powerful state of trance as an end in itself. Many women express a desire to advance to higher spiritual planes, but most do not attempt it. Some claim this is because women are more afraid of pain than men are. (Intense physical pain is universally seen as closely associated with the !Kung trance.) But the erratic course by which girls and women receive n/um and the more limited opportunities available to them to practice their skills are more likely causes.

A girl's first exposure to altered states of consciousness may occur when she is as young as eight years old, when her mother feeds her small quantities of *gwa*, a purportedly psychoactive root. This training tapers off with the approach of motherhood, because n/um is thought harmful to fetuses and young children. If the woman's spiritual education, halted in its (as well as her) infancy, does resume, it is likely to be only when she is in her forties, after her last child has grown. By this time, male healers of the same age, having learned their skills when they were still young, physically strong, and more adaptable, have long since become accomplished.

Despite these obstacles, a handful of older !Kung women have always reached high levels of spiritual mastery. When they lay on hands, their n/um is considered as powerful and effective as that of men of comparable experience and accomplishment. The current interest in the women's dance is likely to encourage even more women to become actively involved. The few successful women healers are promoting this trend by initiating drum dances in villages they visit, by teaching women to trance, by transferring n/um, and by guiding others to lay on hands and cure.

N/UM—THE POWER TO HEAL—is a very good thing. This is a medicine very much like your medicine because it is strong. As your medicine helps people, our n/um helps people. But to heal with n/um means knowing how to trance. Because, it is in trance that the healing power sitting inside the healer's body—the n/um—starts to work. Both men and women learn how to cure with it, but not everyone wants to. Trance-medicine really hurts! As you begin to trance, the n/um slowly heats inside you and pulls at you. It rises until it grabs your insides and takes your thoughts away. Your mind and your senses leave and you don't think clearly. Things become strange and start to change. You can't listen to people or understand what they say. You look at them and they suddenly become very tiny. You think, "What's happening? Is God doing this?" All that is inside you is the n/um; that is all you can feel.

You touch people, laying on hands, curing those you touch. When you finish, other people hold you and blow around your head and your face. Suddenly your senses go "Phah!" and come back to you. You think, "Eh hey, there are people here," and you see again as you usually do.

My father had the power to cure people with trance medicine, with gemsbok-song trance medicine. Certain animals—gemsbok, eland, and giraffe—have trance songs named after them, songs long ago given by God. These songs were given to us to sing and to work with. That work is very important and good work; it is part of how we live.

It is the same with everything—even the animals of the bush. If a hunter is walking in the bush and God wants to, God will tell him, "There's an animal lying dead over there for you to eat." The person is just walking, but soon sees an animal lying dead in the bush. He says, "What killed this? It must have been God wanting to give me a present." Then he skins it and eats it; that's the way he lives.

But if God hadn't wanted, even if the hunter had seen many animals, his arrows would never strike them. Because if God refuses to part with an animal, the man's arrows won't be able to kill it. Even if the animal is standing close beside him, his arrows will miss every time. Finally he gives up or the animal runs away. It is only when God's heart says that a person should kill something, be it a gemsbok or a giraffe, that he will have it to eat. He'll say "What a huge giraffe! I, a person, have just killed a small something that is God's." Or it may be a big eland that his arrows strike.

That is God's way; that is how God does things and how it is for us as we live. Because God controls everything.

God is the power that made people. He is like a person, with a person's body and covered with beautiful clothes. He has a horse on which he puts people who are just learning to trance and becoming healers. God will have the person in trance ride to where he is, so God can see the new healer and talk to him.[1]

There are two different ways of learning how to trance and of becoming a healer. Some people learn to trance and to heal only to drum-medicine songs. My mother knew how to trance to these, although she never learned to heal. There are other people who know how to trance and to heal to drum-medicine songs as well as to ceremony-dance songs. The n/um is the same in both. If a person is lying down, close to death, and someone beats out drum-medicine songs, a healer will enter a trance and cure the sick person until he is better. Both men and women have n/um, and their power is equal. Just as a man brings a sick person back to health, so does a woman bring a sick person back to health.

My father was a very powerful healer. He could trance to both kinds of songs, and he taught n/um to my older brother. He also taught it to my younger brother. But when my father died, he stole Kumsa's medicine from him. He left Dau with it, but not Kumsa. Today, even if someone is lying down sick, Kumsa doesn't try to cure him. Only Dau does that.

My present husband, Bo, doesn't have n/um. He was afraid. People wanted to teach him but he refused. He said it would hurt too much.

N/um is powerful, but it is also very tricky. Sometimes it helps and sometimes it doesn't, because God doesn't always want a sick person to get better. Sometimes he tells a healer in trance, "Today I want this sick person. Tomorrow, too. But the next day, if you try to cure her, then I will help you. I will let you have her for a while." God watches the sick person, and the healer trances for her. Finally, God says, "All right, I only made her slightly sick. Now, she can get up." When she feels better, she thinks, "Oh, if this healer hadn't been here, I would have surely died. He's given me my life back again."

That's n/um—a very helpful thing!

I was a young woman when my mother and her younger sister started to teach me about drum-medicine. There is a root that helps you learn to trance, which they dug for me. My mother put it in my little leather pouch and said, "Now you will start learning this, because you are a young woman already." She had me keep it in my pouch for a few days. Then one day, she took it and pounded it along with some bulbs and some beans and cooked them together. It had a

horrible taste and made my mouth feel foul. I threw some of
it up. If she hadn't pounded it with the other foods, my
stomach would have been much more upset and I would
have thrown it all up; then it wouldn't have done anything
for me. I drank it a number of times and threw up again and
again. Finally I started to tremble. People rubbed my body as
I sat there, feeling the effect getting stronger and stronger. My
body shook harder and I started to cry. I cried while people
touched me and helped me with what was happening to me.

Eventually, I learned how to break out of my self and
trance. When the drum-medicine songs sounded, that's when
I would start. Others would string beads and copper rings
into my hair. As I began to trance, the women would say,
"She's started to trance, now, so watch her carefully. Don't let
her fall." They would take care of me, touching me and helping. If another woman was also in trance, she laid on hands
and helped me. They rubbed oil on my face and I stood
there—a lovely young woman, trembling in trance—until I
was finished.

I loved when my mother taught me, and after I had
learned, I was very happy to know it. Whenever I heard people beating out drum-medicine songs, I felt happy. Sometimes
I even dug the root for myself and, if I felt like it, cooked it
and drank it. Others would ask for some, but if they hadn't
learned how to trance, I'd say, "No, if I gave it to you, you
might not handle it well." But once I really knew how to
trance, I no longer drank the medicine; I only needed that in
the beginning.

When my niece gets older, I'll dig some of the root for
her, put it in her kaross for a few days, and then prepare it.
She will learn how to drink it and to trance. I will stand beside her and teach her.

Unlike my mother, I know how to cure people to drum-
medicine songs. An elderly uncle taught me a few years ago.
He struck me with spiritual medicine arrows; that's how everyone starts. Now when the drum starts sounding, "dong . . .
dong . . . dong . . . dong," my n/um grabs me. That's when I
can cure people and make them better.

Lately, though, I haven't wanted to cure anyone, even when they've asked. I've refused because of the pain. I sometimes become afraid of the way it pulls at my insides, over and over, pulling deep within me. The pain scares me. That's why I refuse. Also, sometimes after I cure someone, I get sick for a while. That happened not long ago when I cured my older brother's wife. The next day, I was sick. I thought, "I won't do that again. I cured her and now I'm sick!" Recently, Dau cured her again. I sat and sang the medicine songs for him. He asked me to help, but I said, "No, I was so sick the last time I almost died. Today, my medicine is not strong enough."

I am a master at trancing to drum-medicine songs. I lay hands on people and they usually get better. I know how to trick God from wanting to kill someone and how to have God give the person back to me. But I, myself, have never spoken directly to God nor have I seen or gone to where he lives. I am still very small when it comes to healing and I haven't made these trips. Others have, but young healers like myself haven't. Because I don't heal very often, only once in a while. I am a woman, and women don't do most of the healing. They fear the pain of the medicine inside them because it really hurts! I don't really know why women don't do more of it. Men just fear it less. It's really funny—women don't fear childbirth, but they fear medicine!

Chapter 14
Further Losses

THE THREAT of unpleasant encounters with the creatures of the bush is a major concern to the !Kung. The semidesert environment of the Dobe area has its share of dangerous animals (lions, leopards, cheetahs, hyenas, buffaloes, and elephants) and poisonous snakes (mambas, adders, cobras, and boomslangs). Wild dogs, wild cats, badgers, jackals, foxes, and other small mammals also abound, as do scorpions, centipedes, spiders, and other stinging insects. None of these species routinely preys upon humans and, except for the buffalo, the rock-python, and a few smaller mammals, most are rarely hunted or eaten by the !Kung. Returning with others from the village to animal kills temporarily abandoned, however, !Kung hunters often encounter lions or other large cats scavenging their kill. Loud noises and flailing with long sticks are likely to drive the cats off without incident. The greatest actual threat is the lone carnivore, too old, sick, or wounded to catch fast game animals, who may turn to humans or domestic animals for prey. Few !Kung have actually been killed this way, but those few are enough to perpetuate a general wariness. Carnivores are a major consideration in their reluctance to travel at night, and even dreams of carnivores, seen as portents of impending danger, may cause the !Kung to limit bush travel for a day or two.

Much more of a threat than wild animals is violence among people. The past is studded with fatalities that everyone knows about or remembers, and the prospect of tempers flaring out of control is dreaded; the fear of it forms an undercurrent in !Kung daily life. Open conflict, therefore, is actively guarded against. The constant talking heard in !Kung camps—people talking to themselves, to others, and even to those already talking, at most times of the day and night—is one way of expressing the normal tensions that build up in daily life. The cathartic release of trance, followed by total physical and psychic exhaustion, probably serves the same function. Even the freedom of movement people of both sexes enjoy helps create distance from escalating conflicts.

Sometimes, however, directness is unavoidable. At such times the good-natured tease—although not innocuous, still a fairly safe option—may be employed. Between two people who have a joking relationship, the following scene might transpire. A young woman walks into the village with a bright strand of beads around her neck. An older woman sees them and jokes, "Oh, those beads are already mine! Your past stinginess is going to be turned around today!" The younger woman returns the tease in the same spirit, "Look who's talking about stinginess! I would die of ugliness before my neck would be adorned with beads given by you!" The exchange develops into an insult match, in which the women level sexual and other verbal barbs at each other. Amusing as it is, the underlying criticisms do not go unnoticed. In a desire to maintain friendly relations, the younger woman gives her antagonist the beads (or something else) later that day. After a few weeks, the gift is reciprocated with one of comparable appeal. The problems between the women are thus resolved for a time.

If the two women are in-laws and have a respect relationship, the situation will be somewhat different. The older woman might sit in her hut and talk loudly to herself: "Does youth need anything to make it beautiful? How is it no one helps this old woman's heart feel young again?" It is likely that her target (or someone close to her) would hear this lament through the thin grass walls of the hut. Or the older woman might sing her criticisms for all to hear, accompanying herself on a thumb piano or pluriarc, while sitting alone in the darkness of the night. In either case, a generous exchange of gifts would probably result.

But of course anger is not always so easily diverted. If an undercurrent of serious unresolved problems existed between the two women, one might resent the other's tease and respond with a direct verbal attack instead of a mild retort. This could easily provoke a heated exchange in which each reviewed old grievances. Serious insults, curses, and threats might follow, or even a physical fight. At this point others would immediately intervene and pull them apart. Although they might continue to shout at each other, the conflict might very well end here. After everyone had cooled off, the two antagonists might actually be found sitting and laughing together later in the day.

Most conflicts are resolved at the verbal stage, but physical fights are nevertheless not uncommon. Women are nearly as likely as men to get into fights, although they initiate them far less frequently; once provoked they are also effective and determined fighters. Most fights between men and women are between husbands and wives, with the husband being the aggressor. Fights are generally spontaneous and passionate in nature and last only a few minutes. Friends and relatives, the only effective authorities, are responsible for physically separating those fighting as well as for preventing further clashes. Determination of guilt is not a major concern, and, except in the most extreme cases, punishment is not meted out. Group pressure makes it very clear, however, that violence is not a respected way to resolve conflicts.

In spite of this attitude, conflicts sometimes develop into violence. Such outbreaks rivet the attention and emotions of the entire community. People take sides, and long-buried resentments surface, provoking secondary arguments and fights, often remote from the original issue. Amid the pandemonium, someone may mention weapons, threatening, "I'm a man. I've got my arrows. I'm not afraid to die." If the brakes are not somehow applied, spears, clubs, knives, and poisoned arrows may enter the fray. (The !Kung have no ritualization of warfare and no weapons designed exclusively for use during violent confrontations.) If arrows are actually shot, they may fly about wildly in the confusion. With no known antidote to the poison, anyone struck by a poisoned arrow has less than a fifty-fifty chance of survival.

!Kung men between the ages of twenty and fifty are the ones most likely to resort to this type of violence (all the weapon-related deaths in the Dobe area during the last fifty years were caused by men). Men were also the usual victims, although an occasional female bystander died after being struck by a stray arrow. Because of the small size of the !Kung villages, the victims were generally known to the killers, but they were rarely close family members. Although most homicides occurred during outbursts of temper, retaliation against earlier homicides also resulted in a few cases of premeditated murder. To end this kind of violence, marriages might be arranged between the two feuding families.

Most of the people responsible for homicide in traditional times moved away from the original village and took up life elsewhere without further violence. If someone proved to be repeatedly dangerous, however, the group might decide that he should be killed. Once Tswana law was established in the area, those !Kung convicted of murder by the Tswana courts were sent to prison. The incidence of !Kung homicide, quite substantial before this time, diminished significantly, and since 1955 there have been no known homicides by !Kung living in the area.

Although comparisons between two cultures on these measures are difficult, what little evidence does exist points to a rate of violence among the traditional !Kung that is comparable to that found in American cities. However, the !Kung do not wage war, and if battle deaths are included in the American figures, our own rate becomes considerably higher. In addition, modern emergency medical procedures prevent many acts of violence in America from entering the homicide statistics, while no such procedures are available to the !Kung. Thus it is possible to enumerate violent acts in such a way as to make the !Kung seem less violent than we are; yet, as in all societies, conflict plays a significant role in !Kung life.

WHEN YOU GIVE birth to a number of children, you know one of them will probably die. That's what happened to me. The little one, the one I first gave birth to, she was the first; she died before I was even pregnant with the others. I mourned for her and cried; I squeezed the milk from my breasts, spilled it out into the sand because the fullness was killing my chest. I mourned for months. Then I started to think, "I'll still have others."

I became pregnant again and my stomach grew. I gave birth to my second child, Nai, and she was growing when I became pregnant with my third, a girl who also died very young. I became pregnant again and gave birth to my last born, Kxau. I took care of him while he grew. He, a little boy and she, a little girl, grew up together.

But they both died. My son was old enough to know about girls and to make love to them. My daughter had become a young woman and menstruated. Her breasts were large and stood straight out; her body was large—she wasn't small like me. She was beautiful! She died before my son did.

Nai and Kxau—two who grew up, two who were old enough to do things and help me. Their deaths made me feel pain. Eh, mother! I almost died of that pain. I mourned for them for many hot seasons. Because they did things with me. We went places together and talked about things. Nai's young brother had just started to go out hunting and bring back meat. Kxau only killed one large animal before he died, a gemsbok, but he had killed many smaller animals—steenbok and duiker. He gave me the meat and we sat around and talked. Kxau's older sister also helped—Nai took the water containers and filled them with water. Other times, even if I just sat, she followed the other women and went gathering. When she came back, she gave me the food she collected.

I remember once when I took her traveling with me in the bush and it was just the two of us; two women alone. It was while I was still married to Besa but had already started with Bo. Besa was always jealous, was always accusing me and yelling at me. One day, my heart simply exploded and I left with Nai, thinking, "She's old enough." Kxau stayed behind with Besa. We walked and walked, a long way, until we arrived where the nin berries grew. We stayed there and gathered them.

Besa left soon after we did. He followed our tracks until he came to us. He said that he had followed us to bring us a burning log, so we would be able to start our own fire in the bush. He said, "I understand you were angry when you left and that you two are traveling alone together. But, you are a woman and will become afraid of being alone in the bush and will make Nai afraid as well. So, for her sake, let me continue on this path with you."

I said, "I don't care what you do, because I don't like you any longer. You're so full of talk! Other people live, but you, you kill me with words! It's in the name of that, that I took the child with me today. If God favors us, if God gives us safe travel, we will continue to walk along this path together." Besa left and returned to the village.

Nai and I walked and walked until we came to a water well where we stopped for the night. I made a fire and Nai played the pluriarc[1] she had carried with her. She lay there, playing, and I sat nearby, eating nin berries. She played for a long time and when she stopped, we just sat together and talked. We talked and talked, so long that the moon set before we lay down to sleep. Nothing hurt us. The two of us just lay there and slept, slept very well. In the morning, we woke and left. We walked until we arrived at my brother's village.

When Dau saw us, he said, "What? What forced you to leave with your daughter, that the two of you would travel alone from your village like this? Did you sleep in the bush or did you walk all night?" Nai answered, "Mother and I left yesterday because she had a fight with Besa. (Nai always called him Besa because he wasn't her true father.) Her heart flew out. That's why we left. We slept at the water well along the way and now we're here." Dau said, "It's true that Besa talks a lot. But an animal or even little things could have killed you and your mother in the bush. The way your mother just took you alone ... something could have killed both of you."

We lived at my brother's village for a while, and while we were there, a Zhun/twa asked to marry Nai. Eventually, he did. I continued to live with my brother, but Nai moved to her husband's village. One day, someone came and told me, "Your daughter has had her first menstruation." I left and went to her. We danced during the days of the flow, danced for her each day. When it was finished, we washed her and she left the hut she had been lying in. When it was over, I returned to my brother's village.

After that, Nai's husband started to bother her for sex. She refused, thinking, "Haven't I just been washed from my first menstruation? Why is this man saying we should make love now?" She refused because of those thoughts. But he kept bothering her.

That's when it happened. One night he became so angry he grabbed her, and tried to take her by force. They struggled and he pushed her very hard. She fell down with a great force, so great that her neck was broken—one of the bones even stood out so you could see it.

She lived only a few days after that and was very sick. Someone came and told me, "Nisa, your daughter is very sick. Go and see her. Her husband struck her, and today, she is just lying still. I don't know where she is sick or what is hurting her, but I came to tell you."

I went back to her village and saw her. She could barely speak. Her arm motioned in the air and her hand showed how her husband had grabbed her. With much difficulty, she said, "My husband wanted to sleep with me, but I refused. He grabbed me, and pushed me, and now my neck is broken." She took my hand and had me feel her neck. I felt the broken bone.

We brought her back to our village where her uncle, Dau, tried to cure her. But he could see there was no cure. He said, "Your child ... the bone in her neck is broken and she is going to die. Now is when you should start crying for her. Yet here you are sitting, still hoping for something to change. It is true that this beauty of hers, this fair-skinned beauty which has always been hers, is still with her as she lies here. Is that why you think she may yet live and haven't started crying?"

He stopped trying to cure her and sat down. I saw that and started to cry. Then I stopped. I said, "No, a Zhun/twa killed my child and I won't cry for her. I'll just wait until that person comes here, maybe tomorrow, and when he does, I'll kill him. Or, maybe I'll do what he did—when his older sister comes here I'll kill her and bury her in the ground."

We stayed with my daughter until she died.[2] It was only two days. When she died, I cried and cried, "What is making this happen? My daughter was old enough to have given birth to a child, a child I could have held and greeted with joy. Yet, this woman who was already grown, this woman who was my daughter, is dead."

The next day, her husband came to us to mourn, came with his older sister. When I saw her, I grabbed her and shoved my knee into her. I cried, "You've already had your chance to give birth to children, but my daughter didn't." I threw her down and started doing it to her—I grabbed her throat; I wanted to break it. She started to shit as others came running and pulled me away from her. I kicked her in the stomach as we separated. Her brother, Nai's husband, said, "Even if Nai's mother seeks revenge, it's justified. I was the one who brought ruin to her."

I went and looked for my digging stick. I grabbed it into my hands, turned it around and around, and hit him with it. (I hit his body, not his head. I was afraid it would crack open and blood would be everywhere. I didn't want that; I was afraid of that.) I hit him, over and over. Finally, I stopped. I said, "I'm finished now. I hurt your sister and I hurt you. Now I'm finished. You and the others, take my daughter's body and bury her. I won't go with you."

That's what they did. They took her and buried her while I stayed in the village and cried.

Later, I went to the Tswana headman and told him what had happened. He called a tribal hearing about it. He asked

Nai's husband, "A young girl refused to sleep with you, yet you tried to take her by force?" Then he said, "You killed her; you robbed Nisa of her daughter. What are you prepared to give Nisa in return, Nisa who is crying beside you?" Nai's husband stood up and answered, "Yes, I was with my wife and told her I wanted to sleep with her. But she refused me."

The headman said, "You fool. When a young girl has her first menstruation, you don't have sex with her. You wait until she has finished with it. Nai knew what she was doing when she refused you. Yet, you went ahead and killed her!" Then he said, "Tomorrow, I want you to take five goats and give them to Nisa."[3]

I screamed, "No, my daughter is dead! This man killed my child. I don't want goats. I want you to take him to prison and kill him there." Then I started to cry, cry and cry and cry.

The headman didn't do that; he didn't really do anything to him. He didn't even beat him. He left him so he could just walk away, which he did. He still lives among us today. But he did come and give me the goats. I took three for myself and gave the others to the headman.

But after, I cried for months; I cried steadily. Only when a distant moon died, did I finally stop.

All I had left, then, was my son. We lived together a long time after Nai died before his chest started up against him. He was already a young man, a "shade expert."[4] He was so handsome all the young women were asking for *him* in marriage!

The sickness started after he returned from a trip with a Herero man to the East. The night he came back, he was fine. The next night, he also slept. But the next day, sickness entered his chest, just as it had his father's.

It started with a beehive he had seen in a termite mound while hunting in the bush. There was some honey in it, partially eaten by a honey-badger who had found it first. What was left in the hive was what eventually killed him. Kxau collected it and ate as he extracted it. That's when God speared his chest with a spiritual arrow. Perhaps God didn't want him

eating the honey the honey-badger had already eaten. Because, when he came back, he said, "Mother, I just saw a little honey that a honey-badger left behind. I ate some of it.
But now my chest hurts. It feels as if something struck me
here, as if a stick entered my chest and is trying to kill it."

My older brother started to cure him. While in a trance,
he saw what the cause of the sickness was. He said, "Yes, it's
the stick God struck him with that's making him sick. God
said he ruined the honey, that it belonged to the honey-badger. He should have left it for the badger to eat."

He was sick for a long time before he died. Day after
day, for months. First one month, then another and another,
each month dying a little more. Uhn, uhn . . . I felt tremendous pain! He was the only one left. I said, "This child is the
only one I have. He's the only one who helps me and does
things for me, who gives me food to eat and leather skins to
wear. And he's dying like this! How terrible this is!" My
brother and others kept trying to cure him. They worked on
him, laying on hands, but the sickness refused to leave his
chest.

It refused and eventually, he died.[5] I cried, "Why is it not
even one child remains with me now? What debt do I owe?
How have I wronged God? I haven't done anything wrong.
Nothing of God's have I hurt, not even a small thing. What
kind of mourning is God leaving with me now, having taken
all my children like this? What will I ever find to cure me of
my pain?"

This time I cried for many more months. My son had
been the only one left. Month after month I cried, until the
tears themselves almost killed me. I cried until I was sick, and
I was near death myself. My older brother came to me and
tried to help. He did medicinal trancing and cured me, laying
on hands and working hard, trying to make me better. Finally,
he said, "When this moon finishes, I want you to stop
mourning. Even God refuses what you are doing now. Even
God says you should stop crying for your son. You must stop
now!" Others told me the same, "Enough! Won't you be finished now?"

I listened to them and soon I stopped. I was exhausted. The mourning had been for all my children and I had no strength left. Asking God why I had been refused had worn me out.

Eventually, I went back to living, to every day living and doing things. Even though I had finished mourning, it was only slightly, because I kept missing them. I missed them when I sat alone and didn't see anyone to talk to. Then my heart would change. I missed them when I had an argument with someone and I was being yelled at. Then, I would think about the two of them. Because, whenever anyone had yelled at me before, Nai always defended me. Even if it was only a child that yelled at me. That's what she was like. After she died and someone argued with me, it would make me think and I would start to cry. Whenever Bo saw, he'd refuse, "Don't do that. If you cry, you'll make yourself sick. Now, don't start that again." The two of them . . . my daughter and my son . . . they caused me terrible pain, a heavy and awful pain.

Today, I rarely think of those who have died. My husband Tashay . . . I don't think of him. Isn't today another time? He isn't in my heart any longer. And even my children, I don't think of them either . . . only sometimes.

Not too long ago, my younger brother, Kumsa, and his wife gave me one of their children, little Nukha, to take care of for a while.[6] They lent her to me so I would help bring her up. His wife was pregnant with their third child and wanted to wean her. But Nukha didn't want to stop and cried all the time. Finally, my brother said, "My older sister, why don't you take care of her for us for a while." That's what I did. I took her and kept her with me. I'm still taking care of her today. I am the one bringing her up; I am the one beside whom she is growing and whom she calls Mother. She says her real mother is just another person, and refuses to sleep in her hut. She stays there during the day, sometimes, but at night she lies down next to me.

Taking care of her has made me very happy; it's as

though I had given birth to her myself. I love children. So, when my brother had his second child, I took her and kept her with me.

In your heart, your child, your mother, and your father are all equal. When any one of them dies, your heart feels pain. When your child dies, you think, "How come this little thing I held beside me and watched all that she did, today has died and left me? She was the only child I had with me; there wasn't another I spent my days with. We two stayed together and talked together. This God . . . his ways are foul! Why did he give me a little one and then take her away?"

You cry out like that and cry and cry and cry. It is the same if it is your mother. You cry for her as you do for your child. You pull off your beads and ornaments so your neck and body are bare. You mourn for her, you miss her, and your heart is miserable. You think, "Mother was the one who helped me with the food I ate; she was the one who gave me presents of beads. Now that she's dead, who's going to help me?" If you are living in your in-laws' village, you have other thoughts. "Here I am living in the heart of other people, not my own relatives. God came, took mother and left. Now people will be unkind to me. They will yell at me, first one person, then another and another."

Your thoughts come from your heart. Isn't this what your heart also says: "What kind of thing ruled that this is the way life should be? God tricked me when he took mother from me. I can see her as if she were still alive, yet God has already taken her."

Perhaps your father is still alive and living with you. But, after time passes, his months are also finished. He, too, gets sick and dies. And your thoughts return to death. "Who is saying this should be so? First my mother died and then my father was the only one who helped me. Now, he has also died. Who's going to help me now? Who's going to help with food to eat and things to wear? God is refusing me. God has done this to my parents and is no longer going to help me."

You cry and mourn for your father, cry and cry and cry.

Finally, people tell you, "Look, even if you continue to cry like this, where do you think your father is? Where do you think you are going to see him? God has already taken him and that's the end. If you keep crying like this, God will take you, too, and then you will be able to see him. How else will your crying help you to see him again?" That's what people say. Soon, you are quiet. You finish mourning and just sit.

It's the same for your husband. When he gets sick, people make medicinal cuts on him and the healers try and cure him. But he dies, nonetheless. You cry for him and for the others as well.

The death of your parents, husband, or children—they are equal in the amount of pain you feel when you lose them. But when they all die and you have no family left, then you really feel pain. There is no one to take care of you; you are completely alone. If your mother dies and your father dies, but your husband is still alive, that's still all right. Your heart says, "Yes, even though my parents are dead, there is still someone to look after me." Or, if your husband dies and your parents are still alive, the death of your husband makes you very unhappy, but after a while, the pain subsides; you know your father and mother are still with you.

It is different with a child, though. Even if the others around you are still alive, the death of your child is tremendously painful. You loved your child and you feel the pain for months. It tugs at you and only leaves when you are sitting and pregnant with another.

The death of any of your family is hard, but if others are alive, after a while your heart stops hurting. But when each one dies until, finally, they are all dead, your pain continues month after month after month. You look at other people who are surrounded by their families and you ask yourself why your whole family had to die. Your heart pains and you cry and can't stop. You cry and don't eat; you become thin, thin to death. Only some far distant moon, when that strikes, do you feel like a person again.

That's the way it is. God is the one who destroys. It isn't people who do it. It is God himself.

Chapter 15
Growing Older

When you think about death, what do you think?
Death is a bad thing. When you die, you can't see. You just go to the place in the sky.
And do what?
That's where people go. How can we know what they do there?
Don't the adults tell you?
No, they just say you go to the sky and live there, live with all the people who died before you.
Is that bad?
Yes, aren't you dead?
Are you afraid?
I'm afraid. Dying is a horrid thing. You can't see anyone or anything.
What about getting old?
That's bad, too. When you're old, what can you do?

> (conversation between the author and a
> fourteen-year-old !Kung girl)

THE PROSPECT OF GROWING OLD is not something many !Kung look forward to, but they recognize that old people have unique things to offer. !Kung culture, humane in most aspects, is no less humane in its treatment of the elderly. Older people are highly respected, often influential in the group, and privileged in some ways that younger adults are not.

For most !Kung, growing old may be considered a luxury: barely over 20 percent of those born ever reach the age of sixty.

(In modern societies, it is closer to 83 percent.) Death therefore is not associated exclusively with the elderly, but befalls people of all ages. Those !Kung who survive to old age are threatened by infectious diseases and accidents, as are !Kung of all ages, but they are free of many diseases common to older people in other cultures, including atherosclerosis, hearing loss, hypertension, and diseases that are more obviously stress-related, such as ulcers and colitis. Many !Kung at age sixty are vigorous and independent (they have been sturdy enough to resist diseases others succumbed to), but more than half have some physical problem that makes them dependent on others. Partial loss of vision is the most common of these. Walking difficulties and respiratory diseases (tuberculosis, chronic bronchitis, and emphysema) are also frequent. Tooth decay is essentially absent, probably because the !Kung eat so little sugar and refined carbohydrates. (They regularly care for their teeth by rubbing them with a plant stem that both cleans and whitens them.) Due to the abrasiveness of many !Kung foods, however, the teeth of many old people are worn down close to the gums.

Those who reach the age of sixty have a life expectancy of another ten years (as compared to almost twenty years in the present-day United States). Of course, some !Kung confound the statistics and live to a ripe old age. During both my field trips, there were many old people actively participating in !Kung daily life and there were even a few "very old" people around—those determined by demographer Nancy Howell to be in their eighties. One man was close to ninety. Nevertheless, old people in !Kung society make up a fairly small portion of the population as a whole (only 10 percent are aged sixty and over, as compared to 16 percent in the United States).

Because women usually marry men five to fifteen years older than themselves, as many as 40 percent of !Kung women over sixty are widows. Although most women widowed in their forties or early fifties remarry within a year or so, an older woman may choose to remain unmarried. If she has no surviving children or if her children, her closest kin, and her friends live far away, she may decide to enter a marriage as a second wife. As a co-wife she will receive companionship and security, but at a cost. Being the newcomer—the junior wife—in a long-standing marriage, she may be expected to do a large proportion of the daily chores, may be less favored by the husband, and is likely to encounter the jealousy of the first wife. If she has children and grandchildren or other close relatives nearby, she may decide against the polygamous life and set up a hut of her own "in the heart of her family."

The !Kung do not think of themselves in terms of chronological age. They measure the passage of time by less precise strokes—the changes of the seasons, the cycles of the moon, and the rhythms of day and night. The human life span is described as an orderly progression of the biological and social events that most people experience. Childhood, for example, is seen as a sequence: the onset of social smiling, sitting alone, standing, walking, and learning to talk. Similar sequences describe adulthood and aging. Although they do not keep track of numerical age, the !Kung are acutely aware of relative age. Since age is associated with status, "who is older"—be it a few years or a few days—is extremely important and affects all relationships. Except for the occasional visitor from a distant area, people usually know the age ranking of everyone around them.

A term of respect—the suffix *n!a* attached to a name—acknowledges the attainment of full adulthood. It may occasionally be applied to a younger person to applaud high achievement (in hunting, trancing, or playing a musical instrument, for example), but it is usually given to people in their forties, a time of great vigor and productivity for both men and women. It may also be used to distinguish them from younger people with the same name. By their late fifties, however, *n!a n!a* may be used to express the greater respect that comes with their advancing age. ≠*Da*, meaning "quite old," describes people in their late sixties, and those who live into their seventies and beyond often joke about being ≠*da !ki*, literally, "so old as to be almost be dead."

For most !Kung, the rate of aging seems comparable to what it is in our own and other cultures. The constant exposure to the wind and sun dries and wrinkles the skin early in life. But when anthropologists' guesses of !Kung ages were checked against painstaking age verifications made by Nancy Howell, the guesses

321

turned out to be quite close. This might be explained by the fact that the !Kung do not put on excess weight as they age, thus keeping a youthful appearance.

An undeniable sign of aging, for women, is the cessation of menses. This seems to occur in the late forties, but its exact occurrence is often difficult to ascertain, even for the women themselves. For those who have their last child in their mid-to-late thirties and menstruate for years after the birth, menopause is usually very clear. For those who give birth in their forties, however (the oldest recorded birth among the !Kung was to a woman of forty-six), nursing their last child may suppress menstruation long enough to conceal menopause. When they stop lactating, menstruation may simply never resume. This picture is compounded by certain illnesses that cause temporary or permanent cessation of menstruation. However, by the age of fifty, most !Kung women acknowledge that their menstrual cycles have permanently ceased.

The feelings with which a !Kung woman faces menopause usually depend on her reproductive history. For an infertile woman or for one with no surviving children, the realization that she will remain childless is painful. For those surrounded by healthy children some of whom may be having children of their own, the end of reproductive life may come more easily. As one woman explained, "When you stop menstruating, your heart is happy not to have more children." Nevertheless, menopause is an inescapable sign of aging, a harbinger of mortality; as such, it is certainly not welcomed.

Most women describe the end of menstruation, like menstruation itself, as a thing of no great importance: "Your body is fine. There is no pain. It's just your moons that stop." When I asked one woman if that made her feel bad, she said, "If I were young, it would. But I'm old." !Kung women do not seem to associate menopause with the physical symptoms reported by women in our own culture. A certain amount of physical discomfort is described for the initial months, but hot flashes and prolonged physical or psychic distress are not reported. It is conceivable, although not likely, that menopause actually affects !Kung women and American women differently, because of diet, or life style, or causes as yet unknown. However, it is also possible that the physiological effects are similar but that the stoical attitude that makes !Kung women aspire to give birth alone also keeps them from recognizing or discussing any physical reactions they do have.

By the age of sixty, life for a !Kung man or woman is substantially changed from what it was at forty. Reproductive activity has long since ceased for women and, although biologically possible for men, it appears to be rare for them as well after the mid-fifties. The !Kung claim that many old people lead reasonably active sex lives, but the irreverence with which certain older people's sexual habits are jokingly discussed may suggest that an active sex life is somewhat unusual.

Economic activity has also slowed by this age. Most old people no longer contribute much food to the group, although many are able to forage for themselves. (They vary in the distances they are able to travel, and those who must forage near the village are likely to find only less desirable plant foods bypassed by younger adults. But because vegetable foods are usually pooled within a family, an older person will probably have the same varied diet as a younger person.) Men who are too old to follow along on the hunt, interpreting tracks and proposing strategies, turn to activities they have engaged in to some extent all their lives—setting bird and animal traps and gathering vegetable foods. Husbands and wives often pursue these activities together as long as their health allows. At more advanced ages, they may become nearly totally dependent on younger family members.

Although some older people complain that their spiritual abilities lessen with age, others claim that their powers continue to strengthen. The latter may be especially true for women, who wait until after their childbearing years before seriously exploring trancing and curing. Older men and women play an essential role in spiritual matters, as well, because they are not bound by food taboos and other restrictions that apply to younger adults. They confidently handle ritual substances (such as those associated with male and female initiation ceremonies) considered too potent for those still involved in having children.

Old people know things. They know the history of the immediate and the more distant past. They know who married whom, how people are related, and who was born when. If something unusual happens, it is likely that an older person was there when it happened before, and will know what to do. Old people also know the year-to-year variation in an area's food resources, so there is a good chance that when conditions are poor they will know where to go for food.

Apart from such knowledge, there is not very much that old people traditionally have. Material possessions, though of value at any one time, are not accumulated over a lifetime. There is also little, if any, material inheritance following death. The mutual exchange of goods characteristic of the !Kung economy continues throughout life, but many of the partners in an older person's exchange network (parents, siblings, close relatives, and peers) will have died. Those who remain may become part of a young person's "inheritance."

Some old people, however, do "own" something that affords them a certain degree of influence. For water and food resources, the !Kung recognize ownership—the right of use, usually held by the oldest person in the group whose family can be traced back longest in the vicinity. It is rare that these rights are contested or that an owner denies others short-term access to the resource; but ownership itself is an influential and desirable position.

Variation in the quality of life among the old is quite substantial. If one's spouse is alive, if one's children have survived, if one's grandchildren live nearby, if there are other close relatives in the village, old age may be quite enjoyable. When younger adults come back from hunting and gathering, they bring enough food for everyone. Evenings can be spent telling stories of the time of the creation, when animals were still people and the creatures of the bush got their markings. Grandchildren too old to sleep innocently with their parents may share their grandparents' blankets, and may be left in their grandparents' care for days or weeks at a time. Advice will be asked for, opinions will be listened to, and affection will be generously offered. Some older women, having survived their husbands but still surrounded by family, are among the most influential members of the group.

For the 5 percent of men and 20 percent of women who survive their spouses and children, however, old age may be bleak. Others may not provide for their needs in the way close relatives would. They may become a burden on the group—food may have to be specially gathered and prepared, travel may have to proceed at a slower pace, and nomadic rounds may have to be kept minimal. It has been suggested that in traditional life those without close kin would be less well cared for in illness and might be less likely to survive times of crisis.

A !Kung woman (or man) growing old today, then, faces an uncertain future: her economic contribution to the group is sure to lessen; she is likely to become a widow; physical disabilities may make her increasingly dependent; she may even have to move to a Tswana or Herero cattle post to rely on the generosity of others to provide for her needs.

But age should still bring her respect, especially as she is looked to for the stories of the past, whether mythic or historical. She was there when the first Herero moved into the region, and twenty-five years later when the first anthropologists arrived. She knows the histories and scandals of people living and dead, and the folktales kept alive by word of mouth from one generation to the next. She will be able to amuse others with ribald accounts of the often zany behavior of the mythic heroes—like the tricks Kauha, the !Kung God, played on his wives before he ascended to the heavens, or the argument between the moon and the hare as to whether death was to be permanent, as the hare wanted, or only temporary, as the moon argued, using the example of his own continual rebirth. By telling these stories and the stories of her life and experiences, she may be able to preserve in some measure the richness of traditions that are in danger of being lost.

AFTER MY CHILDREN DIED, I just continued to live.[1] While I was married to Bo, we almost had a child together. I hadn't seen my period for three months, but then a sickness entered me. I was sick for a while and after that, I miscarried.[2] I even saw it; a tiny little fetus. Bo said I miscarried because I had made love to other men. But I said, "No, I've been sick a long time and that's what caused this miscarriage."

After that, there was nothing more; I didn't get pregnant again. I just kept menstruating, for months, for years. But even that has left me now. It's only been a few months, no more than a handful. One month I felt a little pain and then I menstruated. The next month, I felt even more uncomfortable. After that, the moon left me and I didn't see any more periods. But the discomfort remains. Because, when the moon doesn't come to you, it causes your insides to hurt.[3]

Maybe you could give me some medicine? I'd like to start menstruating again so my insides would stop hurting. Maybe you could also give me some medicine so I could conceive again. I've heard Europeans have medicine like that. If I were to menstruate again, I'd be happy. Then I'd feel healthy again.

Childbirth really hurts; its pain is very bad. For years, now, my heart has been happy that I haven't been pregnant. I've left that blood behind. God has seen very well by having done this to me, by not having given me any more children.

God refused to help me with children. When I gave birth, they died. Born and then, dead. That's because God refused me. I gave birth many times, but he killed them all. He could have left just one. How could I possibly give birth to another now? Even my monthly cycles are gone. God's taken that, too. That's why I know I'm finished with having children, little babies. Because, when you are still menstruating, after a few months, you may get pregnant. But once you stop, you are cut off from that. Then you are old and just continue to live.

That's who I am today. My hair is full of gray; I am an

old woman. That's why I have stopped menstruating and why I am finished with all that.

Today . . . I'm just living.

Not long ago I had a dream[4] that I was pregnant and that I gave birth to a little girl. I thought, "What? Haven't I already stopped menstruating? How could I have given birth to this child, this beautiful child?" Because I gave birth to her as I had my own children. I held her and called her, "My daughter . . . my daughter." I took care of her and she started to grow. Then she died and I cried and cried and cried. I said, "Why is God treating me like this, always refusing to help? Is something trying to kill me by taking this wonderful child?"

I cried and cried and my crying was full of pain. I was sobbing so loudly that I woke myself and realized I had been dreaming.

Why did I dream I was pregnant with a child that died, when I've just now stopped menstruating? Was God trying to fool me with that dream? Was God playing tricks on me? God doesn't want to help me, so why was I asking to be pregnant again?

I dream quite often. A few months ago, I dreamed about an animal that lives in a hole, whose hands and feet are like a person's: an antbear. I dreamed that I struck it with a spear and that it screamed, "Ouw! Who struck me with that spear?" I said, "Bo, listen to that. Listen! Does a person kill an animal and it starts to talk? How come it spoke to me?" Because, although it was an animal, it had the speech of a human.

We started to run, calling out in fear. But as hard as I tried, I couldn't move. Bo was also frightened and ran. The antbear stayed in the hole, talking. Was it a person talking like that? I kept trying to run, but I couldn't. I cried out, "Take my hand . . . take my hand . . ." Bo came back and took my hand, then we ran off together. The antbear just stayed in the hole.

The things God brings, they aren't good for me.

Sometimes I dream every night and then many nights go

by and I don't dream. Sometimes I dream that I've died, that I am sick for a long time and then die. If I dream like that, when dawn breaks, my body feels terrible and I get sick. I live like that for a while, then I get better and my body feels fine again.

Another dream I have is that I walk a long distance to a well, one with an ivory palm tree nearby. I dream that I am with a group of people and that, as we're all sitting near the well, I fall in. I try to get out by holding on to the sides, but each time I lift myself up, I fall down. I try, again and again, but I keep falling back into the water.

Even this morning God struck me with a dream about falling. I dreamed I was climbing a tree, looking for some gum resin to eat, and I fell down. As I fell, a branch struck my leg and I cried out with pain, "Ouw! That branch went right into me!" Because the branch pierced right into my leg and broke off.

Then you, Marjorie, you came and helped me. You said, "Oh, Nisa . . . you're dead!" You called to the others and you all tried to get the stick out of my leg. Finally, you were able to pull it out. You put medicine on it and made it better. Then you gave me other medicine to drink.

The dream woke me up, very early this morning. I was trembling to death from it and my leg was hurting in that very spot. I shook and shook and said, "What use could this dream possibly have? God really likes to trick me, telling me I fell out of a tree." Then I thought, "That Marjorie, she helped me get better."

I just lay there and wouldn't let myself go back to sleep. I was afraid of dreaming the same dream again. I lay there, trying to keep myself awake, until dawn broke, aware of lying there.

When I was a small child, I dreamed but I didn't remember what I dreamed. I probably didn't even know to say, "I'm dreaming," because I wasn't aware of things then. I just dreamed and sometimes I would cry. But I didn't know what was making me cry.

Once I was older, I knew that I dreamed and knew the

names of the things in the dreams. Some days I dreamed that I was living and eating meat. Other days I dreamed that I was crying. Sometimes I dreamed that an animal bit me or that someone hit me.

Marjorie, God's dreams embarrass me (laughs)! I recently dreamed that a man, one who lives here, slept with me. I said, "No, my husband will catch me. Don't sleep with me." But he didn't listen and he wanted me, so we slept together. My husband didn't catch us. But in the morning, I woke and thought, "God is trying to hurt me, having me dream this way about men."

Another night I dreamed that I was sleeping with someone and that my husband did catch us. He hit us, again and again. When I woke, I thought, "The things I dream about! God keeps bringing me these dreams about men!"

Another dream was that my husband was making love to another woman and I saw them. I don't know who she was, I just saw them in the dream. I yelled at him and they separated. After, my husband wanted me and refused the other woman.

Dreams about men are good dreams—it means that men find you attractive and want you. When that happens, you dream about sex.

I dream like that all the time. God really tortures me with dreams (laughs)! But when I dream that someone is making love to me, it makes me happy. It means I have lovers and I like that.

Me, I'm an older woman. But I still have strength. I still have interest in sex. Strength. But it's just a little now. Is it my heart? I don't know. Has my heart already died? Perhaps. Because my heart hasn't been looking for men; it hasn't been seeking a lover. I just sit around, day after day. Then one day, only then does my heart rise and want a little. Only then do I look for a man for some "food"—a man who will stay with me for a while.

But as I am today, my heart is lying down; perhaps it has even fallen asleep. Its excitement hasn't broken loose inside.

When I'm heavier, my heart will stand tall and people will say, "Oh, look at Bo's wife, how beautiful she is! What a beautiful woman Bo is married to!" And I'll wear beads all over my body and I'll take a piece of cloth, a scarf, and tie it around my head. Then I'll walk around and look beautiful. My heart will be so happy ... I'll be just like a young woman again!

Today, I feel old and don't want lovers. I've worn myself out. Today, I feel ugly. Not like before, when I felt beautiful. When I was a young woman, I was truly beautiful! Now I am tired and thin and no longer attractive. It's in the name of all this I'm not looking for sex now.

Maybe another day. Another day when my heart wants, I'll ask someone, "Is it because I'm unattractive that you haven't asked me to sleep with you?"

There are many men who still want me and don't refuse me because I am old. They come to where I sit and talk to me about it. But I refuse them. I tell them that I am old and don't want lovers. They ask, "Why? What's wrong? Other older women have lovers. Why are you saying a man won't make love to you?" I tease, "No, I refuse. Because, if I were to have one of you young men as a lover, you shade experts, I'd die. Your strength, your strong heavy bodies would kill me."

They say, "Don't you know that even cows, when they are old, still have sex? It's the same with an older woman; you still have sex with her, even if she's old. So, what's wrong with you that you refuse to let someone make love to you?" I say, "A cow, when a cow is old and a bull has sex with her, she falls down. Even you have seen a cow falling down on her thighs and just lying there when she is old. So, why do you say you should have sex with me? If you did, you'd kill me."

When the young men hear what I have to say, they go away. Except one young man, he came back again. But I still sent him away.

Another day I'll be interested again. Another day I'll think about men. Then I'll put on some powder and string some

beads to wear. I'll wear the beads and powder and I'll be
beautiful again, so beautiful that the men will say, "Nisa,
aren't you a lovely one!" I'll smell so good they'll say, "Why
is this older woman who smells so sweetly refusing me?" I'll
laugh and say, "Go away! Who's grabbing me? Do I have
something that belongs to you? Who's trying to steal it from
me? I'm old, but it's still mine. I'm not going to give it away.
What's wrong with you that every time we meet, you ask me
for it and even though I refuse, you ask me for it again?" I'll
refuse and chase him away.

That's what happened recently with a man. He asked me,
"Nisa, won't you give me something?" I said, "There's no
food inside my hut today." He said, "I'm not asking for ordinary food." He pointed to me and said, "I'm asking for that
special food, right over there. Won't you give me some?" I
teased, "That food has been finished. People have eaten and
eaten and there's no more left. Today, the fruit has been finished and only the shell remains. There's no nourishment or
sweetness left. It is unsatisfying; it is like an insect that bites."

Perhaps this winter, when it is very cold, I will agree to
him. But today it is still hot and I'll just lie beside my husband. Because an old woman like me doesn't like the cold.
Now, with the hot season here, there's no cold to be afraid
of. But when winter comes, I'll agree. My husband will go out
hunting and I will steal off with my young lover. He's the
only new one I'll have.

There are a few men, a few of my lovers, who still live in
my heart. There's Debe, and there's Kantla, who has been
with me from the beginning. The most important one now,
the one strongest in my heart, is Debe. I really like him. Even
yesterday, while we were sitting around, he came up and
talked to me. His heart really likes me. That's part of why I
like him so much. If he didn't, if his whole heart didn't feel
about me the way it does, then maybe I wouldn't like him as
much as I do.

One time, Bo found out about us. Debe and I had gone
with some other people to live in the mongongo groves for a

few days. When we returned to the village, people saw us
and said, "Oh, you're all already dead! Nisa, you and your
friend are finished. Your husbands are going to kill you." Because my friend was also there with her lover. My heart became miserable. I said, "If that's what's going to happen, then
I'll sit here and when my husband comes, let him just kill
me."

My friend's husband was the first to arrive. He started to
hit her, beating her hard. I wondered what was going to happen to me. I left to get some tobacco and when I came back,
I sat down in a group of people; Debe was also sitting there.
I got up to give some presents of mongongo nuts and when I
sat down again, Bo arrived. He stood for a moment, looking
at us, then he ran past me and grabbed Debe. They started to
fight, grabbing and hitting each other until others separated
them. Drinking anger, Bo came to where I was sitting and
kicked me in the chest. He kicked so hard it sounded,
"Bamm!" and knocked me over so I landed in the branches
of a nearby bush.

Someone helped me up. Someone else yelled at Bo,
"What's the matter with you? Nisa's a woman. What did you
think you were killing when you almost killed her? Don't you
know you could have broken her chest?" I sat there, quietly. I
was afraid of Bo's anger so I didn't say anything. Everyone
else was there, talking about what was happening.

That night, we slept. But the next morning, a Tswana
truck came by on its way back to the East. I thought, "Today,
I'll join the truck's tracks; I'll run away on it when it leaves." I
heard myself thinking these thoughts. I asked myself, "Is that
true?" I answered, "Yes, that's true." I went over to the driver
and said, "I'm afraid my husband will kill me. I'd like to join
these other people and go with you back East."

As the truck started to leave, I got on. My husband saw
and started to run after us, running in the truck's spoor. The
truck kept on until it reached the next village where it
stopped so the drivers could drink some Herero cows' milk. I
was waiting with the others in the back of the truck.

Bo had continued to run, and had followed the tracks in

the sand until he caught up with us. He ran to where the Tswanas were sitting and yelled, "Hey, black man, give me back my wife! Leave her here. Give her back to me." He started to shout, insulting and cursing them, "Have your penises died that you took my wife with you? Death to your genitals, black men! Now, leave my wife here."

Finally, one of the men said, "Here's your wife," and he gave me to Bo. We walked back together to the village and that was all. We continued to live with each other, but since then, I've been afraid of having lovers and have refused new men. I even refused Debe for a while.

Not long after this incident, Debe came to me and said, "Nisa, I want to marry someone now. Should I?" I said, "Yes, marry her." He married and that's how it was. But he still wanted me, even though I refused him. He came to me one time and I chased him away. He came to me again and I told him to leave: "You, yourself, have a young woman for a wife now."

He left but came back again, another night. He said, "Nisa, make the bed so we can lie down." I said no, and he left again. But the next time he came, I finally agreed, I agreed to having him again.

Lovers, yes. I almost died because of Debe. My husband almost killed me that time. What bothered Bo most was that we had gone away together. I don't think he would have been as upset if we had just stolen inside the hut. Sometime after, he even spoke to Debe with words that were very beautiful. He said, "Debe, I almost killed you that time because you did a foul thing—you took my wife and went away with her. That's why I was so angry. But if you don't do that again, if you don't distress me to death, then I won't yell at you again. Because everyone seems to have affairs. You aren't the only one. That's why people no longer argue about it so much, because everyone's doing it. So, now don't say that I am being unfair to you."

After that, he stopped being so jealous, probably because Debe finally married someone—one of Bo's nieces—and wasn't single anymore. Also, Bo really likes me and doesn't want me to leave. Even yesterday, Debe was around our camp and when Bo saw him, he told me he knew that I might go and make love to him. That was all he said. But I could see it was in his heart, his heart which is a man's heart. That's why I won't meet Debe when Bo is around.

Last night, there was a dance in a nearby village and I left it to go and get something from my hut. When I arrived, Debe was there. He asked me to go off with him, but I refused. I said, "No, my husband will yell at me. If he doesn't see me at the dance very soon, he'll yell at me." So Debe kissed me on the mouth and left. My heart was very happy and I went back to the dance.

But I really like him! Maybe I will meet him. Maybe tomorrow night I will cheat, just a little bit—a tiny spoonful!

And Kantla? My heart still goes out to him; he is still an important man in my life. Even now, if my husband goes away, Kantla may come and lie down with me. We met not so very long ago. Neither Bo nor his wife, Bey, knew. But most of the time, we're afraid. When there are a lot of people around, we just look at one another; we glance into each other's eyes and our hearts burn. When that happens, I think, "Oh, my lover. We have to act this way because there are so many people around and we're afraid of Bo and Bey."

Sometimes Bo is jealous and when he sees Kantla, he'll ask me why I have him as my lover. I can see his heart and how full of jealousy it is. That's why I only meet Kantla when Bo and Bey aren't there. But, other times, Bo seems to accept him and even greets him with a friendly greeting. He'll call him "my older brother" even though they aren't related. Because, after all, Kantla started with me long before I started with Bo.

Bey, of course, knows about us, but she isn't jealous. Even long ago, when we were young, she wasn't jealous. Nor is Kantla afraid to come over to me and touch me, even if Bey's sitting right there. But if another woman is with him, Bey yells, "Leave this man alone!" and bites her. So do I. But we've never been that way toward each other. We've always liked each other and we call each other "co-wife."

But today, only a small part of my heart is with Kantla, because his ways have ruined my heart. He is deceitful and bad. He has another woman. What can I do when he's with her? Yesterday, I spoke to him about it. I told him to drop her, but he didn't listen. He said I was being jealous. I said, "No, I'm not jealous. I'm afraid of getting sickness from her."

That's why some days my heart refuses him. But other days, my heart is still very strong for him. I don't know how much longer I will keep him. Should I have him along with Debe? Debe doesn't like it that I have Kantla and he tells me to leave him. And Kantla, he tells me to leave Debe. He says Debe is only a child. But I say, "Debe may be young, but his head is full of sense and I won't leave him."

I feel strongly about both of them. If I go somewhere else, I think about them and miss them. When I see either one, my heart stands strong again. Then, everything is fine.

What I don't understand is what my woman's heart is doing to me! Does it simply like men?

I still want my husband. When he says to me, "Today, I'm going to look to you for 'food,'" then my heart is happy. He comes to me, and after we finish, he lies down and I lie down.

Sometimes, I also refuse him, although the last time I did that was long ago. I told him I was sick, that my body was thin and that maybe we should just leave it for a while. He asked me, "Am I responsible for that? No, God is the one who made you thin and sick." Then we lay down and slept.

Another time, he yelled and said it was because I had other men. I said, "No, that's not true. Does a woman refuse her husband when she has a lover?" He said, "You've got lovers! If you didn't, you wouldn't refuse." I said, "Nonsense! Do you see anyone as thin and sick as I am having sex with someone else?"

That was when he was still sleeping with me often. But for a while, now, he's hardly slept with me at all. He sleeps with me one night, then not again for a long time and we just live beside one another. Only another month, when the

moon first strikes, will he sleep with me again, just one night.
We live again until the next moon strikes. That's what he's
been like.

Perhaps his heart doesn't want me any more. Maybe
that's why he hasn't been sleeping with me more often. I
really don't know what it is or understand why he has so little interest in sex now. When he does sleep with me, it's very
good. Maybe he thinks I'm old? He tells me I'm too thin and
that when I'm heavier again, it will be better.

Whatever it is, it isn't good; it makes me feel very bad.

Because I still have interest in sex, but when I want it, Bo
doesn't help at all. He isn't interested. That's why I have to
look for other men, so I can find it for myself. That's also why
I have Debe and why I like him. He is almost like a husband
to me, and he is someone who knows about work. If you're
with him for the night, he'll have sex with you until dawn
breaks.

My other husbands weren't like Bo. When I was with Tashay, one night we would make love and another we
wouldn't. Sometimes, we made love twice in one night—first,
when we lay down and again, before dawn. And Besa, he was
always interested! He was always aroused, always erect. He
didn't let you rest! As his wife, you never rested. He'd have
sex with you until you were exhausted and worn out. Your
whole body was tired after he did his work. That man, he
really wanted sex! I never could understand him. What do
you suppose he was eating? He would make me so tired! I'd
think, "Why is Besa having sex with me so often? Does he
want to screw me to death?"

Because that man, he really liked sex. Mother!

When Bo and I were still lovers and hadn't married yet,
in one night he would also sleep with me many times. Even
after we married, it was like that. His sexual interest in me
was always good. His heart was full of warmth and his love
for me was very strong. He slept with me often and it was
very good. Even a few months ago it was still like that.

That's why, what has been happening recently, I don't
like, and why I have been asking him, if he can be like that,

what has made him change? I don't know what is wrong. It isn't that he's lost his strength or that he is no longer potent, because he is still very strong in that way. Perhaps it is something in his heart. Perhaps his heart has died, because I've never heard about his being with other women. If he has them, he wouldn't tell me, because Zhun/twasi fear their spouses and don't tell. They just have their affairs and don't talk about them. So I don't really know. But since I haven't heard about him from anyone else, I think he probably doesn't have other women.

Or perhaps he isn't interested in me any more.

It was only four months ago that I asked him about it for the first time. Before that, I saw how often he was with me and how good it was. We were living alone in the bush when it started. I asked, "Even though we're not sleeping where other people live and it's only the two of us by ourselves, why haven't you been wanting to sleep with me? Our hut stands by itself and there is no one else beside us, so why aren't we sleeping together?" He said, "Because I'm sick. If you're sick and have sex, you might die while lying on top. You're talking like a child, saying I should have sex when I'm sick."

After he told me that, I thought I would just stop talking about it for a while, that I'd leave it at that. Because I don't believe that he's sick. There's nothing wrong. He's saying that, but it's not true. Do you understand that that's what he's doing? He's just trying to make me think he's sick. That's why I dropped that talk and didn't ask him again.

But I keep those thoughts in my heart. I still think my thoughts.

I'm fairly sure it isn't other women. Before he was with me, when he didn't have another wife, he had many women. But after he married me, he refused them. Only I am the one who steals. I wonder why . . .

The other day I told him he should have an affair with a young woman, but he refused. He asked, "Why is it, when you see another woman, you want to give her to me?" I said, "Why shouldn't I? I'll let you be with other women. Go ahead, have an affair with that young woman." But he said he wouldn't be with a married woman. If her husband found him in his hut, he'd kill him. I stopped talking about it after that.

Some days, I feel hurt and angry because of all this. That's when he asks, "What's upsetting you? Why are you so angry?" I say, "Because you didn't really marry me. If you had, you would be sleeping with me." He says, "Why are you always mourning for sex? Why are you, a woman, always complaining about wanting sex?" I say, "What did you think you would give me when you married me? Did you marry me with the idea that you'd have sex with me or that we'd just live together without it? Did we marry just to help each other with our daily chores?"

Because, when you marry, your husband asks you to help him do things and he also has sex with you. But if he doesn't have sex with you, your heart dies! If the two of you aren't sharing that together, it pulls your heart away. Do you understand that? If your husband doesn't have sex with you, you become disturbed; your desire upsets your mind. It's only when you are having sex that everything is really fine.

That's why I think, "Eh, a man is someone who has strength. Now, Bo is a man who is strong, yet he doesn't do a man's work. Am I going to keep asking him about it this way every day? Why don't I just leave it and let him sit. I'll do whatever I have to do to help myself, to give something to myself."

Sometimes I think that if I hadn't married Bo, if I had married someone else, someone who slept with me all the time, that I might have gotten pregnant again. Because, when a man sleeps with you all the time, you get pregnant and give birth, get pregnant and give birth. That's something that you, a woman, know about as well. Maybe that's why I didn't get pregnant again, because my husband wasn't sleeping with me often enough.

Bo also thinks about how we haven't had children together. Hasn't he also said he wanted to have a child with me? But I've said, "Look, when you're still menstruating, that's when you get pregnant. But after you've stopped, there are no more children."

He did have a child with another woman. His daughter was very beautiful! She grew up, menstruated, married, became pregnant, and gave birth to a child. But they both died soon after the birth.

I'm the only one he's been with that he hasn't had a child with. Only with me is he without children.

I would never leave Bo. If I found another man I liked, I would have him as an unimportant one, as a lover. Even if another man came and wanted to marry me. I would sleep with him when Bo was away and I would probably let myself like him, but I would never leave Bo. I have no need to do that.

My husband and I argue a lot. We complain and yell at each other, all the time. But it was like that from the beginning. Sometimes we argue about my not working when he asks me to. He tells me to do something and I refuse. He yells at me and then we start fighting. He says, "Aren't you going to get any water today?" When I refuse to go, he says, "Tell me, what do women do? When a man marries a woman, he tells her what work she should do: get water, bring home firewood, and set the blankets down for sleeping. That's what a woman's jobs are. Now, what kind of woman are you that you won't make the bed, fetch water, and bring home firewood?"

But I say, "Don't the other men help their wives? When their wives go out for firewood or water, don't their husbands go with them and help bring home wood and help fill the containers with water? What's telling you that you don't have to help me?" And we'll continue to fight like that.

We have other fights, too. One day he'll ask me for something and I'll refuse to give it to him. He yells at me, "Nisa, you're really bad! Even the other men say you are a bad one. Why is it, when I tell you to do something for me,

339

you refuse? What happened to you that you are such a bad woman? I'll leave you and find another woman to marry, that's what I'll do!"

I say, "Fine! Go! Find yourself another wife. Even if it is true that I am lazy and you decided to leave me and marry another woman, it wouldn't make a difference. I wouldn't care. Do you think I'd feel bad? I wouldn't. I'd have lovers and they'd help me with everything. Do you think you're the only one who's a man?" Then he says, "Yes, it's because of all your lovers that you refuse to work when I ask. They make it so you don't listen to me."

One time, he had a thorn stuck in his foot. He said, "Nisa, come here and help take this thorn out of my foot." I said, "Do it yourself. Why should I do it? Didn't I ask you to take one out of my foot and you refused?" He said I was lying.

Of course, I took the thorn out of his foot, but after, I said, "See, now I've taken this thorn out, but if it had been in my foot and I had asked you, you would have refused and said, 'I'm not going to take it out. Do you ever see a man taking a thorn out of a woman's foot?' And I would have said, 'Nonsense! If I were another woman, you would take a thorn out of her foot. Why do you refuse when I ask?' "

I went and lay down on the other side of the hut from where Bo was lying. He asked, "Why are we fighting like this? Now you're lying way over there and I'm all alone over here. Why did you get up and go away from me?" I said, "Because you're full of nasty talk and aren't nice. You're always yelling at me. Every day. You never stop to rest."

Even yesterday we had a fight. I asked him for his pipe so I could smoke some tobacco. He said I had lost the last pipe and he wouldn't give me his again. I said, "That's a lie. Now, what's wrong with you? Why won't you light your pipe for me?" He said, "Too bad! Be unhappy! Today I won't light my pipe for you." And that was that.

We had another argument in the evening. After we had been at the dance for a while, Bo said he wanted to go back to the hut. I said I wanted to stay and that, if he wanted, he should go back alone. But he wanted me to go with him, so we left together.

We argue so much that my older brother once said, "Nisa, what's wrong with you that you're always yelling at your husband?" I said, "Uhn, uhn. He's the one who yells at me. I am a woman and am not full of anger. He's the angry one." But he said, "No, I really don't like what you're doing, Nisa. It's very bad. You yell at him all the time. What has he done? He's a good person. Why are you always yelling at him?" I said, "Bo's the one who hates me! He yells at me all the time, even over fetching water. He tells me to get him some, but when I do, he doesn't like it and complains."

It's true that sometimes I refuse to work. If Bo wants me to do something and I'm tired, I refuse to do it. But if I'm not tired and he asks, I don't refuse. He thinks the reason we argue so much and why we don't agree more is that I'm not good. But only when it comes to working. That's what I sometimes refuse to do and all he ever really yells at me about.

Our arguments are usually small ones, but we've had a few serious ones, too. One time we were arguing about something and he was yelling at me. He became so angry, he hit me near my eye. I screamed and ran at him. I started to hit him. He picked me up, threw me down, and held me there until people pulled him off. He sat down while I stood, yelling at him. I ran for a stick, wanting to hit him, but others stopped me. So I just stood there, screaming at him where he was sitting.

We had one other bad fight. It was over my niece, little Nukha, that we take care of. Bo and I and my niece had gone with some others to live in the bush for a while. I was near our bush camp, cutting grass for our hut. While I was working, I heard little Nukha crying. I continued to work and she continued to cry. I stopped and ran back to the camp as fast as I could. By the time I arrived, my heart was angry. I said, "Why was little Nukha crying without stopping? Who hurt her? What was she crying about?" I turned to her and said, "Did your grandfather do something to you that you're crying like this?" I turned to Bo again and said, "Who told you to make her cry?" He said, "This little child of yours, this bad thing, is certainly full of tears. Why is she always crying? She started, just like that. I didn't do anything to her, yet you're accusing me of having made her cry."

We started to argue, then to fight. He pushed me and I fell down. I jumped up and grabbed him, then I bit him. That's when he hit me with his fist, so hard that there's still a scar on my head there. I tried to grab him after that and bit his hand; I wanted to break it. But people separated us and that was all.

After, we made up and loved each other again. Everyone said, "Eh, Nisa and Bo do very well. After they fight, they like each other again." It's true. We just continue to love each other and sit beside each other. We don't fight and then hate each other in our hearts. No. We just continue to love each other. We fight and we love each other; we argue and we love each other. That's how we live.

That's my life. That's how it is and that's who I am, still having lovers, still doing many different things. I lived and lived and now I am old. As I am today, I know about many things, the things people long ago spoke in front of me and the things I have seen. Those are the things I have told you about and is the talk you will take from me when you leave.

Epilogue

ACCORDING TO ARCHAEOLOGICAL EVIDENCE, populations culturally similar to the modern-day Khoisan peoples once occupied all of Southern, East Central, and Eastern Africa. Beginning at least two thousand years ago, those in the north were gradually supplanted and pushed southward by iron-using agricultural people from the Sudan, ancestors of the modern-day Bantu-speaking populations. Although this migration continued at a steady pace, Sub-Saharan Africa proved sufficiently hospitable to the gatherers and hunters that they flourished, as a people and as a culture, for centuries. Previous to this, archaeological findings reflect the presence of a gathering and hunting people in southern Africa for tens of thousands of years.

Fierce competition and warfare characterized much of San relations with their Bantu-speaking neighbors prior to the arrival of the Dutch in South Africa in 1652. But it was ultimately the Dutch—ancestors of the present-day Afrikaner population—who were responsible for the near-total extermination of an estimated two hundred thousand South African San within two hundred years. Raids and counter-raids characterized the widening and essentially lawless South African frontier throughout much of the seventeenth and all of the eighteenth centuries. Ultimately, bows and arrows and spears were no match for firearms or for the officially sanctioned volunteer militia (the "commandos") that penetrated the countryside, massacring even the most isolated San.

The political sequence of events for San groups living in neighboring countries was less brutal. Bantu-speaking cattle-herders, the Bakalahari, Tswana, and Herero, armed and mounted, eventually gained control of San territories. But unlike the victory in the south, this conquest was not accompanied by large-scale extermination of San. Today, the total San population—a heterogeneous mix of at least three major linguistic and cultural subgroups—is estimated to be between forty and fifty-five thousand, over half of whom live in Botswana. A few of the most isolated San groups were actually able to carry on as their ancestors had before them. As recently as the early 1950s, a large proportion of the northernmost San population—the !Kung of Botswana, Namibia, and Angola—still maintained themselves by gathering and hunting.

When Richard Lee and Irven DeVore arrived in 1963, many of the !Kung in the Dobe area of Botswana were practicing their traditional way of life. Although pressures for change were being universally felt in 1969, the time of my first field trip, !Kung traditions still dominated. By the spring of 1975, however, when I made my second field trip, the pace of change had increased and changes could be seen everywhere. Gathered and hunted foods were still in ample evidence, but gardens were also being planted, herds of goats were being tended, donkeys were being used to transport food from the bush, and cattle were being bought with money saved from selling crafts. Most of all, the attitude of the people had changed. They were now looking to the agricultural and herding people near them as a model for their future.

These changes came partly as a result of years of contact with the Herero and Tswana, who first settled in the Dobe area in the mid-1920s, when a group of Hereros established permanent residence there. The !Kung were often welcomed into their villages, to provide extra hands for tending their herds; food and shelter were the usual exchanges for !Kung labor. Despite their presence it took a long time for the ability of the !Kung to live by gathering and hunting to be seriously jeopardized. But droughts throughout Botswana and the overgrazing of large tracts of land in more populated areas gradually made the Dobe area, with its unfarmed and ungrazed land, attractive to neighboring populations. Added to this, advancing technology made it easier and cheaper to dig wells. By the late 1960s, the 460 !Kung in the area were sharing all but the smallest of their nine water holes with about 350 Herero and Tswana who themselves owned an estimated 4,500 head of cattle and 1,800 goats. Roots and berries were becoming harder to find, most having been trampled, eaten, or uprooted. Game animals were also frightened away by the herds and by the competition for grasses. To gather or hunt, the !Kung now had to walk farther from the permanent water holes where they had traditionally spent much of their time.

In recent years the impetus for change has come from a number of other sources as well. A store, opened in 1967 for the purpose of buying cattle, also sells food and other goods. The sugar available at the store is used to make beer, and the selling and drinking of beer have become common pastimes. Increased trade and visits from government personnel also mean occasional vehicle traffic to and from the area. A number of !Kung men have sought transport to recruiting stations in the East, where they sign up to work in the gold mines of South Africa. Months or years later, when they return, they bring with them not only money they have earned, but also a new sophistication and awareness of the outside world.

Wage labor is not entirely new to the area. A number of !Kung men and women have worked, over the years, on projects sponsored by the Botswana government in surrounding areas or as short-term laborers in Namibia. The frequent presence of anthropologists from 1963 to 1972 amplified whatever changes were already occurring, both by exchanging wages or goods for labor and assistance and by providing yet another set of outside role models.

Still another push toward change came in the mid 1970s from the Botswana government. Independent since 1966, Botswana is dedicated to a multiracial modernization program in which no one people is favored above another. But the government realized that without help the San would probably continue in the second-class citizenship that had been ascribed to them (although not legally) for generations. On their own, the most unacculturated San, such as the Dobe area !Kung, would probably follow the pattern already seen in other parts of the country, becoming squatters or destitute herders on wealthy farms, too naive politically to maintain a hold on the lands where their ancestors gathered and hunted.

For these reasons the Botswana government created, in 1974, an Office for Basarwa Development within a government ministry. Its first job was to gather statistics on the number of San in the country and to enumerate their needs. Then, with support from international funding organizations, money was earmarked for projects that could substantially improve the lives of the San.

Another source of support came from the anthropologists and others who had worked with the San in various locations throughout the country and who were interested in their future. The founding of the Kalahari People's Fund (KPF)[1] was enthusiastically supported by the Botswana government. Under government supervision, and with the assistance of the San themselves, the KPF helped to develop programs aimed at protecting the !Kung and other San peoples' rights to their land and to their culture. The organization has raised money to fund programs, many of which were initiated by San requests; secured dynamite and other equipment for digging wells, without which legal claims to the land could not be made; supported a liaison officer to improve communication between the Botswana government and the !Kung and to assist in the complicated legal work involved in registering agricultural fields or in applying for water rights; provided scholarships for clothing and school fees for !Kung children; and helped to develop a curriculum on the San people and culture to be used in the schools throughout Botswana. These and other initiatives should enable the San to secure a more favorable future. However, they may not be fully realized as the governments they depend on—themselves vulnerable to economic and political flux—make shifts in their policies and priorities.

But events taking place across the border in South African-controlled Namibia (South West Africa) are much more threatening to the long-term welfare of the !Kung. South Africa, embroiled, since 1966, in a guerrilla war with black militants in northern Namibia, has deliberately fostered antagonisms between !Kung and other native peoples in order to lure !Kung men into enlisting in the South African army as counterinsurgents. Recruitment of !Kung as trackers and scouts has by now included a number of men from the Dobe area. Reports are that they are receiving weapons training and are wielding firearms. If a peaceful political solution to the Namibian conflict is not achieved, the !Kung of Namibia, and those of Botswana as well, may find themselves opposing, and losing their lives to, a people they have little reason to fight.

It is clear that gathering and hunting will not be a viable way of life for future generations of !Kung. Changes beyond their control are accelerating around them. They are no longer isolated from other groups or from the material goods and the social, economic, and political influences of the outside world. Roads with transport trucks, stores, schools, and even a clinic exist in the Dobe area today, and the future promises more of the same. The !Kung welcome this future; they are not only accepting its challenge but actively seeking it out. How much of their cultural heritage will survive into the future, however, is a question that remains to be answered.

In the four years before I had the chance to return to Botswana and to the Dobe area !Kung, I worked on organizing the massive amount of material I had collected. Reviewing the tapes of the other women confirmed my feelings that Nisa's narrative was the most compelling of the group, and I set out to translate, transcribe, and edit the fifteen interviews she and I had completed.

As I worked on the material, however, I also became aware of potential problems with it. First, I was struck by how frequently sexual topics had been discussed. "Teach me what it is to be a !Kung woman," was the way I had presented myself to Nisa and to the other women. How much this had influenced each woman's self-presentation was not clear. After all, another anthropologist had told me that the !Kung depicted me in one of their amusing (and often scathing) character portrayals as someone who ran up to women, looked them straight in the eye, and said, "Did you screw your husband last night?" My reputation was even used, one time, to fuel a man's accusations concerning his wife's infidelities. He asked her, "If you aren't having affairs, what does Marjorie speak to you about all the time?"

There were other questions as well. Nisa did not fairly represent the mainstream of !Kung life, either in her experiences or in her personality. None of the other women I interviewed had encountered as much tragedy as Nisa, or had a comparable extravagance of personal style. Perhaps her story was too idiosyncratic an interpretation of !Kung life; perhaps it didn't generalize to other women. Another problem was that the amount of violence she described—between children, between children and parents, and between adults—seemed excessive. Physical punishment and violent encounters certainly appeared in other women's interviews. Anthropologists were present at times when fists were used and when assault with poisoned arrows was threatened, and a significant number of homicides had even been documented, so the existence of aggression in !Kung life was not the issue. What concerned me was that Nisa might have emphasized negative experiences to the point where her narrative portrayed an extreme view of her culture, one not shared by many others around her. Most published material presented the peaceloving side of the !Kung. Was Nisa's portrayal of the other side accurate? And did I really want to be the one—by publishing her account—to balance the picture?

The last major issue was a moral one: what obligation did I have to discuss with Nisa my intention of publishing her life story? Although I had assiduously changed the names of people and places to conceal their identities, my plans for the book would certainly be affected if she opposed my making her story—in any form—public. It was *my* work, certainly, and she had given what could fairly be called informed consent to it; but it was *her* story. I had told her, as I had the other women I interviewed, that my work with them would be brought back to my country so that people there could learn about !Kung women's lives. Writing seemed implicit in this agreement, which, I felt, justified my having published small parts of the narrative in magazine articles.

The book I was proposing was quite different. Nisa's entire narrative was much more complex than that presented in the articles, and it included discussions of personally compromising issues. Given the concealment of people's identities and the isolation of Nisa's village, it seemed highly unlikely that any repercussions from the book would ever reach her. I nevertheless considered it essential to discuss my plans with her. Perhaps she would ask me to exclude material she felt was too private for publication.

Would she comprehend the world of publishing, print, reading, and publicity? She did understand the concept of writing as a method used to record speech for later interpretation by reading: she had told me that she would ask Richard Lee to write a letter to me, and she had seen other anthropologists and officials of the Tswana courts using writing in various contexts. She also knew enough about the marketplace—buying and selling, making and spending money—to understand the principle of a book as a commodity, like a piece of clothing, that sometimes sells and sometimes doesn't. Since I was planning to set aside a portion of whatever profit the book might make for the Kalahari People's Fund and, in an appropriate manner, for Nisa herself, it seemed important to discuss our shared financial interest in the book's success. All in all, I felt hopeful that when I did talk to her again, she would approve of the project. If not, I resolved that I would abide by her wishes.

A second field trip would allow me to explore these and other questions. Reviewing confusing sequences and missing details in Nisa's life story would also enhance the quality of the final narrative. In addition, it would give me the chance to renew my relationship with Nisa and to hear what had happened in her life since I had left.

I also looked forward to a second trip as a chance to study another aspect of !Kung women's lives. I had learned how !Kung women talked about their past, but I had little information—especially quantitative information—on how they experienced the present. What were their daily lives like practically and physically? Whom did they talk to, play with, and work with? What kinds of daily moods did they experience, what caused them, and how frequently and widely did they fluctuate? Did mood changes have any relation to their menstrual cycles?

I was especially interested in this last question. Studies conducted in the United States and elsewhere had suggested that women's moods, social behavior, physical symptoms, and activity patterns varied somewhat with the phases of the menstrual cycle. I decided to explore this issue among the !Kung. Their environment and cultural conditions were radically different from the ones these studies had looked at and might highlight some of the cultural and biological variables involved. Also, their isolation made it unlikely that Western beliefs, including those about women's cycles, would have gained much ground in their value system.

My husband, a graduate student named Carol Worthman, and I worked out the details of the study: my husband would take periodic blood samples from !Kung women to determine the hormonal profiles of their menstrual cycles; Carol Worthman would receive the frozen samples we shipped and would begin analyzing them in a laboratory; I would interview menstruating !Kung women to learn what kinds of behavioral fluctuations characterized their daily lives. The interviews would review their daily activities, their relationships to people (including all facets of their relationships with their husbands), their health, and their feelings about themselves and others. I hoped to interview each woman every other day and to review everything she could recall having done since she last saw me.

My second field trip was one of the most rewarding experiences of my life. The painful adjustments of the first trip did not have to be repeated, and the limitations of the field situation no longer sparked great emotional turmoil. The sights, the sounds, and the people were unexpectedly familiar and felt like home to a part of myself I had not been in touch with for four years. I was happy to be there and was treated with kindness. (I had not remembered just how generous the !Kung could be.) A few weeks of reacquaintance with the language also brought me back to my previous level of proficiency.

I spent the first few weeks catching up on people's lives and surveying women for inclusion in the study. We set up camp near where we had lived before, an area with four !Kung villages within a half-mile of one another. There were seven women who were neither too young, too old, pregnant, or nursing very young children, who were menstruating regularly, and who were willing to participate in the study. A woman from a village three miles away eventually joined as well.

Most of the women were interviewed through two menstrual cycles; I completed more than two hundred new interviews in all. The task of extracting the important information and interpreting it was left for after our return home. Then, the data were dealt with statistically, with more than one hundred variables isolated and coded.

The results were fascinating. The !Kung did not have any expectation or belief comparable to that held in the West of a premenstrual or menstrual syndrome. Nor did they recognize any effect of the menstrual cycle on women's moods or behavior. They were surprised when asked about it, saying that menstruation was such an unimportant event that it didn't deserve much concern. (I mentioned to one woman that women in my country are occasionally unhappy around the time of menstruation, and she suggested that it might be because their husbands were not having sex with them while they had their periods.) The women felt I was misguided: "Now, pregnancy must be what you mean; that's when a woman's behavior can turn strange." They did associate physical discomfort with menstruation, especially with its onset, but this discomfort, like the concern that others not see their menstrual blood, was described only in practical terms, not in terms of wider psychological ramifications.

These departures from the pattern observed in the West were not caused by major hormonal differences: the blood samples from the eight !Kung women evidenced the same basic monthly hormonal pattern as that reported for Western women. However, the analysis of the interview data showed that the kinds of effects of the menstrual cycle on mood and behavior that were reported elsewhere were, in the case of !Kung women, very small. Knowing what phase of the menstrual cycle a woman was in would enable one to predict little or nothing about her behavior or mood. Much more powerful were such influences as the behavior of husbands, relatives, and friends, or the availability of food and water, or minor illnesses. The effect of the menstrual cycle was statistically significant, but practically unimportant.

Of course, the results were not available to me in the field, and the amount of data collected made it impossible to know even in which direction the results were going. My goal was therefore to collect as complete accounts of the women's lives as was possible. The interviews were very time-consuming and the pace unrelenting, but following the lives of the eight women over the course of two months often felt like an adventure—each woman's life circumstances unfolded with greater clarity and depth for each interview day. What I learned from these detailed interviews forms the foundation for many of the generalizations about !Kung women's lives in the ethnographic sections of this book.

These two hundred additional interviews also offered me a valuable perspective on my earlier discussions with Nisa. The content and slant of her stories were not unusual. All !Kung women, it seemed, loved to talk and joke about sex. I was still willing to talk about it, but I was not quite as interested as I had been four years earlier. I now wanted to focus on less romantic matters: on friendship, on women as providers, on child care, and on avenues for self-expression and creativity—issues that had also become more relevant to my own life.

Although I made it quite explicit that my work involved a broader scope than it had years before, I found conversations drifting, if not being totally diverted, toward sexual topics. Also, the women usually reported on their daily activities in a dutiful manner, but when they discussed their relationships with men—either fanciful or factual—they often expressed delight in our work.

A number of incidents that were separate from the interviews supported this impression. One day a group of women were sitting around my camp, waiting to do some work with my husband. I sat down among them and heard them discussing something about food. The animated tones, the facial expressions, and the laughter, however, quickly signaled that sexual puns using food imagery were the real matter of the conversation. Feeling brave, I joined in, trying to match their clever banter. I must have succeeded, because the women soon started to exclaim that I had truly become a !Kung woman. Praise of my verbal skills rippled through the entire group. My dubious attempts to stop them—through further jesting—only inflamed the situation further. All semblance of conversation soon broke down amid gales of laughter.

Another incident took place one day when I joined a group of women on a gathering expedition. We walked through the nut groves collecting mongongo nuts. After an hour or more, the women dropped their loads in the shade of a large tree and rested. I used the time to organize my own load: camera, lenses, and notebooks as well as nuts, roots, and berries. The women seemed in exceptionally good spirits as they smoked tobacco, talked, laughed, and began to sing. In jest each described the quantity and quality of their gatherings. While I was preoccupied with my bundle, a teenage girl whom I had known for years came over to me and said she thought I might not have enough food. Without looking up, I exclaimed that I could barely handle what I had already collected. Her tone, when she spoke again, made it quite clear that I had missed the point. I looked up, and sure enough, I had: she was standing with her leather apron raised to her waist, revealing her genitals. Trying not to miss a beat, I answered according to the new rules: I surely had enough "food" to keep my husband and me from going "hungry"; and from the look of things, I offered, so did she. Roars of laughter sounded from the others, and were followed by a mock-performance of the dance steps and melodies of the menstrual initiation dance—a time when women repeatedly bare their buttocks and genitals to celebrate their womanhood.

The wonderfully bawdy sexual content of these and other incidents finally helped me to see that my own interest in sexual issues, although substantial in its own right, was probably no greater than and perhaps was even less than theirs. My prior reputation may have magnified their tendency to make sex a prime topic of conversation, but certainly it did not create that tendency.

I also came to see that these moments actually expressed shared friendships, trusts, and even group solidarity. Sex may have been a highly charged topic, but it was not taboo. Talking about it in a general way—to each other and to me—may have been easier than talking about more troublesome matters or about some of the specific experiences I asked about. This seemed to be the case when Nisa and I started working together again. During our first interview, I asked about the years I had been away. She asked, "You mean about men?" I explained that I hoped we would review everything that had happened to her, men included, but that I now only wanted to hear about the truly important things. For the next hour, she talked about lovers, mostly those of the past. No matter how I tried to lead the discussion elsewhere, I met with little success. It was only during later interviews that she seemed to feel comfortable enough with me again to discuss some of the more "personal" issues in her life.

My first contact with Nisa on this second field trip was on the very first day we arrived, soon after we drove into the Dobe area. We passed one !Kung village after another, getting out to greet people along the way. I was concerned when I did not see Nisa at her old village, but others told me she had moved. She came to greet us, along with others, when we stopped our truck near her new village. She looked older, but a familiar vitality of spirit was evident. Bo was beside her. We hugged and she greeted me, "My niece . . . my niece . . ." She asked if I still remembered our talks of years before. With everyone pressed around us, I could only offer a modest yes. Then I added, "I remember them very well. Later, during our stay, if you are willing, I would like to work with you again." She agreed enthusiastically. We would have talked further, but the excitement generated by our arrival demanded my full attention. Before we left to drive toward our old camp, I told her how thrilled I was to see her again: "You are a very important person in my heart." I heard the words, and I felt them. But at the time, I also felt a strange detachment. She seemed so frail and small, almost insignificant amid the animated crowd around her. Was this really the person whose life I had been thinking about and working on for years?

Occupied with setting up the new study, I didn't see Nisa again until a month or so later, when she came by with a generous gift of fresh honey that she and Bo had extracted from a beehive. It had been cleared and strained of its waxy cone, and was considered a choice gift. We talked in very general terms and agreed to work again after I completed my current study.

The next time I saw her was late one afternoon. I had stopped at her village on the way back from chauffering people to a government-sponsored meeting dealing with land rights. As soon as the truck came to a halt near her village, Nisa came running. She greeted me quickly and said that Bo and her niece were very sick. She thought Bo might even be dying. Would I take them to my camp, give them medicine, and watch over them? Bo was lying covered with blankets; it was clear that he was seriously ill. Her niece, sitting nearby, had more strength, but they both seemed dangerously weak. The two of them were helped into the truck, but there were already so many people crowded in it that Nisa offered to walk the six miles to our camp. When she arrived a few hours later, she made a temporary camp for her family a short distance from my camp. After three days of taking medicine, Little Nukha was completely better and Bo had started to regain his strength. Nisa said it was the first time he had walked in weeks. She claimed we had saved his life.

Even living that closely together, we saw little of each other. My daily schedule was packed, and by evening I was exhausted. Nisa, too, was away much of the time, gathering or just socializing in the four !Kung villages in the area. Then one night, while I was relaxing by the fire, two men I knew quite well came from one of the villages to visit. I put up a kettle for tea and we sat together, warming ourselves in the cool night air. Nisa soon joined us, and later Bo and her niece came as well. The atmosphere was

357

friendly, the tea delicious and hot, and the talk relaxed, covering many topics: the differences between !Kung medicine and Western medicine, news of people living in the nearby villages, and incidents in our daily lives.

Thrilled by the chance to renew contact with Nisa in this relaxed and informal way, I watched, carefully, everything she did and said. She looked wonderful and seemed happy, evidently pleased by Bo's renewing health. She flirted, laughed, and carried the conversation along in an energetic and appealing manner. She slowly took command, telling humorous anecdotes about people and events. Her charm was infectious; and our appreciative laughter encouraged her penchant for vivid description even further. Our other guests seemed to be enjoying her as much as I was.

I was riveted, as I tried to reconcile the person in front of me with the voice I had come to know so well from the tapes. Once again, she deeply moved me. It was the first time in months that I had had a chance to think about her, and it felt as though I was discovering her all over again.

As I watched, I became more sure than ever that our work could and should move forward. The interviews I was conducting with other women were proving to me that Nisa was fundamentally similar to those around her. She was unusually articulate, and she had suffered greater than average loss, but in most other important respects she was a typical !Kung woman.

My attention was caught, suddenly, by a flying ant with a long, wormlike body and large, almost transparent wings. It landed in the hot sand beside the fire and, by arching and flexing, managed to pull itself away from the flames. It flew off, then turned and hurled itself once again toward the fire. Again it landed in the hot sand, freed itself, and repeated its dangerous dive toward the red-hot coals.

The conversation slowed and then stopped as we watched; it mesmerized all of us. Finally the insect landed too close to the coals, and no matter how it tried it could not propel itself to safety. In an instant it would be dead. Moving swiftly, Nisa raked it out onto the cool sand beyond the fire. It lay there for a moment, then repeated its same frenzied course. Its next flight landed it again in the coals, and Nisa saved it again.

This time, however, she picked it up and pierced it through half the length of its body with a thin twig, leaving the upper half—with the wings and head—free. She planted the stick, with the skewered insect at the top, upright in the ground and tapped it gently with her fingers. The insect's wings burst into motion, as if in flight, propelling the free parts of its body around and around the stick; then it stopped. Nisa tapped the stick again and again; each time, the insect responded with the same outpouring of energy .

I watched, horrified. On my first field trip I had come to terms, though not easily, with the killing of wild animals for meat. I had also seen this very species of termite being roasted in the coals by the hundreds—a savory treat for !Kung, Europeans, and others alike. But what Nisa was doing was different. It seemed like an inexcusable torture.

My gaze was drawn once again toward Nisa. Her head and the upper parts of her body had begun to move rhythmically. I did not understand what she was doing at first. Then it became clear: as the insect held itself erect, Nisa's body also became erect; when the insect circled, drooped, and strained, Nisa's body did the same. Her face and torso echoed the insect's plight with a wrenching subtlety and her mimicry of its every move-ment was so sympathetic that the situation took on a kind of beauty. My revulsion did not disappear, but it paled against my growing realization of the power her creative spirit had over me. I felt eager to begin work with her again.

Despite my enthusiasm, the incident also reminded me of the cultural gulf between Nisa and me. It raised the probability that some of my questions would not find easy answers, while others might lead to answers I might not like to hear. The differ-ences in our backgrounds, though I sometimes tried to deny them, would always be there.

A few months later, after I completed the interviews for the menstrual cycle study, Nisa and I began to work together. I sum-moned her to my camp, as I had done years before, and Bo and her niece again came with her. They planned to live in our camp until Nisa and I were finished with our work.

The first moments of the first interview were warm and friendly. With the tape recorder on, I told her how well she had spoken years before. I outlined some of the major phases of her life, as I perceived them from our previous discussions. I brought up many specific details, hoping to impress her with the depth of my interest. I joked in !Kung manner about her lack of interest in me: "But, over the years, surely you have forgotten me. Perhaps you no longer care about our working together. Perhaps, when I ask you about things, you will refuse to talk to me."

She surprised me with her answer, remembering almost verbatim part of our last conversation four years earlier. "I haven't forgotten our work nor have I forgotten you. Didn't we agree years ago that while you were away, I would put my thoughts into the things I see and carry them around in my chest until you returned? Didn't you say that we would talk about those things one day when you came here again? As I am now, have I not seen many things that I have carried around to tell you?" It was her turn to question me. "But now that you have come back, you have worked with all the others, but not with me. You yourself are clearly the one who has forgotten me."

I explained that the interviews I had been doing this time were not the same as those she and I had done before. These concerned things younger women did from day to day. For the kind of work we had done years before, concerning the past as well as the present, I told her, she had no equal. That was why I had listened so carefully to her interviews while I was away and why I wanted to work with her again now. My explanation seemed to satisfy her; she spoke with enthusiasm about opening up and looking into the different phases of her life as we had done before. Then we would close them up again and be finished. She warned me to pay careful attention to everything she said.

I suggested that we start by talking about the things she had seen during the years I had been away. The conversation that followed was warm and personal, although low-keyed, and centered mostly on men and lovers, those in her life and those in the lives of other women. She started to mention names, then pulled back, "Perhaps, once you know, you'll tell?" A mere formality, it seemed, because before I could protest she continued where she had left off. She described the recent end of her relationship with Debe, the lover she had started with when I was last there. She also talked about her continued love for Kantla, the man who had been in and out of her life since childhood: "He is a truly important man in my life—the one with the gray hair, the one who is like a husband to me." She mentioned other men, too, but said, "I meet them very rarely. If my husband were to find out, he'd kill me!"

How had it been between them? She said, "My husband and I live and live and live together; only then does he come to me and we sleep together. We go on living and only another, distant day does he come to me again. That is how it has been between us." Then she added, "Because he is the man of my hut." Remembering her complaints from years before, I asked, "Is that good or bad?" She said, "That's good, very good." But years before, hadn't she felt that when her husband didn't make love to her frequently, it meant that perhaps he no longer cared for her? She said, "Even now, I occasionally yell at him for not sleeping with me more often, 'Do you refuse me?' But he says that the way we live is the way it should be. That's how it has been since you left. We live and then we're together, we live and then we're together."

There was no trace of the pain this issue had brought forth years before. I asked, "And your hearts, do they go out toward each other?" She said, "Yes, our hearts love each other and go out toward each other." What about fights? "We rarely fight. When we do, it's usually about food, when I serve too many people. That's when he asks, 'What are you doing, serving everyone? When do others ever serve us? When we have food, we should be the only ones to eat.' But I say, 'You just like to yell about things.' Then he says, 'It's because you are bad, a bad one that sees a person and gives him food, then sees another and gives him food. Don't you know that when you have food, it is for you and your child, that she can eat and be full? You'll wind

up just like a woman with nothing this way.' " Was this an important fight? "No, it's very small. We fight a little, then leave it
and love each other again."

There was a break in the conversation while I adjusted the
tape recorder. When we resumed, she offered, "A woman, if she
doesn't have things to eat ..." She paused, then laughed. I
laughed too—the conversation had turned to sex again. She
continued, "That's the way a woman makes herself alive. But no
one is doing that for me." Wondering if this was her way of expressing dissatisfaction about Bo, I asked again about their relationship. She answered, "Today, my husband makes love to me
very well—with vigor and with pleasure. Even long ago. It was
only because of my periods that he wouldn't come to me." I reminded her that even before our previous talks had started, her
periods had already stopped. Yet her husband had not slept with
her often. She concurred, but went on as if she didn't consider
these events worthy of further discussion: "Making love is not
that important. The man of the night just does it and that's all."
Seeing my questioning look, she added, "Yes, where could its
importance come from?"

She also minimized the importance of menstrual cycling.
"When my periods were over, that was the end of it; they left
easily and without pain." Her memory of the anguish she had
felt at the time of menopause had faded. She did not repeat her
earlier request for medicine to make her fertile, and had evidently come to terms with the end of childbearing.

I asked, "These years I've been away ... have they been
good to you or have they caused you pain?" She answered,
"These years I have been living, I have not been unhappy." She
interpreted the question, once again, as pertaining to involvements with men. "Even though I have been with one man and
passed on to another, my heart has not been hurt." Some men
had wanted her, she explained, and had almost killed themselves
trying to be with her; sometimes she felt the same for them. "Not
all men have a place in their hearts for me. But that has caused
me little pain."

She repeated how important Kantla still was in her life, then
added, with obvious pleasure, "But he is jealous and accuses me

of having too many men. That's because he feels so strongly about me." Her previous husband, Besa, also still wanted her: "He says he's going to take me away from Bo one day." But she brushed his interest aside by telling him, "We separated long ago, so stop talking to me about it today."

After our interview that day, I felt pleased—it had gone quite well. There had been a comfortable accord between us, familiar and easy. She was serious, willing to be personal, and concerned that our work go well: when there was some momentary trouble with the tape recorder, she wanted to be sure her voice was recording clearly before we resumed. It had gone so smoothly that I almost felt as though I had never left.

Yet something was different. It was the tone of her voice: easy, relaxed, and, for Nisa, calm. Qualities had crept into it that I didn't recognize from years before. Things no longer seemed nearly as painful for her. Although nothing much had changed in her relationship with Bo, she no longer seemed very upset by it. Her relationships with other men were also much the same as they had been years before, yet they too were not of great concern. The interviews that followed supported this initial impression that she was happier and more at peace with herself. Various events had caused her pain over the years, and there were things that even now disturbed her. But most of the issues that had involved intense emotions in the past seemed, somehow, to have been resolved.

Life, she said, was basically good. "As I've been living, I haven't been hungry." She ate mostly bush foods, ones that she gathered, although she occasionally asked the Herero living nearby for some of their "softer" foods, like milk and ground corn meal. But she only asked once in a while, because if she were to ask too often they would say, "How come you're a Zhun/twa, yet you ask for food every day?" If either she or Bo were to work for them, they would get more of their food, of course. But neither wanted to. They had done so years before, but, "Working for the Hereros isn't good. I won't do it again. You don't get enough for your work. They only give you food. They don't give you money to buy blankets or clothing."

That was why she and Bo lived apart from the Herero. "We

like living only with Zhun/twasi." That was also why she relied as much as possible on her own efforts to meet her family's needs. "The foods that keep us alive are the mongongo nuts, baobab fruits, and sha and other roots that I gather." But the nut groves were far away and Bo usually accompanied her. Some days she stayed at home and worked on ostrich eggshell beads, wooden (Herero-style) beads, or musical instruments to sell to a government crafts purchaser who made periodic visits to the area. "Then I take the money and buy a blanket at the store." Or she used it to buy shucked corn from the Herero, which she dried, pounded, and cooked for her family. She saw the future as more of the same.

She and Bo had been getting along very well and had been "loving each other": "We like being together sitting and talking." They rarely fought. When they did it was usually about small matters. She admitted that she was the one who most often provoked fights. Usually, it was about food. She would tell him she was hungry : "Why don't you get up and get me some food? Go and set the traps, than maybe we'll have a guinea fowl to eat. Why should the insides of my mouth be dying like this?" When she yelled at him, he would yell back, "The other women gather for their families, why don't you?" The fight would end with her saying, "I don't want to go with the women. They go too slowly. Let's go together, gather some food, and bring it back. If I go without you, I'll only be able to bring back enough for today; tomorrow, I'll have to go out again. If we go together, there will be enough in the hut for days. So, let's go and work hard. After all, we can't pretend we're children who just play." Then they would go gathering in the bush together and bring back enough for themselves and others.

The event that had caused her the greatest pain in the preceding four years was the death of Kxaru, her older brother's wife and her close friend. "My heart has been without anger. Only pain has been there, the kind you feel when someone you love dies." Then she explained, "After you left, Kxaru and I continued to live in our village at Gausha, sitting, talking, and doing things together. That's how we always were with each other. We never fought or argued. But sickness was in her and eventually it killed her. God did it; he grabbed her away from us. When she died, everyone cried—the pain of missing her was so great. I cried and kept thinking how much I had loved her and kept asking why God took her from me. I felt miserable. Her husband—my older brother—finally told me to stop mourning.

"But I missed her and my heart no longer wanted to stay in our village. There was no one there for me to sit with. I didn't see another older person with whom I could talk. Most people there are young and live with the Hereros. When I live with the Hereros, we don't see things the same way. That's why I decided to move to where there were people for me. My heart had fallen and I thought this would be a good place to sit until I was free from mourning, the mourning that comes with death. Now, the pain has stopped, but only a little bit."

After the death, Nisa started taking care of Kxaru's teenage daughter: "I felt very bad for Kxaru's daughter. I saw that she no longer had a mother to help her, so I started doing things for her. Eventually, I brought her to my village. Now she calls me mother and helps me with my chores."

Nisa also still cared for Nukha, the daughter of her younger brother. "Yes, I'm still taking care of her. Her father long ago told me it should be as though I had given birth to her. And that's how it has been—because I truly love this little one I'm raising. When we're together, she tells me things and we talk. I even wanted to take my brother's next younger child, but didn't he refuse?"

Her new village was small, only a few San families, and was at a considerable distance from the Herero villages sharing the same water hole. Emotional as well as practical support came from a cousin, a woman named Kokobe. Kokobe and her husband worked for the Hereros and had three cows. There was little milk because the cows were being grazed and corralled in another village. "When the cows return, Kokobe's husband brings milk and gives some to us." Bo and Nisa had no cows. "We almost had one, but my husband bought a donkey instead." For the first time, she and Bo had goats, which they were keeping in their village. They had even planted some melon fields a few months before, and people bought all she was willing to sell. She had gotten some of the seeds from the Hereros, as well as additional melons and corn.

Nisa and Kokobe were very close. "After Kxaru died, I was looking for a place to go, but I didn't know where. One day Kokobe visited and saw how we were living alone, without anyone. She told us to go back with her and live in her village, so we did." It has worked out well. "All this time I have been here, I have seen someone who takes good care of me. We argue a lot, almost every day—about food—but we never really fight. We usually get along well."

They often argued when one had a particular food that the other didn't have. Accusations of stinginess would fly back and forth: "I've given you honey many times but you never give me any." Or when one asked for something the other would say, "I already gave you mongongo nuts. How come you finished them so soon?" Or it might begin, "The last time you had meat, I didn't bother _you_ with asking." "Yes, but didn't I give you some of the guinea fowl I had the other day? Now, you have meat and won't give me any." These fights usually ended in an easy reconciliation.

The variations in this kind of argument seem almost infinite. Nisa described one in detail. She cooked some food, saying "I'm not giving any of this away today," and she ate it herself. She thought, "When others have food, they don't know how to share. They just eat and eat and eat. I'm the only one who gives. Even then, they always ask for more. So why, when I've cooked this food today, should I give it to them?" She sat eating alone, and didn't give any away, to Kokobe or to others.

The next morning Kokobe came to her and said, "Tell me, are you someone I don't know, perhaps not my kin? Didn't I yesterday see, with my own eyes, that you had something resembling meat? Now, give me some that I can put inside my mouth to taste. If you don't, won't you be wrong and be indebted to me?" Nisa said, "Oh! You are making me weary saying those things. If something is mine, why shouldn't I just eat and eat and eat it? What makes you yell at me and say I have taken something from you when I've only cooked and eaten my own food?"

Kokobe's brother and his wife were also living in the village, and sometimes they too became involved in these arguments. "Once, Kokobe's brother and I yelled at Kokobe together and she started to cry. I saw her crying and scolded her brother, 'Look what we did, getting together like that against her. Now she's crying.' I started to cry and there we were, the two of us, sitting together, crying."

Not all her current relationships with women were satisfying. Soon after Kxaru's death, her older brother remarried. She complained about this new sister-in-law, "We don't really like each other. She never came to tell me she was going to marry my brother. Neither did he." Nisa had visited them only once since her move, when she was sick and needed their help. Powerful healers, they administered the traditional curing ceremony for her. She was cured, but she hadn't been back to see them since.

She was getting along somewhat better with her younger brother's wife and had even hoped that his family would change villages with her. But her brother worked for the Hereros and had refused to move. She felt that if she had stayed, "His wife and I would have fought all the time." Unimportant fights, basically, again only about food. But, she felt, "It would have eventually worn me out."

Nisa was almost as expansive as she had been years before on the subject of sex and men, and the tone of her remarks was light and playful. Even her descriptions of herself as an old woman, "so old as to be almost dead, who occasionally wants men" was more sweet than bitter. In a teasing tone, she told me that her only real problem was an uncomfortable itch in her genitals. Not sure on which level she was talking, I asked her to explain. "You really *don't* know things, do you? The itch is *desire*, desire for a man. Let me teach you, because you are still a child." She continued to tease me, laughing and pointing, "These are your genitals. If a man doesn't take them, they itch and itch and itch! They become aroused and cry out for a man. It's only when he takes them that the itch goes away."

Another day her mood was more serious. She said that she had had a few lovers since I had left, "some new ones and some old ones." It was very important "to go to one who will help you with more than just sex and not to one who never gives anything else he may have." She met them only rarely, when Bo was away or when she went to the bush for wood or water. "Because a woman fears her husband. She has to be clever; she doesn't want to make herself known."

She talked further about Kantla, her man "since the beginning." She said their relationship was still strong, but she was concerned that his involvements with other women exposed him to venereal disease. "I don't think he has it, but I'm afraid other women will give it to him, and to me. That's something I really don't want." He had these involvements, she was certain: "Do you think an older man like Kantla doesn't enjoy being with women?"

He had come to her not long ago, when Bo was away, and asked her to sleep with him, but she had refused. She was taking care of too many children, she explained—Nukha, Nukha's older sister, and Kxaru's daughter—and was afraid one of them might tell. So she chased Kantla off. He was angry and yelled at her, saying she was lying. "But another day, he'll come to me again. I'll put him beside me and the two of us will lie together. Because my heart is with him. Is he not a very important man in my life? One day I chase him, and another I lie down with him. That's how it is."

Toward the end of one long interview in which we had reviewed the past, Nisa paused after describing an illness from which she had recently recovered. Almost as a reflection, she softly said, "That's what my life has been like." Her tone became emphatic as she added, "I'm talking about very big, very important things, things that have caused me pain." She returned to a near-whisper as she recounted some of them: "the children I gave birth to, who grew big and who died, and the older person I sat beside, my husband, whose death almost destroyed me, making me feel terrible pain."

During our last interview, she told me a dream she had had that morning: "I dreamt that I went alone to the well. But as I was filling my water containers, I fell in. I trembled and almost killed myself with fright. I tried to grab onto the sides of the well, but fell down. I tried again and fell down again. I was finally able to grab onto a stick and crawl out. No one else was there."

Later in the interview I brought up the issue of making our work public. I explained that I thought people in my country would like to know about her life. My own friends had even asked me, "Why don't you write a book so that people can find out about the woman you talked to." I told her that I would like to do it; but first I wanted to talk to her about my plans. I hoped to take all the stories from both sets of interviews, translate them into English, and put them down on paper, paper that would be turned into a book. I would change everyone's name so that no one would recognize her or the people she had talked about. It would take a long time, probably a number of years. There was also no way of knowing whether people would buy it when it was finished. If they did, I told her, my plans were to give some of whatever money I might earn to her and some to projects—such as the school and the well—that would benefit all the people in the area. They, too, had been generous with me. But first I wanted to know what she thought of the idea and "Whether you refuse or agree to other people hearing the talks we have done." She asked, "Do you mean the people where you live?" I said, "Yes, mostly. But, because the names will have been changed, even a Tswana reading it would not know whose speech it really was." I asked again, "So, what do you think? Does it sound good or bad?"

At first she didn't seem quite sure what I was asking. The project I was proposing, as she saw it, basically involved only me: "If this is what you want to do, that's good. But you're the one who has to do it, not me." I agreed, but said it was important that she know exactly what I was planning, since it was her life story that would be the focus of the book. She understood. "Yes, that's good. You'll leave here, and while you're away you'll write. Then others will say, 'Eh, so this is what you and that woman talked about. These are her words. This is her name.' And if they like your book, they will buy it and help you with money." I added, "And will help you and others, too." She said, "Yes, because our work has been important and we have done it very well."

I repeated my intention of changing her name and the places where she and others lived, "So that people won't know who you are." I'm thinking of calling you 'Nisa' and saying your home is at . . ." I paused. Immediately taken with the idea, she offered, "Gausha. You'll say that 'Nisa' sometimes lives at Gausha, in the heart of the mongongo groves, the true bush. That, they will like." I said, "Yes, and when I talk about your husbands, I will say, 'This woman was once married to a man named Tashay and is now married to a man named Bo.' " She laughed at the names I had invented for her husbands. "Yes, Bo, who lives at Gausha. Eh-hey, my niece!"

There was still the question of whether there were any stories she would not want to have included. I had deliberately reviewed the major events of her life during this round of interviews, to keep the content of what would be covered in the book fresh in our minds. I asked, "During the days we have been working, we have reviewed the stories of your life, those that we discussed years ago and those we have added this time—those of the present and those of the past. These stories, the happy and not-so-happy ones, are the ones I plan to put in the book, the book you have agreed to my writing. But perhaps some of these things, you don't want me to include, perhaps there are things you don't want others to hear. If so, I can easily take them out. If not, do you think that all of our talk should enter the papers?" She answered emphatically, "All the talk that the two of us have done—all that this tape recorder, this old man, has heard, wants to enter the paper."

I cautioned again about the length of time before the book would be completed and the uncertainty of its making any money, "Because, sometimes, people look at a book and leave it on the shelf." She added, "Yes, they say, 'very nice,' but their hearts don't go out to it. But if they do help the two of us and buy it and you help me, then I will buy a cow." I said, "We will have to wait and see."

She understood that there was a lot of work to be done. "Yes, this old man will help you. He will talk and you will write. Just the two of you, together! Also, the two of us—he and I. We will be the ones talking to you. Because I am the one who is talking, am I not?" I said, "Yes, I will take your talk home with me, and even though I will be alone, I will be able to write."

Delighted, she spun a fantasy of my work—a fantasy that has since proved true. "Yes, you will listen to me and when I say something that makes you laugh, you will laugh aloud and praise me, 'Eh-hey, my aunt! My aunt, I still have you with me, here in my home.' You will feel love for me, because I will be there with you." I agreed, "Yes, I will look at all our talks, from years ago and from today. Some day, we will see how it turns out." She said, "My niece ... my niece ... you are someone who truly thinks about me."

The uninhabited bush just beyond the edge of a !Kung village imposed little of its presence into the living space within. There people abounded, sitting outside their huts in work or leisure, or visiting at other people's huts. Activities took place outside, in the view, if not the company, of others. Children circulated comfortably among adults, or played separately in the cleared center area and in the bush nearby. A constant stream of talk, work, and movement characterized the village during most days; and at night, when dinners were cooked and eaten and fires blazed, the flow of conversation and activity continued.

This was the !Kung world—a world of people. It was perhaps because human ties were so valued that a few !Kung women and men briefly shared their lives with me. I was young, and Nisa talked as if to guide me, as if she were talking to the woman I might become. She treated me with respect, and she gave me a great gift—a window on a complex world that is quickly passing. Almost every experience I have in life is colored and enriched by the !Kung world and the way Nisa looked at it. I will always think of her, and I hope she will think of me, as a distant sister.

Notes

INTRODUCTION

THE FOLLOWING BOOKS provide a balanced overview of gatherer-hunter studies: R. Lee and I. DeVore, eds., *Man the Hunter* (Chicago: Aldine, 1968); M. Bicchieri, *Hunters and Gatherers Today* (New York: Holt, Rinehart and Winston, 1972).

For the history of the San see A. Willcox, "The Bushman in History," R. Inskeep, "The Bushmen in Prehistory," and P. Tobias, "Introduction to Bushmen or San," all in P. Tobias, ed., *The Bushmen* (Cape Town: Human and Rousseau, 1978). Additional material on more recent history as well as descriptions of climate and ecology of the Dobe area can be found in R. Lee, *The !Kung San* (Cambridge: Cambridge University Press, 1979), pp. 31–35. Also see J. Yellen, *Archaeological Approaches to the Present: Models for Reconstructing the Past* (New York: Academic Press, 1977).

The first major publication resulting from Lee and DeVore's interdisciplinary project was R. Lee and I. DeVore, eds., *Kalahari Hunter-Gatherers* (Cambridge, Mass.: Harvard University Press, 1976).

The first anthropologists to collect systematic data on the !Kung were the Marshall family. A number of publications and films have resulted from their work, including L. Marshall, *The !Kung of Nyae Nyae* (Cambridge, Mass.: Harvard University Press, 1976), and E. Marshall Thomas, *The Harmless People* (New York: Knopf, 1959). John Marshall has made a number of excellent films from footage taken of the !Kung beginning in the 1950s; they are available from Documentary Educational Resources, 5 Bridge Street, Watertown, Mass. 02172. One of these films, *N!ai: The Story of a !Kung Woman*, documents the effect Chum!kwe has had on the !Kung.

My account of the !Kung way of life is based on Lee, *The !Kung San;* Lee and DeVore, eds., *Kalahari Hunter-Gatherers;* R. Lee, "Ecology of a Contemporary San People," in Tobias, ed., *The Bushmen;* Marshall, *The !Kung of Nyae Nyae;* and personal observation. The hxaro system of gift exchange is described in P. Wiessner, "Hxaro: A Regional System of Reciprocity for Reducing Risk among the !Kung San" (Ph.D. diss., University of Michigan, 1977).

On !Kung health, disease, and mortality see A. Truswell and J. Hansen,

"Medical Research among the !Kung," in Lee and DeVore, eds., *Kalahari Hunter-Gatherers;* T. Jenkins and G. Nurse, *Health and the Hunter-Gatherers* (Johannesburg: Witwatersrand University Press, 1977); E. Wilmsen, "Seasonal Effects of Dietary Intake on Kalahari San,"*Proceedings of the Federation of American Societies for Experimental Biology,* vol. 37, 1978; N. Howell, *Demography of the Dobe !Kung* (New York: Academic Press, 1979).

An excellent brief account of the clicks used in the !Kung language appears in Marshall, *The !Kung of Nyae Nyae,* pp. xix–xx. For more extensive accounts of the languages of the San peoples see A. Trail, "The Languages of the Bushmen," in Tobias, ed., *The Bushmen;* and E. O. J. Westphal, "The Click Languages of Southern and Eastern Africa," in J. Berry and J. H. Greenberg, eds., *Linguistics in Sub-Saharan Africa* (The Hague: Mouton, 1971).

1. Nisa and all other names of !Kung individuals are pseudonyms for real people. They are typical !Kung names but are given without click notation for ease of reading. Place names are treated in the same way. The Glossary gives the full spelling of the names including clicks.

2. The Dobe area technically refers to an expanse of land in both Botswana (about 75 percent) and Namibia (about 25 percent). Except for statistical computations, when I refer to the Dobe area in the text I mean only the Botswana portion. Nyae Nyae is the name used to refer to the area in Namibia.

3. Although tobacco smoking is not part of the oldest !Kung traditions, it was apparently brought to them by others before they had contact with Europeans. A firmly established desire and even demand for tobacco existed among the !Kung at the time they were first contacted by anthropologists.

4. The kinship terms Nisa used with me were determined by her actual kinship to my namesake, Hwantla (her aunt), whose genealogical equivalent I became when I assumed her name.

5. The !Kung believe in a number of supernatural beings, but one of them is said to rule over the others. This being, called Kauha, I have translated as "God." The various other spirits are called *Ilganwasi.*

1. EARLIEST MEMORIES

Much of this chapter is based on the author's observations and interviews. For additional information on !Kung infancy and childhood see P. Draper, "Social and Economic Constraints on Child Life among the !Kung," in Lee and DeVore, eds. *Kalahari Hunter-Gatherers;* P. Draper, "!Kung Women: Contrasts in Sexual Egalitarianism in Foraging and Sedentary Contexts," in R. Reiter, ed., *Toward an Anthropology of Women* (New York: Monthly Review Press, 1976); M. Konner, "Aspects of the Developmental Ethology of a Foraging People," in N. Blurton Jones, ed., *Ethological Studies of Child Behavior* (Cambridge: Cambridge University Press, 1972); M. Konner, "Maternal Care, Infant Behavior and Development among the !Kung," in Lee and DeVore, eds. *Kalahari Hunter-Gatherers;* M. Konner, "Relations among Infants and Juveniles in Comparative Perspective," *Social Science In-*

formation 15, no. 2 (1976):371–402; M. West and M. Konner, "The Role of the Father: An Anthropological Perspective," in M. Lamb, ed., *The Role of the Father in Child Development* (New York: Wiley, 1976); P. Draper, "!Kung Bushman Childhood" (Ph.D. diss., Harvard University, 1972); Lee, *The !Kung San*, pp. 296, 330–332.

On the grandparent-grandchild relationship, see Marshall, *The !Kung of Nyae Nyae*, ch. 6; M. Biesele and N. Howell, " 'The Old People Give You Life': Aging among the !Kung San," in P. Amoss and S. Harrell, eds., *Other Ways of Growing Old* (Stanford: Stanford University Press, 1979).

On women's carrying and other aspects of women's work load, see Lee, *The !Kung San*, pp. 250–277, 309–330.

1. The memories in this chapter probably reflect Nisa between the ages of three and six (c.1924–1927). Accurate age estimates (within a year or two for adults and within a few months for children and teenagers) were made possible by Nancy Howell, who constructed a calendar based on events with known dates and a strict rank ordering of the ages of all the individuals in the population.

2. beat me to death: Expressions like this one are used as threats, similar in tone to our "If you ever do that again, I'll beat the living daylights out of you."

3. make you shit: The !Kung word *zee*, a colloquialism for defecation, is also used when referring to the fear the speaker will be able to provoke in someone else. It is comparable to the American expressions "make you shit (or piss) in your pants" and "beat the shit out of you."

4. Mother!: An expression that emphasizes the truth of what the speaker is saying, similar to "I mean it" or "I swear." Other forms of this expression are "Grandmother!" and "Our mothers!"

5. stinge: A literal translation of the !Kung verb, k"xung. The archaic word "stinge" (see Oxford English Dictionary) seems to convey the most appropriate feeling even though it is no longer used this way in our language.

6. Actual cases of infanticide were very rare (see Chapter 2).

7. split your face into pieces: A literal translation of a !Kung idiom, similar in meaning to "it will ruin your life."

8. Insults referring to the genitals are common and are given either in jest or in anger. But even when expressed in anger, they are not necessarily very serious.

9. ruin: A literal translation of the !Kung word k"xwia, meaning general disruptiveness.

10. Zhun/twa: The !Kung name for themselves, literally "the true people" or "the real people" (also see Glossary).

2. FAMILY LIFE

For discussion of various aspects of birth spacing among the !Kung see Lee, *The !Kung San*, ch. 11; Howell, *Demography of the Dobe !Kung*, chs. 6, 7, 10, and 11; M. Konner and C. Worthman, "Nursing Frequency, Gonadal

Function and Birth Spacing among !Kung Hunter-Gatherers," *Science* 207 (1980): 788–791; and N. Blurton Jones and R. Sibley "Testing Adaptiveness of Culturally Determined Behavior," in V. Reynolds and N. Blurton Jones, eds., *Human Behavior and Adaptation* (London: Taylor and Francis, 1978).

!Kung infanticide is discussed in Marshall, *The !Kung of Nyae Nyae*, pp. 165–168; Howell, *Demography of the Dobe !Kung*, pp. 119–121; and Lee, *The !Kung San*, pp. 319–320.

The !Kung attitude toward menstruation may be contrasted to the use of the concept of menstrual pollution to restrict women in many other cultures. See D. Hammond and A. Jablow, *Women in the Cultures of the World* (Menlo Park: Cummings 1976), pp. 6–7.

1. The memories in this chapter probably reflect Nisa between the ages of four and eight (c. 1925–1929). lived and lived: A literal translation of a !Kung phrase, often presented in a long string of repetitions, the repeated segments denoting an ever-increasing span of time: a dramatic storytelling device. Sometimes translated in the narrative as "time passed."

2. ejaculate on yourself: A typical insult.

3. Besides a word that specifically refers to menstruation, there are a number of common !Kung idioms that have the same meaning, all referring to the moon: "going to the moon," "seeing the moon," "being with the moon." These expressions highlight the importance of the moon in helping women keep track of their cycles, and reflect their sense of being in time with powerful natural forces.

4. chief: Probably a reference to the Tswana chiefs. No such institution exists among the !Kung.

5. Men as well as women speak of "conceiving" or "giving birth" to children using the same word, // ge.

6. The !Kung are much lighter in color than the neighboring Bantu peoples.

3. LIFE IN THE BUSH

For detailed accounts of the subsistence ecology and environment of the !Kung see Lee, *The !Kung San*, chs. 5 and 6; Lee and DeVore, eds., *Kalahari Hunter-Gatherers*, chs. 1–3; R. Lee, "Ecology of a Contemporary San People," in Tobias, ed., *The Bushmen*; and Marshall, *The !Kung of Nyae Nyae*, chs. 1–4.

The account of hunting among the !Kung is based on Lee, *The !Kung San*, ch. 8; and Marshall, *The !Kung of Nyae Nyae*, ch. 4.

1. The memories in this chapter probably reflect Nisa between the ages of five and eight (c. 1926–1929).

2. The !Kung language has many different and specific words for carrying. The one used here designates the traditional method of hanging heavy strips of meat on sticks carried on men's shoulders.

3. go to the bush: A euphemism for defecation or urination; sometimes a more explicit phrase is used.

4. The first dangers of the bush that come to mind at the sight of a child running and shouting are bites—either of snakes or of carnivores.

5. When a !Kung says "the small acacia thicket near the rise beside the Nyae Nyae baobab," it means something as specific and helpful to the hearer as "the corner of Fifth Avenue and Thirty-Fourth Street in front of Longchamps" would mean to a New Yorker. It is difficult to render in English what the !Kung say about the environment, because their vocabulary has a richness of detail for the terrain and vegetation that has no English equivalent.

4. DISCOVERING SEX

A major source for this chapter is Draper, "Social and Economic Constraints on Child Life among the !Kung San." Additional information comes from Lee, *The !Kung San*, ch. 9; Konner, "Relationships among Infants and Juveniles in Comparative Perspective"; N. Blurton Jones and M. Konner, "Sex Differences in the Behavior of Bushman and London Two-to-Five Year Olds," in J. Crook and R. Michael, eds., *Comparative Ecology and Behavior of Primates* (New York: Academic Press, 1973); Hammond and Jablow, *Women in the Cultures of the World*; and personal observations by the author.

For a discussion of the !Kung use of space see P. Draper, "Crowding among Hunter-Gatherers: The !Kung Bushmen," *Science* 182 (1973).

1. The memories in this chapter probably reflect Nisa between the ages of six and twelve (c. 1927–1933).

2. In the !Kung language the third person singular pronoun, *a*, does not distinguish gender. Where it is used in the narrative as the *indefinite* pronoun, I have translated it as "she" or "her."

3. make love: The phrase here is *are akwe*, literally "love (or like) each other," in this context a euphemism for sexual intercourse. Other euphemisms: *are an/te*, "to like oneself"; *gu akwe*, "to take each other"; *gu an/te*, "to take oneself"; and *du si//kwasi*, "to do their work." The sexual intercourse position described here is considered a discreet method to avoid waking a child.

4. worry about: The !Kung term is *kua*. It is used in contexts where we would use the words "fear," "respect," and "awe."

5. A literal translation of the phrase *n!aro an/te*, the usual way to say "learn."

6. screw: The !Kung word here is *tchi*. It gives the feeling of being very colloquial and slightly, but not very, vulgar.

7. The East is the region more densely populated with other peoples such as the Herero and Tswana; it is associated in !Kung minds with culture contact and change.

8. Since a woman may bear a child after her eldest daughter is already

a mother, it is not uncommon for children to have aunts and uncles among their playmates.

5. TRIAL MARRIAGES

Marriage rules and customs are presented in Marshall, *The !Kung of Nyae Nyae*, ch. 8; marriage statistics in Howell, *Demography of the Dobe !Kung*, ch. 6; Lee, *The !Kung San*, p. 242; and Lee, "Ecology of a Contemporary San People." An account of the history of a !Kung marriage is given in John Marshall's remarkable film *N!ai*, which was shot over a period of twenty years.

1. The memories in this chapter probably reflect Nisa between the ages of twelve and fifteen (c.1933–1936).
2. There is only one instance on record of a !Kung woman having more than one husband.
3. A small percentage of !Kung women marry Herero or Tswana men, usually as second wives. Herero and Tswana women never marry !Kung men.

6. MARRIAGE

For a discussion of !Kung relationships in which reserved behavior is expected, see Marshall, *The !Kung of Nyae Nyae*, ch. 7. Marshall also discusses and compares the marriage ceremony and the menstruation ceremony (pp. 271–279). See Howell, *Demography of the Dobe !Kung*, ch. 6 and p. 179, concerning the onset of !Kung fertility.

1. The events recalled in this chapter probably took place when Nisa was between the ages of fifteen and eighteen (c. 1936–1939).
2. crack open the insides of her ears: Literal translation of the !Kung idiom; no common colloquial English equivalent.
3. The !Kung have little body hair and women have very long genital labia; elongation of the labia rather than appearance of pubic hair signals puberty in girls. (Hence the numerous references to long labia in sexual insults.)
4. Food and eating are universally used by the !Kung as metaphors for sex. However, they claim no knowledge or practice of oral-genital contact.
5. Calling out periodically to one another is the standard procedure for maintaining contact in a group that is scattering over a landscape. Deliberate failure to answer is a quite pointed message.
6. Nisa's reserve at this moment (despite her excitement at seeing her mother) is required by custom during the period between the first and second menstrual periods and their accompanying dances, and for some time afterward.
7. The words "like" and "love" are used here to denote changes in emphasis in Nisa's use of the word *are*, which, like the French *aimer*, is used in contexts where either English word might be appropriate.

7. WIVES AND CO-WIVES

The information in this chapter is drawn from Lee, *The !Kung San*, pp. 452–454; Marshall, *The !Kung of Nyae Nyae*, ch. 8; and Howell, *Demography of the Dobe !Kung*, ch. 12. For a crosscultural perspective on the institution of polygyny see Hammond and Jablow, *Women in the Cultures of the World*, pp. 34–36.

1. The !Kung can easily recognize the tracks of any person they know well, as well as a number of others, and they can tell much about a person's circumstances and behavior by reading this record in the sand.
2. Nisa's grandfather evidently had three wives at once, an extremely rare occurrence.
3. Nisa's experience as a co-wife probably occurred when she was between the ages of seventeen and nineteen (c. 1938–1940).

8. FIRST BIRTH

This chapter is based on the author's own observations; on Lee, *The !Kung San*, ch. 11; and on Howell, *Demography of the Dobe !Kung*, chs. 4 and 6. Also see Marshall, *The !Kung of Nyae Nyae*, ch. 6, for a detailed description of the !Kung naming system.

1. Most of the events recalled in this chapter probably took place when Nisa was between eighteen and twenty-one (c. 1939–1942).
2. Nisa's statements about the customs of peoples other than the !Kung may or may not be accurate.
3. anger at birth: An expression for the pain of childbirth.
4. a woman's heart can leave her: An expression for losing consciousness.
5. Greeting is a formality of central importance in !Kung social life, and the way people greet one another reflects their feelings toward one another.

9. MOTHERHOOD AND LOSS

On !Kung life expectancy and mortality see Howell, *Demography of the Dobe !Kung*, chs. 3–5 and pp. 239–242. For reviews of health and medical studies, see A. Truswell and J. Hansen, "Medical Research among the !Kung," in Lee and DeVore, eds., *Kalahari Hunter-Gatherers*; and T. Jenkins and G. Nurse, *Health and the Hunter-Gatherer* (Johannesburg: Witwatersrand, 1977).

!Kung beliefs about the supernatural are discussed in L. Marshall, "!Kung Bushman Religious Beliefs," *Africa* 32, no. 3 (1962): 221–225; and M. Biesele, "Religion and Folklore," in Tobias, ed., *The Bushmen*.

1. Most of the events recalled in this chapter took place when Nisa was between twenty and thirty (c. 1941–1951).

2. The !Kung believe that much illness in infancy is caused by bird-spirit-possession. Such illness is specifically considered separate from the illnesses caused by the ancestral spirits. It has a unique ritual treatment, and it affects only infants.

3. This move represented a major change in Nisa's life; after it she became much more involved with the Tswana and Herero than she had been before. It probably happened when she was about thirty years old.

4. Tashay was probably between thirty-five and forty when he died. He was survived by both his parents.

5. The !Kung rarely refer to illness as caused by the evil intent of other living persons. This belief is explicitly held by the Tswana, however, and it is possible that the accusation against Kantla and Nisa reflects the influence of the Tswana on the !Kung.

10. CHANGE

For detailed accounts of culture contact and change since the turn of the century among the !Kung and other San peoples, see Lee, *The !Kung San*, chs. 1–3 and 14; M. Guenther, "From Hunters to Squatters," in Lee and DeVore, eds., *Kalahari Hunter-Gatherers*; H. Heinz, "The Bushmen in a Changing World," in Tobias, ed., *The Bushmen*; and G. Silberbauer, "The Future of the Bushmen," in Tobias, ed., *The Bushmen*.

The effects of culture change on women's status are discussed in P. Draper, "!Kung Women: Contrasts in Sexual Egalitarianism in Foraging and Sedentary Contexts," in R. Reiter, ed., *Toward an Anthropology of Women*. For the Kalahari People's Fund, see p. 348.

1. Nisa lived mostly in or near Tswana and Herero villages from this time on.

2. Nisa was probably thirty-one or thirty-two years old when she married Besa (c. 1956).

11. WOMEN AND MEN

The quote from Margaret Mead is from *Male and Female* (New York: William Morrow, 1949).

On !Kung women's status in the community, see Lee, *The !Kung San*, pp. 274–275, 447–454; Draper, "!Kung Women: Contrasts in Sexual Egalitarianism in Foraging and Sedentary Contexts"; Draper, "Cultural Pressure on Sex Difference," *American Ethnologist* 2, no. 4, (Nov. 1975): 602–615; Draper, "!Kung Bushman Childhood"; Marshall, *The !Kung of Nyae Nyae*, pp. 175–179; and Weissner, "Hxaro."

The quantitative data on !Kung father-child relations come from West and Konner, "The Role of the Father: An Anthropological Perspective."

Crosscultural overviews of women's roles can be found in Hammond and Jablow, *Women in the Cultures of the World*; M. Rosaldo and L. Lamphere, *Woman, Culture and Society* (Stanford: Stanford University Press, 1974); L. Lamphere, "Review Essay: Anthropology," *Signs* 2, no. 3 (1977):

612–627; and Reiter, ed., *Toward an Anthropology of Women*. See also the classic works of Margaret Mead, *Male and Female* and *Sex and Temperament* (New York: William Morrow, 1935).

Other information in this chapter comes from B. Whiting and J. Whiting, *Children of Six Cultures* (Cambridge, Mass.: Harvard University Press, 1975), and from M. Biesele and R. Katz, "Male and Female Approaches to Healing among the !Kung," in preparation.

1. This chapter covers about five years, beginning when Nisa was in her early thirties (c. the mid 1950s).

2. In fact, her husband and children were with her.

3. The Rand is a South African currency that was then legal tender in Bechuanaland (pre-independence Botswana). It was worth between $1.20 and $1.50. Five Rand was a very large sum of money to the !Kung at that time—perhaps as much as two months wages at a typical menial task.

4. tastes her: A euphemism for sexual intercourse.

5. The procedure for divorce in traditional !Kung culture would have been less complicated and would have proceeded more quickly.

6. Nisa and Bo married around 1957, when Nisa was about thirty-six years old.

12. TAKING LOVERS

The importance of extramarital sex and sexual jealousy among the !Kung has been independently studied and confirmed by several anthropologists: see Marshall, *The !Kung of Nyae Nyae*, pp. 279–283; Lee, *The !Kung San*, p. 383; and Howell, *Demography of the Dobe !Kung*, pp. 59–61, among others. Sexual joking and verbal sexual abuse are also documented by Marshall (pp. 204–208) and Lee (pp. 372–374).

1. The memories in this chapter cover all of Nisa's adult life.

2. A very strong version of "What kind of a man is he?"

3. Among the euphemisms for orgasm are "finish," "be full," and "be made alive." Such terms apply to both men and women.

4. The !Kung have word for clitoris (*tsun n/u*), and are aware of its functions in sexual arousal.

13. A HEALING RITUAL

For information on the healing ritual see R. Katz, "Education for Transcendence: !Kia-Healing with the Kalahari !Kung," in Lee and DeVore, eds., *Kalahari Hunter-Gatherers;* Biesele and Katz, "Male and Female Approaches to Healing among the !Kung"; and an excellent film by J. Marshall, "N/um Tchai," available from Documentary Educational Resources.

1. Each !Kung healer who has traveled to the world of the spirits seems to bring back an at least somewhat original report of that world.

14. FURTHER LOSSES

Fauna that figure in !Kung life—whether dangerous, useful, or both—are reviewed in Lee, *The !Kung San,* pp. 96–102 and app. C; Marshall, *The !Kung of Nyae Nyae,* ch. 4; and Howell, *Demography of the Dobe !Kung,* pp. 54–59.

Discussions and documentation of violence and its resolution among the !Kung may be found in Marshall, *The !Kung of Nyae Nyae,* ch. 9; Lee, *The !Kung San,* ch. 13; and Howell, *Demography of the Dobe !Kung,* pp. 59–62. P. Draper provides an account of how !Kung culture socializes children with respect to aggression in "The Learning Environment for Aggression and Anti-social Behavior among the !Kung," in A. Montagu, ed., *Teaching Non-Aggression* (New York: Oxford University Press, 1978).

1. A traditional stringed instrument.

2. Nai probably married at about age fifteen and was sixteen or seventeen at the time of her death. No other known deaths have occurred in a comparable manner.

3. The goats were offered in an effort to bring closure to the incident, not as restitution for murder. Indeed, the young man was not accused of murder, but of something akin to homicide. Had he been found guilty of murder, he would have been sent to prison in the East as Nisa urges.

4. "shade expert": A term for young men, who spend much of their time lying around in the shade.

5. Kxau was probably in his mid-teens when he died. Having killed his first buck made him eligible for marriage.

6. This is unusual with such a young child and reflects a strong desire on both Nisa's and her brother's part to replace her own children in some way.

15. GROWING OLDER

A major source for the statistics of the !Kung life course is Howell, *Demography of the Dobe !Kung,* chs. 3, 6 and 12; U.S. data for comparison are from the 1970 Census. For detailed accounts of aging among the !Kung see Biesele and Howell, " 'The Old People Give You Life' "; Lee, *The !Kung San,* pp. 58–61, 242–243; and Weissner, 'Hxaro.' Also see A. Truswell and J. Han—sen, "Medical Research among the !Kung," in Lee and DeVore, eds. *Kalahari Hunter-Gatherers.* A full discussion of !Kung folktales can be found in M. Biesele, "Folklore and Ritual of !Kung Hunter-Gatherers" (Ph.D. diss., Harvard University, 1975).

1. Nisa was about thirty-seven when her son died, leaving her without any living children (c. 1958).

2. This pregnancy occurred when Nisa was about forty. She experienced menopause when she was about forty-nine years old in 1970.

3. This is the only reference made by an !Kung woman to physical dif-

ficulties resulting from menopause. Since Nisa was experiencing it at the time it is likely to be more accurate than retrospective data, in which !Kung women deny any symptoms of menopause.

4. The !Kung phrase for "dream" means literally "a gathering up of the spirits."

EPILOGUE

The material on the menstrual cycle draws heavily on the doctoral thesis of Carol Worthman, one of my collaborators on the study: "Psychoneuroendocrine Study of Human Behavior," Harvard University, 1978. Worthman gives a detailed account of the !Kung study and its results and reviews relevant studies in Western populations.

For the history of the San see Willcox, "The Bushman in History," Inskeep, "The Bushmen in Prehistory," and Tobias, "Introduction to Bushmen or San," all in Tobias, ed., *The Bushmen*. Additional material on more recent history can be found in Lee, *The !Kung San*, pp. 31–35. Also see Yellen, *Archaeological Approaches to the Present*.

1. Kalahari People's Fund c/o Cultural Survival, 11 Divinity Avenue, Cambridge, Mass. 02138

Glossary

apron. A small leather covering for the genital area, tied around the waist.

ant bear (n/a). *Orycteropus afer.* A species of underground mammals hunted by the !Kung. They average about 140 pounds for males, 90 pounds for females.

baobab (≠em). *Adansonia digitata.* A common African tree. Soft wood trunks of gargantuan breadth and height (over 80 feet); excellent shade trees. Its fruit is a major food in the !Kung diet.

Bantu. A major African language family; also refers to Bantu-speakers, who include the cattle-keeping neighbors of the !Kung San of the Dobe area, the Hereros and Tswanas.

Bau. A woman's name. The woman who first confided in me about !Kung life; also, the girl Nisa often fought with in childhood; also, the mother of Nisa's second husband, Tsaa; also, Nisa's third daughter who died as a young child.

Besa. A man's name. One of the boys in Nisa's play group; also, Nisa's fourth husband, who left her when she was pregnant and from whom she later separated.

Bey. A woman's name. The 75-year-old woman who promised to "tell me everything" but never did; also, the wife of Nisa's lifetime lover, Kantla.

Bo. A man's name. Nisa's first husband; also, her fifth husband, to whom she was married at the time of the interviews.

Botswana. An African-ruled country, independent from British rule since 1966, sharing borders with South Africa, Zimbabwe (formerly Rhodesia), Namibia (South-West Africa), and Zambia. The Dobe area, where the !Kung San of this book live is in the Northwest District of Botswana, on the northern fringe of the Kalahari Desert. Preindependence Botswana was known as the Bechuanaland Protectorate.

bush (tsi). A general term referring to all land beyond a village camp boundary; uninhabited, wild.

Bushmen. A term for the San peoples, once common buy now in disuse among scholars because of its negative, racially pointed connotations.

caterpillars. At least six edible species have been identified. About two inches long and with smooth skin, they are highly subject to seasonal variation and when available, are considered a great delicacy.

chon. *Walleria muricata.* A grasslike plant with a small edible root.

Chotana (Tcho/tana). A water hole and village name; the place where Nisa's aunt lived and where there were no children she wanted to play with.

Chuko (Chu!ko). A woman's name. Nisa's mother; also, Nisa's first child; also, the mother of Tashay, Nisa's husband.

colostrum. The thin milky fluid secreted by the breast before and for a few days after childbirth.

dcha. *Citrullus naudinianus.* The bitter root of this crawling vine is pounded into a paste and rubbed on a woman's nipple to discourage a child from nursing. Its fruit—a melon similar in appearance to a prickly pear—is quite sour and is one of the less popular !Kung foods.

Debe. A man's name. A man in the East in whose village Nisa and Besa lived; also, one of Nisa's lovers at the time of the interviews.

Dem. A man's name. A man who wanted Nisa as a second wife; also, one of Nisa's lovers and the younger brother of Kantla, her lover since her youth.

Dau (≠Dau). A man's name. Nisa's older brother.

do (≠). *Eulophia hereroensis.* An edible, abundant root.

Dobe. The area technically refers to an expanse of land existing in both Botswana (about 75 percent) and Namibia (about 25 percent). Except for statistical computations, the Dobe area as used in the text refers only to the Botswana portion. Nyae Nyae is the name used to refer to the area in Namibia.

duiker (/tau). *Sylvicapra grimmia:* gray duiker. A small antelope, 40 to 45 pounds in weight, frequently caught in traps, clubbed down or hunted with poisoned arrows.

eland (n!n). *Taurotragus oryx:* giant Cape eland. A very large antelope, 750 to 1000 pounds, with much fat.

European (/ton). The way a white person is commonly referred to in southern Africa.

Gau (/Gau). A man's name. Nisa's father.

Gausha (/Gausha). A water hole and !Kung village name; Nisa's home at the time of the interviews.

gemsbok (!gwe). *Oryx gazella.* The most frequently killed large antelope, averaging 475 pounds. It is hunted in the classic manner with poisoned arrows, or with the aid of dogs.

giraffe (≠dwa). *Giraffa camelopardalis.* The largest of the big game species traditionally hunted by the !Kung, averaging about 2400 pounds. It was killed occasionally in traditional times, but it has been officially protected, even from the !Kung, for many years.

Goshi (!Goshi). A water hole and !Kung village name; the anthropologists' main camp.

gow (!gau). *Cyperus fulgens.* A small onionlike bulb.

guinea fowl (udi). A bird commonly caught in traps; similar in size to a chicken.

gwea (//guea). *Talinum crispatulatum.* A green vegetable. Both the leaves and the roots are eaten.

Herero (Tama). Bantu-speaking pastoralists who predominated in Namibia before the turn of this century. They were nearly exterminated as a people in 1904 during the genocidal German-Herero war. Survivors fled to Botswana, where they and their families have remained.

honey badger (//hau). *Mellivora capensis.* A commonly hunted mammal weighing approximately 20 pounds.

Hwarïtla (Hwan//a). A woman's name. The author's !Kung name and that of her !Kung namesake.

hxaro. The custom of giving and receiving gifts with designated exchange partners, which forms an elaborate network central to economic life. Gifts are not exchanged between two partners simultaneously, but rather one is given freely and an exchange gift is given only after a suitable delay.

ivory palm tree (!hani). *Hyphaene benguellensis.* The fruit of this palm tree is a major part of the !Kung diet.

jackal (≠tedi). *Canis mesomelas.* The black-backed jackal, a common visitor to the Dobe area, rarely hunted by the traditional !Kung.

Kalahari desert. The eastern portion of the Kalahari-Namib Desert, a half-million-square-mile expanse including southern Angola, most of Namibia, South-West Africa, northwestern South Africa, and almost all of Botswana.

Kalahari People's Fund. Acknowledging that change is inevitable, this organization of anthropologists and others undertakes to facilitate positive change by working with the San and with the Botswana government.

Kantla (Kan//a). A man's name. A trial co-marriage with Kantla and his wife Bey preceded Nisa's marriage to Tashay, and failed but Kantla has remained her lover throughout her life; the father of her husband Tashay.

kaross (chik!na) or blanket. A leather covering made from the hide of a large antelope, usually an eland or gemsbok. The most substantial article of !Kung clothing, it is worn almost exclusively by women. Similar skins are used for sleeping. Draped along the back, two ends are tied at the shoulder, while a rope holds it close over the abdomen. The pouch formed in the upper back is where ostrich eggshell water containers, gathered foods and older children are carried. The remainder of the skin hangs down over the lower half of a woman's body, offering protection and concealment. The leather is often embroidered with beads.

Kashe. A man's name. One of Nisa's lovers.

Keya (!Keya). A woman's name. One of Nisa's childhood friends.

Khoisan. A cultural and racial group that includes both the Khoi-Khoi (Hottentots) and the San.

klaru (//haru). *Lapeyrousia coerulea.* An edible bulb.

Koka (/Koka). A woman's name. Nisa's aunt (her mother's sister).

kua. The feelings or actions associated with ritual events variably translated as awe, fear, or respect; also used to refer to the respect relationship.

kudu (n!hwa). *Tragelaphus strepsiceros:* greater kudu. One of the most frequently killed large antelopes, it weighs an average of 600 pounds for males, 350 pounds for females. It is hunted in the classic !Kung manner, with bow and poisoned arrows.

Kumsa. A man's name. Nisa's younger brother.

!Kung. The name of a language and a people. The !Kung occupy an area covering northeastern Namibia, northwestern Botswana (the Zhun/twasi), and southeastern Angola.

Kunla (Kun//a). A woman's name. One of Nisa's childhood friends.

kwa (!Xwa). *Fockea sp. poss. monroi.* The most abundant water-bearing root crucial to the San's survival in the desert when no standing water is available.

Kxamshe. A woman's name. Nisa's youngest sibling who died as a young girl.

Kxaru. A woman's name. A 35-year-old woman in the initial interview study; also Nisa's aunt.

Kxau. A man's name. Nisa's son.

Kxoma (!Kxoma). A man's name. A field assistant to the author.

medicinal cuts. Small cuts made in the skin of a person suffering from illness, near the source of the pain. The slight bleeding is thought to allow some of the disease to escape. Herbal medicines may also be applied to the cuts.

mongongo (//"xa) or mangetti nut. *Ricinodendron rautanenii.* This abundant nut is available year-round and is in a class by itself as the staple of the !Kung diet. The fruit is also eaten. Only meat rivals this nut for first place in the hearts of most !Kung.

na (≠na). Berries, probably of the *Grewia* species.

Nai (N!ai). A woman's name. A 14-year-old girl in the initial interview study; also, one of Nisa's childhood friends; also, Nisa's second child.

Namibia. The area formerly known as South-West Africa, adjacent to Botswana on the western border and partly occupied by !Kung. This name is recognized by the United Nations as the official name of the country.

Nanau (/N!au). A man's name. One of Nisa's lovers.

Naukha. A woman's name. A 35-year-old woman in the initial interview study.

nehn (n≠h'n). *Pterocarpus angolensis DC.* A tree from which dyes used on leather karosses are made.

nin (n/n). *Grewia flava.* Berries that grow on low bushes and are eaten in huge quantities in summer and fall. The word for the berries is the same word used to mean "sweet" or "pleasant."

Nisa (N≠isa). A woman's name.

Noni (N!oni). A man's name. One of Nisa's childhood playmates.

Nukha (N!unkha). A woman's name. A 20-year-old woman in the initial interview study; also Nisa's niece and her charge; also, the woman who stayed with Nisa at night during her first marriage and made love to her husband; also, her friend in childhood.

n/um. A spiritual force that resides in many material forms, notably inside the bodies of healers who have access to it through trance.

Numshay (N/umshay). A man's name. A lover in the East who became involved with Nisa after Besa, her fourth husband, deserted her.

Nyae Nyae. A large area in Namibia along the Botswana border in which many !Kung San were gathering and hunting when first contacted by the Marshall family in 1951. Since 1960, the !Kung of the area have been settled in Chum!kwe a South African government station.

ostrich eggshell water container (tsun n!usi). A durable and widely used traditional water container. Eggs are found in caches of ten to fifteen at nesting sites. Their contents are extracted through a small drilled hole, then cooked and eaten. The shells are occasionally decorated with etched designs. Broken shells are made into beads.

porcupine (!kum). *Hystrix africaeaustralis.* The most frequently hunted species of underground mammal, weighing an average of 39 pounds.

Saglai (Sag//ai). A woman's name. The woman Nisa's father wanted as a second wife.

San. A term used to replace the somewhat derogatory word "Bushmen." It is derived from the Khoi-Khoi (Hottentot) word for their gathering and hunting neighbors.

sha. *Vigna dinteri.* An abundant root, one of the major plant foods consumed by the !Kung.

springhare (n/hum). *Pedetes capensis.* One of four important species of small mammals hunted below ground. It is more easily captured than the other burrow-dwelling mammals by means of a 12-foot springhare probe, with a metal hook at one end. It weighs an average of 7 pounds.

steenbok (/ton). *Raphicerus campestris.* A small antelope averaging slightly less than 25 pounds. It is hunted with clubs, spears, dogs, and occasionally poison arrows. The !Kung word is the same as the word used for Europeans.

Tasa (/Tasa). A woman's name. Nisa's cousin and childhood friend.

Tashay (/"Tashay). A man's name. Nisa's third husband and the father of her children; also, the !Kung name of the author's husband and colleague.

Tikay (Tikn!ay). A woman's name. A co-wife of Nisa's.

Toma (/Toma). A man's name. A field assistant to the author; also Nisa's cousin with whom she played and fought in childhood; also the lover with whom Nisa's mother ran away.

Tsaa. A man's name. Nisa's second husband; also, one of Nisa's lovers.

tsin. *Bauhinia esculenta.* The bean from this crawling vine, collected in large quantities, is a major food in the !Kung diet. It is the staple food of San peoples living in the Central Kalahari.

Tswana (/Tebi). A Bantu-speaking people, the predominant tribal group of

Botswana, numbering aproximately half a million. They are settled in almost all parts of the country, although most densely in the southeastern region.

Tuka (/Tuka). A man's name. Nisa's grandfather.

Twah (/Twah). A woman's name. The lover of Nisa's husband Besa.

Twi (/Wi). A man's name. Nisa's cousin; also, the younger brother of Nisa's husband Tashay who became her lover; also, a man from the East who became her lover and took her back to her brother's village after Besa deserted her.

warthog (/wa). *Phacochoerus aethiopicus.* The large mammal most frequently killed, either above the ground or in burrows below the ground, by !Kung hunters. About 170 pounds in weight, it has long razor-sharp tusks and is similar in appearance to a wild pig.

water pan. Temporary pools of water formed by the summer rains. In a good rainy season they may reach 4 or 5 feet in depth and several acres in size and may remain full for several months.

wildebeest (!ghi). *Connochaetes taurinus:* blue wildebeest. A species of large antelope weighing about 550 pounds for males 450 pounds for females; one of the commonly killed big game animals.

Zhun/twasi. The name the !Kung use for themselves. It comes from *zhu,* meaning person, and */twa* meaning true or real with *si* providing the plural ending. This refers to the most traditional of the three regional divisions of !Kung including the six thousand in northwestern Botswana and northeastern Namibia. Many of the world's peoples refer to themselves with such a designation, indicating their sense of themselves as central to the idea of what is human.

Acknowledgments

My profound gratitude goes to the !Kung of the Dobe area of northwestern Botswana who tolerated the presence of numerous research workers, including me. Their cooperation made possible the collection of invaluable documentation of their world—one that is fast disappearing. I owe specific thanks to the !Kung women who shared their lives with me and who participated in one or both of my studies. I would like to thank each woman by name, but that would be inconsistent with the protection of their privacy. One of them is Nisa.

Life among the !Kung was made easier by the assistance of a number of !Kung individuals, including !Kxoma, ≠Tuma !Koma, Kopella Moswe, and Kapange, all from Dobe.

Special thanks go to Irven DeVore and Richard Lee, who invited me to participate in the long-term research project and who were generous with help throughout the execution of my own study. Nancy DeVore and Lorna Marshall gave me essential advice preparatory to fieldwork, and fellow field-workers Patricia Draper, Henry Harpending, John Yellen, Megan Biesele, and Polly Wiessner were helpful while I was in the field and afterward. Nancy Howell made available to me unpublished background data on the !Kung, as did Lee, DeVore, Carol Worthman, and others.

For their hospitality while I was in Southern Africa, it is a pleasure to thank Richard Variend, Peter and Isla Jones, Flemming Larssen, George Riggs, Derek and Vera Haldane, and Revel Mason. I owe thanks as well to the government of Botswana for its hospitality extended to members of our expedition over many years: in particular, to Alec Campbell of the National Museum of Botswana, Elizabeth Wily of the Basarwa (San) Development Office, and Isak Utugile, the local Tswana tribal headman, all of whom were extremely helpful.

For encouragement during the translation, editing, and writing, I am grateful to Jerome Kagan, Beatrice Whiting, Cora DuBois, Irven and Nancy DeVore, Paul Trachtman, Herbert and Gertrude Perluck, Laura Smith, Lois Kasper, Penelope Naylor, Robert Liebman, Diane Franklin, Harry Lewis, David Glotzer, Vicky Burbank, Nancy Rankin, Belinda Rathbone, Edna and Jerome Shostak, Lucy Shostak, Marilyn Gilchrist, and Barbara Massar.

The support of a number of women writers, including Harriet Reisen, Celia Gilbert, Barbara Sirota, Janet Murray, Naomi Chase, Claire Rosenfield, Gail Mazur, Beth O'Sullivan, and Laura Shapiro, was of particular importance. Ann Banks read and criticized major portions of the book. For special assistance during the writing, I thank Suzanne Winchester, Anula Ellepola, Carla Burke, and Eleanor Davis. I am also grateful to George and Ann Twitchell for the hospitality of their Vermont retreat, where some of the writing was done.

Elaine Markson and her associate Geri Thoma provided important help and encouragement. Eric Wanner and Camille Smith offered valuable editorial advice that helped shape the book in its final form. Thanks also go to Elyse Topalian and Mary Kelly for assisting with many tasks associated with the book, and to Catherine Tudish, who prepared the index.

I owe thanks to David Maybury-Lewis and the staffs of the Department of Anthropology and the Peabody Museum, Harvard University, as well as Nancy Schmidt and the staff of the Tozzer Library for their hospitality during much of the writing.

Financial support for the first field trip came from the National Science Foundation and the National Institutes of Mental Health, in the form of research grants to Irven DeVore and Richard Lee. The second field trip was supported by the Harry Frank Guggenheim Foundation; I am grateful to Lionel Tiger and Robin Fox, the research directors of that foundation, for their enthusiasm.

An important phase of the work was completed during my year at the Bunting Institute, Radcliffe College. The administrative staff of the Institute at that time included Patricia Graham, Susan Lyman, Hilda Kahn, Doris Lorensen, and Marion Kilson, who were particularly helpful and encouraging. I also benefited from my contact with the community of scholars and artists who were at the Institute when I was there. Their friendship and example were an inspiration to me.

The last year of my work on the book was supported by the National Endowment for the Humanities. I wish to thank the staff of the Endowment, as well as Louise Lamphere, Robert Le-Vine, and Robert Levy, among others previously mentioned, for their support of my proposal.

Finally, my deepest thanks go to Melvin Konner, who shared the fieldwork experience with me. His unwavering support and encouragement, as well as his assistance with the research and writing, were essential in making this book a reality.

Index

Note: Page numbers from Nisa's narrative appear in italic type.

Index

Join our
online community
and help us save paper and postage!

www.earthscan.co.uk

By joining the Earthscan website, our readers can benefit from a range o
exciting new services and exclusive offers. You can also receive e-alerts an
e-newsletters packed with information about our new books, forthcomin
events, special offers, invitations to book launches, discussion forums an
membership news. Help us to reduce our environmental impact by joining th
Earthscan online community!

How? – Become a member in seconds!

>> Simply visit **www.earthscan.co.uk** and add
your name and email address to the sign-up
box in the top left of the screen – You're now a
member!

>> With your new member's page, you can
subscribe to our monthly **e-newsletter** and/or
choose **e-alerts** in your chosen subjects of
interest – you control the amount of mail you
receive and can unsubscribe yourself

Why? – Membership benefits

✔ Membership is free!

✔ 10% discount on all books online

✔ Receive invitations to high-profile book
launch events at the BT Tower, London
Review of Books Bookshop, the Africa
Centre and other exciting venues

✔ Receive e-newsletters and e-alerts
delivered directly to your inbox, keeping
you informed but not costing the Earth –
you can also forward to friends and
colleagues

✔ Create your own discussion topics and
get engaged in online debates taking place in our new online Forum

✔ Receive special offers on our books as well as on products and services
from our partners such as *The Ecologist*, *The Civic Trust* and more

✔ Academics – request inspection copies

✔ Journalists – subscribe to advance information e-alerts on upcoming
titles and reply to receive a press copy upon publication – write to
info@earthscan.co.uk for more information about this service

✔ Authors – keep up to date with the latest publications in your field

✔ NGOs – open an NGO Account with us and qualify for special discounts

Join now?

Join Earthscan now!

name

surname

email address

Earthscan Member

[Your name]

Click to
Change

My profile

My forum

My bookmarks

All my pages

www.earthscan.co.uk